*LEARNING
and
APPLYING*
APL

LEARNING and APPLYING APL

B. Legrand

Ingénieur de l'Ecole Centrale des Arts et Manufactures

Translated by

Julian Glyn Matthews, Linguatech

John Wiley & Sons Ltd
Chichester · New York · Brisbane · Toronto · Singapore

Copyright © 1984 John Wiley & Sons Ltd.

First published 1981 © Masson, Editeur, Paris under the
title Apprendre et appliquer le langage APL
(2eme édition corrigée et révisée)

Drawings by RUMWEISS

Library of Congress Cataloging in Publication Data:

Legrand, B.
   Learning and applying APL.
   Translation of: Apprendre et appliquer le langage APL.
   Bibliography: p.
   Includes index.
   1. APL (Computer program language)   I. Title.
   QA76.73.A27L4413 1984   001.64'24   83-10620
   ISBN 0 471 90243 8

British Library Cataloguing in Publication Data:

Legrand, B.
   Learning and applying APL.
   1. APL (Computer program language)
   I. Title   II. Matthews, Julian Glyn
   III. Apprendre et appliquer le langage APL. *English*
   001.64'24   QA76.73.A27

   ISBN 0 471 90243 8

Printed in Great Britain

A C K N O W L E D G E M E N T S

Gérard LACOURLY and Philip S. ABRAMS led me to take my first steps in APL, when they had just launched, with the success which is well known, the APL service of CEGOS, which has now become SLIGOS. Then, attaching a concrete meaning to meticulous operations such as outer product, decoding, or dyadic transposition, Guy VARIN led me to discover the scope of this language. Without him, APL would still be merely an intellectual toy for me.

I am also indebted to Yann GAUBERT for having been able to write some meaningful lines on CMS files and the Domino function.

When my wife, with endless patience, had read the entire text, Philip ABRAMS was able to let me have his ever pertinent criticisms and suggestions, thus tying up the loose ends. Meanwhile, Alain BILLORET had secured the necessary contacts for publication of the work.

All played their part in the publication of this book; may this page express my deep gratitude to them.

CONTENTS

vii

CHAPTER 7. - INDEX-OF, GRADE UP, GRADE DOWN, ENCODE, DECODE

CHAPTER 8. - COMPUTING AIDS

CHAPTER 9. - THE EXECUTE FUNCTION, PRINTING CONTROL

Exercises 16 – 18 – 22 – 45 – 55 – 71 – 74 – 78 – 88 – 92 –
101 – 125 – 140 – 144 – 155 – 169 – 179 – 197 – 205.

The first public demonstration of an APL time sharing system occurred
more than ten years ago. Since then we have witnessed a blossoming of APL
in North America and Western Europe. Today APL is found on the equipment
of all computer manufacturers and equally on a large proportion of mini-
computers. Some organisations offer conversational APL services, sometimes
on an international scale. The use of APL as a pure algorithmic notation
has been established in some universities and secondary schools, especially
in the United States and Canada. For several years there has been an
international STAPL society concerned solely with APL and there have been
some ten APL congresses.

Although there is an increasing amount of "APL literature" we have
observed some absence of choice of texts for learning the language. This
is the more curious since there is a superabundance of literature on other
programming languages.

Given that the use of APL is more widespread in France than elsewhere
in Europe, we are pleased to welcome this book by Bernard LEGRAND, because
he offers the reader who wants to learn APL another choice, in terms of
style, depth and breadth of treatment. Whilst remaining a textbook, it
also serves as a reference for the already qualified programmer。

We can give credit to the author for the fact that he has not over-
insisted on converting the APL vocabulary into French. I think that he
is wise to recognize that data processing, whether expressed in APL or
not, is a practice which overrides national frontiers.

I think that the reader will appreciate, as I did, the humour and
liveliness with which the author approaches his subject. It is precisely
this rather informal style, despite the weighty message, which makes this
textbook thoroughly comprehensible. Historical perspectives are also dis-
persed amongst the text, as well as some of the author's opinions on the
formation of the language.

Faced with the problem of multiple versions of APL, B. LEGRAND provides an insight into the problem by setting out the significant aspects
of the various systems. He very well demonstrates the immediate need for
standardization of the APL language.

This book will be welcome also to those who wish to acquaint themselves
with APL.

Washington D.C.,

Philip S. ABRAMS

CHAPTER 1

CONVENTIONS, TERMINOLOGY

More than a computer programming language, APL is above all a mathematical notation which has a particular terminology associated with it. It is important to stress the significance of this terminology, just as it is with certain notations which will be used throughout this work.

1-1   PRIMITIVE FUNCTIONS, DEFINED FUNCTIONS

Any operation on one or more pieces of data will be called a FUNCTION. Thus, 4+3 is the application of the function ADDITION to the data 4 and 3. Some functions are more complex, such as calculation of a logarithm, or classifying of a series of numbers in increasing order, while others require a considerable amount of work. Such is the case, for example, with calculation of the pay for employees of a company, which could be considered as a function of hourly rate, grade on the salary scale, rate of legal deductions, taxes, etc...

The mathematical notations in use have given a symbolic notation to a number of relevant functions: addition takes +, multiplication takes ×, etc... For other equally useful functions the use of a key-word was used: sin, cos, log. Other very useful operations are not represented by any particular notation; such is the case when classifying a series of numbers in increasing order.

As it would be inconceivable to invent a symbol for every human activity, a compromise was necessary, and a set of functions of general significance in APL was decided on, to which symbols have been designated.

There are many well-known symbols: + - × ≥ ≠ ∈ ∧ !
There are also some new symbols: ⍋ ⊛ ⌈ | ?

These functions are called PRIMITIVE FUNCTIONS, because they constitute the basic hub of the language. To solve operations which are not covered by primitive functions, the APL user can create new functions which he can baptize as his own (*AVERAGE PAY INDEX-OF*), which will be more or less complex combinations of primitive functions. These functions created by the user will be called DEFINED FUNCTIONS.

1-2   MONADIC AND DYADIC FUNCTIONS

We shall call the values which are applied to a function either ARGUMENTS
or OPERANDS. Hence, in the expression 124+90, 124 and 90 are the arguments or operands of the function ADDITION.

In mathematics, the arguments of a function are indicated between
brackets, following the name of the function: $f(x,y,z,t)$. This notation
permits as many arguments as necessary to be attributed to a function,
but the functions used in present practice have only one or two arguments
and are written:

     cos x

     Log u

     a + b

     p x *q*

This usage has been retained in APL, where each function, whether primitive
or defined can have:

    - either a single argument, in which case the function will be
      said to be MONADIC

    - or two arguments, in which case the function will be said to
      be DYADIC.

For a dyadic function, the arguments will be placed on both sides of the
symbol (*A+B*), for a monadic function the argument will ALWAYS be placed
to the RIGHT of the symbol. This last convention is particularly significant, because it considerably eases computer interpretation of APL by
eliminating certain incoherences of traditional mathematical notations
in which the operation sign is placed:

    sometimes before its operand *(-5)*,

    sometimes after *(4!)*,

    sometimes above ($\bar{A}$),

    and sometimes on both sides ($|x|$),

    or is occasionally suggested by a special index (x^n).

Furthermore, to prevent ambiguity, no operation sign should be omitted.
Hence, the expressions *3x*, *AB* and *(X+1)(Y-3)* should be written: *3xX*,
AxB and *(X+1)* x *(Y-3)*.

1-3   DATA PROCESSING MEDIUM

After being used for more than six years as a formal tool for algorithm
description, APL has been implanted in the computer as a programming
language. It is used in an interactive manner, meaning that expressions
typed on the keyboard by the operator are instantly performed by the
computer, and the result directly printed or displayed on a screen.

For example:

$$451 - 371$$ Expression typed by the operator
    80   Computer's answer

        $$512837 \times 4269803$$ Expression typed by the operator
    2189712961111   Computer's answer

Even though it is conceivable to study APL entirely from books, like any
other mathematical notation, the use of the computer constitutes an
extremely valuable aid, more by the immediate visual appearance of the
results and the precise notification of errors than by the possibility
of direct experimentation which is provided by the instantaneous execution of expressions submitted to the computer.

We would here stress the importance of performing the examples of the
course on the computer and solving all the exercises at the end of each
chapter.

1-4   CONVENTIONS

1 - APL is the only data processing language which distinguishes between
    the SUBTRACTION FUNCTION ($8-3$) and the typographical symbol attached
    to negative values ($^{-}7$), called the negative sign.

    We will see the significance of this distinction in paragraph 3-3.

    The subtraction sign - is placed to the right of the keyboard (key + -),
    the negative value sign $^{-}$ is to the left of the keyboard (key 2 $^{-}$).

    Here is a dialog with the computer, which illustrates this distinction:

        $$34 - 86$$ Expression to evaluate (subtraction)
    $^{-}52$ Computer's answer (negative value)

2 - To be precise, it is irrelevant whether 0.873 or $.873$ is written.

3 - Very large or small values are represented by using an exponent
    and the symbol E indicates by which power of 10 the displayed
    value must be multiplied.

   $^{-}1.43E9$ signifies -1.43×10^{9} and $6.88E^{-}8$ signifies 6.88×10^{-8}

   This representation can be used by the operator.

1-5   USING THE APL TERMINAL

We will not describe the procedure of connection to a computer, since
it varies greatly from system to system. However, the use of an APL
terminal presents some features which are useful to know.

THE MAIN GROUPS OF TERMINALS

There are several modes of communication between a computer and a terminal.
For the operator, some differences are barely visible and the terminals
can be roughly classed into two main groups:

- some terminals send characters typed by the operator one by one to the
  computer. A character which has already been transmitted can be
  corrected only with the help of the computer. We will say that these
  terminals work in CHARACTER MODE.

- other terminals make use of a memory and a local processing unit. The
  characters are transmitted only at the end of a line or a page, on the
  operator's command and they can therefore be corrected in advance. We
  will say that these terminals work in BLOCK MODE (or in PAGE MODE).

END OF A LINE

There is a special key to signal to the computer that a line is completed
and can be processed. By pressing it, the printing head or the screen
cursor returns to the left margin. According to the terminal, it is
engraved RETURN, CR, EXECUTE, TRANSMIT, or ← . For the remainder of
this book, we will call it CARRIAGE-RETURN (by analogy with the first
typewriters).

SYMBOLS

- The keyboard accommodates only capital letters, numbers and special symbols. On many typewriter-style terminals, the letters are in italics, so that confusion is impossible, for example:

    between the letter X and the multiplication sign ×

    or between the letter O and the number zero 0

    or between the letter I and the number 1

- Each key accommodates two symbols: the normal symbol is the lower case one. The upper case symbol is obtained by simultaneously pressing the "SHIFT" key and the selected key.

- A space bar enables blank spaces to be inserted between the characters, called BLANKS.

- Certain special characters are obtained by superimposing two symbols. Hence, ⌹ is obtained by superimposing ÷ and ☐. These are called OVERSTRUCK characters.

The character mode terminals accommodate a BACK-SPACE key engraved BACK-SPACE or ←, which enables you to return to a preceding character to superimpose another (see diagram on previous page). Hence, a wide diversity of composite symbols can be composed, provided that the computer will accept them.

Terminals working in block mode enable composite symbols to be typed in one operation, by simultaneously pressing a special key (sometimes engraved APL ALT) and the key which accommodates the desired symbol, engraved on its FRONT SIDE. Thus only the signs provided on the keyboard can be used. These symbols are, in fact:

I   ⍫   ⍊   ⍙   ⌽   ⍉   ⊖   ⊗   ⍷   ⍋   !   ⌷   ⍞   ⍛   ⍕   ⍀   ⍂   ⌿

INTERRUPTION

There is a key which enables a signal to be sent to interrupt the flow of a process being fed into the computer, or of a print-out being printed on the terminal.

A STRONG interruption causes an immediate stoppage of the work, as with an error. A WEAK interruption causes a stoppage at the end of the line in the program being used (except if the function is locked), or immediately interrupts the print-out in progress.

Some terminals possess the two corresponding keys (engraved AP2 and AP1), but most terminals have only one key, engraved ATTN, INT or BREAK, as may be the case, as on the keyboard represented above. A single press causes a weak interruption, two presses in immediate succession cause a strong interruption.

In the remainder of this work, we will designate the name "INTERRUPTION KEY" for this device.

<u>CORRECTION</u>

A line typed on the keyboard can be modified and corrected provided that the CARRIAGE RETURN key, which starts the operation, has not been pressed.

On screen terminals in block mode, it is sufficient to displace the cursor and to use the replacement facilities, insertion or cancelling of characters present on most screens.

For terminals in character mode, the only method consists of cancelling the last characters typed, and replacing them with others.

For example, if instead of typing *GOOD MORNING*, *GOOD MIRNING* was typed, the six last characters (*IRNING*) must be cancelled and replaced by *ORNING*.

For this you must:

- return to the first incorrect character (*I*) by using the BACK-SPACE key;

- press the special key, which from now on we will call the <u>CORRECTING KEY</u>. This key causes a jump to the next line, printing (on some machines only) a reference character under the cancelled character (V);

- type the correct characters.

According to the terminal, the correcting key is either the same as the interruption key (ATTN or INT on mode 2741 terminals), or a different key engraved LINE-FEED, as on the diagram shown.

1-6   NOTE

You can now start reading this book. You will see that each chapter is followed by a supplement, which often makes reference to ideas which are studied only later in the work.

These supplements are meant for readers who are already experienced and well practiced in APL. We STRONGLY recommend you to totally ignore these supplements during the first reading of this work, and to take up the study of them only when you have acquired some practice in the language.

You will appreciate this particular arrangement, which enables every-thing concerning a given subject to be grouped in a single chapter and its supplement and which makes it easy to locate a precise piece of information.

Good reading!

CHAPTER 2

DATA

2-1   VARIABLES, ASSIGNMENT

In order to store a value which seems significant it must be given a
name to designate it and to retrieve it. This association of a name
and a value constitutes a VARIABLE. It is expressed by the symbol ←.

If we type *PRICE ← 17.20*, the variable *PRICE* takes the value 17.20
and will keep it until it is assigned another value, for example by
typing:

> *PRICE ← 240*

PRICE now equals 240. The value 17.20 is permanently lost.

In order to assign to several variables values deduced from each other,
it is convenient to concatenate the assignments as follows:

> *I ← 1+J ← K ← 21*

J and *K* take the value 21 and *I* takes the value 22.

The value of a variable can also be modified by referring to its present
value:

> *PRICE ← PRICE + 100*

PRICE has been assigned its present value (24) plus 100. Henceforth
PRICE equals 340.

2-2   DIRECT EVALUATION

Any expression typed on the keyboard is instantaneously evaluated. If
the result of the calculations is assigned to a variable name, it is
not printed:

> *I ← PRICE + 60*

This expression gives *I* the value 300 but does not bring about its print-
out. On the other hand if the result is not assigned, it is automatically
printed:

> *J+K*

60

> *PRICE × 3*

1020

Special case: in order to know the value of a variable, it is necessary only to type its name:

> *I*
> 400

A shift of six characters, called an INDENTATION, enables what the person types to be distinguished from what the computer answers, which allows for the easy analysis of written documents.

So as to further improve the readability of this book, anything typed by the person will henceforth be printed on a grey background.

2-3   STRUCTURED DATA

Frequently the data is not presented alone, but in the form of groups which have a common significance. For example, the rise in temperature of a furnace with time every 10 minutes was noted thus:

> 20 35 90 210 360 480 550 580 595 (in °C)

A single variable can serve to designate this set of data and this can be written:

> *DEGREES* ← 20 35 90 210 360 480 550 580 595

A person has recorded his earnings during the first six months of the year as follows:

	JAN	FEB	MARCH	APRIL	MAY	JUNE
Salary	3400	3400	3360	3510	3510	3510
Bonus	200	0	0	380	210	170

A single variable, *MONEY*, can be used to designate this set of numeric data, cleared of the headings. It will not be seen how to constitute this variable until later on; suppose that it has already been introduced and now print it out:

> *MONEY*
> 3400 3400 3360 3510 3510 3510
> 200   0   0   380   210   170

For a last example, suppose that an industrialist had recorded, over four years, the production of car, lorry and aeroplane tyres at his five factories. Here is the data which he could have collected:

1974	LEEDS	DOVER	GLASGOW	HULL	LUTON
Car	3200	0	4100	8340	0
Lorry	420	840	360	0	7420
Plane	0	0	0	0	1280

1975	LEEDS	DOVER	GLASGOW	HULL	LUTON
Car	3120	0	4600	8520	0
Lorry	400	910	380	0	7660
Plane	0	0	0	0	1310

1976	LEEDS	DOVER	GLASGOW	HULL	LUTON
Car	3000	0	4330	9480	0
Lorry	440	970	890	0	8020
Plane	0	160	0	0	1560

1977	LEEDS	DOVER	GLASGOW	HULL	LUTON
Car	2240	0	4460	9660	0
Lorry	440	1040	380	0	8200
Plane	0	280	0	0	1430

A single variable, *TYRES*, can represent this set of values. Suppose that it has already been introduced, now let's print it:

        TYRES

```
    3200       0    4100    8340       0
     420     840     360       0    7420
       0       0       0       0    1280

    3120       0    4600    8520       0        ◀-------- notice that the computer
     400     910     380       0    7660                  passes a blank line
       0       0       0       0    1310                  between each sub-array

    3000       0    4330    9480       0
     440     970     390       0    8020
       0     160       0       0    1560

    2240       0    4460    9660       0
     440    1040     380       0    8200
       0     280       0       0    1430
```

DEGRES, *MONEY* and *TYRES* are called ARRAYS of values.

2-4   DIMENSIONS

The dimensions of these three variables can be expressed in the following manner:

TYRES: 4 times 3 lines of 5 components

MONEY: 2 lines of 6 components

DEGREES: 9 components

The dimensions of these three variables are stated to be respectively:

     for *TYRES*:   4   3   5

     for *MONEY*:   2   6

     for *DEGREES*:   9

The monadic primitive function SHAPE, symbolized by the Greek letter ρ
(Rhô, accommodated on the R key) reveals the dimensions of a variable.
Here are some applications:

          ρ *TYRES*
4 3 5
          ρ *MONEY*
2 6
          ρ *DEGREES*
9

We are accustomed to talking of the first, the second, ... the last
dimension of an array. For *TYRES*, for example, the first dimension
(4) indicates the number of sub-arrays, the first dimension indicates
the number of lines, the last (5) ALWAYS designates the number
of columns.

2-5   RANK

In order to express the dimensions of *TYRES*, three numbers are needed;
we will say that this is an array of three dimensions, or again, a
three rank array.

The rank of an array is equal to the number of its dimensions.

ρ*TYRES*
4 3 5   ← dimensions of *TYRES*

3   ρ 4 3 5

                        ← rank of *TYRES* = number of dimensions

ρρ*TYRES* could have been written directly, which would have given the
answer 3.

In order to express the dimensions of *MONEY*, two numbers are needed; this
is an array of two dimensions or of rank 2.

ρ*MONEY*
2 6
ρρ*MONEY*
2

Finally, in order to express the dimensions of *DEGREES*, only one number
is needed, this is an array of rank 1 (or one dimensions array).

ρ *DEGREES*
9
ρρ*DEGREES*
1

We have discovered arrays of ranks 3, 2, 1; there must also be an array
of rank 0.

Let's try: ρρ95

        0

This experiment shows that the rank of a solitary number is 0. It must
be expected therefore that there is no need for ANY NUMBER to express
its dimensions.

        ρ95
                    ← the computer has answered by leaving a blank
                      line, thus expressing that a solitary number
                      does not have any dimensions.
It can also be said that the set of dimensions of a solitary number is an
EMPTY SET which is usually designated ∅ in mathematics (N.B. ∅ is not an
APL symbol).

2-6   TERMINOLOGY

All data are arrays, but some receive a special name; it is customary to
use the following words:

> Scalar: to designate a solitary number, like 95,
> Vector: to designate an array of one dimension, like *DEGREES*,
> Matrix: to designate an array of two dimensions, like *MONEY*,
> Array: to designate an array of more than rank 2, like *TYRES*.

It is only necessary to talk of four or five dimension arrays in order
to qualify as a hardened mathematician. In order to convince you that
it is not a question of disorderly abstractions, ask the storekeeper
of a large pharmaceutical laboratory how he stores GYNOSTOP pills. He
will answer:

"There are 10 shelves of 8 boxes each one containing 12 cartons of 24
packets, each with 3 cards of 21 sugar-coated tablets of anhydrous
polycarbonyl dimethylaminehydroxybenzoate (stamped Ph 7)" (1)

10 8 12 24 3 21: 6 numbers are needed to describe the dimensions
of this stock, this is an array of rank 6, or of 6 dimensions.

APL enables the use of arrays of rank as high as required: 5, 6, 12 ...,
put another way, values referred to by classifying systems to 5, 6,
12 .... different classifying levels. For our medical supplies, the
classifying levels are the shelf, the box, the carton, etc... For the
letters in a book these are: the work, the volume, the page, the line and
the position on the line.

2-7   SUMMARY

The following array recalls the different types of variable which we
have encountered. It is not a closed array, since the variable rank
can be as high as is required (2).

Usual Name	Example Z	Dimensions ρZ	Rank $\rho\rho Z$
Scalar (number)	258	(empty set $\emptyset$)	0
Vector	*DEGREES*	9	1
Matrix	*MONEY*	2 6	2
Array	*TYRES*	4 3 5	3

It is important to remember that the result of the expression ρZ is
ALWAYS a vector, no matter what Z is.

(1) The author declines all responsibility for the consequences of
     taking this compound.

(2) The only limits are those imposed by the way in which the language
     is implemented in the computer. With IBM, for example, APL
     accepts 17 dimensions.

2-8   DEFINING A VARIABLE

The definition of a scalar variable, or of a vector, can be achieved
directly:

> *AGE* ← 37

> *REFERENCES* ← 11 23 47 9 2 6

This is what would be called, in mathematics, a definition "in extension".
A vector can be defined also by means of the dyadic primitive function ρ
as follows:

> *BIZOU* ← 8 ρ 1 0

This signifies: to create an array of eight elements, filled with the
series of numbers 1 0. Check the result:

> >   *BIZOU*
>   1 0 1 0 1 0 1 0

It can be seen that the list has been repeated as many times as necessary
to obtain a vector of eight components.
Here is another example:

> *OWL* ← 7 ρ 1 8 3 14 5

> >   *OWL*
>   1 8 3 14 5 1 8   Here again the list has been rescanned.

In mathematics this method of defining a variable would be called a
definition "by insight".

In order to create arrays with rank equal to or more than two, it is
imperative to use the function ρ (SHAPE or RESHAPE), because the dimensions of the array required to be constituted must be defined.

For example, here is how to create the array *MONEY*:

> *MONEY* ← 2 6 ρ 3400 3400 3360 3510 3510 3510 200 0 0 380 210 170

> >   *dimensions*   *contents*

This expression signifies: creating an array of two lines and six columns,
filled with the series of numbers 3400   3400   3360 ...

Here is another example:

> >   *PRESSURES* ← 3 4 ρ 11 12 13 2 4 5 0

> >   *PRESSURES*
> >   11 12 13   2
> >   4   5   0 11
> >   12 13   2   4

> >   ρ*PRESSURES*
> >   3 4

2-9   SYNTAX OF THE FUNCTION ρ

- the dimensions of the array to be created are indicated to the left
  of the symbol ρ. This is a vector or a scalar.

- the list of elements used to constitute the array are placed to the
  right of the symbol ρ.
  This list could be:

    - a scalar, in which case the array will be composed of elements
      which are all identical;

    - a vector, as in the preceding examples;

    - another array, where the elements will be used in the order in
      which they appear.

For example, given the array *PRESSURES*, as seen above, the expression
5 2 ρ *PRESSURES* yields the following result:

```
    11  12
    13   2
     4   5
     0  11
    12  13
```

The two operands of the function ρ can be numeric values or designated,
as above, by the naming of a variable. As an illustration, here is
another way of creating the array *MONEY*:

```
LEFT ← 2 6
RIGHT ← 3400 3400 3360 3510 3510 3510 200 0 0 380 210 170

MONEY ← LEFT ρ RIGHT

MONEY
3400  3400  3360  3510  3510  3510
 200     0     0   380   210   170
```

2-10   ALPHANUMERIC DATA

412; 19; or 83 107 91 are numeric data.

On the contrary, *PIERRE DETAILLE, 19 RUE DU BAC - 75006 PARIS*, represents
data comprising numbers and letters; we say that this is ALPHANUMERIC
DATA. It is important to note that 19 or 75006 are not considered as
numbers here, but as character strings, under the same heading as *"RUE"*
or *"PARIS"*. Actually, it is hard to imagine what computing could be
performed with 19 and 75006.

Hence we will be led to distinguish between numeric data and alphanumeric
data, then logical data, which we will discover later on.

An alphanumeric variable can be defined by placing any series of characters
between QUOTES (' character on the *K* key).

For example: *NAME* ← *'GILLIAN FLOOD'*

         NAME
      GILLIAN FLOOD

         ρ*NAME*
      13

It is evident that a series of characters is considered by the computer
as a vector having as many elements as there are characters, BLANK
SPACES INCLUDED.

Letters, numbers and special characters can be mixed without restriction;
however, if the text contains an apostrophe (quotation mark), it must be
doubled so as to distinguish it from the outside quotation marks. At
the time of print-out, a single apostrophe will appear:

         ASK ← *'ISN''T IT ?'*

         ρ*ASK*
      10
         ASK
      ISN'T IT ?

It can be seen that the apostrophe counts as a single character.

         PAMPHLET ← *'PL/1 PROGRAMMER''S GUIDE - REF. 84470**A'*
         ρ *PAMPHLET*
      39
         PAMPHLET
      *PL/1 PROGRAMMER'S GUIDE - REF. 84470**A*

A solitary character is considered as a scalar:

         ρ *'G'*

         ρρ *'G'*
      0

Character arrays of any rank can be created. For example, here is how
to create a matrix of characters by using the dyadic function ρ in the
same way as for a numeric variable:

```
DRAWING ← 3 3 ρ'/¯\|□|‾‾'
DRAWING
```

We have built a dog kennel.

2-11   CLAMP ON

Two names of variables cannot be stuck together, they must be attached
by a function.
For example, if *A* has a value of 5, and if *B* has a value of 3, the
vector 5 3 cannot be constituted either by writing *A B*, or *A* 3 or
5 *B*. The CATENATION function, which will be studied in paragraph
3-17, must be used and it will be written *A,B*.

EXERCISES

[1]   *SHODDY* ← 2 3 5 ρ 5 0 1 6 6 0 0 1 7 9 2 5 12 72 0

Write the value of the variable *SHODDY*. What are its dimensions?
What is its rank?

[2]   What happens if the argument on the right of the function ρ contains
more elements than is necessary, as in the following example:

ARRAY ← 2 5 ρ 9 1 4 3 6 7 4 3 8 2 2 5 2 8

[3]   How can the scalar *S* be transformed to a vector of a single element?

[4]   How can the vector of a single element *V*←1ρ435 be transformed into
a scalar?

[5]   The following tests have been set on the data *X*:

```
      X
1 15 8 3
      ρX
8
```

What is the value of *X*?

[6]   *A*←1+*B*←2×*C*←50+*D*←27   What are the values of *A*, *B*, *C* and *D*?

[7]   What would be the value of   (ρ*MONEY*) ρ (ρρ*MONEY*)

[8]   How can the following matrix be created without typing all 36
       elements?

                         1 0 0 0 0 0
                         0 1 0 0 0 0
                         0 0 1 0 0 0
                         0 0 0 1 0 0
                         0 0 0 0 1 0
                         0 0 0 0 0 1

2-12   INDEXING

With a vector: *SOUP* ← 4 0 7 1 9 4 2 9

SOUP[3] designates the third element of *SOUP*, i.e. 7.

If extraction of the third, second, sixth and then the third element
again of *SOUP* is required, we will write:

             SOUP   [3 2 6 3]
         7 0 4 7

In order to modify the sixth and eighth elements, we write:

             SOUP [6 8] ← 8 5
             SOUP
         4 0 7 1 9 8 2 5

This method of adjustment is called the INDEXING of an array. The values
within square brackets constitute the index, or the set of indices.

An array of any rank can be used as an index. For example, a matrix can
be used:

             TOMATO ← 2 3 ρ 2 1 2 7 3 5
             TOMATO
         2 1 2
         7 3 5

             Z ← *SOUP* [*TOMATO*]

┌──┐
│ RULE: When a vector is indexed by an array, an array of the same │
│   dimensions as the index is obtained, in which each value would │
│   have been replaced by the element of the vector which it │
│   designates.   │
└──┘

This rule will be seen in more detail in the supplement (§ 2-27).

Hence, the 5 of the array *TOMATO*, which is the index, is found to be
replaced by the fifth element of *SOUP* (having the value 9); the 1 is
replaced by the first element, etc... We will check this:

                 Z
         0   4   0
         2   7   9

Here is a second example: INDEX ← 4 2 ρ 5 4 3 2 1 1 8 7

What is the value of   SOUP [INDEX] ?

> INDEX

    5 4
    3 2
    1 1
    8 7

> SOUP [INDEX]

    9 1
    7 0
    4 4
    5 2

It is possible to index character strings in the same way.   Here are two typical examples:

> 'MY HOUSE' [1 5 6 7 8]

    MOUSE   (there was a mouse in my house !)

> CATHE ← '□ Δ∩'
> DRAL ← 5 4 ρ 3 2 2 3 1 2 2 1 1 1 1 1 1 1 1 1 11 4 4 1

> DRAL

    3 2 2 3
    1 2 2 1
    1 1 1 1
    1 1 1 1
    1 4 4 1

> CATHE[DRAL]

    Δ   Δ
    □   □
    □□□□
    □□□□
    □∩∩□

EXERCISES

[9]   What result is obtained by typing: 'LE CHAT'[7 5 2 3 4 6 7]
       (Extract from "INFORMATIQUE PAR TELEPHONE", Philip S. ABRAMS and
       Gérard LACOURLY, HERMANN books, Paris 1972.)

[10]   The vector of the following characters is given: STEAM ← '□ ⌈/∩○<'
       What must be the value of TRAIN, in order to make the expression
       STEAM[TRAIN] print-out the following little train:

                    □ ∩ ⌈
                    <□□□□
                    /○○ ○○

2-13   INDEXING ARRAYS OF RANK GREATER THAN 1

In order to designate the value 8520 to the array *TYRES*, it must be
specified that it is in the second sub-array, on the first row in the
fourth column. We will write:

> *TYRES*[2;1;4]
>
> 8520

The index relating to each of the dimensions must be separated from the
others by a semi-colon.
Failure to include these semi-colons, *TYRES*[2 1 4] would designate three
elements (the second, first and fourth) as a vector, which is very
different. The message "RANK ERROR" would be received.

Likewise, *MONEY*[2;5] designates the value 210. This value can be modified
by typing:

> *MONEY*[2;5] ← 230
>
> *MONEY*
>
> | 3400 | 3400 | 3360 | 3510 | 3510 | 3510 |
> |------|------|------|------|------|------|
> | 200 | 0 | 0 | 380 | 230 | 170 |

Taking the earlier array *PRESSURES*:

> | 11 | 12 | 13 | 2 |
> |----|----|----|----|
> | 4 | 5 | 0 | 11 |
> | 12 | 13 | 2 | 4 |

several terms can be simultaneously extracted from it by writing:

> *PRESSURES*[2 3;2 4]
>
> | 5 | 11 |
> |----|----|
> | 13 | 4 |

The elements situated at the intersections of rows 2 and 3 with columns
2 and 4 have been obtained. There is NO WAY of designating the 5 and 4
without designating the 11 and 13 at the same time.

2-14   CONVENTION

In order to designate all the elements relating to a certain dimension,
it is sufficient to omit the index relating to this dimension, without
omitting, however, the semi-colon which accompanies it:

> *PRESSURES*[2;]
>
> 4 5 0 11   gives the second line
>
> *PRESSURES*[;3]
>
> 13 0 2   gives the third column

TYRES[;;2] will give the second column of all the sub-arrays of *TYRES*,
i.e. the output of DOVER.

                              TYRES[;;2]

                0   840   0
                0   910   0
                0   970   160
                0   1040   280

TYRES[3;;]   gives the third sub-array, i.e. the output for 1976.

                    TYRES[3;;]
            3000   0   4330   9480   0
             440   970   390   0   8020
               0   160   0   0   1560

The output statements for the year 1977 were incomplete; the output for
HULL and LEEDS are actually as follows:

                    HULL   LEEDS

Car   9870   2290

Lorry   0   580

Plane   0   0

In order to modify the array *TYRES* accordingly, the following must be
written:

        TYRES[4;;4 1] ← 3 2 ρ 9870 2290 0 580 0 0

Now check: *TYRES*[4;;]
            2290   0   4460   9870   0
             580   1040   380   0   8200
               0   280   0   0   1430

This example shows that the array situated to the right of the assigning
arrow must have the same dimensions as the extract of the array to be
modified.

Hence, we can write: *MONEY*[1 2;5 1] ← 2 2 ρ 100 200 300 400
but we could not write: *MONEY*[1 2;5 1] ← 100 200 300 400

However, since all the designated elements must be replaced by the same
value, a scalar can be entered to the right of the arrow:

        PRESSURES[3;]
    12   13   2   4

        PRESSURES[3;] ← 27   the third line is replaced by 27
        PRESSURES
    11   12   13   2
     4   5   0   11
    27   27   27   27

2-15   THE NATURE OF A SET OF INDICES

Each list of numeric values comprising a set of indices can be designated
by the name of a variable, can be the result of a calculation or can
itself be an indexed value and can be to as many levels as is desired.

                    CUBE ← 3 3 ρ 1 2 3 4 5 6 7 8 9

Examples: CUBE
        1   2   3
        4   5   6
        7   8   9

                    ONE ← 1 3

                    CUBE[ONE;1+1]   Here, part of the set of indices is
        2 8   a variable, the other part is the result
                                     of calculation. everything happens as if
                                                 CUBE [1 3;2] had been
                    VECTOR ← 5 8 1 9 7 11 2 4   written.

                    CUBE[;VECTOR[3 7]]   Here the set of indices is itself
        1   2   an indexed variable with the value
        4   5   1 2.
        7   9

An indexed variable can, in turn, be indexed. In this case it must be
placed between brackets.

                    (CATHE[DRAL])[3 1 2;]
            ☐☐☐☐
            Δ   Δ
            ☐   ☐

The lines 3, 1 and 2 have been extracted from the array obtained by
CATHE[DRAL], yielding a Roman porch, or very nearly.
The same result would have been obtained by:

                    CATHE[DRAL[3 1 2;]]
            ☐☐☐☐
            Δ   Δ
            ☐   ☐

2-16   THE INDEX GENERATOR

It is so common to have to use the series of natural integers 1 2 3...,
that it was considered important to equip APL with a function which
automatically generates this series. This function, called the "index
generator", is represented by the Greek letter iota (ι), accommodated
on the I key of the keyboard.

            ι8
        1 2 3 4 5 6 7 8

            ι5
        1 2 3 4 5

Hence ιN designates the vector of the first N natural integers. As ιN is a vector of N elements, if N has zero value, a vector of zero elements must be obtained: an empty vector.

        ι0

                                        ← blank line
            ρι0
        0

ι0 is therefore a new way of creating an empty set; the first consisted of taking the size of a scalar.

Among the applications of the index generator, here is how to extract the first N elements of a vector; for example the first 6:

        DEGREES[ι6]
    20   35   90   210   360   480

DEGREES[ι6] is equivalent to *DEGREES*[1 2 3 4 5 6].

The use of empty vectors sometimes results in surprises. When you are more acquainted with APL, consult paragraph 3-10 on this subject.

EXERCISES

[11]   Type on the terminal   A ← 8 5 3 9 7
                                 B ← A[1 3 5]←0

        Now ask for the value of A and then that of B.

[12]   Given the array *TYRES*, display the production of lorry tyres over the 4 years, for the 4 factories which make them.

        Display the production of the LEEDS factory in 1977.

[13]   What is the value of: *TYRES*[1;1 2;1 2 3]
                                TYRES[3 2 1;2 1;1]

[14]   What is the value of: A[A ← 5 4 6 2 1 3]

[15]   Given *M* as follows: M ← 4 4 ρ '*ABCDEFGHIJKLMNOP*'
        Then we perform in succession: M[1;] ← M[;3]
                                         M[;2] ← M[2;]

        What result is obtained?

[16]   What should be done in order to exchange the second and fourth columns of the array *PRESSURES*?

[17]   The variable *ARRAY* is given as follows:

            ARRAY ← 2 5 ρ 9 1 4 3 6 7 4 3 8 2

        What should be done in order to replace the numbers 9, 6, 7 and 2
        by 21, 45, 78 and 11 respectively?

[18]   What is the result of the expression:

            TYRES [3; *DRAL* [1; 4]; *PRESSURES* [2; *SOUP* [7 4]]]

        Use the values stated in this course.

[19]   Given: *A* ← 2 4   What is the value of: *A*ρ(ι14) ?

[20]   Since *V* is a vector, why cannot the expression *V* [1+ι(ρ*V*)]   be
        carried out?

[21]   *X* ← 1 2 9 11 3 7 8
        X [3 5] ← *X* [4 1]
        What is the new value of *X*?

[22]   Given a vector named *ORIGIN*, some terms have been mixed by indexing:

                ORIGIN [3 1 6 5 2 4]
            8 11 3 9 2 15

        What was the value of *ORIGIN*?

[23]   Having been given a vector called *INDICES*, the following operation
        was performed:

                9 2 7 4 5 1 [*INDICES*]
            4 2 9 1 5 7

        What was the value of *INDICES*?

2-17   VARIABLES MANAGEMENT

When working on the computer each APL user has a memory area, which can be
of fixed or variable size according to the system and which is called the
ACTIVE WORKSPACE. This area is for storing the variables and later the
defined functions, as they are created.

After a long working period, we would like to know which variables have
been created and are still available. Therefore it is not a calculation
that we are processing, but a request for information relating to the
management of the contents of our active workspace. This is done by
special instructions called COMMANDS. A chapter will be dedicated to
commands, but we will discover the most useful ones in the course of
our work.

It should be noted that the procedures shown hereafter correspond to the
working of almost all the systems. Nevertheless, some computers require
slightly different commands, in this case, the manuals published by the
manufacturer should be referred to.

In order to obtain the list of workspace variables, it is sufficient to
type the command *)VARS* (commands all start with a closed bracket).

> *)VARS*
A   AGE   BIZOU   BROCHURE   CATHE   CUBE   DEGREES   DIAGRAM   DRAL   I   INDEX
J   K   LEFT   MONEY   NAME   ONE   OWL   PRESSURES   PRICE   RIGHT   SOUP   TODAY
TOMATO   TYRES   VECTOR   Z

All the variables which we have defined are still there. If some have
no further use, they can be erased by means of the command *)ERASE*
followed by their names:

> *)ERASE   A   B   I   J   K   Z   BIZOU   BROCHURE   RIGHT   LEFT   AGE   CATHE*
> *)ERASE   REFERENCES   DRAL   CUBE   TODAY   PRICE   SOUP   TOMATO   ONE   VECTOR*

check that the work has been done:

> *)VARS*
DEGREES   DIAGRAM   INDEX   MONEY   NAME   OWL   PRESSURES   TYRES

We may also wish to erase all the contents of the active workspace in
order to make available a workspace clear of all variables and functions.
The following will be typed:

> *)CLEAR*
CLEAR WS

message from the computer, indicating that the work has been performed.
WS is the abbreviation of workspace.

Check the result:
> *)VARS*
                    ← the reply is a blank line.

2-18   MANAGEMENT OF WORKSPACES

When the user stops work, the active workspace is destroyed and its contents lost. So as not to lose the benefit of the work which has been
accomplished, there must be the ability for long-term storage.

Whereas in other interactive data processing languages each program is
stored separately, in APL all the contents of a workspace are stored
as a whole, so as to preserve the possible interactions between several
functions and several variables.

In order to safeguard a workspace the command)*SAVE* is used, followed
by any designated name which will serve to retrieve this workspace.
For example:
>)*SAVE HOLDALL*
> 13.17.32   09/11/77

Under the name *HOLDALL* an instant COPY of our active workspace has been
stored. The computer has confirmed the successful completion of the
operation by specifying the time and date of the safeguard.

This safeguard copy is added to other workspaces which have been safeguarded
in the past and constitutes the private library of the user.

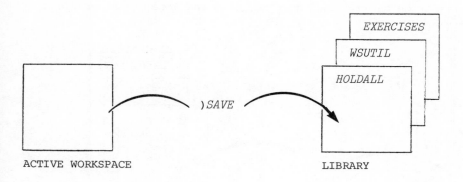

ACTIVE WORKSPACE   LIBRARY

The command)*LIB* reveals the names of the workspaces contained in the user's
private library.

>)*LIB*
> *EXERCISES*
> *WSUTIL*
> *HOLDALL*

If, after a safeguard, the user adds modifications to the contents of
his active workspace, these modifications ARE NOT REFLECTED on the
safeguard copy contained in the library. To retain these modifications,
a new safeguard must be initiated, but it is no longer necessary to
specify the name of the safeguard workspace.

>)*SAVE*
> 13.37.55 09/11/77 *HOLDALL* (confirmation message)

NOTE: Each new safeguard copy replaces the previous one. If in the
      meantime variables have been erased, they will have been
      permanently lost.

2-19   LOADING

The contents of a workspace which has been stored in the library can be
re-used in the course of subsequent work. For this it is sufficient
to type)*LOAD* followed by the name of the workspace.

>)*LOAD HOLDALL*
> *SAVED* 13.37.56 09/11/77

The confirmation message indicates the time and date of the previous
safeguard.

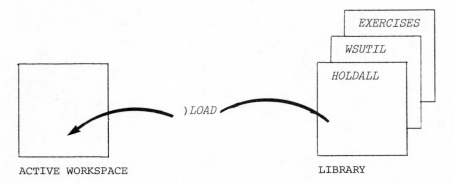

ACTIVE WORKSPACE   LIBRARY

This loading erases all existing at the time in the active workspace.
Finally, a workspace which has no further use can be erased from the library
by the command)*DROP*, followed by the name of the workspace.

>)*DROP EXERCISES*
> 16.29.14 09/14/77

CONTENTS OF A SPACE

The management of workspaces and of their contents will be studied in
detail in Chapter 10. In the meantime, a single workspace will be very
broadly adequate for containing all the data and functions necessary
for studying this book.

It will be advisable generally to group the sets of functions attached
to different areas of activity in different workspaces. This can lead
to the duplication of certain functions in general use, but the documentation and maintenance of workspaces will be considerably eased by
this.

SUPPLEMENTS

TO CHAPTER 2

These supplements are intended for the experienced reader; we would advise beginners to ignore them and return to them when they have acquired some practice in APL. Many paragraphs in the supplements refer to concepts which will be studied in later chapters.

2-21   NAMES OF VARIABLES

A name of a variable must obey certain rules. It must:

1)   Comprise no characters other than the following:

$A\ B\ C\ D\ E\ F\ G\ H\ I\ J\ K\ L\ M\ N\ O\ P\ Q\ R\ S\ T\ U\ V\ W\ X\ Y\ Z$
$\underline{A}\ \underline{B}\ \underline{C}\ \underline{D}\ \underline{E}\ \underline{F}\ \underline{G}\ \underline{H}\ \underline{I}\ \underline{J}\ \underline{K}\ \underline{L}\ \underline{M}\ \underline{N}\ \underline{O}\ \underline{P}\ \underline{Q}\ \underline{R}\ \underline{S}\ \underline{T}\ \underline{U}\ \underline{V}\ \underline{W}\ \underline{X}\ \underline{Y}\ \underline{Z}$
$\underline{0}\ \underline{1}\ \underline{2}\ \underline{3}\ \underline{4}\ \underline{5}\ \underline{6}\ \underline{7}\ 8\ 9$
$\Delta\ \underline{\Delta}$

In particular, no blanks should be inserted.

2)   not start with a number

3)   not comprise more than a certain number of characters, determined by the designer and which is usually fairly high (77 characters on APL SV version planned by IBM).

The following are correct names of variables:

    IBM
    TEMPERATURE
    JANUARY16th1971
    *ONCE*ΔUPONΔAΔTIME
    MONTH
    MONTH
    MONTH
    X1
    Δ*Y*

It is important to note that *MONTH*, *MONTH* and *MONTH* are three different names.

On the other hand, the following names are incorrect:

LITTLE RIDING HOOD	contains blank spaces
11*OCLOCK*	starts with a number
PL/1	contains a special character
C D C	contains special characters

A variable exists only from the moment when a value has been assigned to a correct name. The use of a name to which no value has been assigned constitutes an error which is signalled by the computer:

HORSE + 34

VALUE ERROR

    HORSE + 34
        ∧

The reference *VALUE ERROR* indicates that no value is associated with the name *HORSE*. The computer then repeats the incorrect line and signals the exact position of the error by the sign ∧.

ARRAYS

2-22

PRINTING OF VECTORS

A vector is always printed out on one line, even if it has been obtained by extraction of a column of an array. This is why, in paragraph 2-14, the expression *PRESSURES*[;3] causes 13 0 2 to be printed out, and not 13
                                          0
                                          2

In effect, *PRESSURES*[;3] is a vector of 3 elements.

2-23

ORDER OR SHAPING ARRAYS

When *ARRAY* ← *DIMENSIONS* ρ *CONTENTS* is written, the values are ranked in the array starting with the last dimension, something like the way in which a book is written. The different letters of a line, the lines of a page, the pages of a chapter, etc.

On the other hand, when an element of an array is designed, the order of the indices must follow the normal pattern (plan, row, column, for example). For example, given the variable *PRESSURES*, which has the value:

    11 12 13 2
     4 5 0 11
    27 27 27 27

the expression *PRESSURES*[2;3] designates without ambiguity the value 0 (second row; third column), and not the value 27 (second column; third row).

2-24

EMPTY SETS

An array of any rank is an empty set if any one of its dimensions is nil. Such an array can be created by means of the function ρ as follows:

    EMPTY ← 3 0 7 ρ 12345
    EMPTY   Any value can be used to fill the
                                  array, since it is empty.
    ρ *EMPTY*
3 0 7

The expression *EMPTY* ← 3 0 7 ρ(ι0) is equally correct. On the other hand, an array cannot be filled with nothing and an expression such as 3 5 ρ (ι0) causes print-out of the error message: *DOMAIN ERROR*

Empty vecotrs, or empty arrays are particularly useful as a basis for repeated catenation processing.

INDEXING

2-25   ## RE-EXPLORATION OF AN INDEX

When modifying an array, the same element can be designated several times by the index. In this case, each new value assigned to this element erases the previous one and only the last one remains:

> *A* ← 71 72 73 74 75

> *A*[2 3 2 4 2] ← 1 83 9 47 100

A[3] and *A*[4] take the values 83 and 47 respectively. *A*[2] takes the values 1, 9, and 100 successively.
The following is finally obtained:

> *A*
> 71 100 83 47 75

This result may depend on the system used.

2-26   ## LIMITS IMPOSED ON INDICES

None of the values appearing in a set of indices can be greater than the number of elements of the dimension to which it refers, nor can it be nil or negative.

Check this on the variable *DEGREES*, which has the value:

> 20 35 90 210 360 480 550 580 595
>
> *DEGREES*[3 12 0 5]

INDEX ERROR

> *DEGREES*[3 12 0 5]
>   ∧

The computer indicates an index error relating to the variable *DEGREES*. Neither the value 0 nor the value 12 is acceptable.

Nevertheless, the origin of the indices can be fixed at zero instead of 1. In this case, the first element takes the index 0, the second takes the index 1, up to the ninth, which takes the index 8. This subject will be referred to in paragraph 10-7.

THE RESULT OF INDEXING

Given an array Z, the result of the expression $Z[A; B; C; ...]$ has the dimensions:

$$(\rho A), (\rho B), (\rho C), ...$$

If an index is omitted, one proceeds as if it had the value ιn where n is the omitted dimension. This rule can be readily checked on a known array: *TYRES*. Suppose it is desired to extract the production of lorry and aeroplane tyres over the last three years, in order to compare them. HULL, which does not produce either, is of no interest to us.

YEARS ← 2 3 4	(i.e 1975, 76 and 77)	
TYPES ← 2 3	(i.e lorries and aeroplanes)	
FACTORIES ← 1 2 3 5	(all except Hull)	

EXTRACT ← *TYRES*[*YEARS* ; *TYPES* ; *FACTORIES*]

EXTRACT

```
400    910    380    7660
  0      0      0    1310

440    970    390    8020
  0    160      0    1560

580   1040    380    8200
  0    280      0    1430
```

Check the rule stated above: ρ*EXTRACT* has the value 3 2 4, which is equal to:

$$(\rho YEARS), (\rho TYPES), (\rho FACTORIES)$$
$$\quad 3 \qquad\quad 2 \qquad\qquad 4$$

If only the lorry results had been required, *TYPES* would have been given the value 2, which is a scalar (without dimensions). The result would therefore have been of dimensions 3 4.
We will check this:

TYRES[*YEARS* ; 2 ; *FACTORIES*]
```
400    910    380    7660
440    970    390    8020
580   1040    380    8200
```

Note that in order to replace all the elements of an array by a single value,
the following may be written:

PRESSURES[;] ← 140 or *TYRES*[;;] ← 0

The expressions *PRESSURES* ← 140, or *TYRES* ← 0 would ampunt to creating two
scalars having the values 140 and 0 respectively,which is very different.

2-28   INTERPRETING FEATURES

The interpretation of APL by computers can present slight differences one from
another. Here is one:

The expression (*A* ← 21 34 56) [2] gives the result 34, with any computer. On
the other hand, if we try to use the same method to modify the second element
of *A*, the answers are different:

                    (*A* ← 21 34 56) [2] ← 79
                    A   This system has accepted the instructi
          21   79   56
                    (*A* ← 21 34 56) [2] ← 79
          SYNTAX ERROR   On the other hand, this system has
                 (*A* ← 21 34 56) [2] ← 79 indicatéd an error.
                               ∧

2-29   INDEXING SYNTAX

The notation used for indexing constitutes a distortion of the APL syntax.
In fact it would be natural for a subset of an arrav to be obtained bv means
of a primitive function and not bv the notation:

ARRAY[2   5 ; 1   4   7]

Unfortunately, the set of values 2   5 ; 1   4   7 does not constitute an array
in the sense that we have so far understood and could not be used as an argume
of a primitive function.

Various solutions have been proposed; the most impressive is that available on
experimental svstems using the GENERALIZED ARRAYS concept.

In such svstems, the set of indices can be defined as a generalized array,
and serves as an argument to an indexing function. Hence, it becomes possible
to extract elements which are not positioned at the intersections of the same
lines and columns of the array, a disadvantage indicated in paragraph 2-13.

ALPHANUMERIC VARIABLES

2-30   ## SPECIAL CHARACTERS

We have said that an alphanumeric variable could contain any character.
However, certain characters cannot be placed between quotes. This is so
for example with BACK SPACE and LINE FEED, which are very useful for
creating special effects.

These characters can be obtained by indexing the atomic vector $\Box AV$, which
will be studied on page 277, or the control variable $\Box TC$ if there is one.

Some systems accept that a character string comprises several lines
separated by the carriage returns, counting each one as a character:

         TEXT ← 'I
   AM
   WELL, THANK YOU'
            TEXT
     I
     AM
     WELL, THANK YOU

          ρ TEXT
     20   This shows that both carriage returns are
                                   counted.

With such systems, an isolated quotation makr is frequently inadvertantly
typed, for example, an apostrophe which one forget to double up. From this
moment, all the lines typed are considered by the computer as a long series
of characters and the user has the impression that he is no longer receiving
a response to his instructions. To escape from this deadlock the string must
be enclosed by typing a second quotation mark.

In order to overcome such a disadvantage, most systems over-rule this
possibility and signal an anomaly when a line has an odd number of quotation
marks (except during definition of a function).

Test the reaction of your APL system when faced with the introduction of the
variable *TEXT* above.

Some systems enable special characters to be created by overstriking two
letters. For example '*E*' which is *L* and *F* overstruck, gives the charater
Line Feed. The reading of functions is complicated by this.

2-31   ## NUMERIC ↔ ALPHANUMERIC CONVERSIONS

Numerics and alphanumerics cannot be mixed, except for the functions = ≠ ι ε,
which will be encountered later. Any attempt clears itself by the diagnostic
DOMAIN ERROR which signifies that these two types of variables are essentially

different and may not be associated.

Example:

          NUMBER ← '34'
          NUMBER
   34
          NUMBER + 12
   DOMAIN ERROR
          NUMBER + 12
          ∧

NUMBER is a variable which does not belong to the addition domain. Printing this variable does not indicate whether it is numeric or alphanumeric
and the only way of finding out is to try and use it in an operation.
Subsequently we will write a very useful function, which enables this
discrimination to be made (see the function *NUMER*, paragraph 6-1).

Two functions enable an alphanumeric value to be converted into its
equivalent numeric value (the function EXECUTE: ⍎), or a numeric value
into a character string (the function FORMAT ⍕).

Here is an example using ⍎ :

          12 + ⍎NUMBER   gives the result 46.

These two functions will be studied in detail in chapter 9.

2-32   THE EMPTY ALPHANUMERIC VECTOR

          EMPTY ← ''   No character is left between the
          ρEMPTY   quotes, not even a blank space.
   0

An empty character string has been created. This alphanumeric empty
vector is distinct from the numeric empty vector (ι0). This difference
will be put into effect by the function *NUMER* quoted in the previous
paragraph.

We will end this chapter on an optimistic note:

          PRESENCE ← 'FRIEND'   which proves that a friendly
                                           presence can always fill the
          EMPTY ρ PRESENCE   empty space; but can you
   F   explain it?

CHAPTER 3

BASIC FUNCTIONS

3-1   NOTE

It has been seen that the APL notation comprises a number of primitive
functions which are by way of being the WORDS of the language.

Employing primitive functions, the user can also define functions for
resolving his own problems, which amounts in some ways to writing SENTENCES.

Since the best way to understand the meaning of words is to employ them
for expressing oneself, it is obvious that the best way to master APL
is to create functions for resolving simple problems. This will be the
purpose of chapter 4.
In order however to write sentences, a minimum number of words must be
learnt, at the risk of not immediately grasping all the nuances. We
therefore propose in this chapter quickly to introduce some essential
primitive functions of APL.

The advanced reader, or one who has already had a few hours practice with
APL on the computer, may confine himself to reading only the framed rules
and supplements to this chapter.

3-2   THE SCALAR FUNCTION CONCEPT

The primitive functions of APL are represented by symbols: ι ρ $\lceil$ $\in$ ....
In order to restrict the number of these symbols, and due to the small
number of keyboard characters, two different meanings are associated with
many symbols, depending on whether they are used in a monodic or dyadic
manner. These two meanings usually have a relationship which simplifies
storage.

We have seen that the symbol ρ had two meanings, both connected with the
dimensions of a variable (paragraphs 2-4 and 2-8).

Some functions apply only between two arguments of the same dimensions
and yield a result also of the same dimensions. It is said that such
functions are SCALAR FUNCTIONS.

It is the same with addition, which allows the addition term by term
of the elements of two arrays:

>   3 5 2 + 2 2 6
>   5 7 8

On the contrary, the two arguments and the result of the function ρ have
different dimensions:

>   5 ρ 2 8 4   would yield a result: 2 8 4 2 8

The function ρ is not a scalar function, and it is called a MIXED
function.

SOME BASIC FUNCTIONS

3-3   THE FOUR OPERATIONS

Among the dyadic scalar functions there are the four operations of
arithmetic:

Addition   +

Subtraction   −   (on the same key as +)

Multiplication   ×

Division   ÷

While most DP languages employ * and / to represent multiplication and
division, APL employs the usual symbols × and ÷.

RULE:

> Dyadic scalar functions apply term by term to data of the
> same dimensions. They also apply between a scalar (or any
> array of a single element) and any array; in such a case,
> the result has the dimensions of the latter array.

The following examples illustrate this rule:

>   2 3 4 × 10 ⁻5 6   composition of two data of the same dimensions.
>   20 ⁻15 24

If *M* and *N* are two arrays, the respective values of which are:

21	22	⁻25	30	and	14	19	⁻30	12
12	31	11	0		12	50	50	⁻11

M + N can be calculated, being:

35	41	⁻55	42
24	81	61	⁻11

composition of a scalar and an array:

N ÷ 2

7	9.5	⁻15	6
6	25	25	⁻5.5

Or again:

⁻7 + 23 40 67 11 0 12

16	33	60	⁻1	4	⁻7	5

This brings out the full importance of the distinction made in paragraph 1-4 between the minus sign and the subtraction symbol. If this distinction were not made it would be impossible to say whether the expression 9 7 - 3 6 is a vector of four values one of which is negative (the 3) or whether subtraction of the vectors 9 7 and 3 6 is involved. In APL confusion is impossible:

        9 7 - 3 6 is a subtraction, the result of which is: 6 1
9 7 ⁻3 6 designates the vector of four elements: 9 7 ⁻3 6

Other dyadic scalar functions will be useful to us shortly, these being power, minimum and maximum, relationship functions and logical functions.

NOTES ON DIVISION:

The expression 17 ÷0 will bring about appearence of the message DOMAIN ERROR : 0 does not belong to the field of application of division. On the other hand 0 ÷0 yields the response 1 so that any number divided by itself yields 1.

3-4   POWER

The mathematical notation x^n is written *X∗N* in APL.

This function applies whatever *N* is, whole or decimal, positive, negative or zero, as shown in the following example:

We will write the scalar 4 with a powers vector:

<pre>   4 *2 1.4 0 0.5 ‾1 ‾2.1 5

            16   6.964   1   2   0.25   0.0544   1024
            ↑   ↑   ↑   ↑   ↑   ↑   ↑
</pre>

i.e respectively: 4^2 $4^{1.4}$ 4^0 $\sqrt{4}$ $1/4$ $4^{-2.1}$ 4^5

According to usage 0*0 yields 1.

It is seen that there is no specific symbol for square root $\sqrt{}$, which is obtained by raising to the power 0.5. One cannot of course extract the square root of a negative number:

<pre>   ‾3 * 0.5   will bring about the error DOMAIN ERROR
     ‾125 * (1÷3)   will yield the response ‾5.
</pre>

3-5   MINIMUM, MAXIMUM

The function ∟ (minimum) and ⌐ (maximum) respectively give the smallest and largest of two values whatever the sign.

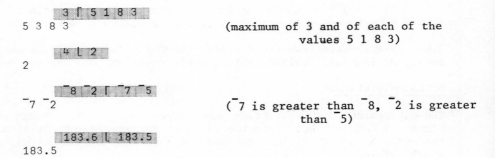

<pre>   3 ⌈ 5 1 8 3
       5 3 8 3   (maximum of 3 and of each of the
                                           values 5 1 8 3)
            4 ∟ 2
       2

          ‾8 ‾2 ⌈ ‾7 ‾5
       ‾7 ‾2   (‾7 is greater than ‾8, ‾2 is greater
                                           than ‾5)
          183.6 ∟ 183.5
       183.5
</pre>

With the arrays M and N on the preceding page, we would obtain:

<pre>   M ∟ N
       14   19 ‾30   12
       12   31   11 ‾11

             M ⌈ N
       21   22 ‾25   30
       12   50   50   0
</pre>

3-6   RELATIONSHIP FUNCTIONS

APL comprises the six relationship functions which can connect two values:

$A < B$ A less than B
$A \leq B$ A less than or equal to B
$A = B$ A equal to B
$A \geq B$ A greater than or equal to B
$A > B$ A greater than B
$A \neq B$ A different from B

These functions yield the value 1 if the relationship expressed is correct
and 0 if it is not:

2 < 8   yields the response 1

5 = 9   yields the response 0

The relationship functions are dyadic scalar functions and therefore vectors
or arrays can be composed from them. The following are some examples:

        3 5 11 > 1 8 3
     1 0 1

This result means that 3 is greater than 1, that 5 is not greater than 8
and that 11 is greater than 3.

        4 ≤ 6 2 9 4 3 1 5 4
     1 0 1 1 0 0 1 1

It is said that the results obtained with the relationship functions are
BINARY values (since they can take only one of the two values 0 and 1),
or again LOGICAL(since they express a logical relationship between two values),
or again BOOLEAN (from the name of the mathematician George BOOLE).
Boolean values are particular numeric values. The use of certain primitive
functions is strictly reserved for them, as we will find.

The functions = and ≠ apply to alphanumeric data:

        'IMPULSIVE'= 'INCENTIVE'
     1 0 0 0 0 0 1 1 1

There would of course be no sense in applying one of the functions < ≤ ≥
or > to alphanumeric data. We will see later how to prepare an alphabetic
classification.

3-7   LOGICAL NEGATION

A binary value indicates whether a relationship is verified or not.   It
may sometimes be useful to refer to the inverse relationship.

For example here is a list of wages:

> WAGES ← 2420 4630 1890 3407 6523 3000 1720 3448

Wages greater than £3000 can be indicated by a vector B obtained as
follows:

> B ← WAGES > 3000
> B
  0 1 0 1 0 0 1

Now if we wish to indicate wages which are not greater than £3000 we can
of course write WAGES ≤ 3000, but it would be quicker to write:

> ~ B
1 0 1 0 0 1 1 0

The monadic function ~ gives the opposite logical value to that of its
argument.   It is called NOT function or again LOGICAL NEGATION.

> ~ 0 equals 1
> ~ 1 equals 0

3-8   MEMBERSHIP

Relationship functions are not the only ones which yield binary results.
The membership function (∈) indicates by 1's and 0's if the elements
of its left operand appear or not in the right operand.

The two operands can be any, both as regards dimensions and type, and
the result ALWAYS possesses the dimensions of the left operand.

Membership therefore is not a scalar function but a mixed function.

Examples:
> 11 8 3 ∈ 17 14 8 2 6 11 8
    1 1 0

This result means that 11 and 8 appear in the right vector but that
3 does not appear there.

		8	14	7	9	2			1 0 1 0 1
If M is the matrix:	5	8	16	16	3	then M ∈ (ι8) will equal:	1 1 0 0 1
		0	1	6	7	4			0 1 1 1 1

Membership can be used with alphanumeric values

'JANUARY' ∈ 'SUMMER'
0 0 0 1 0 1 0

O
17 ∈ '17'   (the types are mixed here)

O O
'17' ∈ 17   ('17'is actually a 2 element vector)

3-9   LOGICAL FUNCTIONS

When binary values are available there are functions which enable
them to be composed from them. These are LOGICAL functions. In this
paragraph we will study only the two main ones, namely the functions
AND and OR.

The function AND is indicated as ∧. It takes the value 1 only if the
conditions expressed by the right operand <u>AND</u> the left operand
are simultaneously verified.

        Thus, 1∧1 equals 1, but 1∧0, 0∧1, 0∧0 equal 0.

For example we have the age and number of children of a certain number
of women:

AGES ← 18 35 41 25 23 52 29 55 32 21 24 47 36 29

CHIL ← 0 2 1 3 1 3 4 0 2 2 2 2 0 3

If we wish to indicate the women who are below 30 and have more than
two children, we proceed as follows:

AGES < 30 equals: 1 0 0 1 1 0 1 0 0 1 1 0 0 1

CHIL > 2 equals: 0 0 0 1 0 1 1 0 0 0 0 0 0 1

(AGES<30) ∧ (CHIL > 2) equals: 0 0 0 1 0 0 1 0 0 0 0 0 0 1
                                         ▲   ▲   ▲

                          Only these persons simultaneously
                          satisfy the one <u>AND</u> the other
                          conditions.

The function OR is marked ∨. It takes the value 1 if one <u>OR</u> the other
of the conditions expressed by its operands equals 1 and a fortiori
if both conditions are satisfied.

Thus, 1∨1, 1∨0, 0∨1 will equal 1, but 0∨0 will equal 0.

If it is required to bring out women who are over 40 <u>OR</u> who have no children the work can be broken down as follows:

AGES > 40 equals: 0 0 1 0 0 1 0 1 0 0 0 1 0 0

CHIL = 0 equals: 1 0 0 0 0 0 0 1 0 0 0 0 1 0

(AGES > 40) v (CHIL = 0) equals: 1 0 1 0 0 1 0 1 0 0 0 1 1 0
                                  ▲   ▲   ▲   ▲   ▲ ▲

Each of these persons conforms to one OR other of the two conditions stated. There is even one who conforms to both conditions.

It is usual to visualise, by a TRUTH TABLE the value taken by the logical functions for each combination of the two operands:

Data		AND	OR
A	B	$A{\wedge}B$	$A{\vee}B$
0	0	0	0
0	1	0	1
1	0	0	1
1	1	1	1

There are other logical functions: the EXCLUSIVE OR, the NOT-OR (called also NOR), the NOT-AND (called also NAND). These functions are treated in the supplements to paragraph 3-27.

Very simple application of binary variables will be found in the exercises at the end of the chapter (see in particular exercise 42).

3-10   ABSORPTION

If a scalar and a vector are composed of a dyadic scalar function, the result possesses the dimension of the vector. Consequently, if a scalar is composed with an empty vector, the result will possess the dimensions of the latter and this will also be an empty vector.

This can be readily checked both on numeric values and on alphanumeric values.

        2 + (ι0)

                ← Blank line.

        ρ(2 + (ι0))

    0

(⍳0) ⌈ 4827

← Blank line, the result is an empty vector.

A ← 439
B ← 9125
(⍴A) = (⍴B)

← Blank line, the result is an empty vector.

Here is the alphanumeric empty vector:

⍴('Q' = '')

0

Our comments can be formalised in the following rule:

RULE:

> Composition of an empty vector and a scalar (or any single element array)
> by means of a dyadic scalar function returns an empty vector. It is
> said that the empty vector is ABSORBANT.

This charateristic can result in very disagreeable surprises as we will
see in paragraph 6-5.

3-11   METHOD OF EVALUATING APL EXPRESSIONS

Custom teaches us that 3×5+1 equals 16 and not 18, since mutiplication
is performed prior to addition. This rule of evaluation is difficult to
apply as soon as calculation becomes slightly more complicated (thus,
what does 5÷3×4÷3-1 equal?), and it becomes inapplicable as soon as
the expression contains functions for which usage has not established any
priority such as ⍳,⍴, * or ⌈.

It thus becomes impossible to say what 9 + 4 ⌈ ⍳ 3 × 8 ÷ 1 + ⍴ 6 7 8 will
equal.

The need to clarify calculation procedures necessitates re-iteration of
established mathematical usages.

In order to calculate *Log sin* $\sqrt{1+x}$, 1+x is first calculated, then the
root is extracted then the sin is calculated and finally the logarithm of
the result is read off. Each function is applied to the result of the
whole of the expression situated to the right. Concatination of functions
is performed therefore FROM RIGHT TO LEFT.

Since all the operations (+ - × ÷ ⍳ ⍴ ⌊ * etc....) are functions, it
was natural that evaluation of APL expressions should follow the same
single rule.

RULE :

> In an APL expression, each function allows for the right operand, the
> result of the whole of the expression situated to the right of it.
> It allows, for the left operand, if it is dyadic, the data situated
> immediately to the left of it, up to the next symbol.
>
> The use of brackets allows, as is the custom, application of another
> order of evaluation. An expression in brackets is considered as a
> whole, which is evaluated before being used in other calculations.

Thus, there remains no other hierarchy nor rule of priority between
functions.

This rule, wrongly called "evaluation from right to left", involves
concatenation of several functions, but each function retains its usual
significance. Thus, 8÷4 signifies that 8 is divided by 4, and not the
reverse.

3-12   EXAMPLES

a)

$$3 \times 5 + 1$$
$$3 \times \quad 6$$
$$18$$

b)

$$5 - 12 \div 3 \times 4 \div 3 - 1$$
$$4 \div \quad 2$$
$$3 \times \quad 2$$
$$12 \div \quad 6$$
$$5 - \quad 2$$
$$3$$

c) The following represents the case of an expression in brackets:

$$((3 \times 7) + 4) - (5 + 2) \times 3 + 1$$
$$21 \quad + 4 \qquad 7 \quad \times \quad 4$$
$$25 \qquad - \qquad 28$$
$$^-3$$

d)

$$9 + 4 \lceil 1\ 3 \times 8 \div 1 + \rho\ 6\ 7\ 8$$

$$1 + \quad 3$$

$$8 \div \quad 4$$

$$3 \times \ 2$$

$$1 \quad 6$$

$$4 \lceil 1\ 2\ 3\ 4\ 5\ 6$$

$$9 + 4\ 4\ 4\ 4\ 5\ 6$$

$$13 \quad 13 \quad 13 \quad 13 \quad 14 \quad 15$$

e)

$$7 \lfloor 4 \lceil 2 + 1\ 5 + 2$$

$$1 \quad 7$$

$$2 + 1\ 2\ 3\ 4\ 5\ 6\ 7$$

$$4 \lceil 3\ 4\ 5\ 6\ 7\ 8\ 9$$

$$7 \lfloor 4\ 4\ 5\ 6\ 7\ 8\ 9$$

$$4\ 4\ 5\ 6\ 7\ 7\ 7$$

This rule of evaluation requires a change of habits, particularly by those who have already used another programming language and we therefore strongly advise you to carry out the following exercises.

EXERCISES

(1) Evaluate the following expressions:

    a) $3 \times 2 + 6 \neq 3 \times 2$

    b) $12\ 6\ 27 \lfloor 11 + 13$

    c) $4\ 5\ 6 \lceil 4 + 2\ 5\ 9 > 1\ 6\ 8$

    d) $7 \lfloor 25\ 6\ 17 - (2 \times 3) + 9\ 3\ 5$

    e) $((8+6) \times 2 + 1) \times 3 - 6 \div 3$

(2) What is the result of the expression: $2 + 2\ \ 2 + 2$?

(3) We have: $A \leftarrow 8\ 2\ 7\ 5$

Are the expressions $1+\rho A$ and $\rho A+1$ equal?

Are the three expressions $^{-}1+\iota\rho A$, $\iota^{-}1+\rho A$, and $\iota\rho A-1$ equal?

(4) Retaining the variable A from the previous exercise, evaluate: $(2\rho\rho A)\rho A$

(5) Evaluate $(\rho 4\lfloor 5) + 4\lceil 5$

(6) Reformulate the following expressions, removing all brackets:

$$((\iota 4)-1) \lceil 3$$

$$7\lfloor(\iota 9) \lceil 3$$

$$1+((\iota 5)=1\ 4\ 3\ 2\ 5)\ 5$$

(7) $A \leftarrow 12\ 7\ 20 - A + \rho\ A \leftarrow 4\ 5\ 6$ What does A equal?

(8) Assuming a variable A, write an APL expression yielding the response 1 if A is a scalar and the response 0 in all other cases.

(9) Assuming two scalars A and B it is desired that C take the value 7 if A is greater than B and otherwise the value 3.

Write the expression yielding C as a function of A and B.

(10) Assuming two scalars A and B it is desired that C:

- be an empty vector if A is zero whatever B is.

- take the value 0 if B is zero, but not A.

- take the value 3 if neither A nor B are zero.

Write the expression yielding C in terms of A and B.

(11) Perform the following two expressions on the computer:

$$(A\leftarrow 2) \times A\leftarrow 17$$

and

$$(A\leftarrow 2) \times \lfloor A\leftarrow 17$$

How does one explain that the two responses are different?

(12) According to the mathematician FERMAT, numbers of the form $2^{2^n} + 1$ are prime numbers. Give the values obtained for n varying from 1 to 5.

(13) In APL how would one write the following mathematical expressions:

$$x = \frac{\dfrac{a+b}{c}}{\dfrac{c}{d} + e}$$

$$y = \frac{\dfrac{-b}{e+1}}{a}$$

$$z = \frac{-b + \sqrt{b^2 - 4ac}}{2a}$$

(14) Write the following APL expressions in conventional mathematical form:

$X \leftarrow A-B\div C+D$

$Y \leftarrow (C\star D) - B$

$Z \leftarrow A\times X\star 2 + B\times X + C$

$T \leftarrow A\times A - (2\times C) + D$

(15) Given the following three vectors G, M and D: $\quad G \leftarrow 1 \; 1 \; 1 \; 0 \; 0 \; 1$

$$M \leftarrow 0 \; 0 \; 1 \; 1 \; 0 \; 1$$

$$D \leftarrow 1 \; 0 \; 1 \; 0 \; 1 \; 0$$

Evaluate the following expressions:

a) $G \lor D$ e) $\dot{G} \land M \lor D$
b) $\sim G \land D$ f) $(\sim D) \land (\sim G)$
c) $\sim G \lor \sim D$ g) $(M\lceil G) = (M\lfloor D)$
d) $D \land \sim G$ h) $(M\lfloor G) \neq (M\lceil D)$

(16) Evaluate the following expressions:

$5 \; ^-3 \; 2 \; 6 > 4$

$^-2 \; 4 \; ^-6 \leq \; ^-4 \; 2 \; 9 \; \lfloor \; ^-2 \; 5 \; 0$

$0 < 0 \leq 0 = 0 \geq 0 > 0 \neq 0$

$3 + 5 < 2$

$7 \times \sim 3 = 1 + \iota 3$

(17) Evaluate the following expressions:

$(4 \neq 4 \; 3 \; 6) \in \iota 3$

$'SUGAR' \in 'SALT'$

$11 \neq '11'$

$'14' \in '41'$

3-13   REDUCTION

Association of the symbol / (REDUCTION) and of a dyadic scalar function involves application of the latter between all the elements of the single operand on the right.

A few typical examples will assist in understanding the importance of this.

Reduction by the sum yields the sum of the terms of the operand:

>   +/ 2 9 4 6
>   21

This notation is equivalent to: 2+9+4+6

Reduction by multiplication yields the product of the terms of the operand:

>   x/ 3 4 6 2
>   144

This notation is equivalent to: 3×4×6×2

Reduction by the maximum yields the highest value of the operand and reduction by the minimum yields the smallest:

>   ⌈/ 8 19 2 14 9 11 7 13
>   19
>   ⌊/ 8 19 2 14 9 11 7 13
>   2

These four examples show that reduction is a standard notation generalising to advantage staggered notations adopted by usage, such as: Σ , Π , *Max* , *Min....*

Reduction is also very important used with logical functions:

Reduction by AND yields the value 1 if all the elements of the operand are equal to 1. Reduction by OR yields the value 1 if one at least of the elements of the operand equals 1. It yields the value 0 if all the elements are zero.

>   ∧/ 1 1 1 1 0 1 1 0 1
>   0
>   ∧/ 1 1 1 1 1
>   1
>   ∨/ 0 0 0 1 0 0 1 1 1 0 0 0 0 0 1
>   1

Returning to the variables AGES and CHIL in paragraph 3-9, if we wish to know whether all women are over 20, we will write:

<pre>   ∧/ AGES > 20</pre>
    O   The response is no.

If we wish to know if there is at least one woman with more than two children we will write:

<pre>   ∨/ CHIL > 2</pre>
    1   The response is yes.

The expression +/ CHIL > 2 would have also indicated that four women were in this category.

Look out for the evaluation of the expressions involving a non-commutative operation. For example $-/5\ 1\ 4\ 9$ is equivalent to $5 - 1 - 4 - 9$, and the rule of evaluation from right to left yields $^-1$.

3-14   APPLICATIONS OF REDUCTION

a) The wages received by the employees of a company are set out below together with their position in the hierarchy, indicated by a value from 1 to 3.

WAGES ← 3630 6140 2410 5930 4150 2180 3200 5730 3840 3750 5240 3200

CATEGS ← 1   3   2   2   1   1   3   3   3   2   2   3

It is desired to increase the wages of those in category 1 by 5%, of those in category 2 by 3% and of those in category 3 by 2%. How much will this cost the company?

SOLUTION

Note the intended rates of increase: RATES ← 0.05 0.03 0.02
Now writing RATES [CATEGS] we obtain:

0.05 0.02 0.03 0.03 0.05 0.05 0.02 0.02 0.02 0.03 0.03 0.02

We have thus obtained the rate of increase relating to each employee. This has to be multiplied by the corresponding wages in order to obtain the increase for each, then performing the sum:

<pre>   +/ WAGES × RATES [CATEGS]</pre>
    1460.1

b) In order to learn whether a number N is between two limits, we can write:
        >/N>L where L is the vector of the two given limits.

This expression yields 1 if $L[1]<N\leq L[2]$

<pre>   >/8>2 11</pre>
    1
<pre>   >/8>2 7</pre>
    O

3-15   REDUCTION OF ARRAYS

When an array is reduced, it is necessary to indicate by an index whithin
square brackets what is the dimension involved in the reduction.

On reducing an array by a dyadic scalar function along its nth
dimension, the dimensions of the result are those of the array,
amputated by their nth element. The rank of the result is thus
equal to the rank of the initial array less 1.

Example

The array EXPENDITURES summarises (in thousands of francs) the costs
involved in paying the personnel of a company. It comprises two sub-arrays
(staff, temporary personnel) each of three lines (fixed wages, overtime,
bonuses) and six columns (the first six months of the year).

EXPENDITURES

161	161	161	164	164	164	fixed	⎫
9	3	11	6	4	4	overtime	⎬ staff
10	17	22	9	11	20	bonuses	⎭

130	132	184	197	163	0	fixed	⎫
1	7	9	10	5	6	overtime	⎬ temporary personnel
21	24	8	11	17	161	bonuses	⎭

ρEXPENDITURES
  2   3   6

a) If it is wished to obtain expenditures for all the personnel combined,
    the two sub arrays have to be added, so as to obtain a summary of three
    lines and six columns. In other words the first dimension of EXPEND-
    ITURES has to disappear by addition:

+/[1] EXPENDITURES

291	293	345	361	327	164	fixed	⎫
10	10	20	16	9	10	overtime	⎬ staff + temporary
							personnel
31	41	30	20	28	181	bonuses	⎭

b) In order to obtain the total of the amounts involved each month in
    each category of personnel the three lines of each sub-array have to
    be added, thus eliminating the second dimension of the EXPENDITURES
    array:

+/[2] EXPENDITURES

| 180 | 181 | 194 | 179 | 179 | 188 | staff |
| 152 | 163 | 201 | 218 | 185 | 167 | temporary personnel |

Fixed + overtime + bonuses

c) In order to obtain the total, classified by type, of the amounts involved in 6 months, the columns have to be added together, thus eliminating the last dimension of the array.

+/[3] EXPENDITURES

| 975 | 37 | 89 | ← staff |
| 806 | 38 | 242 | ← temporary personnel |

↑ ↑ ↑——bonuses
——overtime
——fixed

CONVENTION : By convention, use of the sign / alone indicates a reduction in the last dimension.
In the case of the previous example +/ EXPENDITURES is strictly equivalent to +/[3] EXPENDITURES.

-16   LOGICAL COMPRESSION

Logical compression, represented by the symbol /, is a dyadic function allowing a logical vector for the left-hand argument and any data for the right-hand argument. This yields a result retaining only the elements in the right-hand argument corresponding to the 1's of the left-hand argument.

For clarification, the following are two vector compressions:

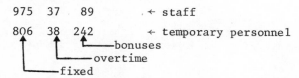

      1 1 0 0 1 0 / 8 2 4 1 6 7
8 2 6

      0 0 0 0 1 1 0 0 0 1 / *'EUCALYPTUS'*
LYS

If the right-hand argument is an array with a rank greater than 1, an index should indicate which dimension is involved in the compression, in the same way as for reduction.

Consider the example:

CHEMISTRY

H2SO4
CACO3
FE2O3

      1 0 1 /[1] CHEMISTRY   and   1 1 0 1 0 /[2] CHEMISTRY
H2SO4   *H2O*
FE2O3   *CAO*
                                        FEO

The second line has vanished   two columns have been
                                            eliminated

In the same way as reduction, the symbol / used alone indicates a compression on the last dimension.

Generally speaking, the left-hand argument is obtained by application of
one of the relationship functions seen earlier. Thus, in order to retain
only values greater than 3 for a vector X we would write:

EXAMPLE:
$X \leftarrow 2\ 9\ 4\ 5\ 2\ 8\ 0\ 8\ 0\ 7$

$(X>3)$ equals : 0 1 1 1 0 1 0 1 0 1

$(X>3)/X$ equals:9 4 5 8 8 7

If one of the arguments is a scalar, it is extended to the dimension of
the other argument.

Thus, 1 0 1 0 0 1/7 is equivalent to 1 0 1 0 0 1/7 7 7 7 7 7 yielding the
result: 7 7 7.

PARTICULAR CASE

If the left-hand argument is a scalar, it applies to the whole right-hand
argument.

1/ [n]$ARRAY$ restores the variable $ARRAY$ in its entirety,
0/ [n]$ARRAY$ restores an array for which the nth dimension is zero i.e an
empty set.

Examples:
$A \leftarrow 2\ 3\ 4\ \rho\ 8$

$\rho\ 0/[2]A$
2 0 4
$0\ /\ 11\ 23\ 45\ 67\ 5$
                                no response: empty set

We will see further that it is important not to confuse REDUCTION and
COMPRESSION despite the similarity of the symbol employed.

3-17   CATENATION OF VECTORS

Catenation symbolised by the comma (,) enables two arrays, the dimensions of
which are compatible, to be coupled in a bigger array. Catenation of arrays
will be considered in paragraph 6-3 (chapter 6) but we will be employing
catenation of vectors from now on.

CATENATION OF NUMERIC VECTORS

$$A \leftarrow 11 \quad 22 \quad 33$$
$$B \leftarrow 6 \quad 3 \quad 8 \quad 9 \quad 5$$
$$A,B$$
11 22 33 6 3 8 9 5

It is seen that $\rho(A,B)$ is equal to: $(\rho A)+(\rho B)$

$$336 \, , \, 21 \quad 602 \quad 78 \quad 900$$
336 21 602 78 9000

CATENATION OF ALPHANUMERIC VECTORS

$$NO \leftarrow {}'IS'$$
$$BODY \leftarrow {}'PERFECT'$$
$$NO, \; BODY$$
IS PERFECT

Since the arguments and result do not have the same dimensions, catenation
is not a scalar function but a mixed dyadic function.

CATENATION OF EMPTY VECTORS

Coupling an empty vector to another vector amounts to not modifying the
latter.
For example:

$$3 \; 5 \; 9 \, , \, (\iota 0) \quad \text{yields : } 3 \; 5 \; 9$$
$$'', \; 'HOTEL' \quad \text{yields : HOTEL}$$

It may be said that empty vectors are neutral elements of the catenation
function. Hence, they are frequently used as the first link in a repetitive
catenation process.

-18   NOTES ON CATENATION OF VECTORS

a) It was stated in paragraph 2-11 that it is incorrect to juxtapose two
    names of variables without separating them by a function. Given the
    variables A and B above, the vector 11 22 33 6 3 8 9 5 can be formed
    only by writing A,B but not writing A B.

b) If a series of values is too long to be typed in a single line, as
    many lines as necessary are catenated end to end. For example:

$$VEC \leftarrow 12 \quad 23 \quad 34 \quad 45 \quad 56 \quad 67 \quad 78 \quad 89 \quad 90$$
$$VEC \leftarrow VEC \, , \, 13 \quad 24 \quad 35 \quad 46 \quad 57 \quad 35 \quad 66 \quad 91 \quad 43$$
$$VEC \leftarrow VEC \, , \, 70 \quad 54 \quad 61 \quad 62 \quad 63 \quad 64 \quad 66 \quad 60$$

At each stage its present value is applied to VEC, catenated to new
values which it is desired to add subsequently.

The following is the result:

> VEC

> 12 23 34 45 56 67 78 89 90 18 24 35 46 57 35 66 91 43 70 54 61 62
> 63 64 66 60

An even quicker method will be considered in paragraph 4-18.

SOME MONADIC SCALAR FUNCTIONS

We have seen that the one symbol may designate two related functions
according to whether it is employed monadically or dyadically. The
following are a few monadic functions which will be of use subsequently.

3-19   EXPONENTIAL

e^X is written *X in APL. This represents monadic use of the asterisk.
it is seen that these two uses are associated with the concept of power,
whence mnemonic placing of the symbol * on the P key.

> * ¯1 0 1 2 3.14
> 0.367879   1   2.71828   7.38906   23.1039

The number of decimal figures displayed is deliberatly restricted here.
Out of curiosity, here is the value of e with the maximum IBM precision
of 16 significant figures:

> *1
> 2.718281828459045

3-20   FLOOR, CEILING

Employed in monadic fashion, $\lfloor$ and $\lceil$ give respectively the immediately
lower or immediately higher integer of their argument (lower and upper
rounding):

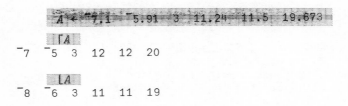

> A ← ¯7.1 ¯5.91 3 11.24 11.5 19.673

> ⌈A
> ¯7 ¯5 3 12 12 20

> ⌊A
> ¯8 ¯6 3 11 11 19

-21   RECIPE

In order to obtain a number rounded to the nearest integral, 0.5 should
be added to it, taking the floor of the result.

          A
    ¯7.1 ¯5.91 3 11.24 11.5 19.673

          A+0.5
    ¯6.6 ¯5.41 3.5 11.74 12 20.173

          ⌊0.5 + A
    ¯7 ¯6 3 11 12 20   Which is the result sought.

EXERCISES

(18) Given a vector *V*, calculate the mean of the *V* elements.

(19) A questionnaire has been completed by several hundred families. On
     analysing them, the number of children in each family has been
     logged in a CHIL vector. How would you go about obtaining the
     percentage of couples with 3 children or less than 3 children. A whole
     number percentage is required, for example 53.

(20) How many times does the letter *S* appear in the phrase *PH* below :
     PH ←'SHE SELLS SEASHELLS ON THE SEASHORE'

(21) The vector *A* and the vector *B* should be identical. They are too
     long to check quickly. What can be done?

(22) Three tests have been carried out on the variable *Z*. Can you deduce
     its value from these?
          Z=9 equals : 0 ; 2ρZ equals : 1 7 ; +/[1]Z equals : 20
                         0
                         1
                         0

(23) FAULTY KEYBOARD: The key (*R*,ρ) of your keyboard no longer functions.
     How is the dimension of a vector *V* to be found?

(24) Three tests have been carried out on the variable X. Can you deduce
     its value from these?

$$X{=}0 \text{ equals : } 0\ 1\ 0\ 0\ ;\ {+}/[1]X \text{ equals : } 8\ 7\ 6\ 5\ ;\ {+}/X \text{ equals: } 20\ 6$$
$$1\ 0\ 0\ 1$$

(25) The co-ordinates of two points A and B of a plan are given by the
     two vectors A and B. A represents the A co-ordinates and B rep-
     resents the B co-ordinates. Find the expression yielding the slope
     of the straight line AB. The slope of AB is obtained from:

$$\frac{y_A\ {}^{-}y_B}{x_A\ {}^{-}x_B}$$

(26) Employing the array *TYRES* of chapter 2, find:
     -   the total production of the 5 plants combined for each category
         of tyre, year by year,
     -   the total production of tyres of all types from each of the
         plants, year by year.

(27) Employing the *EXPENDITURES* array of paragraph 3-15, state how much
     has been expended for staff and temporary employees during 6 months
     for wages, overtime and bonuses combined.

(28) We have the matrix of the names of pupils in a class:

                                         NAMES equals: *MARC*
                                                         JEAN
     We have also in the vector *MARKS*, the marks obtained   *YVES*
     by these pupils in a test.   *ERIC*
                                                         PAUL
                                                         ....

     Print out the names of pupils with a mark higher than 12.

(29) What are the POSITIONS of the letter S in the phrase *PH* of exercise
     20.

(30) Given any vector V. Find a general method for extracting the elements
     of odd indices (1st, 3rd, 5th ......).

(31) How many elements are there in *TYRES* ?

(32) Since 1974 what were the biggest tyre productions for each of the
     three types, all plants combined ?

(33) Evaluate the following expressions:

   2 2 + 2 2   2 , 2 + 2 , 2   2 + 2 2 + 2   2 + 2 , 2 + 2

(34) It is required to eliminate all non-integral values of a vector. How is this done?

(35) In a vector it is required to eliminate all values which are not between 20 and 30. How is this done?

(36) In a vector V, it is required to replace all values less than 20 by 20 and all values greater than 30 by 30. For example:

   66 12 23 42 20 17 22 24 25 23 44 becomes: 30 20 23 30 20 20 22 24 25 23 30

   How is this achieved?

(37) Evaluate the three following expressions: 'A','B' then 'A''B'then'A,B'

(38) The eight expressions below are all abnormal. Why?

   a) 3+(5-(6+2)×4   d) (^-X+5)*2   g) 14 0 $^-$4 ÷ 2 0 1

   b) $B2 - 4AC$ e) (X-3)(X+4)   h) ρA B C

   c) 121÷(14)-3   f) ρ4 5 6+2 3-1

(39) Using an APL expression, set up an arithmetic progression of 17 terms, the first being 23, each term being equal to the preceding plus 11.

(40) Employing an APL expression, set up a geometric progression of 20 terms, the first being 25 and each term being equal to the preceding multiplied by 1.2.

(41) Evaluate the expressions:

   a) 8 , 2 5 + 3   b) 7 6 + 5 , 9   c) 1 + 2 9 6 , 1 5 - 1

(42) A tombola has been organised. The vector *TICKETS* contains the number of tickets printed. The vector *SOLD* contains the number of all the tickets sold. The vector *WINNERS* contains the winning numbers. The vector *FAMILY* contains the numbers of the tickets bought by my family.

   Write the APL expressions answering the following questions:

   a) How many tickets bought by my family are winning tickets?
   b) What are the numbers of unsold tickets?
   c) Have all the winning tickets been sold? (binary response)
   d) How many winning tickets were not sold?

SUPPLEMENTS

TO CHAPTER 3

3-22   DYADIC SCALAR FUNCTIONS

Two comments emerge:

a) On the one hand, 17÷2 gives the result 8.5. APL does not introduce
   the FORTRAN anomaly where the same operation would give 8 as the
   result.

b) On the other hand, while it is possible to use few brackets by a
   judicious arrangement of APL symbols, an additional pair of brackets
   may sometimes save precious calculating time.

   The two expressions $A+B+\iota500$ and $(A+B)+\iota500$ yield the same result.
   However, in order to perform $B+\iota500$, 500 additions have to be made.
   Five hundred more are necessary to add A to this partial result,
   1000 additions in all!
   On the other hand, one addition is necessary to calculate $(A+B)$ and
   500 additions to add $\iota500$ to this result, that is to say a total
   of 501 additions only. This is well worth a pair of brackets!.

3-23   ERRORS OF RANK AND LENGTH

Two arrays of different ranks cannot serve as arguments for the same
dyadic scalar function even if thier dimensions appear the same.

```
      VECTOR ← 6  3  8  1

      MATRIX ← 1  4  ρ  1  2  1  2

      MATRIX
  1  2  1  2

      VECTOR + MATRIX
RANK ERROR
     VECTOR + MATRIX
     ∧
```

These two mathematical expressions, which have the same number of elements,
cannot be added. The computer indicates a rank error. In the same way a
matrix of 4 lines and 1 column cannot be added to a matrix of 1 line and
4 columns:

>   *COLUMN* ← 4 1 ρ 9 8 7 6

>   *MATRIX* + *COLUMN*
> *LENGTH ERROR*
>   *MATRIX* + *COLUMN*
>   ∧

This time a length error is indicated (the rank is correct).
On the other hand, when at least one of the arrays involved in the operation has only one element, the operation is possible:

>   *VECTOR* ← 1 ρ 12

>   *MATRIX* + *VECTOR*
> 13   14   13   14

>   *COLUMN* × 1 1 1 ρ 100
> 900
> 800
> 700
> 600

-24   RELATIONSHIP FUNCTIONS

The functions = and ≠ are the only dyadic scalar functions which accept
a numerical argument, when the other is alphanumeric:

>   1 = '1'
> 0
>   8 3 5 9 6 = 'PUSSY'
> 0 0 0 0 0

>   12 ≠ 'TWELVE'
> 1 1 1 1 1 1

NOTE

In other computer languages such as FORTRAN, there are also relationship
functions but these yield a result T (True) or F (False) instead of 1
and 0 as in APL .

The fact of being able to process the logical values 1 and 0 by means
of ordinary arithmetic functions gives APL an incomparable flexibility
of application.

3-25   LOGICAL FUNCTIONS

The functions AND and OR, combined with logical negation, are adequate
for the majority of current needs. However, for specific needs other
functions are very useful such as EXCLUSIVE OR, NOT-AND and NOT-OR.
These two latter functions will be of particular importance to automatic
control designers who are accustomed to employing them in their relay
circuits.

3-26   EXCLUSIVE OR

The function OR yields the value 1 if one of the operands is equal to 1,
or a fortiori both operands are equal to 1.
The EXCLUSIVE OR function yields the value 1 if either of the two operands
is equal to 1 but not if both are equal to 1.
This characteristic can be demonstrated as follows:

> If A takes the value : 0 0 1 1
>
> If B takes the value : 0 1 0 1
>
> The result will be   : 0 1 1 0

Conventionally this function is indicated by the symbol $\oplus$ in mathematics.
This symbol is completely ineffective since it is immediately seen from
the above example that the function EXCLUSIVE OR is represented perfectly
by the more familiar sign $\neq$.

> 0 0 1 1 $\neq$ 0 1 0 1
> 0 1 1 0

The function $\neq$ will therefore be at the same time the relationship
function (DIFFERENT FROM) and the logical function (EXCLUSIVE OR).

3-27   NOR AND NAND

The function NOR (contraction of NOT-OR) is equal to 1 if <u>neither</u> of the
operands is equal to 1. It is represented by the symbol $\downdownarrows$ (v and ~
overstruck). This representation is due to the fact that $A\downdownarrows B$ is equivalent
to $\sim A \vee B$.

> If A takes the value : 0 0 1 1
>
> If B takes the value : 0 1 0 1
>
> $A\downdownarrows B$ takes the value : 1 0 0 0

The function NOT-AND, better known under the name NAND, is a counterpart
to the function NOR. It is equivalent to $\sim A \wedge B$ and is marked by $\barwedge$ by
overstriking the symbols $\wedge$ and $\sim$.

If A takes the value: 0 0 1 1

If B takes the value: 0 1 0 1

$A \star B$ takes the value: 1 1 1 0

It is seen from this example that the function NAND is equal to 0 only if both the operands are equal to 1.

3-28   NOTE

The functions AND and OR are associative, which means:

$(A \wedge B) \wedge C$ is equal to $A \wedge (B \wedge C)$ and can therefore be written: $A \wedge B \wedge C$
$(A \vee B) \vee C$ is equal to $A \vee (B \vee C)$ and can therefore be written: $A \vee B \vee C$

On the other hand, the functions NOR and NAND ARE NOT ASSOCIATIVE.

$(A \star B) \star C$ is not equal to $A \star (B \star C)$
$(A \blacktriangledown B) \blacktriangledown C$ is not equal to $A \blacktriangledown (B \blacktriangledown C)$

Consequently if $A \star B$ and $A \blacktriangledown B$ are respectively equivalent to $\sim A \wedge B$ and $\sim A \vee B$, this equivalence is no longer verified on the basis of three terms, and $\star/Z$ and $\blacktriangledown/Z$ ARE NOT EQUIVALENT to $\sim \wedge/Z$ and $\sim \vee/Z$.

For example:

$X \leftarrow 1\ 0\ 1\ 1\ 1\ 0$

$\star/X$ equals 0
$\sim \wedge/X$ equals 1

$Y \leftarrow 0\ 0\ 0\ 1\ 1$

$\blacktriangledown/Y$ equals 1
$\sim \vee/Y$ equals 0

The following is a truth table for the logical functions which we have encountered:

A	B	$A \wedge B$	$A \vee B$	$A \neq B$	$A \star B$	$A \blacktriangledown B$
0	0	0	0	0	1	1
0	1	0	1	1	1	0
1	0	0	1	1	1	0
1	1	1	1	0	0	0

3-29   REDUCTION AND COMPRESSION

For compression, in the same way as reduction of arrays, the sign / not
followed by an index indicates that the last dimension is being treated.
The sign $\neq$, obtained by superposition of the signs - and /, indicates
a reduction or compression on the first dimension.

This sign can be followed also by an index, in which case $\neq[n]$ indicates
that the nth dimension is being treated.

+/*EXPENDITURES* and +/[3]*EXPENDITURES* are equivalent.

+/*EXPENDITURES* ,   +$\neq$[1]*EXPENDITURES* and +/[1]*EXPENDITURES* are equivalent

3-30   OPERATOR CONCEPT

Reduction allows a datum for right-hand operand, but for left-hand operand
a FUNCTION :

                    x / 3 4 6 1 7 8

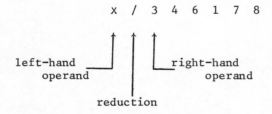

It is said that reduction is an OPERATOR, that is to say a function allowing other functions as operands, whose conditions of application it modifie

APL at present has five operators. The remaining four operators will be
studied in Chapter 5.

Compression is a mixed dyadic function. There could be no question
of confusing it with reduction.

CHAPTER 4

DEFINED FUNCTIONS

-1

DEFINED FUNCTION CONCEPT

There could not be a primitive function for each problem to be solved,
and the APL user can stretch the language by defining new functions
made to satisfy his own needs. These defined functions are not designated
by a symbol such as ρ, ι, or ⌈, but by a name which, when used, will
trigger the calculation process as defined when the function was created.
This process can be very simple or very complicated and invoke numerous
other functions, also primitive, or defined.

-2

FORMAL VARIABLE CONCEPT

When learning the following noteworthy expression: $(a+b)^2 = a^2 + 2ab + b^2$,
a mathematical property must be formalised in an abstract manner; also the
variables a and b, on which this is based, are purely symbolic. These
are FORMAL (or FICTITIOUS) VARIABLES.
In a calculation, the variables actually used will be called perhaps
x and y, 7 and 19, *TRAIN* and *CAR*: these will be EFFECTIVE (or REAL)
VARIABLES.

Equally, formal variables are used in order to create a defined function
as will be seen.

-3

STRUCTURE OF A DEFINED FUNCTION

A defined function comprises two parts:

1st) The HEADER serves to indicate which names apply to the function
      and the formal variables used in its definition. It serves to
      specify whether the function is dyadic, monadic, ... in other
      words what its syntax is.

2nd) The BODY defines the various operations which the function has to
      perform. It comprises a sequence of numbered APL expressions
      involving formal variables, called INSTRUCTIONS. There may be
      only one single instruction and there may be several dozen.

Here is a function which enables the average of the elements of a vector to be calculated:

$$\nabla\ RESULT \leftarrow AVERAGE\ VALUES$$

[1]   *RESULT* ← (+/*VALUES*) ÷ ρ*VALUES* ∇

<u>COMMENTS</u>

- The symbol ∇, called CARROT, or DEL, indicates the beginning and the end of the definition.

- The Header specifies that the function is called *AVERAGE*, that it has a single argument called *VALUES* (it is therefore monadic), and that it gives a result called *RESULT*.

  RESULT and *VALUES* are FORMAL variables.

- The syntax of APL requires that the argument of a monadic function is placed to the right of the function name and no error of interpretation is possible when reading the header: *AVERAGE* is the name of the function *VALUES* is the name of the argument and not the reverse.

- The body of the function comprises a single instruction which indicates how to calculate *RESULT* when the variable *VALUES* is known: its elements must be added (+/*VALUES*) and the total divided by the number of terms (ρ*VALUES*).

4-4   USING A DEFINED FUNCTION

A defined function is used in the same way as a primitive function, with the limitation that it cannot serve as arguments to the operators of the language, as with reduction for example.

The argument can:

- be given numerically: *AVERAGE* 2 9 12 10 13 8 9

- be given by a variable: *AVERAGE DEGREES*

- be the result of calculation, or of another function.

In the same way, the result can:

- be printed, if it is not assigned: *AVERAGE DEGREES*
                          324.44

- be assigned to a variable: *P* ← *AVERAGE* 23 45 56 43 33 44 40

- be used in an expression: *P* ← (5×*AVERAGE W*)*2

- be indexed. It will appear in connection with the function *EXPANSION* which will be written in paragraph 4-9.

Here, for example, is one application of the function *AVERAGE*.

TEST ← 12 43 26 60 77 12 34 43 43 51

M ← *AVERAGE TEST*

M

    40.1

This example clearly demonstrates the fact that EFFECTIVE variables do not have the same name as FORMAL variables (what would be the significance of a function which would only give the average of a single variable called *VALUES*?). It will be seen also in paragraph 13-4 that it is advisable not to give the same name to formal variables and effective variables.

DEFINING A FUNCTION

Two examples will help us understand how to define a function.

FIRST EXAMPLE

A function is required which, applied to an array of any dimensions, reshapes into a vector. This operation is called ravel.

For example, applied to the following array of three dimensions:

    21 32 46
     9 36 27

     3   5 14
    20 11   2

This function will give: 21 32 46 9 36 27 3 5 12 20 11 2

Applied to a vector, it must leave it unchanged.

The required function is visibly monadic; here is how to construct it:

the function, its argument and its result should be named. For example, let us say: *RAVEL*, *ARRAY* and *VEC*.

Hence the header of the function can be typed, starting with the symbol ∇ (DEL), which indicates to the computer that FUNCTION DEFINITION MODE is being used, as opposed to IMMEDIATE EXECUTION MODE, which has been used up to now.

∇ *VEC* ← *RAVEL ARRAY*

   [1]

The computer types [1], thus indicating that it is awaiting the first instruction of the function.

The required result will have the number of elements of *ARRAY* as dimensions
i.e. ×/ρ*ARRAY*, and will be filled with the values of *ARRAY*. Hence, the
single instruction:

[1]   *VEC ← (×/ρARRAY) ρ ARRAY ∇*

A second sign ∇ indicates that definition of the function is closed.
If typing of it had been omitted the computer would have typed [2], and
would have waited for the second instruction. It would still have been
possible to "close" definition by typing the forgotten DEL. For example:

[1]   *VEC ← (×/ρARRAY) ρ ARRAY*
[2]   *∇*

At this stage the instruction introduced is not performed (this would be
impossible since *ARRAY* is a fictitious variable which has no value); it
is stored for later execution.

Definition having been closed, immediate execution mode is re-established,
and the function *RAVEL* can be used by supplying a suitable argument:

```
      RAVEL 9 7 10 11
9 7 10 11
      X ← 2 4 ρ 8 3 0 1 5 3 4 7
      X
8 3 0 1
5 3 4 7
      RAVEL X
8 3 0 1 5 3 4 7
```

It is found that the function *RAVEL* indeed transforms a matrix into a vector and leaves the vectors unchanged. If you have the use of a computer,
type this function and use it before continuing (try *RAVEL DOUGH* and
RAVEL TYRES).

It can be experimentally established that the function *RAVEL* also has the
property of transforming a scalar into a single element vector. This
property derives from a special feature of reduction which will be studied
in paragraph 5-11.

SECOND EXAMPLE

It is required to calculate the gross salaries due to some workers for a
period of one working week. A vector indicates the number of hours worked
by each. The first 40 hours are paid at an identical rate throughout, whi
after the 40th hour each hour is paid 50% more. The hourly rate of pay is
given by a variable.

It is desired that the calculation be committed to a function which will b
called, for example *PAY*. This function will have two arguments:

- the hourly rate, which will be called *HR*

- the hours worked, in the form of a vector *HOURS*.

If it is agreed to call the result *SGROSS*, the header of the function can be written:

- either: ∇ *SGROSS* ← *HR PAY HOURS*

- or: ∇ *SGROSS* ← *HOURS PAY HR*

These two solution are the same. For example, we will choose the first.

          ∇ *SGROSS* ← *HR PAY HOURS*
     [1]

The computer is awaiting the first instruction. We will calculate the number of hours to be paid at the normal rate for each one:

     [1]   *NH* ← 40 ⌊ *HOURS*
     [2]

The second instruction enables us to calculate the number of overtime hours undertaken by each one:

     [2]   *OH* ← *HOURS* - 40
     [3]

The third instruction is the calculation of the gross salary; this is readily understood:

     [3]   *SGROSS* ← *HR* × *NH* + 1.5 × *OH*
     [4]   ∇

The definition mode was closed on line [4]; it could have been equally well closed at the end of line [3].

Here are the 5 lines regrouped, necessary for definition of the function *PAY*.

          ∇ *SGROSS* ← *HR PAY HOURS*
     [1]   *NH* ← ⌊ *HOURS*
     [2]   *OH* ← *HOURS* - 40
     [3]   *SGROSS* ← *HR* × *NH* + 1.5 × *OH*
     [4]   ∇

Now try to execute this function by choosing the data:

          RATE ← 12.40
          H ← 40 40 36 51 18 56 20 38 40 30
          H PAY RATE
     496 496 372 700.6 ‾186 739.6 ‾124 434 496 186

This result is visibly wrong! In such a case the best method of finding the error is to execute the instructions one by one with effective variables and to check the partial results are correct.

          40 ⌊ *H*
     40 40 36 40 18 40 20 38 40 30 This result is correct

          H - 40
     0 0 ‾4 11 ‾22 16 ‾20 ‾2 0 ‾10   here is the error! We obtain
                                        negative values.

The following had to be written: $0 \lceil H - 40$, or better still, subtract *NH* from the total number of hours.

Hence, the line [2] should be corrected as follows: *OH ← HOURS − NH*

4-6   RAPID CORRECTION OF A FUNCTION

In order to correct the instruction [2] which is wrong, you must:

> - reopen the definition mode (∇),
>
> - indicate the name of the function to be corrected, and specify the number of the line to be replaced (*PAY*[2]),
>
> - type the new version of this line, in full,
>
> - reclose the definition mode.

All these options are performed on the one line:

> ∇ *PAY*[2] *OH ← HOURS − NH* ∇

The function has to be called by its name only, stripped of its arguments. The definition mode is closed at the end of the line, or at the following line, without it being necessary to retype the rest. The new version of line [2] will replace the previous one.

This method of correction is useful only for performing simple modifications to short functions. Other more flexible methods which avoid the need to repeat the whole of the incorrect line, will be studied in paragraph 12-1. Meantime, we will make do with the method demonstrated above.

4-7   PRINTING A FUNCTION

For the purpose of checking, it is desirable to print-out the corrected function. In order to do this, the procedure of the previous paragraph should be followed, but replacing the line number by the WINDOW □ (or quad) so as to indicate that the contents of the function are to be displayed. The definition mode is immediately reclosed:

> ∇ *PAY* [□] •∇ request for printing *PAY*.
>
> ∇ *SGROSS ← HR PAY HOURS*
> [1]   *NH←40⌊HOURS*
>   complete print-out supplied
> [2]   *OH   HOURS − NH*   by the computer
> [3]   *SGROSS ← HR × NH + 1.5 × OH*
> ∇

Here again the function is designated by its name only, without arguments.

ILLUSTRATION 69

A further step ebtablishes that the result of the function is now correct:

> *RATE PAY H*
> 496 496 446.4 700.6 233.2 793.6 248 471.2 496 372

It is again observed in this example that *HR* and *HOURS* are fictitious, formal variables, which have no real existence. The values which the function will work on effectively have different names : *RATE* and *H*. In the same way, the variable *SGROSS*, which is used in the function, ceases to exist as soon as the function is terminated. This can readily be checked:

> *SGROSS*

> *VALUE ERROR*
> *SGROSS*
> ^

We will return in detail to these distinctions in paragraph 4-10.

ILLUSTRATION

By way of practice, you are invited to write, and to test on the computer three functions which will be ESSENTIAL in pursuing the study of functions. If you do not succeed with them, consult the proposed solutions.

1) Write a dyadic function which enables the first *N* element of a vector to be extracted. *N* and the vector are the two arguments.
   Example : 3 *TAKE* 15 21 12 43 22 30 60 56 65 78

   > 15 21 12

2) Write a similar function, which enables the first *N* elements of a vector to be ignored.
   Example:
   > 4 *DROP* 5 3 9 7 6 11 2
   > 6 11 2

3) Prompted by exercise 29 of Chapter 2, write a function which indicates in which position(s) a number *N* would appear in a vector *V*.

   Example :
   > 12 *IN* 9 12 21 14 12 3 7 12 0 6
   > 2   5   8

   > 9 *IN* 1 2 3 4 5 6

   > ← empty vector

SOLUTIONS

1) The significant elements are subtracted by indexing:

$$\nabla\ R \leftarrow N\ TAKE\ V$$

[1] $R \leftarrow V[\iota N]\ \nabla$

assume that N is equal to 5, $V[1\ 2\ 3\ 4\ 5]$ gives the first 5 elements of V.

2) The solution to this problem is close to the previous one.

$$\nabla\ Z \leftarrow N\ DROP\ V$$

[1] $Z \leftarrow V[N + \iota(\rho V)-N]\ \nabla$

Taking again the example 4 $DROP$ 5 3 9 7 6 11 2

$(\rho V)-N$	equals :	3
$\iota(\rho V)-N$	equals :	1 2 3
$N+\iota(\rho V)-N$	equals :	5 6 7
$V[5\ 6\ 7]$	equals :	6 11 2 , which corresponds to our expectations.

3) The solution again takes on, in the form of a function, the solution of exercise 29 of the previous chapter :

$$\nabla\ P \leftarrow N\ IN\ V$$

[1] $P \leftarrow (N=V)/\iota\rho V\ \nabla$

For example, if N equals 7, and if V is the vector 5 1 7 0 0 4 3 6 1 2 7

$\iota\rho V$	equals :	1 2 3 4 5 6 7 8 9 10 11
$N=V$	equals :	0 0 1 0 0 0 0 0 0 0 1
$(N=V)/\iota\rho V$	equals :	3 11

It is seen that the solution $(V \in N)/\iota\rho V$ was equally valid.

EXERCISES

[1] Write a function which arranges the elements of a vector in reverse order :

> REVERSE 8 3 2 5 11

    11 5 2 3 8

[2] What result would be obtained if, in error, the function PAY were executed, reversing the two arguments ?

> H PAY RATE

[3] The various diciplines of an examination are marked from 0 to 20, and assigned a coefficient. A vector contains the various coefficients. The marks obtained by the pupils are given in the form of a matrix having as many lines as there are pupils, and as many columns as there are diciplines.
Write a function which enables the overall average obtained by each candidate to be calculated.

Example :

> COEFFICIENTS

    8   5   3   2   2

> MARKS

```
12  14  12   8   9
 9  17  11   9  16
18  14  18  15  11
10  12  11  13  14
12  10  11  13  18
12  12  14  12  10
```

> MARKS EXAM COEFFICIENTS

    11.8 12 16 11.35 12.05 12.1

[4] It has been seen in paragraph 3-21 how to round off data to the nearest whole number. Write a dyadic function which rounds off a datum to N figures after the decimal point. N is given as a left-hand argument.

> 2 ROUND 3.157 4.123 34.1269 0.4498

    3.16 4.12 34.13 0.45

what happens if the left-hand argument is negative ? ‾3 ROUND 8430 19680 47200 It is recommended that this very useful function be retained in a workspace.

[5] Write a function which gives the lengths of all the words of a phrase.

> LENGTHS 'THIS IS THE BEST SOLUTION'

    4 2 3 4 8

[6] A polinomial $a_n x^n + \ldots\ldots + a_3 x^3 + a_2 x^2 + a_1 x + a_0$ can be represented
    by the vector of its coefficients $a_n \ldots a_3\ a_2\ a_1\ a_0$.

Hence, the polinomial $x^4 - 2x^3 + 5x - 3$ can be represented unambiguously
by the vector 1 ¯2 0 5 ¯3. the zero is due to the absence of a term in
x^2.

Write a dyadic function which, from the vector of the coefficients and
the value of x, gives the value taken by the polinomial.

Example :

         1 ¯2 0 5 ¯3 *CALCULATE* 2

      7

7 is the value of the above polinomial for $x = 2$.

[7] The functions ⊃ ∩ ∪ of the theory of sets are not generally implimented
    on APL systems (except on BURROUGHS computers). It is uggested that
    they be simulated in this case by vectors composed of letters of the
    alphabet.

These vectors represent sets, and must not contain the same element
twice (*'BUTTON'* is unsuitable), and the order of the elements is of
little importance (*'CUBE'* and *'BEUC'* represent the same set).

Write the following functions :

    UNION $A∪B$ Set of elements belonging to A or B.

                          'ROSE' UNION 'SPOT'

                     ROSEPT

    INTERSECTION $A∩B$ Set of elements simultaneously belonging to
                          the two operands :

                          'STORM' INTER 'FORCE'

                     OR

    INCLUSION $A⊃B$ Gives the answer 1 if all the elements of B
                          belong to A. Otherwise the answer 0 is given :

                          'STORM' INCLUDE 'FORCE'

                     0

                          'STOMACH' INCLUDE 'SHOT'

                     1

    IDENTITY $A ≡ B$ Gives the answer 1 if the sets A and B are
                          nearly identical with the order of the elements.

                          'BUS' IDENTICAL 'TRUCK'

                     0

                          'SPOT' IDENTICAL 'POTS'

                     1

You can check that all these functions accept numeric arguments.

4-9   FUNCTIONS OF FUNCTIONS

Just as the definition of a function invokes known primitives ($\rho + \iota$, $\lceil$)
it can invoke other defined functions, which can in turn invoke others,
and so on.
A function can even recall itself, which is called RECURSIVITY. This
technique will be studied in detail in paragraph 13-5.
Here is an illustration of the use of defined functions in another function.

A vector, *CASH*, indicates the growth of total income of a company during
the last ten years (in thousands of dollars).
          CASH

       2180 2550 3111 4170 5545 6099 5550 5439 5983 6282

The growth rate of expansion of this company is required, by calculating
the percentage increase of income for each year in relation to the previous
year. This percentage will be rounded off to the nearest whole number.

In the initial stage we will form the following vectors :
          2550 3111 4107 5545 6099 5550 5439 5983 6282
          2180 2550 3111 4107 5545 6099 5550 5439 5983

We will be able now to divide these vectors term by term, in order to obtain
the required relationship. They will be converted into percentages, then
rounded off as shown in paragraph 3-21.

In order to form the two intermediate vectors, the function *EXPANSION* will
involve the functions *TAKE* and *DROP* written in paragraph 4-8.

                  ∇ *RATE* $\leftarrow$ *EXPANSION VECT*

       [1]   *H* $\leftarrow$ 1 *DROP VECT*

       [2]   *VECT* $\leftarrow$ ($^{-}$1+ρ *VECT*) *TAKE VECT*

       [3]   *RATE* $\leftarrow$ $\lfloor$0.5 + 100$\times$(*H*$\div$*VECT*)-1 ∇

Here is an application of this :
          EX $\leftarrow$ *EXPANSION CASH*

          EX

       17 22 32 35 10 $^{-}$9 $^{-}$2 10 5

As stated above, functions can be linked together in the one expression:
          AVERAGE EXPANSION CASH

          13.333

The result of a function can also be indexed: (*EXPANSION CASH*) [5]
which would give the value 10.

EXERCISES

[8] The resistance of an electronic component depends on two parameters
of manufacture, a and b, and the ambient temperature t in accordance
with the following law :

$$R = a.e^{\dfrac{-b}{273+t}}$$

Using the functions *TAKE* and *DROP*, write a function using the vector
of the values a and b as a left-hand argument, a series of temperatures
as a right-hand argument, and giving as the result the resistance
of the component corresponding to each temperature.

        6 154 *RESISTANCE* 16 18 20 22 24 26 28 30

    3.5215 3.53442 3.54721 3.55988 3.57241 3.58482 3.59711 3.60928

[9] As seen in exercise 6 of this chapter, a polynomial can be represented
by the vector of its coefficients.
Using the functions *TAKE* and *DROP*, write a function yielding the
coefficients of the vector corresponding to the derivative of the
polynomial.

For example, the derivative of $3x^3 + x^2 + 2$ is : $9x^2 + 2x + 0$

        DERIVATIVE 3 1 0 2

        9 0 2

[10] Prompted by exercise 5 of this chapter, write a function which extracts
the longest word of a phrase. It would be as well to use *TAKE* and
DROP.

        LONGEST 'THE SILENCE OF THE SEA'

        SILENCE

[11] Write a monadic function *SIGN*, which indicates by ‾1, 0, or 1,
whether the elements of its operand are respectively negative, zero
or positive.
For example, if A is the matrix ‾3 ‾0 2
                                 ‾8 ‾2 0

        SIGN A

        ‾1 ‾0 1
        ‾1 ‾1 0

[12] Using the function *SIGN* as in the previous exercise, write a function
yielding the absolute value of its argument.

        ABS 8 0 ‾4 ‾3 6

        8 0 4 3 6

Is there a direct solution which does not involve the *SIGN* function ?

4-10   LOCAL VARIABLES, GLOBAL VARIABLES

It is required again to use the hours of work vector of paragraph 4-5;

          H

          2550 3111 4107 5545 6099 5550 5439 5983 6282

These values bear no relationship with those expected.
what has happened?

A close inspection reveals that line [1] of the function *EXPANSION* deprives
the argument of its first element, and sets the result in a variable also
called *H*. This explains why *H* is now equal to *CASH* with its first term
removed.

We now find with some diffidence that we were using, for pay, an hourly
rate named *RATE*, equal to 12.40. Has this value been modified by line
[3] of the function *EXPANSION* which uses the same variable name ?

          RATE

          12.40

No, all is well, but why?

The clarification of these phenomena is connected with the idea of local
variables and global variables. It is very important to master this
distinction in order to use defined functions satisfactoraly.

Repeating the definition of the function *EXPANSION* :

               ∇ *RATE ← EXPANSION VECT*

     [1]   *H ← 1 DROP VECT*

     [2]   *VECT ← (⁻1+ρVECT) TAKE VECT*

     [3]   *RATE ← ⌊0.5 + 100×(H÷VECT)−1*

               ∇

On performing the function by typing *EX ← EXPANSION CASH*, the computer
makes a copy of the value *CASH*, and assigns to it the new name *VECT*. It is
on this copy that the function will work; it will be discarded on completion.
It is said that *VECT* is LOCAL to the function.

This set of copies explains :

          - that the formal argument and the effective argument do not
            necessarily have the same name, since it is the value which is
            transmitted, and not the name.

          - That modifications applied to the formal argument have no
            repercussions on the effective argument.

Hence, in line [2], the value of *VECT* is modified. Hence, it is a copy
of *CASH* which is modified, and not *CASH* itself. The contrary would be
a nuisance, since a precious datum would thus be destroyed.

In the same way, *RATE* is a local variable, created by the function in line
[3]. When the function is completed a COPY is made of it, which is assigned
to the variable *EX*, and *RATE* is immediately discarded.

If there is another variable *VECT* or *RATE* in the workspace, they are not
mistaken for the local variables in the function; the function has no access
there, and they retain their initial value.

Hence, although the function *EXPANSION* has created a variable *RATE*, which
was a vector of the rate of expansion, this has not modified the variable
RATE which was already in the workspace, and was equal to 12.40.

On the other hand, if in a function, a variable name appears which does
not feature in the header, a variable of the workspace is involved, which
will be worked on DIRECTLY, without copy. All modifications applied to
it will subsist after completion of the function. It is said to be a GLOBAL
variable for the function.

For example, the variable *H* which appears on line [1] of the function
EXPANSION does not appear in the header; hence a global variable is involved
and the value which it takes (a series of income figures) discards the old
one (a vector of hours worked).

The concept of local variable is a relative concept. If during use, a
function *EXT* calls, for a function *INT* (just as *EXPANSION* calls for *TAKE*
and *DROP*), the variables local to *EXT* behave like global variables for *INT*.

These peoperties can be summarised as follos :

---

1) Effective arguments can have names different from formal arguments;
   this is in fact advised.

2) The effective result can have a name different from the formal
   result.

3) Modifications applied to LOCAL variables do not affect either the
   effective arguments of which they are copies, nor the GLOBAL variables
   which may have the same name.

4) Modifications applied by a function to a GLOBAL variable subsist
   after completion of the function.

5) If a local variable and a global variable have the same name, a
   function has access to the LOCAL variable only, which "masks" the
   global variable.

6) A variable which is local to a function is GLOBAL for all other
   functions which it calls for during its execution.

4-11   DECLARATION OF LOCAL VARIABLES

The formal arguments and result of a function are local variables. However
some intermediate variables used in the function can also be declared
local. This prevents the values taken by these variables from distorting
the variables of the workspace.

In order to declare a variable local, its name must be made to appear
in the header of the function by separating it from the arguments by a
semi-colon.

Example :   ∇ *R ← COMPUTE PRO; A; SIZE; DENSITY*

This function header indicates that *R* is the formal result, that *PRO* is
the formal argument and that *A, SIZE* and *DENSITY* are equally local variables.

The header of a function is considered as instruction number zero, and can
thus be corrected like any other instruction :

              ∇ *EXPANSION*[0] *RATE ← EXPANSION VECT ; H* ∇

H has become a local variable ; Now check this :

              H ← 1 2 3 4 5

              EX ← EXPANSION CASH

              H

       1 2 3 4 5   it can now be established that execution
                                 of the function *EXPANSION* no longer modifies
                                 the value of *H*.

┌───┐
│   │
│   Henceforth, unless deliberately intended (see paragraph 13-3)   │
│   ALL, variables entering into a function will be systematically   │
│   declared LOCAL to the function, from its creation.   │
│   │
└───┘

Application of this working discipline prevents unpleasant surprises, and
prevents the command)*VARS* from producing a host of insignificant variables
arising from intermediate calculations in defined functions.

On requesting the list of variables by the command)*VARS* before and after
processing a function, the names of variables which may have been forgotten
to be declared local will appear.

EXERCISES

[13] Write a function which enables two matrices to be coupled one above
the other, into a larger matrix. It is assumed that their dimensions
are compatible.

Example : if *A* equals :   2 5 3   and if *B* equals : 4 3 8
                              9 2 6   2 0 0
                                                           5 1 1

then *A* on *B* will equal :   2 5 3
                                9 2 6
                                4 3 8
                                2 0 0
                                5 1 1

[14] A global variable called *TEXT* is given. Write a function which
replaces all the appearences of a given character by another character.

Example : *TEXT*

    A LOT OF SLICES

      'P' REPLACES 'L'

      TEXT

    A POT OF SPICES

[15] Give yourself a global variable called *VALUES*, which equals 2 5 9 4 5 8.
Now write a function which enables one or more values to be inserted
into this vector, at a position which will be specified by the
left-hand argument :

      3 INSERT 7 1

      VALUES

    2 5 9 7 1 4 5 8

This function will allow values to be inserted at the head of the
vector by typing, for example : 0 *INSERT* 3. *VALUES* will then equal
3 2 5 9 7 1 4 5 8.

[16] In exercise 7 of this chapter you constructed certain functions of
the theory of sets. It is required to construct the function
COMPLEMENTATION, which indicates which letters must be added to a set
in order to reconstitute the alphabet. The alphabet will be the
global variable *ALPHA*.

      ALPHA ← 'ABCDEFGHIJKLMNOPQRSTUVWXYZ'

      COMPLEMENT 'VERY MUCH'

    ABDFGIJKLNOPQSTWXZ

      COMPLEMENT COMPLEMENT 'VERY MUCH'

    CEHMRUVY

               (remember that the order of letters is unimportant)

INPUTS AND OUTPUTS OF A FUNCTION

The following paragraphs will enable us to discover the various ways in which a function recieves the values of its environment (INPUTS), and in which it returns the results which it has formulated (OUTPUTS).

-12   USE OF ARGUMENTS AND RESULT

Although functions without arguments exist, as we will see, most functions have one or two arguments. Furthermore, many functions give a result. Hence, a function on input receives the value of the effective arguments, and transmits the value of its result at output.

For example :

$$\nabla \ RESULT \leftarrow AVERAGE \ VALUE$$

[1] $RESULT \leftarrow (+/VALUES) \div \rho VALUES$

$$\nabla$$

$$AVERAGE \ 4 \ 12 \ 23$$

13

We introduced the values 4 12 23 into the function, and the value 13 emerged from it.

This input/output mode is the most natural for APL; it enables the defined functions to be used as a primitive function, as was seen in paragraph 4-4.

The number of arguments is limited to two, which is one of the major defects of APL, but it should be remembered that these arguments can be arrays, and that the number of values thus transmitted can be very large.

-13   USE OF GLOBAL VARIABLES

We found in paragraph 4-10 that a function can use the value of global variables (input), and can change their value (output). Hence, the function *EXPANSION* informed us of the result (undesirable) of its first instruction in the form of the variable *H*.

This property can be utilised as a means of input/output of the function, as will be   demonstrated by the following example.

A company has consigned the prices of the articles which it produces to a
vector called *PRICES* :

      PRICES

    1.2 12.4 37.5 8.1 6 12 14.3 17.5 84 41.8

A function named *RISE* allows for a certain percentage increase to be applied
to the articles whose numbers are given. This function is :

      ∇ *RATE RISE NUMBERS ; A*

    [1] *A ← (1+RATE ÷ 100)×PRICES [NUMBERS]*

    [2] *PRICES[NUMBERS] ← A*

      ∇

The function receives as arguments the desired rate of increase and
the numbers of the articles to be increased.
Furthermore, in line [1], this function receives the global variable
PRICES, the values required to formulate the local variable *A*; it therefore
uses *PRICES* at input. *A* represents the new prices of the articles
affected by the rise. In line [2], the function modifies certain elements
of *PRICES*, thus leaving the trace of its action; it therefore uses *PRICES*
at output.

Here it is in use : we are going to increase articles 1 8 2 and 5 by 10%

      10 *RISE* 1 8 2 5

      PRICES

    1.32 13.64 37.5 8.1 6.6 21 14.3 19.25 84 41.8

It is seen that the required prices have been modified.

4-14   IMPLICIT AND EXPLICIT FUNCTIONS

It is found that no explicit result appears in the header of this function;
this explains why its execution did not result in the print-out of any
value. It was necessary to request the value of *PRICES* in order to establish
that the function had had an effect.

RISE is said to be an IMPLICIT function. On the other hand, a function
yielding a result will be called EXPLICIT.

4-15   IMMEDIATE OUTPUT

At most a function gives a single explicit result, but the intermediate
results can be of great interest. These values can be printed during
processing of the function.

There are three ways of causing these intermediate values to be printed :

- they can be called explicitly : the instruction [9] *PERIOD* would
  cause the value of the variable *PERIOD* to be printed.

- By not assigning the result of an instruction. For example, the
  instruction [17] *VxP*-100 will cause the result of the calculation
  to be printed.

- Finally, the value required to be printed can be assigned the
  symbol ☐. For example, here is a function which is prompted by the
  function *AVERAGE*, and which also causes the intermediate results
  to be printed :

$$\nabla\ RES \leftarrow AVG\ VECT$$
$$[1]\quad RES \leftarrow (\boxed{}\leftarrow+/VECT) \div \boxed{}\leftarrow\rho VECT\ \nabla$$

$$AVG\ 12\ 13\ 14\ 15\ 16$$

5	← print-out of ρ*VECT* ⎫ The order may
70	← print-out of +/*VECT* ⎬ depend on APL
14	← print-out of the result. system used. ⎭

The symbol ☐ is called QUAD, BOX or WINDOW. This last name indicates that
this symbol is a WINDOW OF COMMUNICATION between a function and the APL
user.
The values assigned to a quad are printed, and are also transferred to the
left following the instruction. Hence, a quad can be inserted in an
expression as a variable name would be, although it is not one.

PRINTING HEADERS AND MESSAGES

Like all values, a vector of characters is printed if it is not assigned. This
is an easy way. to print messages by a function. Hence, the instruction
[3] *'ANOMALY IN THE DATA'* would cause the corresponding message to be printed
during execution of the function.

16

MIXED PRINT-OUT

There is often occasion to have several values printed in the same line,
and in particular to have mixed numeric and alphanumeric values printed,
for example :

   THE RESULT IS 145.78 *AFTER* 11 *MINUTES*

This line comprises two numeric values and three alphanumeric values. This
is usually called mixed print-out.

There are two methods of obtaining such a result, but in both cases it is
essential that the rank of the values to be printed is less than 2.

FIRST METHOD

APL logic requires that the data to be printed be put in the form of a
character string. However, since numeric values and characters can not be
catenated, it is essential first to convert the numbers to vectors of
characters.

Conversion is achieved by the FORMAT function, which is written ⍕, by
overstriking the characters ⊤ (encode) and ° (jot).
This function will be studied in detail on page 224: we will use only its
monadic form here, which transforms a numeric variable into a vector (or an
array) of characters identical to the print-out which the computer would
perform.

For example :

```
        ⎕ ← NUM ← 23.67 10 0 1 84
   23.67  10   0   1   84

        ⎕ ← CHAR ← ⍕NUM
   23.67  10   0   1   84
```

It is seen that the print-out of *CHAR* is identical to the print-out of *NUM*
but *NUM* is a numerical variable, whereas *CHAR* is a character string, which
can be catenated to other characters.

To illustrate,the function *BREAD* has been created, performing the same work
as the function *PAY*, but with a detailed presentation of the calculations.

```
          ∇ HR BREAD HOURS ;NH ; OH
[1]       'NORMAL HOURS    : ', ⍕ NH ← 40⌊HOURS
[2]       'OVERTIME HOURS : ', ⍕ OH ← HOURS-NH
[3]       ''
[4]       'GROSS SALARIES : ', (⍕ HR×NH+1.5×OH), ' DOLLARS'
          ∇
```

```
     RATE BREAD H
NORMAL HOURS    : 30 36 40 40 18 40 20
OVERTIME HOURS : 0  0  0  16  0  0  0

GROSS SALARIES : 372  446.4  496  793.6  223.2  496  248 DOLLARS
```

Observe that the print-out of an empty vector (instruction [3]) causes a
blank line to be included in the presentation of the results.

Thought should be given to including blanks WITHIN character strings being printed, otherwise numbers and texts would run together :

'*LENGTH*',(⍕*L*),'*METERS*' would print   *LENGTH67METERS*

'*LENGTH* ',(⍕*L*),' *METERS*' would print   *LENGTH 67 METERS*

SECOND METHOD

The FORMAT function has been created relatively recently : the semi-colon occupied the role of print-out separator on early systems.

If, in a function, several expressions are separated by semi-colons, the results of these expressions will be printed on a single line, even if they are assigned to a variable.

Hence, we can write : [23] '*TOTAL PRICE* = ' ; *TP←UP*×*QTY* ; '*DOLLARS*'.

The value of *PT* will be printed in the form : *TOTAL PRICE* = 1245 *DOLLARS*

Despite symplicity in use for the beginners, the very special syntax of the semi-colon has led to it being abandoned on many systems (IBM in particular). In the remainder of this book, we will be using only the method employing the FORMAT function, which is currently the most wide-spread.

If your system allows the use of the semi-colon, turn to page 111 where some particulars about this symbol are stated.

As a guide, here is how line [1] of the function *BREAD* would be written, using a semi-colon :

    [1]   '*NORMAL HOURS* : ' ; *NH*←40 ⌊*HEURES*

-17   # DIRECT INPUT

In the same way as we can interrupt the course of a function in order to print intermediate values, there may be occasion to interrupt its course so as to introduce values directly. The appearence of a ⎕ in a function, other than to the left of an arrow (⎕←) , causes interruption of the function so that the user can introduce a value, a variable, or any expression yielding a result. With the value introduced through the window of communication, which the ⎕ is, processing of the function will continue normally.

Before allowing the user to type the value which he wishes to introduce, the computer types the characters

$$\square :$$

This is a warning symbol, intended to inform the user that he must introduce his data. It is usual to have this warning preceeded by a more explicit message regarding the nature of the data to be introduced. This enables functions to be formed called INTERACTIVE or CONVERSATIONAL, the use of which can be entrusted to personnel unfamiliar with APL.

For example, here is a conversational function which accomplishes the same treatment as the function *RISE* seen above :

```
        ∇ BIGRISE ; R
[1]     'WHAT RISE DO YOU WANT TO APPLY (IN o/o) ?'
[2]     R←□
[3]     'ON WHICH ITEMS ?'
[4]     R RISE □
[5]     ''
[6]     'NEW PRICES : ', ⍕ PRICES
        ∇
```

The first $\square$ will serve for introduction of the rate of increase. The value introduced will be assigned to the variable R. The second $\square$ which enables the numbers of articles to be introduced, is employed directly as the right hand argument of the function *RISE*.

Here is how this function works. You will observe how clumsy it is, as compared with the function *RISE*.

```
      PRICES
1.60   21   48.50   37   8.40   6.30   11.20   14

      BIGRISE
WHAT RISE DO YOU WANT TO APPLY (IN o/o) ?'
□:
      10
ON WHICH ITEMS ?
□:
      3  4  5  6
```

NEW PRICES :   1.6   21   53.35   40.7   9.24   6.93   11.2   14
With the procedure we observe the warning symbol ($\square$:) printed by the computer each time it meets a QUAD in the function.

As with the function *BREAD*, written earlier, *INCREASE* is an implicit function because it does not yield a result. Notice that it does not have any arguments either; it is said to be a NILADIC and IMPLICITE function.

Such a function can be called a data processing PROGRAM.

-18
SPECIAL FEATURES OF THE QUAD

It is possible by means of a quad, to type any APL expression yielding
a result : this expression will be performed by the computer, and its
result will be introduced into the quad. The typed expression can thus bring
other defined functions into play.

For example, assuming that the same original values are used, the function
INCREASE can be performed in the following manner :

        BIGRISE
WHAT RISE DO YOU WANT TO APPLY (IN o/o) *?*
□:
        AVERAGE 7 9 11 13   (which gives 10)
ON WHICH ITEMS ?
□:
        2 + ι4   (which gives 3   4   5   6)

NEW PRICES : 1.6   21   53.35   40.7   9.24   6.93   11.2   14
The results obtained are the same.

This special feature is extremely significant in the design of conversational
programmes. This will be seen in the chapter "Styles, Methods and Advice",
and in paragraph 4-24 of this chapter (see exercise 22 also).

While the essential use of the quad is to allow for the input - outputs
of a function, it can also be used in direct execution mode :

        - in order to visualise a variable which is in the process of
          being created :

              □ ← *TAB* ← 2 3 ρ 6 1 5 2 4 3
        6 1 5
        2 4 3

        - in order to introduce excessively long data by catenating a
          a quad at each line, which initiates a request for values from
          the computer.

              LONG ← 9 1 8 2 7 3 6 4 5 , □
        □:   ← Request from the
              0 0 0 1 3 2 5 4 , □   computer
        □:   ← Request from the
              8 1 2   computer.
              LONG
        9 1 8 2 7 3 6 4 5 0 0 0 1 3 2 5 4 8 1 2

This method is simpler than that presented in paragraph 3-18. It also informs
us that an expression typed by means of a quad can itself invoke a quad.

4-19   NOTE

Printing of a value by a function must not be confused with transmission
of an explicit result.

We have already met the function *AVERAGE*, and here is a function which
resembles it but which does not yield an explicit result :

            ∇ *AVIMPLI VECT*
    [1]   (+/*VECT*)÷ρ*VECT* ∇

            AVERAGE 2 3 4
    3

            AVIMPLI 2 3 4
    3

Performance of these two functions does not display any difference. Actuall
the result of line [1] of *AVIMPLI* not having been assigned, is printed.
This function however, does not transmit an explicit result, and it is
impossible to include it in an expression, or to give a name to its result.

Here is an illustration of this :

            2 + *AVERAGE* 3 4 5
    6

            2 + *AVIMPLI* 3 4 5
    4
    VALUE ERROR
          2 + *AVIMPLI* 3 4 5
                ∧

It is found that *AVERAGE* gives a result which has been added directly to 2.
On the other hand, *AVIMPLI* results in printing the value 4 calculated in
line [1], but does not transmit any value which could be added to 2, which
causes an error message to appear.

One should therefore endeavour to write EXPLICIT functions whenever possibl

4-20   INPUT OF ALPHANUMERIC VALUES

Alphanumeric values can be introduced by means of a quad :

            □:
                '*IT IS FINE*'

However, the constraint of placing the character string between quotes
considerably impairs simplicity of the answer. Also, each time the
introduction of an alphanumeric value into a function is initialed a QUOTE-
QUAD (⍞) is used in preference to a simple quad.

AS its name indicates, the quote-quad is obtained by overstriking a quote
with a quad : ▯ . As with the quad for numeric values, the quote-quad
causes interruption of the function, and requests the user to introduce
an ALPHANUMERIC datum.

The quote-quad does not cause any warning symbol to be printed comparable
with ▯ : of the quad . It takes ALL the characters typed by the user
as data, without concerning itself with any evaluation, up to carriage
return excluded. If the user types only a carriage return, the computer
considers this as being an empty character vector.

Here is an example :

```
         ∇ HELLO ;NAME
   [1]   'HELLO, WHAT IS YOUR NAME ?'
   [2]   NAME ← ▯
   [3]   'PLEASED TO MEET YOU, MR ', NAME
         ∇
```

This function is a good way for the beginner to make contact with the
computer.:

```
         HELLO
   HELLO, WHAT IS YOUR NAME ?
   KAMIECZKATZ
   PLEASED TO MEET YOU, MR. KAMIECZKATZ
```

In line [2] , the quote-quad enabled the user to type his name in a
perfectly normal way, without quotes. This name was placed in the variable
NAME, then catenated to the welcome message.

Moreover, the variable *NAME* could be dispensed with, and lines [2] and [3]
could be regrouped into a single line, as follows :

```
   [2]   'PLEASED TO MEET YOU, MR ',▯ ∇
```

We have recived various means of input and output of values of a function.
There is one more method, which consists of reading or writing these values
on what are called FILES. This will be studied later however.

EXERCISES

[17] Given a vector, it is desired to know its size, the average of its elements, and the number of elements greater than a given limit.

> 90 *CONTROL* 34 80 82 91 60 120 117 63 96 52

       10 *VALUES*

       AVERAGE = 79.5

       4 *VALUES GREATER THAN* 90

Write the function *CONTROL* ; the limit imposed is placed as a left hand argument.

[18] A matrix of 12 columns contains the names of a certain number of people, a vector contains a series of registration numbers associated with each of these people.

Example :
        771   *SMITH*
        725   *PERKINS*
        943   *ROSENTHAL*
        387   *GOODMAN*
        400   *COOPER*
        732   *ANDERSON*
        831   *JACOBSON*

The vector is called *REG*, the matrix is called *NAMES*. Write a function which enables the name of a person whose registration number is given to be modified, according to the following pattern :

>   *MARRIAGE*
>   *REGISTRATION ?*
>   ☐:
>   387
>   *NEW NAME ?*
>   *SPARK*

It can be seen that the matrix has been modified :

   SMITH
   PERKINS
   ROSENTHAL
   SPARK
   COOPER
   ANDERSON
   JACOBSON

[19] Is the expression ☐[2]←8 valid ?

[20] Write a function which indicates the value and the position of the largest term of a matrix (assuming that this term is unique) according to the following pattern :

> POSIMAX M
> *THE GREATEST ELEMENT IS* 71
> *ROW* 2 , *COLUMN* 5

[21] A diferent flight number is assigned to each air connection between the towns of a country. The array below indicates how these flight numbers are assigned for the first eight towns, numbered from 1 to 8 for convenience.

	1	2	3	4	5	6	7
2	1						
3	2	3					
4	4	5	6				
5	7	8	9	10			
6	11	12	13	14	15		
7	16	17	18	19	20	21	
8	22	23	24	25	26	27	28

Hence, to go from town 7 to town 5, flight number 20 is taken, and to go from town 3 to town 6, flight number 13 is taken. For 50 towns, a matrix of 2500 elements would be needed, which would be very cumbersome. It is preferable therefore to write a function which automatically gives the flight number, according to the following pattern :

> CONNECTION
> *ORIGIN, DESTINATION ?*
> ☐:
> 3 8
> *TAKE FLIGHT* 24

Write this function. It is assumed that one never asks to go from one town to the same town.

[22] The articles in a catalogue are referenced by a three-figure code number the first of which is a heading number. These numbers are contained in a vector *CODES*, which is classified in increasing order.

A numeric matrix called *RENS*, each line of which corresponds to an article in the catalogue, comprises three columns which gives respectively the stock, the price and the suppliers code for each product.

PART ONE

Write a function which enables this information to be consulted according to the following pattern :

> HEADING 5
> *THIS HEADING CONTAINS THE FOLLOWING CODES* : 501 508 529 530 566
> *WHICH ONES DO YOU WANT ?*
> ☐:
> 508 566 501

CODE	*QTY*	*PRICE*	*SUPPL.*
508	620	8.10	34021
566	53	151.00	22710
501	307	27.50	13200

The number of the heading consulted is therefore given as an argument; then
the function indicates which codes feature in this heading. A selection
is then presented to the operator.
It will be observed that the article codes are in increasing order but not
consecutive.

PART TWO

Write three functions named *TO*, *ALL*, and *EXCEPT*, enabling the question
"WHICH ONES DO YOU CONSULT ? " to be answered, in any one of the following
ways :

> 710 741 763 as in part one,
> *ALL*   in order to consult all the articles of the heading
> 733 *TO* 741   in order to consult the articles included between
>   733 and 741,
> *ALL EXCEPT* 742 788 or (733 *TO* 741) *EXCEPT* 737 if it is desired
>   not to display certain articles.

It is possible to write the function *HEADING* in such a way that the function
ALL becomes superfluous.

DRAWING BY RUMWEISS

The quote-quad causes interruption of the function
so that the user can introduce data.

21

JUMP INSTRUCTIONS

Use of the computer is justified only for substantial tasks requiring
repetitive calculations. In order to be able to repeat the execution of
all or part of the instructions of a function, special instructions, called
JUMP or BRANCH INSTRUCTIONS, enable the usual order of execution of the lines
to be broken, by returning to any part of the function.
Hence, the instruction [9] →5 causes the computer to undertake execution
of the function at line 5, instead of line 10 as would have been natural.
The value 5 is called ADDRESS or DESTINATION of the jump.

In the case where a previous part of the function is reverted to, as here,
the calculation process will be repeated each time this jump instruction
is again reached. Hence, a repetitive process will have been initiated
(also called ITERATIVE), called a loop.

Example :

                    ∇ *EXAMPLE*
        [1]   *instruction*
        [2]   *instruction*
        [3]   *instruction*
        [4]   *instruction*
        [5]   *instruction*
        [6]   → *4*
                    ∇

In such a function, the instructions 1 to 6 would be executed, then the
instructions 4 - 5 - 6 would again be taken up and the cycle would recommence
indefinitly.

22   SYNTAX OF BRANCHES

A jump instruction is defined by means of the branch arrow, followed by a
scalar or a vector, in which case the FIRST element of the vector which
is taken as the destination of the jump.
The destination must be a NON-NEGATIVE INTEGER, or an EMPTY VECTOR.

The instruction →8 4.5 ⁻9 67 is thus correct, since the first element of the
vector is a non-negative integer.

The following array indicates what the effect of the instruction →A is in
terms of the value of the address A.

Value of the address A	Effect of the instruction $\rightarrow A$
Number of a line of the function	Jump to the line indicated
Zero, or value greater than the number of lines of the function	End of execution of the function
Empty vector	No jump; pass to the next line

The following exercises, which merely require only application of these rules, are for practice in the understanding of jump instructions.

EXERCISES

[23] In a function, the following instruction is encountered : [17] $\rightarrow 3 \times A > B$
To which instruction will execution of the function proceed if A is larger than B; and if A is less than or equal to B ?

[24] The same question for the instruction : $\rightarrow 4 \times \iota A > B$

[25] In a function the instruction occurs : [8] $\rightarrow$ (10=□)/5
To which line will execution proceed in terms of the value introduced by means of the quad ?

[26] The same question for the instruction : [14] $\rightarrow$ 8 15 0 19 [4⌊□⌈1]

[27] Write an expression which would be equal to a given scalar X if I is positive, and would otherwise be an empty vector.

[28] Write an expression which would be equal to 3 if all the elements of a vector V are equal to 1, and would otherwise be equal to 0.

-23   CREATING A LOOP

The various possibilites of jumping shown above allow precise control of
the running of a function ; a simple example will help us to understand
how.

The account numbers of the REGIONAL DAIRIES BANK constitute a vector called
ACCOUNTS. The state of these accounts is noted in the vector BALANCES.
Here they are set out one under the other :

64881	25344	98001	23317	47209	15227	34562	etc...
766.03	4400.34	2671	3102.62	1275.13	‾273.97	3953.43	

In order to inform the clients of the state of their account, the following
function has been written :

```
          ∇ CONSULT ACCTS ; A
    [1]   'ACCOUNT NUMBER ?'
    [2]   A ← ☐
    [3]   'BALANCE : ',(▼ BALANCES[A IN ACCTS]), ' DOLLARS'
    [4]   ''
    [5]   →1
          ∇
```

COMMENTS

After printing the message [1] , the client's account number is introduced
by the quad [2]. The function IN written in paragraph 4-8 is employed to
search for the position of this number in the right hand argument, which
will be the vector ACCOUNTS, and this index is used to display the corresponding balance [3]. Line [4] produces a blank line to punctuate the
presentation, and the instruction [5] causes the process to recommence
at line [1], thus creating a loop.

Execution of this function is as follows :

          CONSULT ACCOUNTS
    ACCOUNT NUMBER ?
    ☐:
          25344
    BALANCE : ‾273.97 DOLLARS

    ACCOUNT NUMBER ?
    ☐:
          15227
    BALANCE : 4400.34 DOLLARS

    ACCOUNT NUMBER ?
    ☐:

Since there are no means of leaving the loop, execution of the function
will revert indefinitely to line 1, which is a nusiance. This vicious
circle can be terminated simply by typing →, as will be seen in paragraph
4-34, but this example clearly shows the need to have better control
of the performance of a loop.

4-24   CONTROL OF A LOOP BY THE USER

We will modify the function :   a)   ∇*CONSULT*[0]
                                     b)   [0]   *CONSULT ACCTS*;*A*;*STOP*
                                     c)   [1]   [0.5] *STOP* ← *1
                                     d)   [0.6] [2] →(*STOP*=*A*←□)/0 ∇

In (a), it is requested that the header of the function be corrected
so as to establish a fresh local variable : *STOP* (b). In (c) the computer
requests line [1] ; this proposal is cancelled by introducing any number
between 0 and 1, the effect of which will be TO INSERT an extra line
between the header and line [1]. In this line any decimal value is given
to *STOP*, for example * 1 which equals 2.71828 (see § 3-19). The computer
continues numbering of the lines by the immediately higher value [0.6].
This proposal is again cancelled by introducing a modification of line
[2], and the function is closed.

Here is the result :

        ∇ *CONSULT ACCTS*;*A*;*STOP*
[1]   *STOP* ← *1
[2]   '*ACCOUNT NUMBER ?*'
[3]   →(*STOP*=*A*←□)/0
[4]   '*BALANCE* : ',(▼ *BALANCES*[*A IN ACCTS*]),' *DOLLARS*'
[5]   ' '
[6]   →1
        ∇

The computer having renumbered the lines 1 by 1, line [1] has become line
[2], which necessitates correction of line [6] which has become false :

        ∇ *CONSULTATION* [6] →2 ∇

We will now study the meanings of the modifications applied to this
function.

Line [1] gives *STOP* a value which can in no way be equal to an account
number, which is why a decimal value was chosen.

During execution of line [3], if a client's account number is typed in
response to the quad, the equation $STOP = C$ is never verified, and gives
the value 0.

($STOP = A \leftarrow \square)/0$ is then equivalent to 0/0, and gives an empty vector. The
branch → *empty vector* results in passing to the following line [4],
as in the first version of the function, and the loop thus follows through
as many times as is desired. If the operator however, types *STOP* in response to the quad (since any APL expression can be typed), *C* takes the
value of *STOP*. Hence $STOP = C$ equals 1.1/0 gives 0. And →0 causes the
function to terminate : the loop has been ended.

This is how the function behaves :

            CONSULT ACCOUNTS
    ACCOUNT NUMBER ?
    □:
            23317
    BALANCE : 3102.62 DOLLARS

    ACCOUNT NUMBER ?
    □:
            47209
    BALANCE : 1275.13 DOLLARS

    ACCOUNT NUMBER ?
    □:
            25344
    BALANCE : 4400.34 DOLLARS

    ACCOUNT NUMBER ?
    □:
            STOP

This method of controling a loop is particularly significant, since this
for the user, is reflected in a natural act : type *STOP* to end a repetitive
process.

The instruction [3] is called TEST or again CONDITIONAL JUMP, since the
jump out of the function is made only under certain tested conditions.
On the other hand, the instruction [6] → 2 would be called UNCONDITIONAL
JUMP.

CONTROL OF A LOOP BY A VARIABLE

The values successively taken by a variable can also be tested to decide
whether to continue or interrupt a loop. This variable can be one which
actually occurs in calculations, or it can be created specially for this
purpose. For example, a variable is often created in order to count the
number of passages in a loop (or ITERATIONS), in which case this
variable is called a COUNTER.

Assuming that we wish to print-out a multiplication table, we could write the following function :

```
        ∇ MULTABLE N ;I
[1]     I←1
[2]     (⍕N),' TIMES ',(⍕I),' = ',⍕N×I
[3]     →(10≥I←I+1)/2
        ∇
```

```
        MULTABLE 7
7 TIMES 1 = 7
7 TIMES 2 = 14
7 TIMES 3 = 21
7 TIMES 4 = 28
7 TIMES 5 = 35
7 TIMES 6 = 42
7 TIMES 7 = 49
7 TIMES 8 = 56
7 TIMES 9 = 63
```

In line [1] the variable I is initialized, serving both as a counter and as a calculation variable.
Line [2] is the "calculation" part of the loop.
In line [3], the counter is increased by one unit and it is compared with 10.
In so far as I is less than 10, (10>I)/2 equals 2, and line 2 is jumped to.
As soon as I equals 10, (10>I)/2 gives an empty vector, and the function is left, since there are no more lines to execute after [3].

This method allows for infinate variants, according to the associated uses which can be made of the counting variable : it can be made to increase, decrease, made to undergo any possible treatment.
This is a classical step in data treatment programming, but it is not really natural to man, and it can be frequently despensed with in APL by using vectors and arrays, and by using language operators, reduction, scan, and inner and outer products.

4-26   ENDLESS LOOPS

The first version of the function *CONSULTATION* comprises an endless loop. This loop was not particularly cumbersome since, interrupted at each cycle by the quad, it consumed only a small amount of calculation time. Far more pernicious endless loops could be established inadvertantly.

As an example, we will write a function which calculates the product of the first N whole numbers by a series of successive multiplications.

```
        ∇ R←FACTORIAL N;I
[1]     R←I←1
[2]     R←R×I
[3]     →(N≥I←I+1)/2
[4]     ∇
```

initializing R and I to 1
multiply R by I
repeat until I equals N

```
        FACTORIAL 6
720
```

Imagine that we want a header to be added by inserting an instruction.

```
        ∇ FACTORIAL [0.5] 'THE RESULT IS : ' ∇
```

```
        FACTORIAL 8
THE RESULT IS :
```

Nothing happens, and the course of the function must be interrupted after a
few seconds calculation by pressing the interruption key.
The computer signals that we have interrupted the function by the following
message which specifies at which line the execution has been suspended :
        FACTORIAL [3]

If the function is printed, it is found that the line which we inserted has
brought about renumbering of all the lines, and that the jump which returns
to line [2] has had the effect of returning I perpetually to the value 1.
Hence this variable will never attain the value N.

```
        ∇ R←FACTORIAL N;I
[1]     'THE RESULT IS : '
[2]     R←I←1
[3]     R←R×I
[4]     →(N≥I←I+1)/2
        ∇
```

An endless loop such as this is particularly pernicious, because NOTHING
warns the user that the computer is "going round in circles" consuming
costly calculating time. Hence it is important to know the normal response
time of the machine which is being worked on, and to quickly interrupt the
running of any function which appears to be taking an abnormally long time.

As a guide, all the exercises in this book should be completed in less than
5 to 10 seconds according to the speed of the computer being used.

-27   LABEL CONCEPT

We have just established that modification of a function can lead to renumbering
of the lines, and have disturbing consequences. In order to avoid having to
correct the jump instructions the addresses of which have become false, it is
preferable to reference the lines which are required to be returned to by a
name called LABEL.

This label is separated from the rest of the instruction by a colon (:).

In the instruction   [11] *BRANCH*3 : *X* ← (*AVERAGE U*) *2 the name *BRANCH*3 is a label. It will be reverted to by the instruction →*BRANCH*3.

It is strongly recommended to use these lables to designate jump addresses, and to abstain from writing direct jumps such as →5 (except for returns to line 0 when it is desired to leave a function).

Here is the function *CONSULTATION* modified accordingly :

```
        ∇ CONSULT ACCTS;A;STOP
 [1]    STOP ← *1
 [2]    MORE: 'ACCOUNT NUMBER ?'
 [3]    →(STOP=A←□)/0
 [4]    'BALANCE ',(▼ BALANCES[A IN ACCTS]),' DOLLARS'
 [5]    ''
 [6]    → MORE
        ∇
```

IMPORTANT : a label is a LOCAL VARIABLE which has as value the number of the line on which it is positioned. It can thus be used like any other local variable, but it may not be assigned a value.

For example :

```
        [3]    LAB: K←ιL/X          LAB is a label
        [4]    X←LAB×3+P        ⎫
        [5]    →LAB+3×A=5       ⎬   these instructions are correct
        [6]    P←□←LAB+P        ⎭
        [7]    LAB←9                this instruction is incorrect
                                                  (syntax error)
```

4-28   CONDITIONAL PROCESSINGS

Processings to be accomplished may differ according to the values taken by certain variables. Each eventuality, which must be foreseen, will be associa with a series of instructions. Reversion to the equivalent sequence will be obtained by a test enabling the suitable address to be selected. In some cases several successive tests may be necessary.

Example : a function called *PRINT* has been written, enabling a numeric matrix and a matrix of characters to be printed according to the presentation on the following page (it is not disclosed how the function *PRINT* is created).

TOWNS

LONDON
CARDIFF
TAUNTON
GRIMSBY

DISTANCES

0	540	220	110
540	0	700	470
220	700	0	230
110	470	230	0

TOWNS PRINT DISTANCES

	LONDON	*CARDIFF*	*TAUNTON*	*GRIMSBY*
LONDON	0	540	220	110
CARDIFF	540	0	700	470
TAUNTON	220	700	0	230
GRIMSBY	110	470	230	0

In order for this function to be used, on the one hand the numeric matrix must be square and, on the other hand, both the matrices must possess the same number of lines. A function is required to be written which possesses these controls and undertakes printing if everything is correct, or which prints a message specifying the nature of the anomaly otherwise.

Here are three different processings, of which only one must be executed :

- everything is correct

- the numeric matrix is not square

- it is square, but of dimensions which are incompatible with those of the matrix of characters.

Here is a possible solution to this problem (there are several others) :

```
        ∇ ALPHA FRAME NUM ;N
[1]     →(=/N←ρNUM)/SQUARE
[2]     'THE RIGHT OPERAND IS NOT A SQUARE MATRIX'
[3]     →0
[4]     SQUARE: →((N=ρALPHA)[1])/OK
[5]     'INCONSISTENT DIMENSIONS'
[6]     →0
[7]     OK: ALPHA PRINT NUM ∇
```

In this function the three processings mentioned can be seen; two successive tests were necessary. Having executed any one of these processings, it would be ill-timed to continue by the processing situated lower down in the function; this is why each processing is terminated by a jump instruction (except the last).
This precaution must never be forgotten when drawing up a function which presents processings which are exclusive from each other.

4-29   SOME TYPICAL JUMPS

There are infinite ways of drawing up a test, the only limit being the
imagination, and the only rule legibiliy. The following methods can simply
be advised; they are in current use :

INSTRUCTION	EFFECT
[11] →(*condition*)/23	Jump to line 23 if the condition is met, pass to the following line if it is not.
[11] →23×ι *condition*	Same effect, but works only in origin 1.
[14] → 23 × *condition*	Jump to line 23, or end of execution of the function if the condition is not met.
[17] → 7 18 0 9 [*expression*]	According as to whether the expression equals 1, 2, 3 or 4, jump to 7, 18, 0 or 9.

A little astuteness can often prevent a jump, as demonstrared by exercise
[29] of this chapter.

4-30   LIST OF FUNCTIONS

Just as the command)*VARS* reveals the list of variables in the workspace,
the command)*FNS* prints the names of the functions, classed alphabetically.
The command)*ERASE*, already met, erases variables as well as functions.

)*FNS*

AVERAGE   AVG   AVIMPLI   BIGRISE   BREAD   CONSULTATION   EXPANSION

FACTORIAL   FRAME   HELLO   IN   INCREASE   LEAVE   LIN   MULTAB   PRINT

PAY   RISE   TAKE

EXERCISES

[29] In many cases, a little astuteness can avoid recourse to a jump in order to solve a conditional processing.

Conversion of degrees Fahrenheit to degrees Celsius is achieved by means of the relationship :

$$C = \frac{5}{9} (F-32)$$

Write a function called *DEGREES* which ALWAYS restores a temperature to degrees Celsius, no matter in what unit the temperature is expressed, in an argument. For example :

        51 *DEGREES* C   No conversion
  51

        86 *DEGREES* F   Conversion Fahrenheit → Celsius
   30

This function will be written without a jump instruction.

[30] Modify the function *INSERT* found in exercise [15], in such a way that it produces an explicit result which will be :

- 1 if the operation has been accomplished,
- 0 if the operation could not be performed, the left hand argument being negative or greater than the size of the vector.

[31] Write a function which causes *WON*, *DRAWN* or *LOST*, to be written according to the respective values of its arguments, as indicated below :

        7 *AGAINST* 2
  WON

        8 *AGAINST* 9
  LOST

       11 *AGAINST* 11
  DRAWN

[32] Write an implicit monadic function which, applied to a number X, prints its root if X is a perfect square or, on the contrary, a message indicating that X is not a perfect square.

Example :

       SQUAROOT 289
  17

       SQUAROOT 91
  91 *IS NOT A PERFECT SQUARE*

[33] It is a tedious obstruction to introduce into the computer a matrix
of large dimensions, of which nearly all the elements are nil, by
means of the function ρ. Write a conversational function which :

- Creates a matrix of suitable dimensions filled with zeros.

- fills this matrix with the values introduced on the keyboard.

Example :

            MAT ← FILL
WHAT ARE THE DIMENSIONS OF THE MATRIX ?
□:
        5 10
GIVE THE ROW NUMBER, THE COLUMN NUMBER, THE VALUE
□:
        1 3 14

□:
                                    For each value required to be introduced
        3 5 28   its position (row and column), then its
□:   value are indicated. Hence, 3 6 29
        3 6 29   causes the value 29 to appear in row
□:   3, column 6, as can be seen.
        4 7 33
□:
        4 8 34
□:
        5 10 54
□:
        STOP

        MAT
    0   0 14   0   0   0   0   0   0   0
    0   0   0   0   0   0   0   0   0   0
    0   0   0   0 28 29   0   0   0   0
    0   0   0   0   0   0 33 34   0   0
    0   0   0   0   0   0   0   0   0 54

This function has required the introduction of 18 values, while the
use of the dyadic ρ would have required the introduction of 50 values.

[34] Modify the function *CONSULTATION* in such a way that the introduction
of an account number which does not feature in the vector *ACCOUNTS*
makes the message *ACCOUNT NO. UNKNOWN* appear. The function must
therefore pass on to the next client.

[35] Modify the function *CONSULTATION* so that the reference *"BALANCE"* is
replaced by *"CREDIT BALANCE"* if the amount remaining in the account
is positive, or by *"DEBIT BALANCE"* if it is negative.

            CONSULT ACCOUNTS
ACCOUNT NUMBER ?
□:
        25344
CREDIT BALANCE : 4400.34 DOLLARS

[36] To carry out the addition of the first N whole numbers, $+/\iota N$ should
     be written. Write a function which achieves the calculation by means
     of a loop. N will be the argument of the function. If necessary
     take guidance from the function *FACTORIAL* (§ 4-26), and consider
     that in FORTRAN, COBOL, BASIC, PL/1, which are classic programming
     languages, you would not have any other solution!

DRAWING BY RUMWEISS

4-31   HOW TO CONTINUE

You have now acquired a sound basis in APL; there only remains for you to
discover new primitive functions, new operators, and to learn methods of
working. But your progress will be all the more rapid as you will be able
to attempt to solve problems which are of direct interest to you. Hence,
you risk the chance of running into difficulties which will not appear
until further on. Here are some guidelines which can help you :

            1 - If you feel the need to modify and correct the functions you
                write in a quicker way than has been demonstrated upto now,
                if you want help in applying this, jump directly to chapter 12.

            2 - If you want to print the results in a way agreeable in use,
                with a strict presentation, consult chapter 9.

            3 - If you want to handle large quantities of data, or if the
                data which you are processing are valuable and must be subject
                to systematic safeguards, the files could be useful to you.
                For this consult chapter 11.

It is obvious that efficient use of these chapters assumes a level of
understanding which you have not yet aquired, but a quick reading can give
you immediately useable information.

Finally, if you want to persue the study of APL normally, have a quick look
at chapter 12 nonetheless, and continue your reading normally with chapter
5.

                          GOOD READING.

4-32   DEFINING FUNCTIONS

Function names must correspond to the same criteria as variable names.   This
matter is referred to in paragraph 2-21.

The instructions of a function are not analysed at the time of the defining
of the function, except on some rare systems; any errors which they may
contain will not be detected until the time of execution.

It is sometimes advantageous to represent certain important constants by
an explicit niladic function, rather than by a variable. Actually, the
value of a variable can be modified by mistake.
On the other hand, if the constant 17.3 is necessary in a certain workspace
it can be represented thus :

$$\nabla\ R \leftarrow COEF$$
$$[1]\ R\ \leftarrow 17.3$$
$$\nabla$$

This function works like a variable, but it cannot be modified by mistake:

$$COEF\ \text{x}\ 100$$
1730

$$COEF \leftarrow 80$$
SYNTAX ERROR

$$COEF \leftarrow 80$$
$$\wedge$$

This rather clumsy proceedure can be avoided on some systems by "locking"
the variable by means of a system-function. This is so with APL proposed
byCONTROL DATA, where the function $\Box LOCK$ enables functions to be locked
as well as variables.

The function *COEF* below constitutes the last type of function which we will
meet.   The table below sumerizes these six types. For each possibility,
the form of the header is shown (on the first line) and the name of a
function belonging to this type (on the second line).

FUNCTIONS	IMPLICIT	EXPLICIT
NILADIC	∇ *FONC* *BIGRISE* (§ 4-17)	∇ *R←FONC* *COEF* (below)
MONADIC	∇ *X FONC Y* *CONSULTATION* (§ 4-23)	∇ *R←FONC* *AVERAGE* (§ 4-4)
DYADIC	∇ *X FONC Y* *FRAME* (§ 4-28)	∇ *R←FONC X* *PAY* (§ 4-5)

We will finish by specifying that the formal result of a function can not hav
the same name as one of the formal arguments. A function which would have
the header ∇ *R←FONC R* or ∇ *R←R FONC S* would cause an error at the time of its
execution.

INPUTS AND OUTPUTS

4-33   CARRIAGE RETURN

A carriage return is not an acceptable response to a quad, and the computer
will request that the data be entered, as it does when it ascertains any
error in the form of the data entered.

```
          ∇ R←EXAMPLE1
     [1]   R←□+1
          ∇
```

        EXAMPLE1

□:   ← question
                                ← the user types a carriage return
□:   ← the computer asks the question again
        4   ← correct answer
5   ← result of the function

On the other hand, a carriage return is a valid response to a quote-quad, and
is assumed to be an empty vector.

```
          ∇ R←EXAMPLE2
     [1]   R←⍞
          ∇
```

     ⍴ EXAMPLE2   ←   the user types a carriage return

     0   ←   the result is a zero vector

4-34   UNWANTED LOOPS

A programming error can create an endless loop, as in the function *FACTORIAL*
(§ 4-26), and the interruption key (ATTN) must be pressed in order to stop
its execution. If an input of data is required during this loop, it is
often impossible to resort to this method.

As would have been the case with the first version of the function *CONSULTATION*
If we had wished to interrupt it.

In the same way, in order to pull out the unwanted loop :

> - if a NUMERIC input is requested (⎕), type → and carriage
> return.

> - if an alphanumeric input is requested, type O, backspace;
> U, backspace, T and carriage return (or OUT, by superimpo-
> sing the three letters in that order). This invalid
> character has the effect of interrupting the running of
> the function.

On the IBM 5110 computer, a key marked ⎕ is provided for this purpose.
On other systems, the interruption key, followed by a carriage return
produces the same effect. On some rare systems, the "ESCAPE" key plays
this role.

4-35   BARE-OUTPUT

The printing of a message is always followed by a carriage return, which
causes a question and its answer to be on two successive lines:

> *WHAT IS YOUR NAME?*

> *PAUL-EMILE VICTOR*

A message can be deprived of its final carriage return (whence the name bare
output) by assigning it to a quote-quad which will cause it to be printed.

```
          ∇ R←EXAMPLE3
     [1]  ⍞←'WHAT IS YOUR NAME ? '
     [2]  R←⍞
          ∇
```

> *RESULT ← EXAMPLE3*
> *WHAT IS YOUR NAME ? CAMEL*

According to the APL system used, the result comprises :
> - either all the characters of the line :

> *RESULT*
> *WHAT IS YOUR NAME ? CAMEL*   (28 characters)

> - or only the users answer, preceeded by as many blanks as the
> printed message had letters;

> *RESULT*
> *CAMEL*   (28 characters)

But in both cases, the question and answer are on the same line, which enables
conversational applications to be reduced in volume, making their use more
acceptable, and improving the legibility of the dialogue written on paper.

JUMP INSTRUCTIONS

4-36   NILADIC BRANCHING

If it is not followed by a value, the branch arrow (→) causes the output of
a function and all the functions which call it, which the instruction →0
does not allow.
The comparison of the executions of the two versions of the function *INSIDE*
below, shows the difference between these two uses of branching.

```
              ∇ OUTSIDE
        [1]   'START OF CALLING FUNCTION'
        [2]   INSIDE
        [3]   'END OF CALLING FUNCTION'
              ∇
```

```
        ∇ INSIDE                          ∇ INSIDE
[1]   'CALLED FUNCTION'          [1]   'CALLED FUNCTION'
[2]   →0                         [2]   →
[3]   'END'                      [3]   'END'
        ∇                                 ∇
```

```
  OUTSIDE                           OUTSIDE
CALLING FUNCTION                  CALLING FUNCTION
CALLED FUNCTION                   CALLED FUNCTION
END OF CALLING FUNCTION
```

Here, the instruction →0 causes   Here, the instruction → causes an
an escape from the function   escape from the function *INSIDE* and
INSIDE and the execution of   from the function *OUTSIDE*. The last
OUTSIDE follows on normally.   instruction is not executed.

4-37   SOME CLASSIC JUMPS

JUMP TO A SINGLE ADDRESS

The following three instructions cause a jump to the label indicated if the
condition expressed is verified, or a pass to the following line if it is
not.

```
        [6]  → condition / labal
        [6]  → condition ρ label
        [6]  → label × ι condition
```

The last method works only in origin 1, and we advise against it's use.

JUMP OR ESCAPE

[11] → *label* x *condition*
This instruction causes a jump to the label indicated, or escape from the function.

JUMPS TO SEVERAL ADDRESSES

[14] → *(cond1 , cond2 , cond3 ...)/ label1 , label2 , label3* ...
This instruction causes a jump to the address corresponding to the first verified condition starting from the left, or a pass to the following line if no condition is verified.

[17] → *(label1 , label2 , label3 ...)/ [expression]*
[23] → *expression* φ *label1 , label2 , label3* ...

In both these instructions, it is the value of the expression which determines the address of the jump, by indexing or rotation of an address vector.

4-38   PARTICULAR CASES

- A jump instruction can have its own line number as an address :

[11] →*(condition)*/11
[18] *LOOP:* → *LOOP* x *condition*

This type of instruction is met more often when a function is required to be executed until its result complies with a given condition :

[7]   → (100 > *FUNC X→X+1*)/7

- A label can be used to achieve a relative jump :

[8]   → *LABEL + J*   where *J* is a whole number
we advise against the use of such a method.

- Labels, being normal variables, cannot be juxtaposed, they must be catenated.
  Hence, the instruction [9] → *LOOP MORE END*   is invalid
  It sould be written :   [9] → *LOOP,MORE,END*

- Finally, for any FORTRAN language nostalgics the instruction IF (A)11,17,3
  is translated in APL by : → 11 17 3 [2+x*A*]

4-39   NOTES

Notes can be inserted into a function. They do not modify its execution,
but can supply useful information when the function is printed. For example,
they can specify the role of this or that variable, or the significance of
a particular calculation, so as to facilitate eventual corrections.

Any character string preceeded by the symbol *LAMP* ⍝ , formed by ∘ superimposed
on ∩, is considered as a note.

```
                         ∇ FOREXAMPLE X
        [1]          ⍝   DEMONSTRATION FUNCTION
        [2]              X × 100 10 1
        [3]          ⍝ IN THE EVENT OF AN ERROR, CALL YOUR MOTHER
        [4]              X + 1 10 100
                         ∇
```

      FOREXAMPLE 45
    4500   450   45
    46 55   145

Some systems accept that the note should be placed to the right of an
instruction:

        [7]   P ← A×Q*H1-H2   ⍝ *PRESSURE CALCULATION*

4-40   INSTRUCTIONS SEPARATOR

Some APL systems accept several onstructions on the same function line,
provided that these instructions be separated by the DIAMOND symbol.
This symbol ◊ does not appear on the standard APL keyboard, and can thus be
replaced by ⌺ which is a the superimposition of < and >.

        [12]   → *LOOP* ⌺ ⎕←'DIMENSION ERROR' ⌺ *POINT←POINT*-1

Line [12] above comprises three instructions.

According to the system used the three instructions will be executed from
left to right (which complicates the computer's work of analysing the
expression), or from right to left, which has been assumed in this example.

The use of the diamond too often leads to barely legible functions, and we
advise that it only be used with moderation, especially as there is no standar
as regards the direction of execution of this type of instruction.

4-41   THIS STRANGE SEMI-COLON !

We have pointed out in paragraph 4-16 that the use of the semi-colon as a
printing separator was prohibited on some systems. If your system allows
it to be used, the following points could be useful to you.

    - A semi-colon can be placed neither on the right of an assigning
      arrow, nor in an instruction containing a branch :

      [25] *A←;4+5*
      [26] *→0;'THIS ARTICLE IS NOT IN THE DIRECTORY'*

      Both these instructions are hence invalid.

    - The semi-colon causes the value of the expressions which it separates
      to be printed, even if this value is assigned to a variable :

      [27] *A←A+1 ; B←P⌊S*   causes *A* and *B* to be displayed
      [28] *;X← 1 2 3 4*   causes *X* to be displayed

    - The expressions are EVALUATED from right to left, but PRINTED in the
      order in which they occur.
      We will imagine, for example, that a function possesses the following
      instruction :

      [29] *POP←9 ; POP←5*

      During execution, the computer will print 95, but the final value
      of *POP* will be 9, thus indicating that *POP* has first taken the
      value 5, then the value 9.

4-42   LOCKED FUNCTIONS

By overstriking the symbol NO (~) on the carrot which opens or closes a
function, this function is locked ▽. It can no longer be printed nor modified
it can only be used or completely erased.

This possibility is used in order to place a function at the disposal of
somebody whilst preventing him from knowing the contents of it or from
modifying it. On some systems, a locked function can be modified by typing
▽ again when it is called, provided that one is in the workspace where the
function was created, and not in a copy of this workspace.

The function ☐*LOCK* of CONTROL DATA Corp., already mentioned in paragraph
4-32, also enables functions to be locked, and produces the same effect
as ▽.

Any attempt to print or modify a locked function brings about the diagnostic
"definition error" : *DEFN ERROR*.

CHAPTER 5

OPERATORS

Operator is the name given to a function when one at least of the arguments
is a function or another operator. Hence the notation +/A indicates that
the operator / applies to the function +. The whole +/ comprises the
RESULTANT FUNCTION, the operand of which is A.

Present versions of APL include five operators. Since REDUCTION has been
studied on pages 48 to 51 and 62 this chapter will introduce the four other
operators, namely the axis operator, scan, outer product and inner product.

In the following, the signs ● and ■ (which are not APL symbols) should serve
to represent any dyadic scalar functions. These signs will therefore replace

+ - × ÷ * ⊛ ⌈ ⌊ ! | < ≤ = ≥ > ≠ ∨ ∧ ⍱ ⍲ ○

5-1   THE AXIS OPERATOR: [I]

This operator indicates on which dimension of an operand should a primitive
function of an operator apply:

> Φ[1]A indicates that the primitive function Φ applies to the first
> dimension of A. This function will be considered later.

> +/[2]B indicates that the resultant function +/ applies to the
> second dimension of B.

If the axis operator is omitted, the operation relates always to the last
dimension of the operand.

The axis operator applies to the following funcitons and operators:

reduction and compression (/ and ⌿), scan and expansion (| and ⊦), catenation
and lamination (,), reversal and rotation (Φ or ⊖).

5-2   SCAN: ●/A

Scanning of an array by a funciton yields the array of successive reductions
of the n first elements (or lines, or columns) of the array. Hence, in the
case of a vector, the nth term of the result is equal to the reduction of
the n first terms of the vector.

FIRST EXAMPLE

A housewife pays out the following sums during the course of a week:

$EXP \leftarrow$ 21 9 12 56 14 37 8

She wishes to know from day to day her total expenditures. Scanning by the sum instantly yields the result.

$+/EXP$

21 30 42 98 112 149 157

It is found that the third term is equal to: +/21 9 12

SECOND EXAMPLE

The company mentioned in paragraph 4-9 has observed the following rates of expansion during the last ten years:

$EX \leftarrow$ 17 22 32 35 10 ‾9 ‾2 10 5

Since the income during the first year was 2180 the future development can be obtained from the following calculations:

        1st year: $\lfloor$2180
        2nd year: $\lfloor$2180 × 1.17
        3rd year: $\lfloor$2180 × 1.17 × 1.22
        4th year: $\lfloor$2180 × 1.17 × 1.22 × 1.32
        etc.

It will be quicker to write: $\lfloor$×\ 2180 1.17 1.22 1.32 1.35 ....
Or again:

        $\lfloor$×\2180 , 1 + EX÷100

2180 2550 3111 4107 5545 6099 5550 5439 5983 6282

THIRD EXAMPLE

For our final example, assume that during its execution, a defined function inquires the name of the person at the keyboard:

        WHAT IS YOUR NAME ?
                LOUIS THE FOURTEENTH
        ↑ ↑ ↑

Having little skill in the handling of a typewriter, the user has entered three undesirable blanks prior to his response. The expression $(R \neq '\ ')/R$ is not suitable for removing them, since it yields the following results:

        LOUISTHEFOURTEENTH   (R represents the user's response).

Scanning by the function OR will enable the head blanks to be eliminated without eliminating the remainder.

$R \neq$ ' '

0 0 0 1 1 1 1 1 0 1 1 0 1 1 1 1 1 1 1 1 1 1

$v \backslash R \neq$ ' '

0 0 0 1 1 1 1 1 1 1 1 1 1 1 1 1 1 1 1 1 1 1

$(v \backslash R \neq$ ' ' $) / R$

LOUIS THE FOURTEENTH (which was required)

CONVENTIONS

Scanning applies to arrays. In this case, all conventions relating to reducti
are also valid for scanning.

a) An index specifies the direction of scanning of the array:

$M \leftarrow 3 \ 4 \rho \iota \ 12$

M	$+\backslash [1]M$	$+\backslash [2]M$
1 2 3 4	1 2 3 4	1 3 6 10
5 6 7 8	6 8 10 12	5 11 18 26
9 10 11 12	15 18 21 24	9 19 30 42

b) The index can be omitted when treating the last dimension. Thus, $+\backslash M$
   is strictly equivalent to $+\backslash [2]M$.

c) A - sign can be superposed on the bar when treating the first dimension.
For example $+\backslash M$ and $+\backslash [1]M$ are equivalent.

NOTE:

As in the case of reduction, care should be taken regarding the use of scanning
with non-associative operations.

$-\backslash 8 \ 2 \ 4$ not equal to 8 6 2 but 8 6 10.

Actually, taking the precaution to calculate the elements one at a time:

$-/8$	equals	8
$-/8 \ 2$	equals	6
$-/8 \ 2 \ 4$	equals	10

In the same way $>\backslash 5 \ 4 \ 8$ yields the result 5 1 1.

PARTICULAR CASES

With boolean vectors, we witnessed the use of a scan by OR. Other operations
are of interest: $<\backslash B$ gives the position of the first 1 of B and $\leq\backslash B$ gives a
vector of 1, except for placing of the 0 of B

OUTER PRODUCT: $A°.\bullet B$

The outer product enables each element of the left-hand argument to be composed
with each element of the right-hand argument, by any dyadic scalar function.
This is a type of generalized pythagoras table.

The arguments can be of any rank and dimension.   At present we will restrict
ourselves to pure examples relating to vectors.

       2 3 5 °.+ 5 8 2 6

This operation yields the table of addition of the two vectors.   For greater
clarity the arguments in italics have been repreated:

+	5	8	2	6
2	7	10	4	8
3	8	11	5	9
5	10	13	7	11

Replacing + by × we obtain a multiplication table:

       3 2 ¯1 °.× 6 4 ¯2 1

×	*6*	*4*	*¯2*	*1*
3	18	12	¯6	3
2	12	8	¯4	2
¯1	¯6	¯4	2	¯1

A relationship function can also be employed, = for example, in which case each
term of the left hand argument will be compared with each term of the right-hand
argument:

       (ι4) °.= (ι4)

=	*1*	*2*	*3*	*4*
1	1	0	0	0
2	0	1	0	0
3	0	0	1	0
4	0	0	0	1

From now on we will no longer indicate the arguments in italics but this
presentation is recommended when seeking the result of an outer product.

Like reduction and scan, the outer product is generalized to all dyadic scalar
functions.   The following are characteristic examples.

5-4   APPLICATIONS OF THE OUTER PRODUCT

FIRST EXAMPLE

During a study trip, students have spent the following amounts:

$EXP \leftarrow$ 800 1300 950 2600 1600 3200 1340 2000 850

It is decided to reimburse them completely for sums less than 1000 Francs a
50% of sums between 1000 and 1800 Francs. In order to obtain the amount
owed to each, the following procedure can be adopted:

The expression 1000 1800 $^\circ.\llcorner$ EXP will yield the following array:

800 1000 950 1000 1000 1000 1000 1000 850
800 1300 950 1800 1600 1800 1340 1800 850

The sum of the two lines of the array yields twice the result sought. It i
therefore sufficient to multiply by 0.5 to obtain the final result:

0.5 +/ 1000 1800 $^\circ.\llcorner$ EXP
800 1150 950 1400 1300 1400 1170 1400 850

SECOND EXAMPLE

Given a sample of 2000 persons, it is required to classify them according to
age. For example, we want to know how many persons are in the following
ranges:
15-30; 30-40; 40-50; 50-65; and over 65 years.

The *RANGE* function provides the following simple calculation.

```
        ∇ REP ← T RANGE A
[1]     REP ← +/ T°.≤A
[2]     REP ← REP-1 DROP REP, 0
        ∇
```

Application is as follows:

   15 30 40 50 65 *RANGE* 27 51 44 60 73 14 23 52 17 66 35 52 41 39 26 33 81
4 3 2 4 3

Calculation of the first instruction can be broken down as follows:

≤	27	51	44	60	73	14	23	52	17	66	35	52	41	39	26	33	81
15	1	1	1	1	1	0	1	1	1	1	1	1	1	1	1	1	1
30	0	1	1	1	1	0	0	1	0	1	1	1	1	1	0	1	1
40	0	1	1	1	1	0	0	1	0	1	0	1	1	0	0	0	1
50	0	1	0	1	1	0	0	1	0	1	0	1	0	0	0	0	1
65	0	0	0	0	1	0	0	0	0	0	0	1	0	0	0	0	1

The sum of the columns yields: 16   12   9   7   3

Finally, in the second instruction,   16   12   9   7   3   -   12   9   7   3   0   yields
the result sought: 4   3   2   4   3

Knowing this classification in ranges of age, assume that we wish to plot a
bar chart (often incorrectly called "histogram").

Try: 4 3 2 1 °.≤ 4 3 2 4 3

```
1  0  0  1  0                              2  1  1  2  1
1  1  0  1  1   by adding 1 we obtain:     2  2  1  2  2
1  1  1  1  1                              2  2  2  2  2
1  1  1  1  1                              2  2  2  2  2
```

Using the latter matrix as index for a string of two characters, for example
'⎕', the 1 will be replaced by a blank and the 2 by a quad.
TThe result is as follows:

'⎕'[1+ 4 3 2 1 °.≤4 3 2 4 3]

We have now obtained the required chart.   This method will be used in paragraph
6-8 for the *HISTO* function.

-5   DIMENSIONS OF THE RESULT

The arguments of an outer product can be of any dimensions.   The following rule
indicates the dimensions of the reult.

$$\rho\ A°.\bullet B \quad \text{is equal to} \quad (\rho A),\rho B$$

> $\bullet$ represents any dyadic
>   scalar function.

An example will demonstrate this rule:

⎕←A←2 6ρ'ALBERTMARCEL'

ALBERT
MARCEL

B←'MARC'

R← A°.=B

The R value framed by the arguments giving rise to it are:

=	M	A	R	C
A	0	1	0	0
L	0	0	0	0
B	0	0	0	0
E	0	0	0	0
R	0	0	1	0
T	0	0	0	0

ρR is equal to 2 6 4, representing catenation of ρA and ρB: 2 6 and 4.

M	1	0	0	0
A	0	1	0	0
R	0	0	1	0
C	0	0	0	1
E	0	0	0	0
L	0	0	0	0

5-6   THE INNER PRODUCT: $A\bullet.\blacksquare B$

The inner product generalizes the mathematic matrix product for all dyadic scalar functions and data of all dimensions.

We will demonstrate with an example.

A coffee roaster markets three brands of coffee named AROME, LUXE and DEGUSTATIO obtained by blending Robusta and Arabica coffees. The following weight matrix indicates the quantities of Robusta and Arabica necessary for making up 250g packet of each blend.

	AROMA	LUXE	DEGUSTATION
Robusta	200	150	100
Arabica	50	100	150

The coffee roaster receives four orders, indicating the numbers of packets of each blend required. The ORD matrix summerises the orders.

Orders →	N°1	N°2	N°3	N°4
AROME	50	600	100	20
LUXE	20	300	40	5
DEGUSTATION	20	200	60	0

In order to obtain the quantity of Arabica necessary for example for making
up an order number three we can write:

$$(50 \times 100) + (100 \times 40) + (150 \times 60)$$

Or better: *+/WEIGHT*[2;]×*ORDER*[;3]

The calculation can then be restarted for the four orders and the two blends of
coffee. The inner product directly handles the necessary sums and products.

This is written:

> *WEIGHT +.× ORDER*

```
15000   18500   32000   4750
 7500    9000   18000   1500
```

<u>DEFINITION</u>   (two-dimensional arrays)

In the inner product $A \bullet.\blacksquare B$, the elements of each A line are composed with the
elements of each B column by the operation $\blacksquare$.   The values obtained are then
reduced one by the operation $\bullet$.   The succession of the two operations is
expressed by hte symbols $\bullet.\blacksquare$.

The following symbolic presentation illustrates this calculation procedure.

It is seen quite clearly on the diagram that the operation is possible only
if the number of *WEIGHT* columns is equal to the number of *ORD* lines.

COMPATIBILITY OF OPERANDS

> An inner product can be performed between two data A and B taken in
> this order if the last dimension of A is equal to the first dimension
> of B.   The result will have the dimensions of the catenation of the
> dimensions of the operands with their common value eliminated.
> One of the arguments (or both) can be a vector or a scalar.

Hence, we can compose two data of dimensions:

2 7 5̲ and 5̲ 2 8 4   the result will be of dimensions: 2 7 2 8 4
8 7 6̲ and 6̲ 3   the result will be of dimensions: 8 7 3

However two arrays cannot be composed with dimensions: 6 3̲ and 4̲ 3

The rule remains valid for vectors as shown in the following calculation:

A householder purchases 2 litres of milk, 5 pats of butter, and 3 kilos of potatoes, costing respectivley 1.50 Francs per litre, 4.80 Francs per pat and 0.80 Francs per Kg. (1).
She will have spent in all:

        2 5 3 +.× 1.50 4.80 0.80
    29.4

Two examples will demonstrate the way in which the inner product is generaliz̶ to other functions than + and ×.

5-8   APPLICATIONS OF THE INNER PRODUCT

Search for a name in a table

We have a matrix of names or words:

        RECIPE
    FLOUR
    SUGAR
    EGGS
    WATER
    SALT
    MILK

It is required to know whether the word "*WATER*" appears in this matrix, which could be greater.

        RECIPE ∧.= *WATER*
    0 0 0 1 0 0

The result clearly indicates that the word sought appears in the fourth position.

The calculation can be broken down for any two elements of the result, the 3r̶ and 4th for example:

    ∧/ '*EGGS*'='*WATER*'   yields 0
    ∧/ '*WATER*'='*WATER*' yields 1

(1) The author confesses complete ignorance of household economy.

The operands were of dimensions 6 5 and 5, the result is of dimension 6,
readily confirming the rule set out above.

ROADS IN A GRAPH

Six warehouses are distributed within a town. The following diagram plots the
distances separating the warehouses. The no entry directions mean that it
is no longer to go from A to B than from B to A.

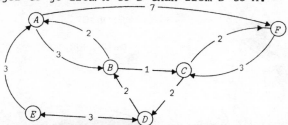

This diagram can be represented by a distances array. The blank squares indicate
that there is no road between the two points, while the value 0 indicates that
the distance from a point to itself is zero.

		DESTINATION					
		A	B	C	D	E	F
	A	0	3				7
	B	2	0	1			
ORIGIN	C			0	2		2
	D		2		0	3	
	E	3			3	0	
	F			3			0

As blank squares cannot be represented in a matrix they are replaced by an
arbitary value, 1000 for example, so as to penalize use of a road which does
not exist,
We thus obtain the representative matrix $T1$.

$$
\begin{array}{cccccc}
 & T1 & & & & \\
0 & 3 & 1000 & 1000 & 1000 & 7 \\
2 & 0 & 1 & 1000 & 1000 & 1000 \\
1000 & 1000 & 0 & 2 & 1000 & 2 \\
1000 & 2 & 1000 & 0 & 3 & 1000 \\
3 & 1000 & 1000 & 3 & 0 & 1000 \\
1000 & 1000 & 3 & 1000 & 1000 & 0
\end{array}
$$

INNER PRODUCT

OUTER PRODUCT

DRAWING BY RUMWEISS

This matrix yields the distance from one point to another in a single stage.
In order to obtain the shortest route in two stages an inner product is formed:

$\Box \leftarrow T2 \leftarrow T1 L. + T1$

```
   0      3      4   1000   1000      7
   2      0      1      3   1000      3
1000      4      0      2      5      2
   4      2      3      0      3   1000
   3      5   1000      3      0     10
1000   1000      3      5   1000      0
```

We will break down the calculation of one of the elements for example,
calculation of the shortest road from D to A.

In order to make up this route one of the following roads can be followed:

$$
\left.
\begin{array}{lll}
D \to A \to A & \text{distance :} & 1000 + 0 \\
D \to B \to A & \text{distance :} & 2 + 2 \\
D \to C \to A & \text{distance :} & 1000 + 1000 \\
D \to D \to A & \text{distance :} & 0 + 1000 \\
D \to E \to A & \text{distance :} & 3 + 3 \\
D \to F \to A & \text{distance :} & 1000 + 1000
\end{array}
\right\}
$$

These values represent

$T1[4;]+T1[;1]$

Reduction by the minimum would yield the shortest road. The operation has
therefore been performed:

$L/T1[4;]+T1[;1]$

Repetition of this calculation for all lines and all columns is reflected
completely by the notation $T1$ L.+ $T1$.

It should be noted that the shortest route is automatically obtained in one
and two stages since the presence of zeros on the diagonal enables one of the
two stages to be performed while remaining on the same point.

The shortest road in three stages at most will be obtained in the same way:

$T3 \leftarrow T2$ L.+ $T1$
$T3$

```
   0      3      4      6   1000      6
   2      0      1      3      6      3
   6      4      0      2      5      2
   4      2      3      0      3      5
   3      5      6      3      0     10
1000      7      3      5      8      0
```

It is found that one cannot always go from F to A in three stages. Finally the shortest route in four stages at most:

$$\square \leftarrow T4 \leftarrow T3 \lfloor .+T1$$

```
0  3  4  6  9  6
2  0  1  3  6  3
6  4  0  2  5  2
4  2  3  0  3  5
3  5  6  3  0  8
9  7  3  5  8  0
```

This matrix shows that it is preferable to go from A to F passing through B and C.

An additional stage in the calculation would teach us that the distances cannot be reduced further.

OTHER INNER PRODUCTS

It will be seen later that it can be learnt whether a vector is classified in increasing order by means of the expression $V<.>1\phi V$ involving an inner product.

If, in the matrix representing the previous graph the distances between points are no longer shown but merely the existance or otherwise of a road, a boolean matrix $B \leftarrow T1 \neq 1000$ may be adequate. Now the existence of a road of length 2 (at most) can be determined by the expression $B\vee.\wedge B$. We continue then for roads of lengths 3,4 etc.

Other interesting examples will be found of inner products in exercise 12 of this chapter and in paragraph 6-12.

5-9   IMPORTANCE AND HAZARDS OF OPERATORS

Operators make it possible to avoid most of the loops necessary in other languages. In this respect they are valuable tools. Care should be taken however, as regards the large number of operations brought about by an inner or outer product. Furthermore, the result of an outer product may be very large. The outer product of two vectors of 100 elements gives rise to a matrix of 10,000 elements which may unnecessarily burden the memory . It is also sometimes pertinent to replace an outer product by an iterative process.

We have given a few examples of inner products: $+.\times \wedge.= \lfloor.+ <.> \wedge.\vee$; all dyadic scalar functions can be combined in pairs but it cannot be said in advance what will be the significance of certain combinations. Only the nature of the data and of the problem to be resolved can lead to a given inner or outer product being used.

EXERCISES

1) Find a solution to exercise 6 of chapter 4, using an inner product.

2) A string of characters is given. Write an expression providing the level
   of bracketing of each character. For example, the vector printed in italics
   under each character will be made to correspond to the string of characters
   shown below:

   $C \leftarrow 'B \times (U * (D-A) + U) - U'$

   Characters: $B \times (U * (D - A) + U) - U$

   Level   : 0 0 1 1 1 2 2 2 2 2 1 1 1 0 0

3) How can the following matrix be prepared in a simple manner?

   ```
   1 1 1 1 1 1 1 1 1 1
   2 2 2 2 2 2 2 2 2 2
   3 3 3 3 3 3 3 3 3 3
   4 4 4 4 4 4 4 4 4 4
   ```

4) Exercise [39] of chapter 3 required the formation of an arithmetic progression
   of 17 terms, the first one being 23, and each term being equal to the
   preceding one plus 11. Find a solution employing the scan operator.

   In the same way, resolve exercise [40] of chapter 3.

5) What are the values of the following expressions:

   ```
   -\1 1 1 1 1 1
   -\5 4 3 2 1
   ×/+ 6ρ1
   ```

6) Given the matrix M as follows: 8 2 5 1 4
                                        3 7 1 5 0
                                        4 3 6 0 6

   What are the values of the following expressions?

   ```
   ⌈/M
   ⌊/+/M
   ×/⌊/[1]M
   ×/ρM
   ```

Check your assumptions on the computer.

7) A questionnaire of Q questions has to be distributed among 3 to 4,000
    persons. It is possible to reply to each of the questions in R
    different ways, including the reply "no opinion".

    For each question, it is desired to obtain the number of replys of each
    type. For example:

	R1	R2	R3	R4	
					··········
Question 1	29	233	67	85]	··········
Question 2	560	106	7	129	··········
Question 3	344	79	216	904	··········

    ...etc...

    Provide a simple means for entering the replies in the computer and
    calculating the array of results. The results will be printed out in the
    form of a simple matrix without any header.

    The functions will be designed so that the person collecting the replies
    may interrupt the work in order to spread it over several days. It
    is also important that the work should be as simple as possible.

    Test your own solution with $Q=6$ and $R=3$.

8) In what way can the following matrices be formed?

    ```
    0 1 1 1           0 0 0 1
    0 0 1 1   and     0 0 1 0
    0 0 0 1           0 1 0 0
    0 0 0 0           1 0 0 0
    ```

9) What are the values of the following expressions?

    ```
    ∧/1 1 1 0 1 1
    ∧ 1 1 1 0 1 1
    =/0 1 1 1 0 1 1
    ```

10) It is desired to know whether an array of characters contains at least
    one completely blank line. How can this be done?
    Same question for a column.
    The use of an inner product is advised.

11) It is decided to eliminate from a matrix all columns containing only
    zeros. How can this be done?

    For example:

    ```
    8 2 0 0 0 9             8 2 0 9
    5 0 0 4 0 5   yields:   5 0 4 5
    6 0 0 0 0 2             6 0 0 2
    ```

12) In paragraph 3-14 b) a method was indicated for determinining whether a
number N is between two limits given by a vector L. Find another method
using the inner product.

13) Calling the three sides of a triangle a, b, c and p the semi-perimeter
$0.5 \times (a+b+c)$, its area can be calculated by the formula:

$$S \quad \sqrt{p \ (p-a) \ (p-b) \ (p-c)}$$

Write a function yielding the value of S when the vector of the three
lengths a, b, and c is given for it.

14) Faulty keyboard: the ⍳ I key of the keyboard is out of order. Write
a *YOTA* funciton to replace the monadic ⍳ function.

15) It is desired to know whether the elements of a vector V are all different
from each other (reply 1 or 0).
Find a solution using the outer product.
Can an inner product also be used?

16) MOBILE AVERAGES

We have a vector V containing measurements taken at regular intervals.
This may, for example, represent the prices of a commodity or temperatures
or, again, production figures for articles manufactured over the 365
days of a year. These figures often contain daily fluctuations rendering
determination of their global variation over the year difficult.
A simple method for reducing such daily variations consists in replacing
the measurements by a sequence of averages relating to 3, 4, 5, 10
values or more.
For example, the first value will be replaced by the average of the values
1 to 10, replacing the second value by the average of the values 2 to 11,
the third by the average of the values 3 to 12 and so on.
In this way, only 355 values will be obtained, called mobile averages.

Write a function for calculating mobile averages of a vector V over
N elements (in the above example N equals 10).

17) The previous exercise can be resolved without a loop by means of the
scan operator. This solution is not only more elegant but is also much
quicker.
Find this solution.

18) How can the following matrix be formed in a simple manner?

```
1 2 3 4 5 6
2 2 3 4 5 6
3 3 3 4 5 6
4 4 4 4 5 6
5 5 5 5 5 6
6 6 6 6 6 6
```

SUPPLEMENTS

TO CHAPTER 5

5-10

THE OPERATOR CONCEPT

An operator is a function, one at least of whose arguments is itself
a function or an operator. The association thus formed is called RESULTANT
FUNCTION.
For example, in the notation $+/A$, the symbol / is the operator and $+/$ is the
resultant function (monadic in this case). In the notation $A+.\times B$ the operato
(.) is applied to the functions $+$ and $\times$ to form the resultant function $+.\times$,
which is dyadic.

This concept was derived only recently and in principle nothing prevents it
being generalized to mixed functions and even defined functions. Some APL
experimental versions possess an extension of operators to mixed functions.

Thus the expression $3\ 2\ 6\ ,\ .\ 5\ 4\ 7$ yields the result:
$5\ 5\ 5\ 4\ 4\ 7\ 7\ 7\ 7\ 7\ 7$
that is to say: $(3\rho 5),(2\rho 4),(6\rho 7)$

It is not difficult to imagine the importance of such an extension of the
language.
It may be observed that these extended versions of APL also include new
operators.

5-11

REDUCTION

Reduction checks the feature that $\bullet/A,B$ is equal to $(\bullet/A)\bullet(\bullet/B)$

However, if B is an empty vector, $\bullet/A,B$ is equal to $\bullet/A,\iota 0$, hence to $\bullet/A$.

Calling a the value of $\bullet/A$ and v the value of $\bullet/\iota 0$, the property expressed
above is expressed by:

$$\bullet/A \ \equiv \ \underline{a \ \equiv \ a\bullet v} \ \equiv \ (\bullet/A)\bullet(\bullet/\iota 0)$$

Such an identity is possible only if v is the neutral element of the function
$\bullet$. Hence the rule:

> Reduction of an empty vector by a function yields the neutral
> element of this function, if there is one. If this function
> does not have a neutral element there is a domain error.

It is found on a specific example that ×/(8 3 2),(5 7) is actually equal to
        (×/8 3 2) × (×/5 7)

In the same way it is necessary that ×/(8 3 2),(ι0) be equal to (×/8 3 2) ×
(×/ι0).

It is now obvious that (×/ι0) is equal to 1, neutral element of multiplication.

The following table shows the result of reduction of an empty vector for all
dyadic scalar functions.

●	●/ι0	NOTES
+	0	
−	0	Neutral element on the right
×	1	See note 1
÷	1	Neutral element on the right
*	1	Neutral element on the right
⊛	nil	Result in domain error
|	0	Neutral element on the left
!	1	Neutral element on the left
⌈	¯7.2370E75	These values are the smallest and greatest
⌊	7.2370E75	numbers which can be represented (here on IBM equipment)
∧	1	
∨	0	
⍲	nil	Results in domain error
⍱	nil	Results in domain error
<	0	Neutral element on the left
≤	1	Neutral element on the left
=	1	
≥	1	Neutral element on the right
>	0	Neutral element on the right
≠	0	
○	nil	Results in the domain error

for boolean (applies to the bracketed group: <, ≤, =, ≥, >)

(1)   This explains how the RAVEL function appearing in paragraph 4-5 may apply
      to a scalar. If *ARR* is a scalar ρ*ARR* is equal to ι0, hence ×/ρ*ARR* is equal
      to 1 and 1ρ*ARR* yields a single element <u>vector</u>.

NOTE

The axis operator is affected by a change in the origin of indices:

+/[1]A +/[2]A +/[3]A become respectively, with origin 0:

+/[0]A +/[1]A +/[2]A

On the other hand the notations +/A and +/A are not affected by the change in origin of indices.

5-12   THE INNER PRODUCT

The dimensions of operands and of the result of an inner product observe the following rule:

$R \leftarrow A$ •.■ B

Conditions of dimensioning: $(-1\uparrow\rho A) \equiv (1\uparrow\rho B)$

Dimensions of the result: $(\rho R) \equiv (-1\downarrow\rho A)$, $(1\downarrow\rho B)$

(the symbol $\equiv$ designates the mathematical identity).

An interesting example of the use of the inner product and of the outer product will be shown in relation to the polynomial regression paragraph 8-5.

5-13   CASE OF SCALARS

If one of the two operands of an inner product is a scalar, it is extended to a vector, so that the condition of dimensioning expressed above is observed

If M is the following matrix: 1 2 4
                                    3 6 9

M +.× 5 is equivalent to M +.× 5 5 5 and is equal to: 35   90

5 +.× M is equivalent to 5 5 +.× M and is equal to: 20   40   65.

CHAPTER 6

SELECTIONS AND TRANSFORMATIONS
IN ARRAYS

TAKE AND DROP

The two functions TAKE (↑) and DROP (↓) are used to extract certain parts
of a datum. They broadly generalize the functions of the same names which we
have written and used in chapter 4.

Application to a vector is as follows :

          5 ↑ 8 2 7 1 4 6   extraction of the first 5 terms
    8 2 7 1 4

          4 ↑ 'RESTORE'   extraction of the first 4 terms
    REST

          4 ↓ 8 2 7 1 4 6   expulsion of the first 4 terms
      4 6

Two examples will show that the result of TAKE and DROP, applied to a vector,
is also a vector, even if only one element remains :

          ρ 1↑'BOX'
    1

          ρ 5↓8 2 7 1 4 6
    1

If their left hand argument is negative, the functions TAKE and DROP apply
starting from the end of the right hand operand.

          ¯2 ↑ 8 2 7 1 4 6   extraction of the last two terms
      4 6

          ¯1 ↓ 8 2 7 1 4 6   expulsion of the last term
    8 2 7 1 4

The result can be an empty vector in both the following cases :

    - No element is taken :   0 ↑ 6 3 9 2

    - More elements are dropped than there are :5 ↓ 2 8 6

                                        or : ¯4 ↓ 1 2 3 4

Finally :

> If the left hand argument of the function TAKE is greater than the
> dimension of the right hand argument, the latter is suplemented by zeros
> (or blanks in the case of an alphanumeric vector).

        ¯8 ↑ 3 4 ¯1
    3 4 ¯1 0 0 0 0 0

        ¯6 ↑ 2 2 4 1
    0 0 2 2 4 1

        ¯6 ↑ *'TILT'*
      TILT
    ↑↑

Two blanks have been inserted.

This property extends to the case where an element is taken where there aren't
any :

        1 ↑ ι0   Here, the value 0 is obtained
    0

        ρ 1 ↑ ''   Here, a blank character is obtained
    1

APPLICATION

The function below indicates whether its argument is numeric (1) or not (0).

         ∇ *R←NUMER ARG*
    [1] *R←0=1↑0ρARG*
         ∇

In effect, $0↑ARG$ gives an empty vector of the same nature as the argument,
that is to say, ι0 if the argument is numeric, or '' if it is alphanumeric.

Hence, $1↑0↑ARG$ gives either a zero, or a blank.

If the argument was numeric, 0=0 gives 1.
If it was alphanumeric, 0='' gives 0.

Examples :

        NUMER 1 2 3
    1

        NUMER '39 64'
    0

        NUMER NUMER 'ZERO'
    1

This function may be of great service, and it is advised that you keep it in
your workspace .

6-2

APPLICATION TO ARRAYS

TAKE and DROP apply to arrays, each element of the left hand argument relating to the corresponding dimension of the right hand argument.

Hence, $A \uparrow B$ or $A \downarrow B$ can be written only if ρA is equal to $\rho\rho B$.

In the following examples, a diagram causes the part of the matrix affected by the function to appear on a grey background.

We will use the matrix M as follows :

```
1  2  3  4
5  6  7  8
9  2  3  0
```

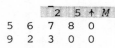

```
1  2  3
5  6  7
```

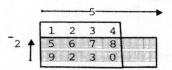

Extraction of two lines and three columns has taken place.

The following represents extraction of the last two lines, and 5 columns :

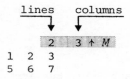

```
5  6  7  8  0
9  2  3  0  0
```

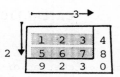

Extraction of the first line, and the last 6 columns :

```
‾1    6 ↑ M
0  0  1  2  3  4
```

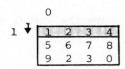

Expulsion of a line and no column :

```
1  0  ↓ M
5  6  7  8
9  2  3  0
```

In order to expel the first line and the last two columns, proceed as follows :

$$1 \; {}^{-}2 \; \downarrow M$$

```
5  6
9  2
```

Finally, in order to expel two columns without modifying the number of lines:

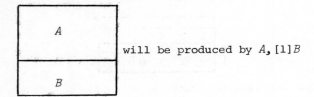

$$0 \; {}^{-}2 \; \downarrow M$$

```
3  4
7  8
3  0
```

6-3   CATENATION OF ARRAYS

We have studied the catenation of vectors in paragraph 3-17, but arrays of
any rank can also be catenated, if their dimensions are compatible, by
specifying by an index on which dimension the catenation takes place.

If there are three matrices A, B and C,

+-------------+
| |
| A |
| |
+-------------+   will be produced by $A,[1]B$
| |
| B |
| |
+-------------+

+---------+-------+
| | |
| A | C | Will be produced by $A,[2]C$
| | |
+---------+-------+

In order to accentuate the visual effect, we will work on matrices of characters

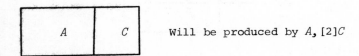

$$A \leftarrow 3 \; 4 \; \rho \; 'A'$$

$$B \leftarrow 2 \; 4 \; \rho \; 'B'$$

$$C \leftarrow 3 \; 2 \; \rho \; 'C'$$

         A,[1]*B*   *A*,[2]*C*

         AAAA   *AAAACC*
         AAAA   *AAAACC*
         AAAA   *AAAACC*
         BBBB
         BBBB

RULES

Two arrays *A* and *B* can be catenated along their *I*th dimension
provided that they are of the same rank, and that all their
other dimensions are identical.

Equally an array *B* of rank n-1 can be catenated to an array
A of rank n without it being necessary to reshape it. Therefore,
the catenation must without fail, occur along the dimension
of *A* which is absent from *B*.

According to this last rule, a vector can be catenated to a matrix :

         'VECT',[1]*A*   *A*,[1]*'ROSE'*

         VECT   *AAAA*
         AAAA   *AAAA*
         AAAA   *AAAA*
         AAAA   *ROSE*

In effect $\left\{\begin{array}{l} \rho A \text{ equals } 3 \quad 4 \\ \rho \text{ '}VECT\text{' equals} \quad\quad 4 \end{array}\right.$

catenation had to be undertaken according to the
1st dimension of *A*.

In the same way we will take an array of three dimensions : $T \leftarrow 2\ 3\ 4\ \rho\ 'T'$

ρT equals 2 3 4
ρB equals 2   4

catenation will have to be undertaken on the 2nd dimension.

         T,[2]*B*

    TTTT
    TTTT
    TTTT
    BBBB

    TTTT
    TTTT
    TTTT
    BBBB   The same reasoning indicates that *A* could have been
                     catenated to *T* according to its first dimension.

A scalar, or an array comprising only a single element, can be catenated to any array; it is thus automatically extended to the appropriate dimension

$$('S',[1]A),[2]'*'$$

```
SSSS*
AAAA*
AAAA*
AAAA*
```

Using this principle, here is a function which can be very useful :

```
       ∇ R ← WRAP X
[1]    X ← (¯2↑1 1,ρX)ρX
[2]    R ← '|',[2]('¯',[1]X,[1]'_'),[2]'|'
       ∇
```

Note that the first instruction transforms the argument into a matrix

```
|----------|
|THE PARCEL|
|_____|
```

Up to now we have demonstrated examples relating to arrays of characters, but it is evident that numeric arrays can be catenated.

$$(2\ 3\rho 1),[1]0$$

```
1 1 1
1 1 1
0 0 0
```

CONVENTION

If the catenation symbol is not followed by any index, the catenation is undertaken according to the last dimension.
Hence, $A,[2]C$ can also be written A,C :

6-4   LAMINATION

Catenation of two data gives a result of the same rank as the data of the highest rank. For example, catenation of two matrices also gives a matrix; catenation of two vectors gives a vector.

The operation which consists of juxtaposing two data in order to obtain a result of a HIGHER rank is called LAMINATION; it is obtained by specifying a catenation axis which is NOT A WHOLE NUMBER.

Here are some points of reflection.

By laminating two vectors, a matrix is obtained :

       1 2 3 4 ,[0.2] 5 6 7 8
  1 2 3 4
  5 6 7 8   Any axis between 0 and 1 would have given the same
                  result.

       1 2 3 4 , [1.6] 5 6 7 8
  1 5
  2 6
  3 7   Any axis between 1 and 2 would have given the same
  4 8   result.

If M and N are two matrices, an array of rank 3 will be obtained by laminating them.

	1 2 3 4			11 12 13 14
M equals :	3 9 0 7		N equals :	13 19 10 17
	4 8 5 5			14 18 15 15

      $M,$ [0.5]N
  1   2   3   4
  3   9   0   7
  4   8   5   5   Here, juxtaposition is performed plan by plan.
                   Dimensions of the result : <u>2</u> 3 4
 11 12 13 14
 13 19 10 17
 14 18 15 15

      $M,$ [1.41]N
  1   2   3   4
 11 12 13 14

  3   9   0   7   Here, juxtaposition is performed line by line.
 13 19 10 17   Dimensions of the result : 3 <u>2</u> 4

  4   8   5   5
 14 18 15 15

Finally, juxtaposition can be obtained column by column by specifying an axis between 2 and 3. This is done on the following page.

The result will have 3 4 <u>2</u> as dimensions.

$M, [2.3]N$

```
1  11
2  12
3  13
4  14

3  13
9  19
0  10
7  17

4  14
8  18
5  15
5  15
```

In paragraph 6-14 of the supplement will be found a formal definition which specifies the dimensions of the result of a lamination.

Lamination extends like catenation in the case when one of the operands is a scalar. For example :

$M, [1.1]0$

```
1  2  3  4
0  0  0  0

3  9  0  7
0  0  0  0

4  8  5  5
0  0  0  0
```

Lamination is used each time that two arrays have to be joined to form an array of higher rank, for example in order to print them facing each other.

For example, here is a vector V. It is required that V and $V>200$ be printed

V

```
183 217 113 266 819 161 161 400
```

$V>200$

```
0 1 0 1 1 0 0 1
```

The above presentation is hardly readable ; this is better :

$V, [0.5]V>200$

```
183  271  113  266  819  161  161  400
  0    1    0    1    1    0    0    1
```

A use of lamination will be found in paragraph 6-12 (application).

6-5   RAVEL

The expression ,*A* restores the vector of the elements of *A*, no matter what its
dimensions.

            M
        1 2 3 4
        3 9 0 7
        4 8 5 5

            ,*M*
        1 2 3 4 3 9 0 7 4 8 5 5

            ρ*SCALAR* ← 81   The dimension of a scalar is the empty vector.

            ρ,*SCALAR*   The ravel has transformed the scalar into a
                                 vector of a single element.

This property is often useful in the writing of defined functions, so much so
that our function *AVERAGE* is false.

            AVERAGE 8 9
        8.5   all is normal

            AVERAGE 7
                                  no answer

In effect, in the calculation (+/7)÷ρ7 , ρ7 is an empty vector, which is
absorbant (see paragraph 3-10) and the expression restores an empty vector.
Hence, we advise you to correct this function by transforming the argument
to a vector before any other processing.

            ∇ *RESULT* ← *AVERAGE VALUES*
        [1]   *RESULT* ← (+/*VALUES*) ÷ ρ*VALUES* ← ,*VALUES*
            ∇

            AVERAGE 7
        7

            AVERAGE M   *M* being the matrix seen above, the average of
        4.25   its terms is obtained.

There are numerous similar uses, in particular it is often preferable to ravel
inputs of data in a function in order to avoid the phenomenum above.
Hence, it would be better to write *U*←,☐ or *U*←,⍞ than *U*←☐ or *U*←⍞

EXERCISES

[1] The following matrix P is given :   1 9 3 6 5
                                          4 8 2 3 0
                                          0 7 2 6 1

How can the following matrices be formed by means of the single function
↑;

   3 6 5   4 8 2 3   9 3 6
   2 3 0   0 7 2 6   8 2 3
                                 7 2 6

[2] Same question but using only ↓.

[3] The following matrix Q is given :   1 2 3
                                          4 5 6

Give two methods of forming this matrix : 0 0 0 0
                                           1 2 3 0
                                           4 5 6 0

[4] It is often necessary to form matrices of characters, for example, lists
of names, without knowing in advance what the longest name will be.
Write a function which enables, by means of a loop, such a matrix to be
formed line by line.

Example :

            R ← GETWORDS
       ENTER WORDS :
       SMITH
       FISHER
       PRICE
       ROLLS

           R   a carriage return serves to close the list.
       SMITH
       FISHER
       PRICE
       ROLLS

[5] Write a function which enables a header above a matrix of characters to
be written. It will have to be centered, and separated from the matrix
by a dotted line.

         'NAMES' HEADER 2 9 ρ 'FORD   CHEVROLET'
       NAMES

       FORD
       CHEVROLET

[6] The matrix *NAMES* is given for the names of the participants in a game, and the vector *SCORE* for the points obtained, classed in increasing order :

BRUNIER	123
FOULET	124
PIGEON	131
LOMBARD	139
LION	139
SARGEL	142
PONTIER	144
PLOUQUE	150

Write a function which will modify this matrix and this vector, in such a way that a new participant can be inserted in the position where his performance places him.

For example *'CREMEL' OBTAINS* 143 will insert this candidate and his score between *SARGEL* and *PONTIER*.

[7] *LOCO* is the following matrix : ▢ ∩ ⌈
<▢▢▢▢▢
/oo oo

WAGON equals :   +|_____|
oo   oo

Form a train comprising the locomotive and two goods wagons. Be careful of dimensions, *LOCO* and *WAGON* are of dimensions 3 6 and 2 9 respectively.

▢ ∩ ⌈
<▢▢▢▢▢+|_____|+|_____|
/oo oo   oo   oo   oo   oo

[8] An array is required which gives the speed of a car (in km.p.h) in relation to the time taken to cover one kilometer. For example :

time in seconds	speed in km.p.h
60	60
65	55.38
70	51.43
75	48
80	45

Write the expression giving this array for times of 20 to 100 seconds, every 5 seconds.

[9] Write a function which prints a vector of characters underlining all the numbers with an arrow :

SHOW '1971 JANUARY 16TH'

1971 *JANUARY* 16*TH*
↑↑↑↑   ↑↑

[10] CONTRACTION OF HOLLOW MATRICES

A matrix is said to be hollow when it consists mainly of zeros, as
is the case with the matrix *GRUYERE* as follows :

        0 0 8 0 0 3
        0 7 0 0 0 0
        6 0 2 0 5 0
        0 0 0 0 4 0

Such a matrix occupies a lot of wasted space in the storage. If
it is ravelled, only the value of the non-zero elements of the vector
and their positions can be retained :

    0 0 8 0 0 3 0 7 0 0 0 0 6 0 2 0 5 0 0 0 0 4 0

values   : 8   3   7   6   2   5   4
positions : 3   6   8 13 15 17 23

If the indication of the dimensions of the original matrix (4 6)
is used as a header, all the significant elements are present in a
compact form :

        4   8   3   7   6   2   5   4
        6   3   6   8 13 15 17 23
        ↑
         dimensions

Write a function which contracts a hollow matrix in this method.

[11] Write a function which re-establishes a hollow matrix on the basis of
its contracted form, as defined above.

COMPACT	RESET COMPACT
3 6 3 5	6 0 0 0
4 1 7 12	0 0 3 0
	0 0 0 5

[12] Two arrays A and B of the same rank are catenated.
Write the expression giving the value of $\rho(A, [I]B)$

6-6   LOGICAL COMPRESSION

Logical compression may be classed among methods of selection in an array.
This function has been studied in detail in paragraphs 3-16 and 3-29; we
advise the reader to refer back if necessary.

To remind you, here is the compression working on a vector :

        1 0 0 1 1 0 / 'ANSWER' gives AWE
        0 1 0 1 1 / 8 3 9 1 5 gives 3 1 5

LOGICAL EXPANSION

The logical expansion of an array T by a boolean vector B according to its Ith dimension is written $B\backslash[I]T$; it is similar to compression.

The left hand argument is a boolean vector possesing as many 1's as the Ith dimension of T posseses elements, and 0's which indicate the positions where zeros must be inserted (or blanks for an array of characters) in the right hand argument.

For example :

      0 0 1 0 1 1 \ 3 1 5   gives 0 0 3 0 1 5

      1 1 1 0 1 \ '*CASE*'   gives *CAS E*

If T is the following array :   1 2 3 4
                               5 6 7 8

      0 1 0 1 0 \ [1] T gives 0 0 0 0
                              1 2 3 4
                              0 0 0 0
                              5 6 7 8
                              0 0 0 0

and 1 1 0 0 1 1 \ [2] T gives 1 2 0 0 3 4
                                    5 6 0 0 7 8

It is clearly seen that each zero of the left hand argument causes the insertion of zeros between the elements of the right hand argument.

CONVENTIONS

As with logical compression, the symbol \ used alone, without an axis, indicates expansion on the last dimension; the symbol ⊢ obtained by superimposing \ on - indicates an expansion on the first dimension.

CONDITIONS OF APPLICATION

The expression $B\backslash[I]T$ is acceptable only if there are as many 1's in B as there are elements in the Ith dimension of T, since the 1's indicate the position of the elements of T in relation to the zeros which are inserted.

This condition is expressed by : $(+/B) \equiv (\rho T)[I]$

($\equiv$ designates mathematical identity)

However, as with compression, when the right hand argument is a scalar, it is extended to the dimensions of the left hand argument, and expansion can take place :

      1 0 1 1 0 \ 7 is equivalent to 1 0 1 1 0 \ 7 7 7 and equals 7 0 7 7 0

PARTICULAR CASE

Expansion of an empty vector gives 0 or a blank, according to whether this
empty vector was numeric or alphanumeric.
The left hand argument can contain only zeros, since there is no element in the
right hand operand.

$$0\backslash\iota0 \qquad \text{gives } 0$$
$$0\backslash'' \qquad \text{gives the blank character.}$$

This property can be used in order to write a different version of the function
NUMER seen in paragraph 6-1.

$$\nabla \ R \leftarrow NUMER \ ARG$$
[1] $R \leftarrow 0 = 0\backslash0/ \ ,ARG$
$$\nabla$$

You will notice that the advice given in paragraph 6-5 has been followed, and
that the argument has been ravelled, which enables this function to be applied
to any array.

EXERCISES

[13] Write a function which will replace every appearence of a given character
in a string of characters by blanks.
Example :   `'*' OUTOF 'BED*AND*BREAKFAST'`
    BED AND BREAKFAST

[14] Write a function which enables two vectors to be intercalated one in the
other in terms of the indications given by the global variable *MODEL*.
The 1's of *MODEL* represent the positions of the terms of the first vector,
the 2's of *MODEL* represent the positions of the terms of the second vector.

    `MODEL ← 1 2 2 1 1 1 2 1`
    `70 71 72 73 74 MIX 18 19 20`
    70 18 19 71 72 73 20 74

[15] A string of characters and a numeric vector indicating the position of the
ends of the words of this string are given. Write a function which divides
this string in the form of a matrix of characters.

    `6   9   15   19 SPLIT 'LITTLEREDRIDINGHOOD'`

    LITTLE
    RED
    RIDING
    HOOD

There is an interesting solution without a loop.

[16] Aided by the previous exercise, write a function which puts a string of
     characters in the form of a matrix by cutting it up at the positions
     marked by a symbol given in the left hand argument.

                `'/' CUT 'HOW/NOW/BROWN/COW'`

       HOW
       NOW
       BROWN
       COW

[17] A current problem consists of finding totals in an array. For example,
     the array below is given :

```
11    8    9    5   10    6   10   12    5
 8    8    9   10    9   10   11   14   13
12   16   11    9    9   10   14   13    5
```

A partial total of the first 3 columns is required, then a partial total
of the first 5 columns, and the overall total of the nine columns.

Write a function *ADDING* which has the vector of the columns of which
the totals are required (here 3 5 9) as a left hand operand, the name
of the array as a right hand operand, and which gives a larger array
in which the required totals will have been inserted as a result.
For example :

              `3 5 9 ADDING T`

```
11    8    9   28    5   10   43    6   10   12    5   76
 8    8    9   25   10    9   44   10   11   14   13   92
12   16   11   39    9    9   57   10   14   13    5   99
```
          ↑   ↑   ↑

      The partial totals have been inserted at the required
     places.

                                 DRAWING BY RUMWEISS

         It is important not to confuse
         reduction and compression

6-8   REVERSAL

The REVERSAL function is written ϕ or $\ominus$, which is obtained by superimposing
o ("orange" of the o key), and | or -.

In a monadic way, $\phi[I]A$ inverts the elements of A in relation to its Ith
dimension, as the following examples demonstrate.

                    ϕ 11 27 14   9   6
        6   9   14   27   11

                    ϕ 'MY FOOT'
    TOOF YM

                    MATRIX
        1   9   3   5
        2   6   7   4

                    $\phi[1]$ MATRIX
        2   6   7   4
        1   9   3   5

                    $\phi[2]$ MATRIX
        5   3   9   1
        4   7   6   2

Finally, we will work on the three dimension array T :   ABCD
                                                           EFGH

                                                           IJKL
                                                           MNOP

$\phi[1]T$ equals *IJKL* $\phi[2]T$ equals *EFGH* $\phi[3]T$ equals   *DCBA*
             MNOP   *ABCD*   *HGFE*

             ABCD   *MNOP*   *LKJI*
             EFGH   *IJKL*   *PONM*

CONVENTIONS

ϕA used alone, without axis, causes A to be reversed on its LAST dimension.

$\ominus A$ causes A to be reversed on its FIRST dimension.

For vectors, either symbol can be used.

APPLICATION

In paragraph 5-4, we discovered a means of drawing a bar chart, using a vector
of frequencies F, which equalled 4 3 2 4 3.
For this the vector 4 3 2 1 had to be formed.   This was readily attained by
the expression $\phi\iota\lceil/F$.

Thus it becomes possible to write a general function to draw such diagrams:

```
        ∇ R←HISTO F
 [1]    R←' □'[1+(φ\iota\lceil/F)∘.≤F]
        ∇
```

HISTO 1 2 1 0 3 5 7 6 6 3 4 2 1 2 0 1

```
        □
        □□□
        □□□□
        □□□□ □
        □□□□□□
 □      □□□□□□□□ □
 □□□ □□□□□□□□□ □
```

The significance of such a function is immediately apparent.

5-9   MONADIC TRANSPOSITION

In addition to the functions ϕ and $\ominus$, the function ψ causes the transposition
of an array, that is to say permutation of all its dimensions.

Given an array T of n dimensions, this is expressed by :

$$(\psi T)[i;j; \ldots ;m;n] \equiv T[n;m; \ldots ;j;i]$$

It is deduced from this that $\rho\psi T$ is equal to $\phi\rho T$.

The symbol ψ is obtained by superimposing the symbols \ and O ("orange").

The function TRANSPOSITION has no effect on a vector.

        ψ 1 2 3 4
    1   2   3   4

If *MATRIX* equals   1 9 3 5   then ⊗*MATRIX* will equal 1 2
                     2 6 7 4   9 6
                                                                 3 7
                                                                 5 4

If *T* is the array *ABCD*
                    EFGH

                    IJKL
                    MNOP   then ⊗*T* will equal   *A I*
                                                               E M

                                                               B J
                                                               F N

                                                               C K
                                                               G O

                                                               D L
                                                               H P

It is established that the rule announced previously has been verified:

   T[1;2;4] is equal to (⊗*T*)[4;2;1]   (this is the character *H*)
   T[2;1;3] is equal to (⊗*T*)[3;1;2]   (this is the character *K*)

It is also verified that ρ*T* (or 2 2 4) is equal to φρ⊗*T*

NOTES

1) The symbols φ ⊖ ⊗ exist, but there is no ∅ symbol.

2) The function ⊗ does not make use of an axis, since, by definition, it acts
   on all the dimensions of its operand.

6-10   THE ROTATION FUNCTION

The symbol φ used in a monadic way causes the complete reversal of all the
elements of its argument; used in a dyadic way, it brings about the circular
permutations of the elements of its right hand argument.

We will study, as a first step, its action on vectors.

The significance of $R \phi V$ can be explained by imagining that the elements of V are placed on a loop, and that they are displaced by R positions in one direction or another, according to whether R is positive or negative.

We will work, for example, on the following vector V : 8 2 5 3 9 4 6

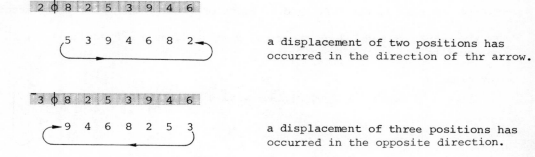

a displacement of two positions has occurred in the direction of thr arrow.

a displacement of three positions has occurred in the opposite direction.

Furthermore it can be said that if R is positive, the first R elements of V pass to the end, whereas if R is negative, it is the last R elements which pass to the head of V.

              ‾2 ϕ 'ROTATE'
        TEROTA

If the left hand argument is zero, no rotation takes place.

-11   ROTATIONS IN ARRAYS

In the case of an array, an index must specify to which dimension the rotation applies.

The expression $R\phi[I]T$, where T is an array of n dimensions, assumes that R is an array of rank $n-1$ the dimensions of which are those of T with their Ith element removed.

To each element of T is thus applied a displacement along the Ith dimension. The value of this displacement, and its direction, are given by the R element having the same coordinates, minus their Ith term.

To illustrate these rules, we will work first of all on an array of two dimensions, which we will call TAB.

```
     TAB
11  18  14  13   1
26  23   2  25  27
39   0  33  32  35
 4  42  47   5  44
```

TAB is of rank 2, the left hand argument of the rotation must be a vector.

If a rotation is made along the first dimension, as ρ *TAB* equals 4 5, ρR must be equal to 5.

For example :

         1 0 ‾1 3 1 ⌽[2]*TAB*   will give :
```
26  18  47   5  27
39  23  14  13  35
 4   0   2  25  44
11  42  33  32   1
```

The applied rotations vector is repeated in italics.   *1   0 ‾1   3   1*

In the same way, if a rotation is made along the second dimension, ρ*TAB* being equal to 4 5, the rotation vector will be of dimension 4.

For example :

        2 ‾1 0 ‾3 ⌽[2]*TAB*   will give :
```
14  13   1  11  18    2
27  26  23   2  25    1
39   0  33  32  35    0
47   5  44   4  42    3
```

The applied rotations value is repeated on the right in italics.

The rule on the previous page will be even more apparent on an array of rank 3 for which the left hand operand will therefore be of rank 2.
We will work on the array *THREE*, of which the value is :

```
7  6  1  5
0  0  1  3
5  2  8  4


3  9  6  7
2  5  4  1
9  0  2  8
```

If the rotations matrix is called *ROT*, and a rotation is required on the third dimension,

                 ρ*THREE* being equal to : 2 3 4

             then ρ*ROT* must be equal to : 2 3

For example, *ROT* could be the matrix   1 0 ‾2
                                    0 2 ‾1

Recalling the values of the rotations in italics, the transformations can be represented as follows :

```
7  6  1  5    1                        6  1  5  7
0  0  1  3    0                        0  0  1  3
5  2  8  4    2                        8  4  5  2
                  ─ ROT φ[3] THREE ►
3  9  6  7    0                        3  9  6  7
2  5  4  1   ‾2                        4  1  2  5
9  0  2  8   ‾1                        8  9  0  2
```

As was said, the rotation value applied on line *THREE*[2;3;] is given by *ROT* [2;3], and it can be said that *THREE*[2;3;] has become equal to :

ROT[2;3]φ*THREE*[2;3;].

CONVENTION

As with reversal, omission of the index (*R*φ*T*) indicates that the rotation is applied to the last dimension of *T*, whereas *R*⊖*T* would indicate a rotation along the first dimension.

PARTICULAR CASE

If the left hand argument is a scalar, a uniform rotation is applied to the entire *I*th dimension of the array.

```
        MAT←[]←3 5ρ⍳15
  1    2    3    4    5
  6    7    8    9   10
 11   12   13   14   15

        ‾1 ⊖ MAT
 11   12   13   14   15
  1    2    3    4    5
  6    7    8    9   10

        2 φ[2] MAT
  3    4    5    1    2
  8    9   10    6    7
 13   14   15   11   12
```

6-12   EXAMPLE OF APPLICATION

A series of points situated in one plane is referenced by the vectors of their
coordinates.

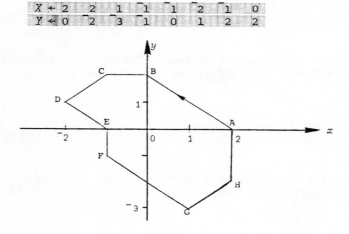

$$X \leftarrow 2 \quad 2 \quad 1 \quad {}^{-}1 \quad {}^{-}1 \quad {}^{-}2 \quad {}^{-}1 \quad 0$$
$$Y \leftarrow 0 \quad 2 \quad 3 \quad {}^{-}1 \quad 0 \quad 1 \quad 2 \quad 2$$

The algebraic surface of the outline which joins these points is given by :

$$0.5 \times (X-1\phi X) +.\times (Y+1\phi Y)$$
$${}^{-}11.5$$

A positive value would be obtained by going round the outline in the opposite
direction.

The perimeter of this outline is given by :

$$((M-1\theta M \leftarrow X [1.5]Y) +.\ast 2) +.\ast 0.5$$
$$13.9$$

Notice the lamination joining the X and Y axes in the form of a matrix.

The first formula results from the calculation of the algebraic sum of the
surfaces of the trapezia formed by the sides of the outline and the Y axis;
the second formula is only the strict application of Pythagores' theory.

-13   DYADIC TRANSPOSITION

Dyadic transposition is certainly, along with the encode and decode functions
and the domino function, one of the most complex functions of APL. Its study
will be divided into two parts : the relatively simple part will be studied
here, the other more complex part being removed to the supplement, in paragraph
6-17.

RE-ARRANGEMENT OF AN ARRAY

Repeated here is the array *TYRES*, which is one of the first we worked on :

```
3200      0  4100  8340     0
 420    840   360     0  7420
   0      0     0     0  1280


3120      0  4600  8520     0
 400    910   380     0  7660
   0      0     0     0  1310


3000      0  4330  9480     0
 440    970   390     0  8020
   0    160     0     0  1560


2290      0  4460  9870     0
 580   1040   380     0  8200
   0    280     0     0  1430
```

This array represents over 4 years, for 3 types of tyres, the production of
5 factories.
It could be interesting to present these values in a different way, by
arranging them according to other priorities. We will imagine, for example,
that a presentation is prefered where for the 3 types of tyre, and for the 5
factories, the production of the last 4 years, would appear.

The array *TYRES* has the following dimensions :

The desired result will have the dimensions :

In other words :

    - the present first dimension will become the 3 rd

    - the present second dimension will become the 1 st

    - the present third dimension will become the 2 nd

The required result will be obtained by writing :   3 1 2 ◊ *TYRES*

         3 1 2 ◊ *TYRES*

3200	3120	3000	2290
0	0	0	0
4100	4600	4330	4460
8340	8520	9480	9870
0	0	0	0

    car tyres

420	400	440	580
840	910	970	1040
360	380	390	380
0	0	0	0
7420	7660	8020	8200

    lorry tyres

0	0	0	0
0	0	160	280
0	0	0	0
0	0	0	0
1280	1310	1560	1430

    aeroplane tyres

    ▲   ▲   ▲   ▲

   1974 1975 1976 1977

It is seen that the result conforms to our expectations.

By using the dyadic transposition $A◊B$ with a left hand argument equal to ιρρλ taken in the disorder, an arrangement of the right hand argument is obtained

---

The left hand argument of $A◊B$ indicates which position each one of the dimensions of the initial array will occupy in the result.

The end of the dyadic transposition will be found in paragraph 6-17.

EXERCISES

[18] The following instruction is met in a function: [8]   →$A\phi$ 3 9 0
What does this instruction bring about ?

[19] The following array of characters M is given : *OGN*
                                                                                                        GV
    SUV
     ZA
    AEE

what would the expression :   ⍉ ¯1 0 1 0 ¯1 ϕ[2] ¯1 0 2 ⊖ M give ?
check this on the computer.

[20] In exercise 17 of this chapter it was proposed that a function *ADDING* be
written, which adds up the columns of an array.
Write a function which executes the same work on the lines, in a very
simple way.

[21] The array *TYRES* is required to be arranged by years, factories, and types
of tyres. What must be written ?

[22] The elements which have equal indices are called the main diagonal of a
matrix. For example, in the array T below, the main diagonal consists of
the numbers 11   3   6

   11   2   5
    1   3   0
    8   4   6

write a function which directly gives the sum of the terms of the main
diagonal of a matrix (called the *TRACE* of the matrix).

     TRACE T
  20

[23] In exercise 3 of chapter 5 the creation of the following matrix was proposed :

   1 1 1 1 1 1 1 1 1 1
   2 2 2 2 2 2 2 2 2 2
   3 3 3 3 3 3 3 3 3 3
   4 4 4 4 4 4 4 4 4 4

Find a simpler solution.

[24] <u>TOTALIZING WITH RUPTURES</u>

Catalogue articles are referenced by a code number. The sales of the day
are represented by a vector *REF* containing the codes of the articles
sold, and a vector *QTY* containing the quantities sold. The identical
references have been regrouped.

REF ←	160	160	160	509	509	509	509	147	662	662	780	781	781
QTY ←	2	5	4	6	1	1	5	14	3	6	1	1	2

It is required to know how many articles of each sort have been sold
(here, 11 13 14 9 13 must be found). This problem, is very common in
data processing.
Write the function which will enable this work to be accomplished.

> *REF SUM QTY*
11 13 14 9 1 3

Note: The vectors given can be very large, so any solution calling upon
an outer product is out of the question.

[25] A phrase which remains identical to itself when the order of its letters
is reversed is called palindrome (ROTOR being an example). In French,
there are usually only pseudo-palindromes, which remain identical to
themselves if the blanks are not taken into account :

Hence,   ELU PAR CETTE CRAPULE
becomes : ELUPARC ETTEC RAP ULE

Write a function which indicates by a binary result (0 or 1) if a phrase
is a pseudo-palindrome or not.

> *PALINDROME 'SURELY NOT'*
0

> *PALINDROME 'ET LA MARINE VA VENIR A MALTE'*
1

[26] Write a function which allows only one blank to be left between the words
of a phrase. The blanks at the head or tail will be treated in the same
way.

> *CUTDOWN 'IF   I WERE   A   RICH   MAN'*
IF I WERE A RICH MAN

[27] Write a function which locates the appearances of a word in a phrase,
or of one numeric vector in another. This function must restore the
index of the first element of the word in the phrase.

> *'OU' INTO 'YOU SHOULD DO IT YOURSELF'*
2 7 19

[28] Write a function enabling a matrix of characters to be divided in height, so as to print the n sections thus obtained side by side. n will be given as a left hand argument.
Here, on this very limited example, is how this function should operate:

M is the matrix below

```
| BOLT
| SCREW
| BOX SPANNER
| BRACE
| CLIP
| PISTON
| JOINT
| TAP
| CASING
| HANDLE
```

4 *DIVIDE* M should cause the following matrix to be printed :

```
| BOLT         | BRACE  | JOINT  | HANDLE
| SCREW        | CLIP   | TAP
| BOX SPANNER  | PISTON | CASING
```

[29] The array *CHARS*, of dimensions 27 7 5, comprises 27 matrices of 7X5 characters representing the enlargement of the 27 letters of the alphabet and the blank.

For example :

```
      o
     o o
    o   o
    o   o
    ooooo
    o   o
    o   o
```

Write a function which uses the array *CHARS* to "enlarge" a phrase or a header. 3 blank spaces should separate the letters.

Example :

ENLARGE 'THE HOLE'

```
ooooo  o   o   ooooo     o   o   ooo    o      ooooo
  o    o   o   o         o   o  o   o   o      o
  o    o   o   o         o   o  o   o   o      o
  o    ooooo   ooo       ooooo  o   o   o      ooo
  o    o   o   o         o   o  o   o   o      o
  o    o   o   o         o   o  o   o   o      o
  o    o   o   ooooo     o   o   ooo   ooooo   ooooo
```

[30] A comparative array gives the prices of 10 commodities (numbered from 1 to 10) in six shops (numbered from 1 to 6) :

> PRICES
>
> | 61 | 60 | 76 | 59 | 94 | 78 |
> |----|----|----|----|----|----|
> | 92 | 42 | 89 | 57 | 66 | 73 |
> | 24 | 25 | 31 | 26 | 27 | 40 |
> | 40 | 41 | 50 | 28 | 29 | 26 |
> | 61 | 62 | 71 | 70 | 67 | 65 |
> | 33 | 32 | 30 | 45 | 41 | 39 |
> | 84 | 91 | 92 | 67 | 72 | 81 |
> | 17 | 27 | 20 | 23 | 15 | 16 |
> | 56 | 58 | 53 | 59 | 64 | 57 |
> | 63 | 42 | 44 | 49 | 47 | 72 |

For each commodity, the number of the shop which sells it the cheapest, and the corresponding price is required to be displayed.

> COMPARE PRICES
>
> | 1 | 2 | 3 | 4 | 5 | 6 | 7 | 8 | 9 | 10 | ← commodity |
> |----|----|----|----|----|----|----|----|----|----|----|
> | 4 | 2 | 1 | 6 | 1 | 3 | 4 | 5 | 3 | 2 | ← shop |
> | 59 | 42 | 24 | 26 | 61 | 30 | 67 | 15 | 53 | 42 | ← price |

We will assume that no two shops ever sell the same commodity at the same price.
Write a function COMPARE. It should accept any number of shops and commodities.

[31] BROKEN KEYBOARD

The ε key of your keyboard no longer works. In order to find out whether the elements of a vector G appear in a vector D, one can proceed as follows :

We will imagine that G is the vector : 9   2   6
        and that D is the vector : 8   2   1   9   2

The two following matrices are formed :

```
8  2  1  9  2            9  9  9  9  9
8  2  1  9  2    and     2  2  2  2  2
8  2  1  9  2            6  6  6  6  6
```

Their comparison gives : 0 0 0 1 0
                          0 1 0 0 1
                          0 0 0 0 0

The lines where the 1's appear indicate the G elements which belong to D.

Write a function which achieves all of these operations. For example :

> G MEMBEROF D

1 1 0

> 'PRICE' MEMBEROF 'COMPARE'

1 1 0 1 1

[32] The function of the previous exercise is designed for vectors. Modify it, in such a way that it accepts arguments of any dimensions, as is the case for the function ε.

$$(2\ 3\rho\iota6)\ MEMBEROF\ 6\ 2\ 7\ 0\ 4\ 3\ 6$$

```
0 1 1
1 0 1
```

[33] At the club MEDITEBASANE, numerous pursuits are available to the residents : sailing, riding, volly-ball, water skiing, etc... In order to best distribute the schedule for these diverse activities, it is required to know how many people intend to practice which activity AND which other; for example water skiing and pottery, sailing and tennis, etc...

All the residents were asked to fill in a form for their intentions, where they could mark with a cross the activities interesting them. This list has been converted into a boolean matrix as follows :

activities proposed

```
        0 0 0 1 0 0 0 0 1 0
        1 0 0 0 0 1 0 0 0 1
        0 1 1 0 1 1 0 0 1 0
        0 0 0 0 0 0 0 1 0 0
        1 0 1 0 0 0 0 0 0 0
        0 0 0 0 1 0 1 0 0 1
        0 1 0 0 1 0 0 0 0 0
        0 0 0 0 0 0 0 0 1 1
        0 0 0 0 0 0 0 1 0 1
        0 0 1 0 1 0 1 0 0 1
        0 1 1 0 0 0 1 0 1 1
        1 0 0 0 0 1 0 0 0 0
        0 0 0 0 0 1 0 0 1 0
        1 0 1 0 0 0 0 0 0 0
        0 1 0 0 1 0 0 0 1 0
```
choice of the residents

This is limited to 10 activities and 15 people here. This array is called *M*. Write the expression which gives the array of 10 lines and 10 columns containing the numbers of people having simultaneously chosen two activities:

```
4 0 2 0 0 2 0 0 0 1
0 4 2 0 3 1 1 0 3 1
2 2 5 0 2 1 2 0 2 2
0 0 0 1 1 1 0 0 2 0
0 3 2 1 4 0 1 0 1 1
2 1 1 1 0 5 0 0 1 2
0 1 2 0 1 0 2 0 1 2
0 0 0 0 0 0 0 2 0 1
0 3 2 2 1 1 1 0 6 2
1 1 2 0 1 2 2 1 2 6
```

For example, it is established from this result that 3 people have simultaneously chosen activities 5 and 2. The terms of the diagonal indicate how many people have chosen each activity : 4 for number 1, 5 for number 3, etc...

6-14   CATENATION AND LAMINATION

Only numerics can be catenated between themselves, or characters between
themselves; and this restriction applies to lamination.
However, there is one exception to this rule in the case where one of the operan
is an empty vector :

       `' ' , 2 5 7`   is correct and gives the result 2 5 7
       `(ι0) , 'MAD'`   is correct and gives the result *MAD*

RESULT OF A LAMINATION

We have indicated in paragraph 6-4, what forms the result of the lamination
of two arrays take. Here are these observations formalized; we will leave
it to the reader to adapt these rules for scalars.

In order to carry out the lamination $R \leftarrow A,[I]B$

1) It is essential that $(\rho A) \equiv (\rho B)$ (except for scalars)

2) I must be a non-whole number value, between 0 and $1+\rho\rho A$ (at origin
   0, I must be between $^-1$ and $\rho\rho A$)

3) The dimension of the result R is given by the expression :

$$(\rho R) \equiv ((\lfloor I) \uparrow \rho A) , 2 , ((\lfloor I) \downarrow \rho A)$$

The symbol $\equiv$ designates mathematical identity.

From examination of the second point, it is clearly evident that the axis
which is assigned to the lamination symbol can be negative, at origin 0.
This is the only case where an axis can be negative.

Example :

       `☐IO ← 0`

       `8 2 3 ,[¯0.3] 6 6 1`
  8 2 3
  6 6 1

-15

ROTATION AND REVERSAL

The use of the symbol ⊖ is usually reserved for ratations and reversals on the first dimension of an array. However, it is possible to add an axis to this function.

In this way : A ⊖$[n]$ X is equivalent to: A ⌽$[n]$ X

⊖$[n]$ X is equivalent to: ⌽$[n]$ X

-16

MONADIC TRANSPOSITION

In the first versions of APL, the transposition of an array of rank greater than 2 only operated on the last two dimensions.

For example :

	T		
1	2	3	4
5	6	7	8
9	10	11	12
13	14	15	16
17	18	19	20
21	22	23	24

	⍉T	
1	5	9
2	6	10
3	7	11
4	8	12
13	17	21
14	18	22
15	19	23
16	20	24

In present versions, all the dimensions of the array are affected by the transposition, in such a way that the mathematical identity :

$$(A+.\times B) \equiv ⍉ (⍉B)+.\times(⍉A)$$

remains true for arrays of rank greater than 2.

One should beware of this change of definition, in re-writing algorithms which may have been written on old systems.

6-17   DYADIC TRANSPOSITION

We have already used the dyadic transposition in order to carry out a
different arrangemant of the elements of an array. For such a use, the
left hand argument of $A \between B$ must be such that :

$A \in \iota\rho\rho B$ ⎫   The elements of A are equal to those of $\iota\rho\rho B$ taken
$(\iota\rho\rho B) \in A$ ⎬   in a different order.

Dyadic transposition can also be used to accomplish selections in an array.
The elements selected then belong to a diagonal section of the array : two
or more of their indices are equal.

For example, we will consider the following array G :

               G
     1   2   3   4
     5   6   7   8
     9   10   11   12

    13   14   15   16
    17   18   19   20
    21   22   23   24

The expression 1 1 2 $\between G$ would give the following matrix : 1   2   3   4
                                                                      17   18   19   20

It can be stated that the elements of this result are respectively :

$G[1;1;1]$ $G[1;1;2]$ $G[1;1;3]$ $G[1;1;4]$ $G[2;2;1]$ $G[2;2;2]$ $G[2;2;3]$ $G[2;2;4]$

All those elements have the common property that their first two indices
are equal, which is the reflection of the expression 1 1 2 $\between G$ in
which the first two elements of the left hand argument are equal.

The use of this form of transposition is rather delicate; here are some rules
to study :

In order to carry out the transposition $R \leftarrow A \between B$ the following
must apply :

1) $(\rho A) \equiv (\rho\rho B)$ as before,

2) $A \in \iota\rho\rho B$ the elements of A are whole numbers less than or
                      equal to the rank of B.

3) $(\iota\lceil/A) \in A$ the elements of A must be a series of consecutive
                      whole numbers starting with 1.

Hence, for the array G, which is of rank 3, the only acceptable left hand arguments will be :

1 1 1 ; 1 1 2 ; 1 2 1 ; 2 1 1 ; 1 2 2 ; 2 1 2 ; 2 2 1

The arguments 2 2 2, or 1 3 1, would bring about a domain error.

If these conditions are observed, transposition will take place in two stages :

1) The elements of the array of which the indices designated by the left hand argument are equal are selected.

A left hand argument equal to 1 1 2 or 2 2 1 will bring about extraction of the elements of which the first and the second indices are equal.

A left hand argument equal to 1 2 1 or 2 1 2 will result in extraction of the elements, the first and the third indices of which are equal.

1 2 2 ⍉ G and 2 1 1 ⍉ G will result in the extraction of the values :

$$\begin{array}{ccc} 1 & 6 & 11 \\ 13 & 18 & 23 \end{array}$$ of which the 2nd and 3rd indices are equal.

2) A re-distribution of these values is therefore accomplished, by using as a left hand argument the sequence of values which, in the initial argument, are different from one another, when they are taken from left to right.

The array below summarizes this transformation :

Value of A in $A \, ⍉ \, B$	Values used for re-distribution of the extracted values of B.
1 1 1	1
1 1 2	1 2
1 2 1	1 2 *
2 1 1	2 1
1 2 2	1 2
2 1 2	2 1 *
2 2 1	2 1

In the lines marked *, it is the right hand value which vanished to the benifit of that on the left.

In the case of 1 2 2 ◊ *G* it is the vector 1 2 which serves to re-distribute
the extracted values. Hence they are not modified, and the result obtained
is :

```
 1   6  11
13  18  23
```

In the case of 2 1 1 ◊ *G* it is the vector 2 1 which serves to re-distribute
the extracted values. They are thus transposed :

```
 1  13
 6  18
11  23
```

PANORAMA

In order to illustrate all these transformations, we have carried out all the
dyadic transpositions, other than the simple re-distributions, that are possible
with the array *G*. Here they are :

```
        G            1   2   3   4
                     5   6   7   8
                     9  10  11  12

                    13  14  15  16
                    17  18  19  20
                    21  22  23  23
```

```
    1 1 1 ◊ G        1  18
```

```
    1 1 2 ◊ G        1   2   3   4
                    17  18  19  20
```

```
    2 2 1 ◊ G        1  17
                     2  18
                     3  19
                     4  20
```

```
    1 2 1 ⍉ G          1    5    9
                      14   18   22


    2 1 2 ⍉ G          1   14
                       5   18
                       9   22


    2 1 1 ⍉ G          1   13
                       6   18
                      11   23


    1 2 2 ⍉ G          1    6   11
                      13   18   23
```

In the case of a two dimensional array the dyadic transposition is a simple
way of extracting the main diagonal, as demonstrated below :

```
        ⎕ ← SQUARE ← 5 5 ⍴ 7 0 0 2 3 1 1 0 0 6 0 0 8 0 0 9 1 0
7 0 0 2 3
1 1 0 0 6
0 0 8 0 0
9 1 0 7 0
0 2 3 1 1

        1 1 ⍉ SQUARE
7 1 8 7 1
```

CHAPTER 7

INDEX-OF, GRADE UP, GRADE DOWN, ENCODE, DECODE

7-1 THE INDEX-OF FUNCTION

The INDEX-OF function $V \iota D$ is a mixed function which accepts a vector V as
a left hand operand, and any data D as a right hand operand.
The result, which has the dimensions of D, indicates the position of the
first elements of D in V.
If certain elements do not appear in V, the answer given is $1+\rho V$.

```
      VECTOR ← 3  19  5  1  8  5  6  4
      VECTOR ι 1  5  2
   4   3   9
```

This answer indicates that 1 is the 4th element of $VECTOR$; that the first
5 appears in the 3rd position, and that 2 does not appear (9 is equal to
$1+\rho VECTOR$).
Notice that only the first appearance of 5 is mentioned.

```
         CITRUS
   11   3   2  12   6
    5   2   9   8   8

         VECTOR ι CITRUS
    9   1   9   9   7
    3   9   9   5   5

      'ABCDEFGHIJKLMNOPQRSTUVWXYZ' ι 'BUTTER'
    2  21  20  20   5  18
```

The INDEX-OF function accepts different types of operands, as is shown by these
two examples :

```
         'ABC' ι 9
   4

         1  2  4  6 ι '1246'
    5   5   5   5
```

This last answer shows that none of the 4 terms of '1246' appears in the left
hand vector, which is numeric.

The use of the INDEX-OF function should always be followed by a test to compare
the value of the result obtained with the dimension of the left hand argument.
This precaution can be dispensed with if the nature of the problem processed,
or the origin of the data is such that all the terms of the right hand argument
belong to the left hand argument.

7-2   THE GRADE UP, GRADE DOWN FUNCTIONS

The GRADE UP function is a mixed monadic function. It is written ΔV and
accepts only vectors as operands.
ΔV restores the vector of the indices which enable the elements of V classed
in increasing order to be obtained as a result.

$$\Delta \quad 3 \quad \bar{5} \quad 1 \quad 0 \quad 9$$
$$2 \quad 4 \quad 3 \quad 1 \quad 5$$

In other words, the smallest element is the 2nd
                              then comes the 4th
                              then comes the 3rd
                              then comes the 1st
                    Finally, the largest is the 5th

The GRADE DOWN function, written Ψ, gives the indices of the elements sorted
in decreasing order.
The symbols Δ and Ψ are obtained by superimposing $\triangle$ or ∇ with $|$.

If several elements of the operands are equal, they are classed from LEFT to
RIGHT.

$$V \leftarrow 8 \quad 3 \quad 5 \quad 2 \quad 5 \quad 7 \quad 0 \quad 2 \quad 2$$
$$\Psi V$$
$$1 \quad 6 \quad 3 \quad 5 \quad 2 \quad 4 \quad 8 \quad 9 \quad 7$$

We will check that the classifications stated are infact obtained by indexing:

$$V[\Delta V]$$
$$0 \quad 2 \quad 2 \quad 2 \quad 3 \quad 5 \quad 5 \quad 7 \quad 8$$

$$V[\Psi V]$$
$$8 \quad 7 \quad 5 \quad 5 \quad 3 \quad 2 \quad 2 \quad 2 \quad 0$$

It should be noted that ΨV is not equal to $\phi \Delta V$. This would be the case only
if all the elements of V were different from one another.

$$(\Delta V),[0.5]\phi \Psi V$$
$$7 \quad 4 \quad 8 \quad 9 \quad 2 \quad 3 \quad 5 \quad 6 \quad 1$$
$$7 \quad 9 \quad 8 \quad 4 \quad 2 \quad 5 \quad 3 \quad 6 \quad 1$$

7-3   APPLICATIONS

The advantage of using a set of indices rather than an already arranged vector
is shown in the following three examples.

FIRST EXAMPLE

The salaries and ages of ten people are given :

SALARIES ←	3110	4580	3320	4940	2651	3945	3512	2305	4607	6903
AGES ←	28	53	38	58	32	41	42	27	39	56

The expression *SALARIES*[⍋*AGES*] gives the respective salaries of the ten people arranged in order of increasing age :

   2305   3110   2651   3320   4607   3945   3512   4580   6903   4940

It appears as though generally the salaries increase with age, but that is not an absolute rule.

SECOND EXAMPLE

The expression ⍋⍋*V* (or ⍒⍒*V*) indicates which position the elements of *V* would occupy if they were classed in increasing (or decreasing) order.

Example :

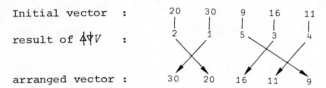
          2   1   5   3   4

A diagram will show th significance of this result better :

   Initial vector   :   20   30   9   16   11
                              | | | | |
   result of ⍒⍒*V*   :   2   1   5   3   4

   arranged vector :   30   20   16   11   9

This process is very useful each time an order number is required to be attributed to individuals in terms of diverse criteria. Thus, if the salaries and the ages given in the first example are used again, the RANK occupied by these people in the hierarchy of salaries and ages can be interesting.

We will then write: *SALARIES* , *AGES* , (⍋⍋*SALARIES*) , [1.5] (⍋⍋*AGES*)

The following matrix will thus be obtained, each line of which corresponds to an individual, and the columns of which respectively represent salary, age, and rank within salaries, and rank within ages :

       3110   28   3   2
       4580   53   7   8
       3320   38   4   4
       4940   58   9   10
       2651   32   2   3
       3945   41   6   6
       3512   42   5   7
       2305   27   1   1
       4607   39   8   5
       6903   56   10   9

This method has the defect of giving different ranks to people who have the same salary or the same age. For example :

      ⍋⍋ 31   45   27   31
        2   4   1   3

EXERCISES

[1] Write a function which converts the APL symbols into the letters of the alphabet positioned on the same key.
Example :

$$TRANSLATE \ '\sim\Delta\iota\lceil\ \iota\lceil\ \alpha\ \sim\rho\alpha\tau\lceil\square\alpha\sim\iota o\tau'$$
THIS IS A TRANSLATION

[2] Write a function which regroups the letters of a phrase in alphabetical order.

SORT 'SOME LIKE IT HOT'
EEHIIKLMOOSTT

[3] Find a way of eliminating repetitions of elements in a vector, as shown below :

CLEAN 9 7 14 21 7 3 21 11 7
    9 7 14 21 3 11

[4] Use the data of exercise 6 chapter 6. What are the names of the people who obtained the scores 131 144 123 ?

[5] Find a new solution to exercise 14 of chapter 6, which uses the function ⍋.

[6] a) Find a function $F1$ which gives the numeric vector corresponding to a string of numeric characters.
For example :

    $F1$ '245' should give the result 2 4 5

b) Find a function $F2$ which transforms a numeric vector into a scalar according to the following model :

    $F2$ 2 4 5 should give the result 245

c) Using $F1$ and $F2$, convert a string of characters into a number :

    2+VALUEOF '1205'
    1207

[7] Any two vectors are given. Write a function which combines them into a single vector, the terms of which are classed in decreasing order.

[8] A being a vector, what is the value of ⍋A[⍋A]

7-4   ENCODE AND DECODE

APL possesses two functions, ENCODE and DECODE, which enable the passage of
a decimal numeric value to its representation in any other numerical base,
and vice versa.

Before studying these functions, it is advisable to specify what the encoding
of a number in another numerical base is; some examples will be of help here.
Later we will study the applications of these functions (calculation of
polynomials, alphabetical classifications etc...).

EXAMPLE N° 1

8839 seconds represent 2 hours 27 minutes and 19 seconds. The same length
of time can be expressed in two different ways :

> - 8839 in our decimal system
> - 2 27 19 in a non-uniform system of numeration comprising 24 hours
>   of 60 minutes of 60 seconds each.

The passage from 8839 to 2 27 19 is called ENCODING.
The passage from 2 27 19 to 8839 is called DECODING.
The vector 24 60 60 is the NUMERICAL BASE which is used for these two
transformations.

NOTES

1) The encoding of a scalar (8839) gives a vector (2 27 19). In other words, a
   encoded value in a non decimal base could not be expressed in the form of
   a single number. Hence, in the same way as 22719 is not written, but
   2 27 19, a value expressed in the binary system could not be written 101011,
   but 1 0 1 0 1 1.

2) The elements of an encoded value can be greater than 9 (27 and 19 for
   example) if the base itself contains elements greater than 10.

3) If a day contained only 18 hours, or if it contained 36, 8839 seconds
   would still represent 2 hours 27 minutes and 19 seconds. That is to say
   that the result of encoding is independant of the first term of the
   base.

7-5   THE DECODE FUNCTION

Knowing the vector 2 27 19, and the vector *BASE* ←24 60 60 the decoded value
8839 is obtained by the following operation :

> (3600 X 2) + (60 X 27) + 19

or again :

> 3600 60 1 +.X 2 27 19

The vector 3600 60 1 represents the value in seconds of one hour, one minute
and one second respectively. This is said to be a vector of *WEIGHT*. It
is obtained starting from the base by the operation :

$$\Phi\ 1,x\backslash\ \Phi\ 1\downarrow BASE$$

This expression confirms the third note stated earlier : the first term
of the base is of no importance.
The DECODE function, written ⊥, directly accomplishes these calculations:

        BASE ⊥ 2 27 19
     8839

EXAMPLE N° 2

Eggs are packed in cartons of 6 lots each containing 6 boxes of 6 eggs. If
one has 2 complete lots, 5 boxes and 3 seperate eggs, this represents :

        (36X2) + (6X5) + 3   equalling 105 eggs.

It could also be written :

        36 6 1 +.X 2 5 3
     105

but it is simpler to use the DECODE function :

        6 6 6 ⊥ 2 5 3
     105

In this example, the numerical base is uniform : 6 6 6. Thus it can be more
simply written :

        6 ⊥ 2 5 3
     105

2 5 3 is the representation of 105 in base 6.

EXAMPLE N° 3

If it is simultaneously required to know what the values of 2 hours 27 minutes
19 seconds and 5 hours 3 minutes 48 seconds are, a matrix with these values
will be formed :

        ☐ ← M ← 3 2 ρ 2 5 27 3 19 48
     2   5
    27   3
    19   48

        BASE ⊥ M
     8839 18228

This example shoes how to decode several values expressed in the same numerical
base.

EXAMPLE N° 4

The same value can also be decoded in several different bases :

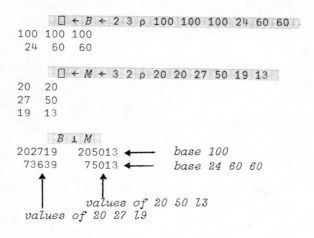

$$\square \leftarrow BB \leftarrow \lozenge 4\ 3 \rho\ 5\ 6\ 7$$

```
5 5 5 5
6 6 6 6
7 7 7 7
```

$$BB \perp 4\ 3\ 2\ 1$$

```
586   985   1534
```

EXAMPLE N° 5

By combining these last two examples, it should be possible to decode simultaneously several vectors, in several different bases.

$$\square \leftarrow B \leftarrow 2\ 3\ \rho\ 100\ 100\ 100\ 24\ 60\ 60$$

```
100 100 100
 24  60  60
```

$$\square \leftarrow M \leftarrow 3\ 2\ \rho\ 20\ 20\ 27\ 50\ 19\ 13$$

```
20   20
27   50
19   13
```

$$B \perp M$$

```
202719   205013  ⟵   base 100
 73639    75013  ⟵   base 24 60 60
   ↑        ↑
         values of 20 50 13
 values of 20 27 19
```

7-6   CONDITIONS OF USE OF THE DECODE FUNCTION

1) Since the DECODE function replaces an inner product, its arguments must obey the same rules of conformity :

        - the last dimension of the left hand argument is equal to the first dimension of the right hand argument,

or :   - one of the arguments is a vector verifying the preceeding condition,

or :   - at least one of the arguments is a scalar.

It can be verified, in example N°5, that the matrices B and M verify this condition.

2) The dimensions of the result of $B \perp M$ are equal to $(^{-}1 \downarrow \rho B), (1 \downarrow \rho M)$. Consequently, since the first dimension of the right hand argument disappears, it is easy to remember that it is along this dimension that the elements of a value to be decoded must be set out.

Hence, in example N°3, the values 2 27 19 and 5 3 48 have been represented in the form of columns in a matrix.

3) The formula which enables the vector of weights to be obtained, $\phi 1, X \backslash \phi 1 \downarrow B$, clearly indicates that the first term of the base is not used :

$$
\begin{array}{rrrl}
0 & 60 & 60 & \perp X \\
24 & 60 & 60 & \perp X \\
17 & 60 & 60 & \perp X
\end{array}
$$

would give the same result.

This unused element serves, on the one hand, to conserve the conformity of the dimensions between the two operands, and, on the other hand, to assure that the same base vector can be used in encoding (which will be studied later) and in decoding.

4) All bases, whole numbers or decimal, positive or negative, are accepted. Some examples of these will be found in the next paragraph.

7-7   APPLICATIONS OF DECODING

In the computer, each whole number occupies a certain space in the memory. The values 3,29748 and 12 occupy exactly the same space.

If small, but numerous values must be stored, it can be advantageous to group them in blocks of 3 or 4 values, or even more.

For example :

$$100 \quad 1000 \quad 10 \quad 100 \perp 27 \ 144 \ 8 \ 61$$
27144861

$$100 \quad 1000 \quad 10 \quad 100 \perp 15 \ 81 \ 7 \ 9$$
15081709

The single number 27144861 condences the values 27 144 8 61, but occupies a quater of the space.
This process must be used only if these values do not have to be consulted too often, because the gain in space would be obtained at the expense of a large consumption of calculation time. The compacting of data will be used only if the storage space for data is small.

Sometimes this method is used to compact dates. Hence, 9 12 77 can be compacted to 91277.
In reality, the following is preferred :

$$100 \perp \phi \ 9 \ 12 \ 77$$
771209

This representation in fact enables dates to be sorted in increasing order with the function GRADE UP, which the notation 91277 would not allow.

CALCULATION OF POLYNOMIALS

In example N°2, the expression 6 ⊥ 2 5 3 accomplishes the following calculatio

$$(2 \times 6^2) + (5 \times 6) + 3$$

This is nothing other than the calculation : $2x^2 + 5x + 3$ when $x=6$.
The DECODE function thus enables any polynomial represented by the coefficient
of a variable to be calculated, arranged in order of decreasing powers.

If it is required to calculate $3x^4 + 2x^2 - 7x + 2$ when $x=1.2$, the following
would be written :

        1.2 ⊥ 3 0 2 ¯7 2
      2.7008

Care must be taken with the coefficients : 0 indicates that there is no term
in x^3, and ¯7 indicates a negative coefficient.
Here is an elegant solution to exercise 6 of chapter 4.

This method enables the value of the polynomial to be calculated for several
values of x, subject to the placing of these values in a matrix, as shown
below :

        (10 1 ρ 0.2 × ι10) ⊥ 3 0 2 ¯7 2
      0.6848   ¯0.4032   ¯1.0912   ¯4.4409E¯16   2.7008   7.6448
      15.5808   27.3728   44

The very small value ¯4.4409E¯16, can be replaced by zero.

ALPHABETICAL CLASSIFICATION

DRESS, DROP, CHESS, DREAM are required to be classified in alphabetical order.

It can be said that each one of these words is the writing of a number in a
strange numerical system, in base 27, where 1 would be written A, where 2
would be written B, where 26 would be written Z, and where zero would be a
blank character.

          AL ← ' ABCDEFGHIJKLMNOPQRSTUVWXYZ '

In order to clarify words, their representation in decimal numbering needs
to be found. We will construct a matrix with these words :

          WORDS
      DRESS
      DROP
      CHESS
      DREAM

Look for the position of the letters in the alphabet :

          AL ι WORDS
      19 16 20 20   6
      19 16 10   1   1
      19 16 20   6   1
      19 16   3   6   1

So that the blank takes the value 0, A the value 1, etc... 1 must be subtracted from this result. Furthermore, so that each word is arranged in a column, the matrix must be transposed.

$$\Phi \quad {}^-1+AL \iota \ WORDS$$

5	5	4	5
19	19	9	19
6	16	6	6
20	17	20	2
20	1	20	14

It is sufficient to decode these values in order to make its equivalent decimal correspond to each word :

$$27 \perp \Phi \ {}^-1+AL \iota \ WORDS$$

   3036116   3043306   2307845   3035624

Thus a function enabling words to be classified in increasing order of their equivalents can be defined , in other words, in alphabetical order.
This solution is hardly advantageous; it is preferable to produce only the set of indices necessary for this classification, as with the function $\spadesuit$ for numbers.
Moreover, if the subtraction of 1 is satisfactory for coherent reasoning, it does not change the result of the classification, and thus constitutes useless work; we will dispense with it.

```
        ∇ R ← SORT M
[1]     R← ♠ 27 ⊥ Φ ALιM
        ∇
```

        SORT WORDS

    3   4   1   2

        WORDS[SORT WORDS;]

    CHESS
    DREAM
    DRESS
    DROP

LIMITS

This method suffices for most classifications. However, if the words to be classified are too long, their numerical equivalents are represented in an exponential form, and two adjacent words can no longer be distinguished.

        27 ⊥ AL ι 'ZYWOLSKOWITZ'
    6.927444706015344*E*16
        27 ⊥ AL ι 'ZYWOLSKOWITS'
    6.927444706015344*E*16

The function *SORT* enables names of a maximum of 11 letters to be classified. In reality, a classification of 6 letters enables more than 80% of everyday names to be classified, a supplementary classification for the 6 following characters (or more) enables possible problems to be solved.

7-8   THE ENCODE FUNCTION

The ENCODE function is written T, it effects inverse transformation of DECODE

                    24 60 60 T 8839
             2   27 19

Hence, all the examples demonstrated with the DECODE function can be reused
one by one when the opportunity arises.

Two values can be encoded in the same base :

                    24 60 60 T 8839 18228
              2   5
             27   3
             19   48

The representation of a same number can be sought in several numeric bases :

                    [] ← *BASES* ← 4 3 ρ 2 3 10
          2   3   10
          2   3   10
          2   3   10
          2   3   10

                  BASES T 7
        0 0 0
        1 0 0
        1 2 0
        1 1 7

The three columns represent 7 encoded in the bases 2, 3 and 10 respectively.

                BASES T 5 12 9 7 3
        0 1 1 0 0
        0 0 0 ⓪ 0
        0 0 0 0 0   Each term of the right hand operand is encoded in
                            the three bases 2, 3 and 10, on 4 representative
        1 1 0 1 0   numbers. The result has 4 3 5 as dimensions :
        0 1 1 ⓪ 0
        0 0 0 0 0   - 4 numbers per encoded value,
                              - 3 encodings per value,
        0 0 0 1 1   - 5 values to encode.
        1 1 0 ② 1
        0 1 0 0 0   By way of example, the representation of 7 in base
                            3, has been circled, that being : 0 0 2 1.
        1 0 1 1 1
        2 0 0 ① 0
        5 2 9 7 3
        ↗ ↗ ↑ ↖ ↖
        5 12 9 7 3

The base has 4 3 for dimensions, the vector to be encoded has 5 for a dimension, the result has 4 3 5 for dimensions.

One can also have a matrix, or any array of higher rank as a right hand argument. In order that the example remains readable, we will work in a single base, for example that which enables us to convert seconds into hours and minutes.

We will try to convert the matrix *SEC* as follows :   1341   5000   345
                                                          3600   781   90

24 60 60 ⊤ *SEC*

0   1   0 } *hours*
1   0   0 }

22 23 5 } *minutes*
0   13 1 }

21 20 45 } *seconds*
0   1 30 }

-9   CONDITIONS OF USE OF THE ENCODE FUNCTION

The result of *B*⊤*M* has (ρ*B*),(ρ*M*) for dimensions.   The elements of each encoded value are arranged along the first dimension of the result.

The dimensions of the operands are not subjected to any rule of conformity; however, it is necessary that the last dimension of the left hand operand (the base) is at least equal to the number of figures necessary for the representation of the encoded values.

For example :

24 60 60 ⊤ 8839 **equals**   2 27 19

   60 60 ⊤ 8839 **would equal**   27 19

      60 ⊤ 8839 **would equal**   19

The last two results are truncated to the dimension of the base, but nothing indicates that they are incomplete.

To avoid this disadvantage, a limited encoding can be undertaken, but which does not truncate the result, taking 0 as the first element of the base.

0 60 ⊤ 8839

147 19

This result indicates that 8839 seconds represents 147 minutes and 19 seconds
Hence, one can, either be content with this result (partial encoding), or
state that 147 minutes is more than one hour, and start again:

$$\begin{array}{ccccc} 0 & 60 & 60 & \top & 8839 \end{array}$$
$$22719$$

There is no easy way of knowing in advance the number of figures which will
be necessary for encoding.

7-10   APPLICATIONS OF ENCODE

1) encoding enables numeric values which have been compacted by a decoding
    to be separated.

    This could be the case for a date :

$$\phi \ \ 100 \ \ 100 \ \ 100 \ \top \ 771209$$
$$91277$$

2) The whole number part and the decimal part of a number can be separated:

$$0 \ \ 1 \ \top \ 127.83$$
$$127 \ \ \ 0.83$$

    In the same way, partial encoding can be used to extract the last figures
    of a number :

$$100 \ \top \ 34561$$
$$61$$

    This is a useful method of extracting the last figures of a list, when
    these have a proper meaning.
    For example, the codes of the articles of a catalogue can be constructed
    thus :

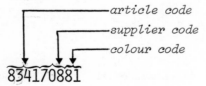

                      —article code
                 —supplier code
             —colour code

834170881

    Access to the supplier will be obtained by : $1\uparrow1000 \ \ 100 \ \top \ CODE$

3) Finally, we will assume that we were seeking the position of a number
    in a matrix.

$$MAT$$

12	34	71	90	92	45
33	40	6	80	88	89
21	22	62	17	83	85
97	42	54	50	56	77

The position of the values 92, 42, 88 and 33 are being sought.

      $\Box \leftarrow I \leftarrow (,MAT) \iota$ 92 42 88 33
5 20 11 7

      1+ (ρMAT) τ I-1
1 4 2 2
5 2 5 1

Each column of a result gives the position of a value ; row index and column index.
Hence, 92 is on the first row and 5th column; 42 is on the 4th row and 2nd column, etc...

A function can be created from this :

      ∇ $R \leftarrow V$ *LOCATE* M
 [1] $R \leftarrow$ 1+(ρM) τ $^-$1+(,M)ιV
      ∇

      50 40 89 77 *LOCATE MAT*
4 2 2 4
4 2 6 6

      4568 *LOCATE MAT*
 1 1

This last result is tedious, because it gives the impression that 4568 appears in *MAT*.
In reality, (,MAT)ι4568 will give the number 25, from which 1 is subtracted.
A complete encoding of 24 would give :

      0 4 6 τ 24
  1 0 0

The function executing an incomplete encoding, only 0 0 remains, which becomes 1 1 by adding 1.

Could you modify this function so that it gives the answer 0 0 each time that a value does not appear in the matrix ?

      50 99 12 *LOCATE MAT*
 4 0 1
 4 0 1

EXERCISES

[9] Can you explain the result of :   0 $\bot$ 12 34 60 77 19

[10] Can you explain the result of :   1 $\bot$ 12 34 60 77 19

[11] Write a function which enables the complete series of indices of a
     matrix to be produced.

```
        INDICES 2 3 ρ 1 0 0 0 1 1
   1 1 1 2 2 2
   1 2 3 1 2 3
```

[12] In order to analyse the contents of a computer memory, it is useful
     to group the binary values in fours. Each group of four binary values
     can represent a value from 0 to 15; in other words, one of the values
     of the base 16 numerical system, also called HAXADECIMAL.
     It is customary to represent the value 10 by A, 11 by B, 12 by C,
     13 by D, 14 by E and 15 by F.

     The memory analyses appear in the following form : 1A5C C20F EB79...

     It is sometimes advantageous to convert these values into decimal
     numbering, and vice versa. Write the functions which perform this
     work.

```
        HEXENCODE  18430  225  6429
   47FE 00E1 191D
```

```
        HEXDECODE '1A5C C20F EB79'
   6748   49679   60281
```

     It is well to note that all the hexadecimal values are represented
     by four figures.

[13] In exercise 6 of this chapter, it was required to convert a string
     of characters into a number. Write a function which accomplishes
     the reverse operation, that is to say, transforms a number into a
     string of characters :

```
        CONVERT 29
   29
        '(' , (CONVERT 8040) , ')'
   (8040)
```

THE INDEX-OF FUNCTION

The result of $A\iota B$ is ALWAYS of the dimension of B. If B is a scalar, $A\iota B$
will be a scalar, whereas $(A\equiv B)/2\rho A$ would give a vector of an element.
Application: here are two ways of extracting a name from an array:

$$N1 \leftarrow NAMES[CODES \iota 387 ;]$$
$$N \leftarrow NAMES[(CODES=387)/_\iota\rho CODES]$$

N] is a vector, whereas $N2$ is a matrix of one line. As a result :

-   it can be written :   '*THE NAME IS*' , $N1$

-   it cannot be written : '*THE NAME IS*' , $N2$

It is necessary to write :   '*THE NAME IS*' , , $N2$

The left hand argument of the INDEX-OF function must necessarily be a vector,
never a scalar, nor a matrix.

      `7 ι 7`

RANK ERROR

      7 ι 7
      ^

The case of empty vectors is also interesting.

      `8  9  6 ι (ι0)`
                        The result is also an empty vector.

      `(ι0) ι 2 3 5`
1 1 1   In both these examples, since the right
                           hand argument does not belong to the
      `'' ι 'A'`   left hand argument, the result is equal
1   to the dimension of the last (zero),
                           increased by 1.

Finally, we will note that the result of the INDEX-OF function depends on
the index origin.

In origin 1, 8 9 6 1 1 ι 6 8 3 equals :   3 1 6

In origin 0, this same expression would equal : 2 0 5

7-12   GRADE UP AND GRADE DOWN

Like the INDEX-OF function $\triangle$ and $\triangledown$ do not accept scalar nor a matrix argume
In the case where it is desired to classify the lines of a matrix in terms
of the values of the first column, then the second, then the third, and so
on until the last, recourse will be had to a defined function.

Here is a classical example :

```
        ∇ R ← GRADEUP M;C
[1]   R←ι1↑ρM
[2]   C←(ρM)[2]
[3]   NEXT: R←R[▲M[R;C]]
[4]   →(0<C←C-1)/NEXT
        ∇
```

        MESS

```
2 40 8
8 31 7
5 55 2
2 33 9
7 20 2
8 12 6
5 55 1
5 52 9
2 40 9
7 18 8
7 21 1
7 20 1
```

        MESS[GRADEUP MESS;]

```
2 33 9
2 40 8
2 40 9
5 52 9          It is established that the result is a matrix of which
5 55 1          the terms of the first column are classified in increa
5 55 2          ing order, and such that, for a same value in the firs
7 18 8          column, the terms of the second column are classified
7 20 1          in increasing order, and so on.
7 20 2
7 21 1
8 12 6
8 31 7
```

Like the INDEX-OF function, GRADE UP and GRADE DOWN give a result which
depends on the index origin.

For origin 1, 4 3 5 2 9 3 equals : 3 1 5 2 4
For origin 0, this expression equals : 2 0 4 1 3

GRADE UP and GRADE DOWN are both greedy functions in calculating time, it is thus prudent to limit the classifications requested of the machine.

-13   ENCODE AND DECODE

If a zero appears in the base of a decoding, the elements situated to the left of this zero are ignored.

              2 5 0 3 4 2 1 1 2 3 2 5 1
       99
              8 6 0 3 4 2 1 1 2 3 2 5 1
       99

In effect, *BASE* ι *VECT* is identical with $(\phi 1, \times \backslash \phi 1 \downarrow BASE)$ +.× *VECT*

It is apparent, in the calculation of the vector of weights, that the appearance of a zero confers a nil weight to all the left side elements.

2 5 0 3 4 2 1 *VECTOR* is strictly equivalent to 0 0 0 3 4 2 ι *VECTOR*

This property is used to justify texts on the right, that is to say, to align the words at the right hand margin.
For example , here is a matrix of characters called *POEM* :

MARY HAD   *MARY HAD*
A   one would want to obtain: *A*
LITTLE   *LITTLE*
LAMB   *LAMB*

              POEM = ' '

       0 0 1 0 0 0 0 0
       0 0 0 1 1 1 1 1
       0 0 0 0 0 0 1 1
       0 0 1 0 0 0 0 1

If the previous property is used, (*POEM* = '')ι1 , will give the same result as if the isolated 1's were zeros :

       0 0 0 0 0 0 0 0
       0 0 0 1 1 1 1 1
       0 0 0 0 0 0 1 1
       0 0 0 0 0 0 0 1

The result will be 1 8 3 5, or 1 more than the desired reversal. The necessary term is deducted from it :

         (1-(*POEM*=' ')⊥1) ⌽ *POEM*
   MARY HAD
        A
    LITTLE
      LAMB

PARTICULAR CASES

  0 ⊥ *V*   is equivalent to :   ‾1 ↑ *V*

  1 ⊥ *V*   is equivalent to :   +/ *V*

 ‾1 ⊥ *V*   is equivalent to :   -/ *V*

Normally, the elements of a vector to be decoded should not be greater than the corresponding elements of the base (it is difficult to imagine a time to be expressed as 7 hours, 83 minutes and 127 seconds). However, if this is the case, the calculation is performed in the same way :

         6 6 6 ⊥ 7 5 10
    292

         24 60 60 ⊥ 7 83 127
    30307

Finally, even though we have not explicitly stated this, it goes without saying that the ENCODE function accepts decimal bases.
For example:

         5.2 5.2 5.2 ⊤ 160.23
    5   4   4.23

7-14   THE CASE OF NEGATIVE VALUES

We will imagine that it is required to encode various values in base 10, and with 6 figures; for positive values we know the result will be :

         (6ρ10) ⊤ 17
    0 0 0 0 1 7

         (6ρ10) ⊤ 431
    0 0 0 4 3 1

For negative values, the ENCODE function gives a result such that the sum of two opposite values remains nil.

$$(6\rho10) \top {}^-17$$
$$9 \quad 9 \quad 9 \quad 9 \quad 8 \quad 3$$

This result is not surprising : in base 10, if the addition of two numbers exceeds 9, a number is carried which is used when adding the numbers immediately to the left. Here is what the addition of the encoding of 17 and ¯17 would give :

```
  1  1  1  1  1  1  ◄─────────── numbers carried

     0  0  0  0  1  7

  +  9  9  9  9  8  3
    ─────────────────
  =1 0  0  0  0  0  0
```

If only 6 figures are kept, as agreed, it is seen that the result is composed only of zeros (on a grey background).

In the same way :

$$(6\rho10) \top {}^-431$$
$$9 \quad 9 \quad 9 \quad 5 \quad 6 \quad 9$$

In another base, the process is similar. For example, in base 5 :

$$\Diamond (6\rho5) \top 68 \quad {}^-68 \quad 129 \quad {}^-129$$

```
0 0 0 2 3 3
4 4 4 2 1 2
0 0 1 0 0 4
4 4 3 4 4 1
```

Remember that in base 5, 3+2 gives 0, with 1 carried.

It is this convention of representation which is used by the computer to represent whole numbers. With IBM computers 32 binary positions are reserved for the representation of each whole number lass than 2147483647 and greater than ¯2147483648.
The inner representation of these numbers is therefore obtained by :
$(32\rho2) \top NUMBER$.

173	is represented by :	00000000000000000000000010101101
2147483647	is represented by :	01111111111111111111111111111111
¯173	is represented by :	11111111111111111111111101010011
¯2147483647	is represented by :	10000000000000000000000000000001

The rule remains valid for decimal values.

        ⍉ (5⍴10) ⊤ 15.8 ¯15.8
    0   0   0   1   5.8
    9   9   9   8   4.2

This method of representation leads to a few frustrations during decoding
if precautions are not taken :

        10 ⊥ (6⍴10) ⊤ 143   equals   143

but   10 ⊥ (6⍴10) ⊤ ¯143   will equal 99857

The sum of these two results does not give 0, but 1000000, or 10*6.

As a result, when retaining values in an encoded form so as to decode them
later, and some of these values are possibly negative, it is advisable to
provide one more figure than is necessary, and to test the value of it.

Hence, the binary representation of numbers in the computer is such that the
possitive numbers start with 0, and the negative numbers with 1.   In base 10,
possitive numbers start with 0, and negative numbers with 9.   A general
function is derived from this in oder to decode encoded values in a uniform
base:

               ∇ R←BASE DECODE V;P
    [1]   R←BASE⊥V
    [2]   P←1↑⍴V
    [3]   R←R-(BASE*P)×(R>¯1+BASE*P-1) ∇

        V ← (6⍴10) ⊤ ¯417.42 26 32 ¯1654 0 3 ¯55

        10 ⊥ V
    999582.58 26   32 99834 0 3 999945   ◄———————altered negative values

        10 DECODE V
    ¯417.42 26 32 ¯1654 0 3 ¯55   ◄————————correct decoding

CHAPTER 8

COMPUTING AIDS

The principle primitive functions of APL were studied in the previous chapters.
Among the functions still to be discovered, will essentially be found functions
useful for mathematical processings.
However, all these functions are equally likely to interest readers working
on the daily management problems of companies. Such is the case, in particular,
with the DOMINO function to which a significant part of this chapter is dedicated.

1   THE DOMINO FUNCTION

If a square matrix is multiplied by a matrix possessing only 1's on its main
diagonal, it remains unchanged.

	12	50	7
If A equals :	44	3	25
	30	71	80

	1	0	0
and if I equals :	0	1	0
	0	0	1

Then $A+.\times I$ and $I+.\times A$ are equal to the matrix A:

12	50	7
44	3	25
30	71	80

It is said that I is the neutral element of the product of the order 3 matrices,
just as 0 is the neutral element of the addition of scalars, or as 1 is the
neutral element of multiplication.
It is also said that I is the order 3 unit matrix.

INVERSE MATRIX

Some matrices possess an INVERSE MATRIX, that is to say that their product
reinstates the unit matrix of the same order.

For example, for order 2 matrices, the two matrices $M1$ and $M2$ below are the
inverse of one another :

$M1$ equals : $\left\{\begin{array}{cc} 2 & 1 \\ 4 & 1 \end{array}\right.$

$M2$ equals : $\left\{\begin{array}{cc} {}^-0.5 & 0.5 \\ 2 & {}^-1 \end{array}\right.$

$M1 +.\times M2$

1	0
0	1

Now, here are two order 3 matrices, *MAT* and *TAM*, which are the inverse of one another.

MAT

1	0	2
0	2	1
0.5	3	1.5

TAM

0	‾3	2
‾0.25	‾0.25	0.5
0.5	1.5	‾1

TAM +.× MAT

1	0	0
0	1	0
0	0	1

The expression *MAT +.× TAM* would give the same result.

8-2   THE MONADIC DOMINO

The DOMINO function ⌹ is obtained by overstriking the symbol ÷ and □ . It gives the value of the inverse of a matrix directly.

```
      ⌹ MAT
 4.680539832E‾16   ‾3.000000000E0    2.000000000E0
‾2.500000000E‾1   ‾2.500000000E‾1   5.000000000E‾1
 5.000000000E‾1    1.500000000E0   ‾1.000000000E0
```

The inversion of a matrix is a complex operation, which often requires a lot of computing, precision of which tends to diminish. This is the reason why the result often appears in an exponential form. It is immediately establis that values with high negative powers assigned to them, like E^{-16}, are very close to zero, and that the result above is equal to the matrix *TAM*.

In order to eliminate this difficulty of reading, the function below will ro off the computed values to their second decimal place, which will be suffici for the examples chosen.

```
        ∇ R← ROUND X
[1]     R←0.01 ×⌊0.5+ 100×X
        ∇
```

By way of checking :

$$ROUND \boxminus MAT$$

0	‾3	2
‾0.25	‾0.25	0.5
0.5	1.5	‾1

Just as the zero scalar has no inverse, some matrices, called singular, have no inverse. A domain error will appear if an attempt is made to invert such a matrix.

$$\boxminus 3 \ 3 \ \rho \ 1 \ 3 \ 5 \ 3 \ 4 \ 15 \ 2 \ 7 \ 10$$
DOMAIN ERROR
$$\boxminus \ 3 \ 3 \ \rho \ 1 \ 3 \ 5 \ 3 \ 4 \ 15 \ 2 \ 7 \ 10$$
$$\wedge$$

SOLVING SIMULTANEOUS EQUATIONS

Three linear simultaneous equations with three unknowns x_1, x_2, and x_3, are represented here in the classical form :

$$\begin{cases} ^-8 = 3x_1 + 2x_2 - x_3 \\[2mm] 19 = x_1 - x_2 + 3x_3 \\[2mm] 0 = 5x_1 + 2x_2 \end{cases}$$

This set can also be expressed in the manner of a matrix. We will call VC the vector of constants :

$$VC \leftarrow {}^-8 \ 19 \ 0$$

We will call CF the matrix of coefficients of x_1, x_2, and x_3 : $\begin{cases} 3 & ^-2 & ^-1 \\ 1 & ^-1 & 3 \\ 5 & 2 & 0 \end{cases}$

To solve the simultaneous equations above now amounts to finding the vector X of the three unknowns x_1, x_2, and x_3, so that VC is equal to CF +.x X

It can be found, working manually, that the product CF +.x X reinstates the three equations of the set.

This matrix presentation will enable us to find a solution.

Suppose that CF possesses an inverse matrix, which we will call FC.

If it is used in order to multiply by matrices the two terms of the equation

Since VC is equal to : CF +.× X

FC+. VC must be equal to $\underline{FC\ +.\ \ \ CF}$ +.× X

FC being the inverse of CF: $\underline{I\ \ \ \ \ \ }$ +.× X

and I being the unit matrix : X

It is concluded that the solution sought X is equal to FC +.× VC.
Which can also be expressed by :

$$\boxed{X \leftarrow (\boxplus CF)\ +.\times\ VC}$$

$$\begin{array}{ccc} & X & \\ 2 & {}^-5 & 4 \end{array}$$

The doubting reader will be able to verify manually that these are indeed
the three values sought.

8-4   THE DYADIC DOMINO

In its dyadic form the DOMINO function directly performs the calculation
which we have just detailed; hence it enables systems of n linear equations
of n unknowns to be rapidly solved.

$$\begin{array}{ccc} \multicolumn{3}{c}{VC\ \boxplus\ CF} \\ 2 & {}^-5 & 4 \end{array}$$

Naturally, this method assumes that the matrix CF is invertable, in other
words, it assumes that the system does not have a solution, a domain error
will be signalled.

The solution of a system of n linear equations of n unknowns of which CF
is the matrix of the coefficients, and VC the vector of the constant terms,
is given by :

$$\boxed{X \leftarrow VC\ \boxplus\ CF}$$

8-5   DOMINO AND CURVE MATCHING

As a preliminary, we invite you to study a complicated method of solving a
simple problem. This is, of course, with the intention of generalizing this
method for the solving of an everyday problem in statistical studies.

It is intended to find the coefficients of the straight line which passes
through two points P and Q, of which the coordinates are given:

$X \leftarrow 2 \quad 4$ vector of the x-axis of P and Q.

$Y \leftarrow 2 \quad 3$ vector of the y-axis of P and Q.

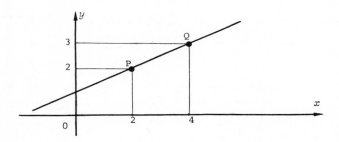

The general equation of a straight line being $y = b + ax$, in the case of the
two points given the following is obtained :

$2 = b + 2a$

$3 = b + 4a$ two simultaneous equations of which the unknowns
are a and b.

We will solve this set by the method demonstrated in paragraph 8-3.

The matrix M of the coefficients of the unknowns is equal to : $\begin{matrix} 1 & 2 \\ 1 & 4 \end{matrix}$

This can be obtained by an outer product starting from the vector X.

*	0	1
2	1	2
4	1	4

This outer product is written : $M \leftarrow X \circ .* \; 0 \; 1$

a and b can thus be computed by using the dyadic DOMINO : $C \leftarrow Y \boxplus M$
Or again :

$$\square \leftarrow C \leftarrow Y \boxplus X \circ . \star 0\ 1$$
    1   0.5

It can be seen on the figure that these are the values sought. The method
may seem tedious, but the next paragraph will show its scope.

A USE OF THE INNER PRODUCT

Having found the coefficients of the straight line, it is now required to
calculate the y-axis ordinates of several points of which the x-axis
ordinates are known.

$$X \leftarrow {}^{-}2\ \ 3\ \ 6$$

The coefficients of the straight line have been obtained by a calculation of
form : $C \leftarrow Y \boxplus M$ which is strictly equivalent to : $C \leftarrow (\boxplus M) +.\times Y$

Multiplying by the two terms of this expression matricially M, it is seen tha

$M +.\times C$ is equal to : $\underline{M +.\times (\boxplus M)} +.\times Y$

                                          $\underbrace{I \qquad\qquad +.\times Y}$

$M +.\times C$ is therefore equal to : Y

Y will therefore be obtained by $M +.\times C$ or again : $Y \leftarrow (X \circ . \star 0\ 1) +.\times C$

In the case of the four given points :

$$(0\ \ {}^{-}2\ \ 3\ \ 6 \circ . \star 0\ 1) +.\times 1\ \ 0.5$$
    1   0   2.5   4

8-6   LINEAR REGRESSION

We will now imagine that there are no longer two points, but eight :

$$X \leftarrow {}^{-}1\ \ 3\ \ 1.5\ \ 2\ \ 4\ \ {}^{-}1\ \ 0.5\ \ 2$$
$$Y \leftarrow {}^{-}3\ \ 3\ \ {}^{-}1\ \ {}^{-}1\ \ 8\ \ {}^{-}1\ \ 0\ \ 1$$

This time, the matrix $X \circ . \star 0\ 1$ will have more lines (8) than columns (2),
and the simultaneous equations will not allow any solution, which means that
no straight line can join all these points.

In such a case, it can be advantageous to locate a straight line which best represents the spread of points. Generally a straight line is sought such that the sum of the squares of the deviations of ordinates between the given points and the straight line is called minimal. This straight line is called the LEAST SQUARES LINE.

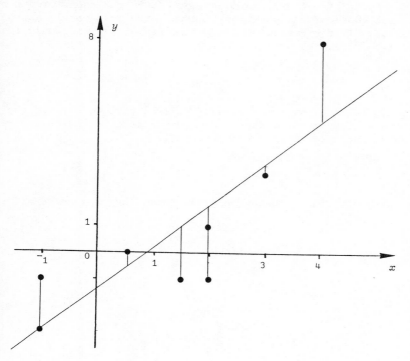

To find this line, the dyadic DOMINO is used again. In effect, the expression which enables the coefficients of a line of which two points are given to be found, automatically gives the coefficients of the least squares line relating to a spread of points.

In the case of the eight points given :

$$Y \boxdot X \circ . \star 0 \ 1$$
$$^-1.416201117 \quad 1.575418994$$

It is these values which were used to trace the line of the figure above.

8-7
POLYNOMIAL REGRESSION

If the matrix of the coefficients is extended to powers higher than X, by writting, for example $X °.* 0 1 2 3$, we no longer obtain the coefficients of a straight line, but those of the polynomial curve which most nearly approac the spread of points. In the case of the eight points given, one would look for example, for a third degree curve, writing :

$$\Box \leftarrow C \leftarrow Y \boxdiv X °.* 0 1 2 3$$
    ‾0.6681529243   0.4885029093   ‾0.5502792157   0.2452272994

As in the previous paragraph, an inner product will be used to compute the Y ordinates of a certain number of points of the curve, those of which the x-a is X for example, so as to facilitate the plotting.

$$ROUND (X °.* 0 1 2 3) +.× C$$
    ‾1.95   2.47   ‾0.35   0.07   8.18   ‾1.95   ‾0.53   0.07

It is seen that the deviations between the given points and the curve are ve small.

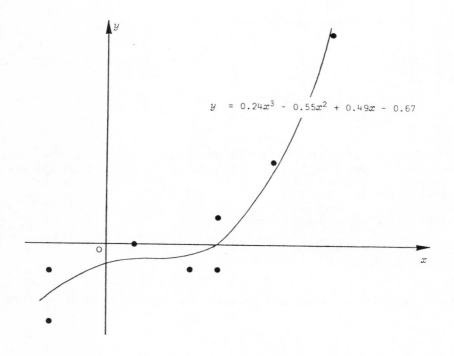

$$y = 0.24x^3 - 0.55x^2 + 0.49x - 0.67$$

GENERATING RANDOM NUMBERS

Creating sets of data in order to test a function is often a long and labourious
task which one would willingly leave to the computer, provided that the values
thus created are sufficiently selected at random so as not to fall into
particularly awkward circumstances.
For certain statistical studies, or to simulate certain natural phenomena, or
certain random events, it is equally useful to use values taken at random.
This is the reason which has lead to inserting, in most computers, programs
which generate series of random numbers. There is such a program in APL.

Anyone who knows this program would be able, of course, to forsee the succession
of values generated by the computer; also the term "random" should be taken
in a restricted sense. In the following pages, we will therefore mean by
"random values" a succession of values which cannot be foreseen by an analysis
of the preceeding values generated, and of which the frequency of distribution
does not favour any value.

Having made this statement, we can study the DEAL and ROLL functions.

THE DEAL FUNCTION

The DEAL function is written ? it is a dyadic mixed function which only accepts
two whole scalars as arguments, or arrays of a single whole element.

The expression $N \: ? \: A$ gives N whole numbers taken randomly amongst the elements
of the vector $\imath A$.

```
      4 ? 12
   3  10  1  7
```

```
      4 ? 12                    Three successive uses of this function
   9  8  12  1                  hence gives three generally different
                                results.
```

```
      4 ? 12
  10  2  4  8
```

The random values are generated without repetition. It is hence obligatory
that N is less than or equal to A.

Example :

```
      8 ? 8
   6  1  4  7  8  5  2  3
```

```
      9 ? 8
DOMAIN ERROR
   9 ? 8
   ^
```

The DEAL can be used to mix up the elements of a vector; this will be the
subject of exercise 5 of this chapter.

8-10   THE ROLL FUNCTION

The monadic ROLL function *?* accepts any numeric argument, and reinstates a
result of the same dimensions : it is a monadic scalar function.

?A is a value of the same dimensions as *A*, each element of *A* giving a random
whole number taken from ι*a*.   Each element having been generated independently
of the others, it is possible to obtain a sampling with a repetition.

Examples :

```
      ? 8  17  4  3  9  12
   7  3  3  1  8  12
```

```
      ? 4  4  4  4  44  4
   1  4  3  4  4  1 3
```

More generally, in order to generate *N* random values at the most equal to *P*,
with repetition, *?NρP* is written.   This time, there are no restrictions on
the respective values of *N* and *P*.

```
      ¯1 + ? 12ρ2
   1 0 0 0 1 0 1 1 0 1 1 0
```

A random boolean vector has been generated.

If it is required to obtain a matrix of 4 lines and 7 columns comprising value
between 100 and 110, the following is written :

```
      99 + ? 4 7ρ11
   102  107  110  102  108  108  105
   101  107  102  101  100  110  104
   103  108  109  110  101  105  103
   103  107  102  107  109  102  104
```

Finally, to generate a series of characters at random, a vector of characters
must be indexed by a series of random numbers, as shown below :

```
      CHARS ← 'ABCDEFGHIJKLMNOPQRSTUVWXYZ -,.'
      MIXTURE ← ? 6 8 ρ 30

      CHARS [MIXTURE]
   GQQUV,ZE
   IOPWV.AQ
   EFQOENCL
   U SCXKKT
   P,Z DCXH
```

EXERCISES

[1] Find the solution to the following simultaneous equations :
$$\begin{cases} x - y = \ \ 5 \\ y - 2x = \ ^-7 \\ z - x = \ \ 2 \end{cases}$$

[2] The three variables a, b and c, verify the following three expressions :

$$a - b + 3c = 13 \qquad\qquad 4b - 2a = -6 \qquad\qquad a - 2b + 2c = 10$$

Can you establish what the value is of the expression : $3a + 5b - c$?

[3] The temperature of an oven has been noted over a period of time :

MINUTES ←	0	1	2	5	7	10	12	15	17	19	20	25	31
DEGREES ←	20	33	45	68	91	130	172	208	270	287	289	308	319

It is required to know what temperature this oven would have reached in 40 minutes. For this, an attempt would be made to find what curve best represents the increase in these temperatures, and the value taken by this curve will be sought for the x-axis 40.

A trial will be run with a straight line, then with polynomials of degrees 2, 3 and 4.

Do you think that such a method of extrapolation is very reliable ?

[4] The generation of random points is undertaken four times in succession in the plane by the following formula :

```
X ← 0.5 X ι12
Y ← (2×X) + ? 12ρ3
```

For these four trials find the parameters of the least squares lines.
Find the least squares line of the 48 points obtained.
Compare the results. The results should be close to 2 2.

[5] Write a function which mixes up the elements of a vector. For example :

         MIX 'YOUR TEA'
     UTO RYEA

[6] What would be obtained by the expression : 10 + ? (10 + ?10) ρ 10

[7] Generate the random values answering to the following criteria :

- 12 values between 8 and 30, without repetition

- a matrix of 4 lines and 6 columns of values between 37 and 47, with repetition.

- a matrix of 5 lines and 2 columns of values between $^-5$ and 5, without repetition.

[8] Generate a vector of 15 random numbers between 0.01 and 0.09, with three significant figures each, and with repetition.

[9] Write a function which gives fortuitously from 6 to 16 random numbers, all between 3 and 40 inclusive, with repetition.

[10] Same problem, but all the values generated must be different.

[11] Create a vector of 5 elements taken at random from among the following values :

$$L \leftarrow 12 \quad 29 \quad 5 \quad 44 \quad 31 \quad 60 \quad 8 \quad 86$$

A result is required without repetition, then a result with repetition.

[12] It is required to obtain a matrix of 2 lines and 12 columns, filled with random values. The values of the same line will all be different , but it is accepted that identical values will appear in different lines. Write the required expression. The values will be between 1 and 21.

[13] It is desired to use APL in order to create decorative motifs. Write a function which will print out a matrix of characters chosen at random from a given list. The dimensions of the matrix are given as argument.

'α?ω⊂⌈⊃∊⌊∩ρ_∪~∇⊥↑ΔT↓ο₁Ο⎕*|<≤=≥>≠∨∧÷-' *HIEROGLYPH* 5 30

```
Δω⊥?Ο=↑∪⊥⌊÷≤TU≠⌈_≤≠∇ο?|ρ∪α⊃ω*↑
=⌊∪ω<⌈∩≠ο∩⊥⌊_?⌈↑∧∧-ο⎕↑>~⊥∩⌊<=≤
∨ω∩?_αρ⌈T∪Δ_~∊↓↓*Tω|?ο<_⌊∪≥Δ∪T
⎕αω=Δ∩<⌈≠∇T∩≤⌊≠⊥_∪|ω⌈∪∩-⌊_⌈÷_α
₁∩≤ω∩⌈∧∇Δ?ρ⌊T⊥∧≥>_T≤=⌈∩?ο>∨_₁∩
```

[14] It is desired to create again a decorative motif, but this time triangular: one character on the first line, three on the second, five on the following. The number of lines is given as an argument.

'α?ω⊃⌈⊂∊⌊∩∪×ρ~∇⊥TΔ↑↓ο÷₁Ο⎕*|' *TRIANGLE* 6

```
      ~
   ₁÷|
  ⊂ω×T*⌊
 ↓α?*Δρ⊃∩
⊃⎕⌈∇↑∪↓∊ο×
ρ~∩÷⎕ο*⊃T∊~Δ          A function without a loop would be welcome !
```

[15] Write a function whose role is to extract an arbitary value from a matrix, and to indicate its position.
For example :

GENERATE 3 5ρι15

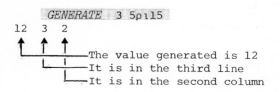

12   3   2

The value generated is 12
It is in the third line
It is in the second column

[16] A niladic function called *GAME* is required to be written which functions as follows :

- When the function is called it chooses 10 letters of the alphabet at random,

- the user is invited in turn to choose three letters,

- if the letters chosen by the user belong to the list drawn up by the function, he has won, if not he has lost.

In all cases, the function prints out the characters it has chosen.

> GAME
> ENTER 3 LETTERS : GHQ
> LOST, I HAD CHOSEN NASQKIOPHW
>
> GAME
> ENTER 3 LETTERS : ZUT
> WON, I HAD CHOSEN VYUSWTFZAP

Write this function. You will notice that the question and the user's answer are on the same line (this subject is referred to in paragraph 4-35).

[17] Two controls are required to be included in the function *GAME*, so as to rule out any cheating :

- the player must introduce exactly three letters (not more, nor less)

- the three letters must be different.

If these conditions are not met, the player is again invited to introduce three letters.

8-11   COMPUTING UTILITIES

8-12   IDENTITY

$+A$ is equal to A, no matter what numeric A is. The function IDENTITY, which is therefore the monadic +, is of little use; it simply allows values to be given a positive sign without the fear of a syntax error.

> + 125.78

125.78

8-13   OPPOSITE

$-A$ is equal to $0-A$ no matter what numeric A is. This is a way of giving values a negative sign or of obtaining the opposite of a value while maintaining the usual mathematical conventions.

$$- 4 \quad \text{equals} \quad ^-4$$
$$- \ ^-3 \quad \text{equals} \quad 3$$
$$-X \leftarrow 2 \quad \text{equals} \quad ^-2$$

8-14   INVERSE

÷A is equal to 1÷A no matter what the non-zero A is.   The symbol ÷ thus
represents the INVERSE function.

        ÷4
    0.25

        ÷ ‾0.2 1 8 100
    ‾5 1 0.125 0.01

IDENTITY, OPPOSITE and INVERSE are three monadic scalar functions.

8-15   SIGN

The SIGN function is a monadic scalar function, represented by the symbol
X.

$$\chi A \text{ equals} \begin{cases} 1 \text{ if } A \text{ is positive} \\ 0 \text{ if } A \text{ is zero} \\ {}^-1 \text{ if } A \text{ is negative} \end{cases}$$

        X 2 ‾1 0 3.2 ‾6.7
    1 ‾1 0 1 ‾1

χA is strictly equivalent to $(A>0)-(A<0)$.

8-16   ABSOLUTE VALUE

The ABSOLUTE VALUE of a numeric datum is supplied by the monadic scalar functi⟨
| .

        |3 0 ‾6.7 8.2 ‾9 ‾30 0
    3 0 6.7 8.2 9 30 0

|A is strictly equivalent to AxχA

8-17   RESIDUE

The RESIDUE function, which is written $D|A$, gives the remainder of the complet⟨
division of A by D.   If D is zero, the result supplied is the value of A.

$$8 \mid 23 \quad 12 \quad 9.3$$
$$7 \quad 4 \quad 1.3$$

$$1.2 \mid 2 \quad 5 \quad 6 \quad 3.1$$
$$0.8 \quad 0.2 \quad 0.7$$

$$0 \mid 6 \quad 17 \quad {}^-2$$
$$6 \quad 17 \quad {}^-2$$

In the case of nagative values, a problem arises. In effect, when 27 is divided by $^-5$, it can be written that 27 is equal to :

- either $(^-5 \times {}^-6)-3$ in which case the residue is $^-3$
- or $(^-5 \times {}^-5)+2$ in which case the residue is 2

In the first version of APL (APL/360), the smallest whole POSITIVE R satisfying the relationship $A \equiv (D \times Q)+R$ was adopted. In the example above, the residue would have been 2.

This choice has been abandonned, and in modern versions of APL, the residue given by $D \mid A$ is ALWAYS between 0 and D. With this convention, $^-5 \mid 27$ gives $^-3$ for a result.

A formal definition of the RESIDUE function will be found in the appendix which explains the reason for this choice.
Here are some examples demonstrating this :

$$R \leftarrow D \mid A \qquad\qquad\qquad\qquad A \equiv R + D \times Q$$

$5 \mid 43$	equals : 3	In effect : $43 \equiv 3 + 5 \times 8$
$^-5 \mid 43$	equals : $^-2$	In effect : $43 \equiv {}^-2 + {}^-5 \times {}^-9$
$5 \mid {}^-43$	equals : 2	In effect : $^-43 \equiv 2 + 5 \times {}^-9$
$^-5 \mid {}^-43$	equals : $^-3$	In effect : $^-43 \equiv {}^-3 + {}^-5 \times 8$

In every case, R and D have the same sign.

APPLICATIONS

In the same way that the whole number part of a decimal number is obtained by $\lfloor N$ its decimal part can be obtained by either $1 \top N$, or by $1 \mid N$.
If N can be negative, it is then advisable to work in absolute value : $1 \mid\mid N$.

Rotation of 123 elements applied to a vector of 17 elements (123ϕV), is equivalent to $(17 \mid 123)\phi V$ or $4\phi V$.

Here, is a simpler example :

```
        4 | 13
   1
       13 ⌽ 5 6 7 8
  6 7 8 5
       1 ⌽ 5 6 7 8
  6 7 8 5
```

8-18   LOGARITHMS

The base B logarith M of A is written: $L \leftarrow B ⍟ A$. This is a value such that $B*L$ is equal to A.

The LOGARITHM function is a scalar function. The symbol ⍟ is obtained by overstriking the symbols O and * if it is not on the keyboard.

```
       10 ⍟ 1000
    3
       3 ⍟ 81
    4
       10 ⍟ 2
 0.3010299957
```

NATURAL or NEPERIAN LOGARITHMS

Base e logarithms (e=2.71828), also called Neperian or natural logarithms, are a special type of much used logarithm. They are obtained by the monadic form of the LOGARITHM function.

```
       ⍟ 10
 2.302585093
       ⍟ * 1
    1
      (*1) ⍟ 10
 2.302585093
```

Between the natural logarithm of A and its base B logarithm, there are the following relationships:

$$N \leftarrow ⍟ A$$
$$L \leftarrow B ⍟ A$$

1) $N \equiv L \times ⍟B$

2) $L \equiv N \times B⍟e$ with e = 2.718281828459045

FACTORIAL

The product of the first N whole numbers is called the FACTORIAL of the number N. It is written $!N$ in APL (the symbol $!$ being formed by overstriking . and ').

```
    ! 5
120
```

As is customary, $!0$ is equal to one.

```
   ! 0 1 2 3 4 5 6
 1  1  2  6 24 120  720
```

If the argument is not a whole number, $!N$ gives the value of the GAMMA function of $N+1$. This point is dealt with in the supplement, in paragraph 8-28.

COMBINATIONS

$!N$ represents the number of ways in which it is possible to arrange N objects.

If P objects are taken from N, the number of possible combinations is equal to :

$$(!N) \div (!P) \times (!N-P)$$

This value usually written C_N^P in mathematics, is written : $P!N$

For example, there are $13!52$ possible deals for a bridge player, i.e exactly: 635013559600 deals.

If P is greater than N, the result of $P!N$ is of course zero

$(0,\iota N)!N$ gives the coefficients of the expansion of $(x+1)^N$, also the expression $P!N$ is called the binomial coefficient.

The succession of these coefficients can be obtained as follows :

```
  φ (0,X) °.! X ← ι4
1  1  0  0  0
1  2  1  0  0
1  3  3  1  0
1  4  6  4  1            coefficients of the expansion of (x+1)⁴
```
coefficients of the expansion of $(x+1)^4$

8-21   TRIGONOMETRIC FUNCTIONS

The constant Pl is very useful in many technical studies.

In the same way that e is obtained from *1, the constant π is obtained from
01.

Hence, the function on gives the value of πXn.

> o 1 2 0.5
>   3.141592654 6.283185307 1.570796327

It is possible to use the trigonometric functions $sinx$, $cosx$, $tanx$, and their
inverse $Arcsinx$, $Arccosx$, $Arctanx$. Similarly, there are hyperbolic trigonometric functions, which are written hsx, hcx, htx, and their inverse : $Arghsx$,
$Arghcx$, $Arghtx$.

All these functions are supplied by the dyadic scalar function o. According
to the value of F, the expression FoA gives one of the trigonometrical or
hyperbolic functions of A.

                2 o A   signifies $cos\ A$

                5 o A   signifies $hs\ A$

               $^-$2 o A   signifies $Arccos\ A$

The table below gives the significance of FoA as a function of F.

F	FoA	F	FoA
0	$(1-A*2)*0.5$	0	$(1-A*2)*0.5$
1	$Sin\ A$	$^-$1	$Arcsin\ A$
2	$Cos\ A$	$^-$2	$Arccos\ A$
3	$Tan\ A$	$^-$3	$Arstan\ A$
4	$(1+A*2)*0.5$	$^-$4	$(^-1+A*2)*0.5$
5	$Hs\ A$	$^-$5	$Arghs\ A$
6	$Hc\ A$	$^-$6	$Arghc\ A$
7	$Ht\ A$	$^-$7	$Arght\ A$

The positive values of F give direct functions, whereas the negative values
give inverse functions. However, take notice that $(-FoA)$ is different from
$(-F)oA$.

It is important to specify that for circular functions (F = 1, 2 or 3), the operand A must be given in RADIANS. For inverse circular functions (F = ‾1 ‾2 or ‾3), it is the result which is given in radians.

Examples :

                          1 2 3 o o÷3
         0.8660254038 0.5 1.732050808   (that being sin π/3 , cos π/3 , tan π/3)

NOTE : the notation o÷3 does not signify that the symbol o in itself represents the value π. This is the function o applied to the result of ÷3, i.e 0.333.

                          1 2 o o÷2
         1   1.743934249E‾16   (that being sin π/2 and cos π/2)

The last result shows a rounding off fault in the operations which leads to the computing of the trigonometrical lines. The result will be taken as equal to 1 0.

                          8 o 2.1
            DOMAIN ERROR
                 8 o 2.1
                 ∧

The value 8 is not acceptable as a left hand argument of the function o.

                    (‾3 o 1) = (o 0.25)
            1

This result confirms that $Arctan$ 1 is equal to $\frac{\pi}{4}$.

EXERCISES

[18] In order to place a number N in relation to two given limits in the form of a vector L, one of the following results is sought :

                    ‾2 if N is less than the two values

                    ‾1 if N is equal to the lowest

                    0 if N is between the two values

                    1 if N is equal to the highest value

                    2 if N is greater than the two values.

     Write the necessary expression.

[19] Explain why the sequence of the four functions + - X ÷ , carried out
in any order, gives the result ¯1 when it is applied to any positive
whole number.

¯1   + X - ÷ 4

¯1   X ÷ - + 6

¯1   - ÷ + X 7

[20] A value close to $cos x$ can be computed by the following limited expansion
(in conventional notation) :

$$cos\ x \simeq \frac{x^0}{0!} - \frac{x^2}{2!} + \frac{x^4}{4!} - \frac{x^6}{6!} + \frac{x^8}{8!} - \cdots\cdots$$

Write the APL expression which accomplishes this calculation, by extending the expansion upto the power $2N$.

[21] Calculate the following expressions, then check on the computer :

(1 ○ ○ ÷ ι4) * 2

¯8 | 15 ¯31 19

2 X 0.5 + ¯2 ○ 1 ○ 0.5

[22] The degree of acidity of a solution is represented by a quantity which
is called pH, and which is the decimal logarithm of the inverse of
the concentration of hydrogen ions in the solution. If C is this
concentration, which expression gives the pH ?

[23] Find all the factors of a whole number N.

[24] How can one extract the elements of a vector which deviate by more
than 10% above or below the average of the terms.

[25] How can the two elements with the smallest difference between them
be extracted from a vector ? Assume that there is only one answer.

       MINIDIFF 12 34 51 78 42 37 91 70 55 62
   34   37

[26] A set in table-tennis is played to 21 points. However, if the two
players have a difference of only one point, the set is continued until
one of the players has two points more than the other.

The vector of the points obtained by both players A and B is called
SCORE. For example SCORE equals 14 19.
Write an expression which indicates whether the set is over or not
by a binary result (1=over, 0=not over).

[27] Two systems enable the sensitivity of a photographic film to be
     represented : the DIN standard, and the ASA standard.

     The DIN degrees increase arithmetically : 15 16 17 18 ...
     whereas the ASA degrees increase geometrically : 25 32 40 50 64 80 100..

     The increase of 3 DIN degrees corresponds to the doubling of the
     sensitivity expressed in ASA.

     Knowing that 15 DIN equals 25 ASA, write the two expressions which
     convert DIN degrees into ASA, and vice versa, and calculate the ASA
     sensitivities which correspond to DIN degrees from 15 to 30.

     As an indication, here is this table of corresponding values. The
     values are rounded off so as to be more handy for photographers.

DIN	ASA	DIN	ASA
15	25	23	160
16	32	24	200
17	40	25	250
18	50	26	320
19	64	27	400
20	80	28	500
21	100	29	640
22	125	30	800

DRAWING BY RUMWEISS

8-22   INVERSION OF RECTANGULAR MATRICES

In paragraphs 8-5 to 8-7 we discovered the use of the DOMINO function which
assumes that a rectangular matrix possesses an inverse matrix.
Moreover, the polynomial regression, as described in paragraph 8-7, is only
a very special case of multi-linear regression.

The following pages are intended to specify the mathematical bases of the
concepts studied in chapter 8, and to extend the scope of applications of
the DOMINO function.

8-23   A PROBLEM ALREADY SOLVED

A company director enamoured of mathematics tries to understand what factors
determine the total travelling and official entertaining expenses of the
different commercial agencies of his company, certainly with the ulterior
motive of knowing which agencies are well and badly managed.

He maintains that these expenses are explained according to four factors only
(what touching naïvety), which are :

        - the number of commercial travellers in the agency (PERS),

        - the geographical size of the area covered by the agency,
          which is measured by the distance which seperates the agency
          from its furthest client (Km),

        - the number of clients of the agency (NCLI),

        - the annual turnover of the agency, expressed in thousands
          of Dollars (TURN).

Therefore, it is a question of finding five coefficients a_0, a_1, a_2, a_3, and
a_4 such that the total of the expenses is equal to :

$$a_0 + a_1 PERS + a_2 Km + a_3 NCLI + a_3 TURN$$

Here is the array of the elements available :

EXPENSES	PERS	Km	NCLI	TURN
40420	25	90	430	2400
23000	20	50	87	9000
28110	24	12	72	9500
32460	24	12	210	4100
25800	14	30	144	6500

Therefore a set of 5 equations must be solved of which the 5 unknowns are a_0, a_1, a_2, a_3, and a_4.

We will call Y the vector of the involved expenses.

If we call FAC the matrix of the explanatory factors (last 4 columns of the above array), then the matrix of the coefficients of the unknowns is obtained by :

$$\Box \leftarrow M \leftarrow 1, FAC$$

```
1   25   90   430 2400
1   20   50    87 9000
1   24   12    72 9500
1   24   12   210 4100
1   14   30   144 6500
```

The 1's indicate that a_0 is always assigned to the coefficient 1.

The coefficients sought by our technocrat are thus obtained by a dyadic DOMINO; this is a problem which we have already solved.

$$\Box \leftarrow ROUND\ C \leftarrow Y\ \boxminus\ M$$

```
3159.69  194.89  ‾130.04  93.67  1.59
```

The expenses Y would be obtained by the product :

$$M\ +.\times\ C$$

```
40420  23000  28110  32460  25800
```

-24   MULTI-LINEAR REGRESSION

Unfortunately, this company does not have 5, but 12 commercial agencies. On the following page, the vector Y of expenses and the matrix FAC of factors which attempt to explain these are printed.

40420	25	90	430	2400
23000	20	50	87	9000
28110	24	12	72	9500
32460	24	12	210	4100
25800	14	30	144	6500
54980	29	130	621	3500
52300	28	14	633	3200
49910	28	214	509	5300
31580	21	12	401	3500
31840	13	14	388	2500
27120	20	50	207	6200
47680	30	150	501	1600

Y FAC

There are now more equations than unknowns, and the system no longer has a
solution. But, it can be demonstrated mathematically that it is possible
to find other coefficients C such that the expression M +.× C no longer
restores Y (which is impossible), but a vector of estimates $ESTY$ such that
the sum

          +/ $(Y-ESTY)$ * 2   is minimal.

In other words, the sum of the squares of the distances between the estimated
values and the actual values is minimised.

It is also shown :

> 1) that the coefficients C are obtained on the basis of Y by
>   linear application, hence a matrix product :

$$C \leftarrow W +.× Y$$

> 2) that the matrix W is unique

> 3) that it is equal to :

$W \leftarrow (\boxdot\ (\lozenge M)+.×M\ )\ +.×\ (\lozenge M)$

          or again :

$W \leftarrow (\lozenge M)\ \boxdot\ (\lozenge M)\ +.×\ M$

In effect one has the right to apply the DOMINO function to the product
$(\lozenge M)+.×M$, which gives a square matrix.

Thus it is said that a multi-linear regression has been achieved. We will
carry out these calculations on the data displayed above:

$$M \leftarrow 1,FAC$$
$$W \leftarrow (\lozenge M)\ \boxdot\ (\lozenge M)\ +.×\ M$$

    $C \leftarrow W +.\times Y$

 3804.417444   609.4792591   15.69507624   45.13488095   0.51340338606

The estimated values of expenses would be :

    $ESTY \leftarrow M +.\times C$

    $\lceil 0.5 + ESTY$

 41094 25326 26747 30204 22645 53345 51303 49923 36688 30743
         29305 47877

In order to know how the agencies are placed in relation to the estimated
values, the relative differences can be calculated (in percentages) :

    $\lceil 0.5 + 100 \times (Y-ESTY) \div ESTY$

  ¯2 ¯9   5   7   14   3   2   0   ¯14   4   ¯7   0

The fifth agency is very much below the normal rate, whereas the second and
ninth agencies appear to be very economical.

IMPORTANT PROPERTY

-25

FIRST PROPERTY

We have said that W is obtained by : $(\boxminus (\lozenge M)+.\times M) +.\times (\lozenge M)$

The product $W+.\times M$ would thus equal : $(\boxminus \underline{(\lozenge M)+.\times M}) +.\times \underline{(\lozenge M)+.\times M}$

We will call U the product $(\lozenge M)+.\times M$: $(\quad \boxminus U\quad) +.\times \quad U$

By definition, the unit matrix   is obtained : I

If $W+.\times M$ gives a unit matrix, it is because W is the LEFT INVERSE OF M.

It is easy to verify this with the values obtained :

         $ROUND\ W+.\times M$

    1 0 0 0 0
    0 1 0 0 0
    0 0 1 0 0
    0 0 0 1 0
    0 0 0 0 1

SECOND PROPERTY

Since W is such that $+/,(Y-ESTY)*2$ is minimal, we will replace $ESTY$ by its value $M+.\times C$, and replace C by its value $W+.\times Y$.

Hence, $Y-ESTY$ can be written: $Y - M+.\times W+.\times Y$
We will replace Y by $I+.\times Y$, where I is the adequate unit matrix:
$Y-ESTY$ is written $(I+.\times Y)-M+.\times W+.\times Y$

Making Y a factor : $(I-M+.\times W)+.\times Y$ is obtained.

By definition, the sum $+/,((I-M+.\times W)+.\times Y)*2$ is thus minimal. Now as W is calculated independantly of Y, this property must remain true no matter what Y is. This is possible only if $+/,(I-M+.\times W)*2$ is itself minimal. This can]
confirmed by replacing Y by I.

W behaves like a pseudo-inverse of M on the right, such that $+/,(I-M+.\times W)*2$ is minimal.

> In APL, W will be called an inverse matrix of M, and the
> DOMINO function will be extended to the calculation of such
> an inverse: $W \leftarrow \boxdiv M$

SUMMARY

In APL, a matrix M having more lines than columns has an inverse, which is calculated by $\boxdiv M$. This value is strictly equal, within rounding off errors,
to the following two forms:

$$(\boxdiv * \lozenge M)+.\times M\ )\ +.\times\ (\lozenge M)$$

$$(\lozenge M)\ \boxdiv\ (\lozenge M)\ +.\times\ M$$

This matrix is the left inverse of M, which signifies that the product $(\boxdiv M)+.$
gives a unit matrix.

This is a pseudo-right inverse of M, that is to say that the product $M+.\times(\boxdiv M)$
does not give a unit matrix, but a matrix J such that the sum of $+/,(I-J)*2$
is minimal.

The result of this is to minimise any expression of the form:

$$+/,((I-J)+.\times Y)*2$$

This last property explains the use made by the DOMINO function to accomplish
linear, multi-linear or polynomial regression calculations.

PARTICULAR CASES

POLYNOMIAL REGRESSION

Multi-linear regression expresses a value Y in terms of several explanatory
factors $F1$, $F2$, $F3$, ... which are independant of one another.
However, these factors may not be independant. This is the case when columns
which make up the matrix of the explanatory factors are the successive powers
of the same vector of explanatry values. Thus it is this particular aspect
of regression that we used to accomplish a polynomial regression in paragraph
8-7.

SCALARS AND VECTORS

A scalar will be treated in such a way that $S⌹$ is equal to $÷S$, with the
difference, however, that $0÷0$ equals 1, while $0⌹0$ causes a domain error.

Vectors are treated like matrices of a single column.

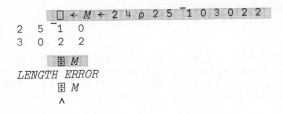

```
      ⎕ ← CEV ← ⌹ VEC ← 2 ¯1 0.5
0.380952381  ¯0.1904761905  0.09523809524

      CEV +.× VEC
1

      VEC +.× CEV
1
```

SINGULAR MATRICES

If simultaneous equations comprise more unknowns than independent equations,
it is understood that there is an infinite number of possible solutions.
Consequently, it will not be possible to define a single inverse to the
matrix of the coefficients.
A matrix with more columns than lines has no inverse.

```
      ⎕ ← M ← 2 4 ρ 2 5 ¯1 0 3 0 2 2
2  5 ¯1  0
3  0  2  2
      ⌹ M
LENGTH ERROR
      ⌹ M
      ∧
```

A direct result of this is that we if we try to carry out a regression of a sp
of n points by a polinomial of degree n or more, an error will be diagnosed
by the computer.

On the other hand, if n points are situated exactly on a polynomial of
degree p (with $p<n$), and we attempt to adjust them by a polynomial of a higher
degree, the surplus coefficients will be zero.

        $X \leftarrow 0,18$
        $Y \leftarrow (X-1)\times(X-5)$

        $Y \boxminus X \circ .* \; 0 \; 1 \; 2 \; 3 \; 4 \; 5$
    5 ‾6 1 ‾1.694233326E‾15   2.428354161E‾16   ‾1.278799058E‾17

SIMULTANEOUS SYSTEMS

In all our examples of solving simultaneous equations, the constants were
always represented by a vector, nothing prevents the simultaneous solution
of several simultaneous equations having the same matrix of coefficients,
using a matrix of constant terms instead of a vector.

This possibility is of little significance. On the other hand, the same set
of explanatory variables can be used to explain several results. Hence, in
the example of paragraph 8-24 , the same matrix of factors could be used to
try to explain other phenomena, such as the rate of absenteeism of commercial
personnel.

It is sufficient, in such a case, that Y should no longer be a vector, but
a matrix.

8-27   GENERATING RANDOM NUMBERS

The algorithm of generation of random values employs an initial value called
the random ROOT. Each time a new value is generated, the root is changed.
However, when a user starts a working session, the random root is given by
the APL system, and always takes the same value (which is 7^5 on IBM computers,
for example).

If this APL user types the same expression after several days interval he
will obtain the same results, since the initial root will be the same. This
can be useful if it is wished to return to the exact conditions to where
a job had developped, but this can also be a handicap.

To escape from this repetition, or to produce it voluntarily, it is possible to arbitarily fix the random root at any time. One easy way of obtaining different working conditions each time consists of generating a variable number of random values before any job. These numbers will not be used, but $\Box RL$ will have taken any value.

> $USELESS \leftarrow \Box TS[6] ? 100$

This method is valid no matter which algorithm is used by the system being worked on. This instruction can be contained in $\Box LX$.

-28

COMPUTING UTILITIES

RESIDUE

Formally, $D|A$ is strictly equal to $A-D\times\lfloor A\div D+D=0$

From this expression it is ascertained that if D is zero, $D|A$ is equal to A.

It is equally established that this definition is such that the result R of $D|A$ is ALWAYS of the same sign as D. This rule has already been stated.

GAMMA FUNCTION

In mathematics, the gamma function of a positive variable x is defined by the following formula :

$$\Gamma(x) \quad = \quad \int_0^\infty t^{x-1} e^{-t} dt$$

This is a function which verifies the recurrence relationship :
> $\Gamma(x) = x, \Gamma(x-1)$

For the whole value of x, it is found that $\Gamma(x) = (x-1)!$

In APL, the function ! gives the value of the GAMMA function directly.

> `! 2.4  3  3.2  3.4`
> 2.981206427 6 7.756689536 10.13610185

The dyadic use of ! with non-whole values, gives the BETA function.

CHAPTER 9

THE EXECUTE FUNCTION

PRINTING CONTROL

Upto now, numbers and characters could be associated only for comparisons
(= ≠ ε ι), or for the needs of printing in a defined function.
This seperation can sometimes be a handicap, and APL systems which appeared
in the early 70's have included functions which convert numbers into characters
(FORMAT function ⊤ , seen in paragraph 4-16), or numeric characters into
numbers (EXECUTE function ⍎ which is studied below).

We will now study these possibilities in detail.

9-1   THE EXECUTE FUNCTION

The EXECUTE function is represented by the symbol ⍎, ∘(jot) and ⊥(decode)
overstruck, on terminals not having the symbol ⍎ . It is a monadic function
which only accepts a vector of characters as an argument. If this string of
characters is an APL expression of correct syntax, the EXECUTE function will
cause its evaluation, in the same way as if these characters had been typed
on the keyboard in execution mode.

An example will clarify this :

>   *LETTERS* ← '5+6×2'
>   *LETTERS*
> 5+6×2
>
>   ⍎ *LETTERS*
> 17

The EXECUTE function has brought about the evaluation of the expression
5+6X2.

The APL expression given as argument can contain :

> - numeric values, or names of variables,
>
> - primitive functions,
>
> - defined functions,
>
> - assignments, print-outs, value requests (⎕ and ⍞),
>
> - it can even contain further calls for the function ⍎ .

      ♠ '3 + AVERAGE 8 9'   the argument contains a function

 11.5

      ♠ '□ ← 3+X ← □'   the argument contains a value request

□:   and a print-out order.

      27

 30

It can be confirmed that the execution below has given rise to a variable X.

     X

   27

The EXECUTE function enables numeric data to be gathered in a string of characters, and to transform them into numbers. It is therefore advisable to be careful to seperate the successive values by blanks, to avoid combining them into a single value. Here are two attempts to illustrate this use :

     OPINION ← 'MRS ARTHUR IS 32 OR 33 YEARS OLD'
     NUMER □ ← OPINION⌈15 16⌉
   32
   0

The use of the *NUMER* function, written in paragraph 6-1, confirms that the part of the vector extracted is not numeric.

      □ ← AGE ← ♠ OPINION⌈15 16 21 22⌉
   3233

We have to seperate the characters by blanks, and Mrs ARTHUR is approximately attributed the age of RAMESES II ! A fresh attempt will be better :

      □ ← AGE ← ♠ OPINION⌈15 16 17 21 22⌉
   32 33
      NUMER AGE
   1

The result is a numeric vector of two elements.

9-2   CONDITIONS OF USE

It has already been said that the argument of the EXECUTE function must be a
vector. If the syntax of the expression represented by this vector is incor
rect, an error message is issued.

>   ⍎ '(3+2]×5'
> ⍎ *SYNTAX ERROR*
>   (3+2]×5
>   ∧

The argument can not be a command of the system, nor can it contain a define
function opening, nor a semi-colon. Hence, the following expressions will
be rejected :

>   ⍎ ')*SAVE*'

>   ⍎ '∇ *AVERAGE*[□]∇'

>   ⍎ '5+1 ; 2+2'

Finally in order for the EXECUTE function to produce a result, the string of
characters executed must itself produce an assignable result. Thus the
result of the expression ⍎*A* can be assigned or used on condition that *A*:

>   - is not an empty vector or comprising only blanks,

>   - contains neither branching (→) nor comment (⍝),

>   - is not an implicit function.

The expressions below are   On the other hand, the following
    therefore correct :   expressions will produce an
                                                            error :

>   ⍎ ''   *T* ← ⍎ ''

>   ⍎ '   '   *3* ↑ ⍎ '   '

>   ⍎ '→3'   *JUMP* ← ⍎ '→3'

>   ⍎ '*CONSULT*'   ρ ⍎ '*CONSULT*'

9-3   USES OF THE EXECUTE FUNCTION

The EXECUTE function has numerous applications, of which the following are
the most common. Other applications will be studied in the supplement.

USE OF THE QUOTE-QUAD

The introduction of a value in a function through a QUAD causes print-out of
the symbol □: . This leads to a significant consumption of paper on the
printing terminal, or skipping and disappearence of the messages and values
introduced, in the case of a cathode ray screen terminal.

Here is a characteristic example of an entry accomplished in this way:

```
SURNAME, FORENAME        ?
BONAZEAU PAUL
DATE OF BIRTH ?
□:
       42
SERVICE ?
□:
       11
MONTHLY HOURS ?
□:
       172


SURNAME, FORENAME        ?
```

            etc........

The use of the quad can be replaced by a quote-quad followed by an EXECUTE.
In a way ⍎⍞ replaces □ . If the "bare-output" shown in paragraph 4-35 is
used, it can result in a far more agreeable entry, of which the principle is:

```
          ∇ R ← CALL MSG
[1]       ⍞ ← (24↑MSG),': '
[2]       R ← 26↓⍞
          ∇


          ∇ ENTRY
[1]       NA ← CALL 'SURNAME, FORENAME       '
[2]       YR ← 1900+ ⍎ CALL 'DATE OF BIRTH'
[3]       SCE ← ⍎ CALL 'SERVICE'
[4]       MH  ← ⍎ CALL 'MONTHLY HOURS'
[5]
          continuation of the function
```

Here is what the preceeding entry would look like with this method of working:

```
SURNAME,     FORENAME    : MILANO SYLVIE
DATE OF BIRTH            : 49
SERVICE                 : 8
MONTHLY HOURS           : 87

SURNAME,     FORENAME    : MIALON ELIANE
```

            etc ......

It can be seen that the presentation is more compact, and the reading of it
is greatly eased by the alignment of the operator's answers.
This method also has its dangers; if the operator makes a mistake and types ,
for example, an incorrect character (17.518.4 instead of 17.5 18.4), he will
cause the function to be interrupted and the transmission of an error diagnostic.

If a simple quad had been used, the same diagnostic would have appeared, but the function would not have been interrupted and the computer would again await a value.

In the same way, the introduction of a carriage-return is not restricting for a simple quad, whereas it causes an error in the function *ENTRY*, since the application of EXECUTE to an empty vector does not give an assignable result.

To escape from this snag, most frequently the following will be written :

$$1\uparrow\pm(CALL\ MSG),'\ 0'$$

If the operator types a carriage-return, the value introduced is 0.

DYNAMIC ASSIGNMENT

A function can dynamically create variables whose names are defined at the moment of its execution.

```
        ∇ COMPUTAVERAGE ; NOP
[1]     'OPERAND NAME ?'
[2]     ON ← ⍞
[3]     'RESULT NAME ?'
[4]     ⍎ ⍞ , '←(+/' , ON , ')÷ρ' , ON
        ∇
```

We will imagine that we wish to calculate the average of the elements of an array *COSTS* of which the value is :

```
        COSTS
120   95   110   240   225   100   220   180   160   160
```

```
        COMPUTAVERAGE
OPERAND NAME ?
COSTS
RESULT NAME ?
 AVG
```

No answer appeared, but the average of the vector has been calculated and assigned to a variable *AVG* created for this circumstance.

In effect, in line [2] of the function, *ON* takes the value *'COSTS'*. In line [4], the catenation of *'AVG'* and the other character strings give :

$$AVG \leftarrow (+/COSTS) \div \rho COSTS$$

The EXECUTE function thus causes the execution of this expression, as can be verified after the function has been completed:

```
        AVG
```

SELECTIVE EXECUTION OF FUNCTIONS

A use, very close to the previous one consists of the user choosing a
computing process.
We will imagine that three methods enable an approximate value of a variable
to be calculated. Three functions *CAL1*, *CAL2* and *CAL3*, are each used to
accomplish one of these calculations. If we wish to leave it to the operator
to choose the method of computing which appears to him as the most appropriate
in terms of the partial results already obtained, a function having essentially the following structure must be constructed :

> ...   *beginning of the function*
>
> [10] *'WHICH METHOD DO YOU SUGGEST ?'*
> [11] →(*L1,L2,L3*)⌈□⌉
> [12] *L1: R←CAL1 X*
> [13] →*NEXT*
> [14] *L2: R←CAL2 X*
> [15] →*NEXT*
> [16] *L3: R←CAL3 X*
> [17] *NEXT:* ... *continuation of the function* ....

The use of the EXECUTE function enables this function to be considerably
simplified by omitting lines [12] to [16].

> ...   *beginning of the function*
>
> [10] *'WHICH METHOD DO YOU SUGGEST ?'*
> [11] ⍎ *'R←CAL'* , ⎕ , *' X'*
> [17] ... *continuation of the function* ....

If the operator answers 2 to the question which has been asked, line [11]
forms, then executes, the character string : *R←CAL2 X*

CONDITIONAL EXECUTION

Some APL users use a similar means to avoid jumps in the functions.
If the function *IF* is created

> ∇ *R ← A IF COND*
>
> [1]   *R←COND/A*
>
> ∇

The series of instructions opposite

> [7]   →(*X*=0)/9
> [8]   *FUNCTION*
> [9]   *next* .....

can be replaced by :   [7]   ⍎ *'FUNCTION' IF X≠0*
                                     [8]   *next ....*

This proceedure is attractive because it gives a clear programming. However, it is strictly not advised because of the large amount of work required of the computer each time the EXECUTE function is called. The repeated use of this form of programming leads to a heavy consumption of computing time.

There are other uses of the EXECUTE function. These will be stated in the supplement of this chapter.
To conclude, here are three functions which have become classics, whose only aim is to entertain :

```
          ∇ IF CONDITION
[1]    ⍎ ⍎ 'FV'[1+CONDITION]
          ∇

          ∇ R←A THEN B
[1]    R←A
[2]    V←B
          ∇

          ∇ R←A ELSE B
[1]    R←A
[2]    F←B
          ∇
```

Here are two examples of how these can be used :

        IF (A≡B) THEN 'R←AVERAGE T' ELSE 'A←A+1'

        IF X>0 THEN 'A←10' ELSE 'B←30'

We will examine the last example :

The variables *F* and *V* take the values '*B←30*' and '*A←10*' respectively.

If *X* is, for example, negative; (*X>0*) equals 0. This is the value of *CONDITIC*

        '*FV*' [1+*CONDITION*]   thus equals   '*F*'

        ⍎ '*F*'   gives the value   '*B←30*'

        ⍎ '*B←30*'   has the effect of giving the value 30 to *B*.

DRAWING BY RUMWEISS

9-4   THE FORMAT FUNCTION

In APL, presentation of numeric results is taken over by the computer.   Thi
presentation does not always conform to what the user would like.   Moreover
this presentation is almost unforseeable, which prohibits the computer from
filling in pre-printed documents, such as invoices or pay slips.

As an example, here is the print-out of a matrix by the computer; it can be
seen that a lot of space is wasted: .

```
      1                     4                     0.5
      2                    ‾1                     0
      0                     1                     6
```

Here are two matrices which are identical in appearance.   The first comes
from multiplying a matrix by its inverse.   The l's and 0's are actually
rounded off numbers of fairly complex values, and the computer gives them
a very spacious presentation (space used for the decimal values).   The seco
is obtained by an operation giving a boolean result; the computer represent
them in a compact space.

```
        □←M←0.01×⌊0.5+100×(⍉T)+.×T←3 3ρ1 4 0.5 2 ‾1 0 0 1 6
  1        0      0
  0        1      0
  0        0      1

        1 2 3 ∘.= 1 2 3
    1 0 0
    0 1 0
    0 0 1
```

In order to enable the APL user to impose the presentation suited to him,
APL versions after 1970 have means of putting the data into shape.   The mos
widespread means is the FORMAT function, which is written ⍕ , by superimpo
ing ∘ (Jot) on ⊤ (encode).

Furthermore, this function has the effect of converting numeric values into
arrays of characters.   Thus it makes possible the catenation of character
strings to numeric values converted into characters.   This use of the FORMA
function is demonstrated ⍳n paragrph 4-16.

On the S.T.S.C APL*PLUS system a function for putting into shape called □F
carries out the same type of work.   This is a function which performs far
more refinements of presentation, but whose use is far more awkward.
Some systems offer their fortunate users both these possibilites, we hope
that you are one of those.

NOTE : APL*PLUS is the registered trade-mark (U.S) of the time sharing
service of Scientific Time Sharing Corporation.

-5

IMPLICIT PRESENTATION

The FORMAT function used in its monadic form simply converts its argument into a character string identical to the print-out which the computer would give. This use was mentioned in paragraph 4-16.

Example :
```
      'MRS ARTHUR IS ', (⍕30+2) , 'YEARS OLD'
   MRS ARTHUR IS 32 YEARS OLD
```

It was possible to catenate the numeric value to characters. This property is equally true for matrices and arrays of higher rank. Thus the function *WRAP*, studied in paragraph 6-3 can be used.

```
      WRAP ⍕ 2 4⍴⍳8
 |----------|
 | 1 2 3 4|
 | 5 6 7 8|
 |_____|
```

In this form, the FORMAT function enables numbers and characters to be printed simultaneously, but does not enable the presentation to be checked, which is still accomplished by the computer. In order to obtain a thorough check of the printing produced, the dyadic form of FORMAT must be used.

We can say that the monadic FORMAT function has no effect on a character string.

```
       ⍕ 'FORMAT'
   FORMAT
```

EXPLICIT PRESENTATION

6

In its dyadic form, FORMAT accepts the name of the variable to be printed as a right hand argument, and a vector of numeric descriptors used to specify the desired presentation as a left hand argument :   *DESC ⍕ VARIABLE*

If the variable to be printed is a vector of n elements, or an array of n columns, the left hand argument will be a vector of n PAIRS of descriptors, each pair of numbers describing the presentation of a column of the result.

  - The first number of each pair indicates the width of the paper
    (measured in number of characters) which will be set aside
    for the value to be printed.

  - The second number of each pair indicates with how many decimal
    places this value will be printed.

For example, the expression 5 2 9 3 8 0 ▼ 2.6 153.0897 78.37 is used to
indicate that :
  - the value 2.6 will be printed on 5 characters, with two decimal

  - the value 153.0897 will be printed on 9 characters with three
    decimals,

  - the value 78.37 will be printed on 8 characters without
    decimals.

Here is the result produced. We have indicated the zones reserved for each
value by the small numbers printed underneath the computer's answer.

      5 2 9 3 8 0 ▼ 2.6   153.0897   78.37

   2.60   153.090   78

  12345
       123456789
                12345678

It can be seen that the computer has carried out the necessary rounding offs.

CONDITIONS OF USE

The width of the zone reserved for each value must be sufficient to contain:

          - the whole number part,

          - the number of decimal places requested,

          - the decimal point, if decimal numbers have been requested,

          - possibly the minus sign, if the value is negative.

If this is not the case, a DOMAIN ERROR will be diagnosed.

In the case of a matrix (or of an array of higher rank), the same width being
assigned to all the elements of the same column, it is advisable to define
a width sufficient for the element which requires the most space.

      3 0 11 2 7 4 ▼ 3 3ρ2 7.122 0.4 9.2 918273 2.0017 144.1 3 7

       2   7.12 0.4000
       9   918273.00 2.0017
     144   3.00 7.0000

It is also advisable to count, in the space reserved for each element, a width sufficient for at least one space to seperate two successive values. In this respect, the preceeding example is hardly readable, and a more spacious presentation would be desirable.

In the case of negative values, the FORMAT function rounds off the ABSOLUTE VALUE of the number to be printed. Here is an application of this :

```
      U
  2.3    2.8    6.81    6.87    9.34    7.5
 ‾2.3   ‾2.8   ‾6.81   ‾6.87   ‾9.34   ‾7.5


    6 1 ▼ U
  2.3    2.8   6.8    6.9    9.3    7.5
 ‾2.3   ‾2.8  ‾6.8   ‾6.9   ‾9.3   ‾7.5
```

In this last example, the left hand argument comprises a single pair of numbers. In such cases, all the elements of the array will be printed in the same format.

PARTICULAR CASES

If the second number of a pair of descriptors is zero, the computer undertakes the printing in such a way that a single blank column will seperate the columns of printed values. The number of decimal places remains fixed as before.

```
   H ← 3 4 ρ 3.6 12.333 5 0 1 107 ‾2 45.7 51.29 ‾66 2 33

      0 1 0 2 0 0 0 8 2 ▼ H
  3.6  12.33   5    0.00
  1.0 107.00  ‾2   45.70
 51.3 ‾66.00   2   33.00
```


This is the most compact presentation possible; it is best to avoid using it.

Another particular case will be demonstrated in the supplement, in paragraph 9-16.

9-7   THE PRINTING CONTROL FUNCTION $\Box FMT$

The FORMAT function enables print-outs to be quikly checked, but does not allow a great subtlety of presentation. Some APL systems, prompted by the *APL*PLUS* system introduced by Scientific Time Sharing Corporation, have a printing function called $\Box FMT$.

□*FMT*   is usually available in the same way as other control functions (see chapter 10) or the primitive functions, by simply calling its name.

□*FMT*   enables print-outs to be checked by a series of descriptors.   These descriptors look like :

> - either the FORMAT instructions of the FORTRAN language (§9-9),
> - or the PICTURE instructions of the COBOL language (§9-11).

The following paragraphs deal with the study of the principle possibilities offered by □*FMT* .

9-8   SYNTAX OF THE PRINTING CONTROL FUNCTION

□*FMT*   is a dyadic function.

> - its left hand argument is a string of characters comprising descriptors separated from each other by commas,
>
> - its right hand argument is a variable name to be printed, or a list of variable names, separated by semi-colons, placed in brackets.

For example :   '*desc1 , desc2 , desc3 , ...* ' □*FMT* (*var1* ; *var2* ; *var3* ; ....

'*6A1 , 3I6 , I9 , F7.2*' □*FMT* (*NAME* ; *NUM* ; *RATE*)

Matrices are printed normally, the presentation of each column being controlled by a descriptor. On the other hand, as many data processing print-outs comprise columns of numbers, the □*FMT* function prints vectors VERTICALLY.

Each descriptor comprises,

> - a letter, which is the SPECIFICATION OF TYPE of the variable to be printed (characters, whole numbers, decimal numbers,...)
>
> - numeric values specifying the extent of the zones reserved for the printing, and its form,
>
> - qualifiers and decorators which will be studied later,
>
> - possibly a repetition factor, which enables the same descriptor to be applied to several columns of the result.

9-9   STUDY OF THE MAIN SPECIFICATIONS

THE *I* AND *F* SPECIFICATIONS

The printing of whole numbers is controlled by the *I* specification, which is written :

$$nIp$$

p = size of the zone reserved for the printing of a column,

n = number of columns of the result which will have to be printed in accordance with this format (repetition factor)

The printing of a decimal value is controlled by means of the *F* specification, which is written :

$$nFp.d$$

p = total size of the zone reserved for the printing of a column,

. = decimal point,

d = number of decimals to be printed (d<p),

n = repetition factor indicating how many columns will be printed according to this format.

We will apply these two specifications to an example.

We have a matrix of numbers (*BREAD*), the vector of the horizontal totals carried out in this matrix (*SUM*), a vector of the rate of contributions applicable to these sums (*RATE*) and the vector of the contributions due, obtained from the product :

$$CON \leftarrow SUM \times RATE \div 100$$

In order to have the total contributions, the following was carried out :

$CON \leftarrow CON$, +/*CON*

To print these data, the following format, for example, will be used :

$$'3I6 , I9 , F7.2 , F12.2'$$

3*I*6   the three columns of the matrix will be printed on 6 characters

*I*9   to assure that the totals are seperated, 9 columns are reserved for them

*F*7.2   the contribution rates will be printed with 2 decimals, on 7 characters

*F*12.2   the contributions due will be contained in a zone of 12 characters, with 2 decimals.

'3*I*6 , *I*9 , *F*7.2 , *F*12.2' ☐*FMT* (*BREAD* ; *SUM* ; *RATE* ; *CON*)

1200	530	0	1730	2.50	43.25
2300	210	540	3050	10.20	311.10
1820	0	0	1820	0.45	8.19
3450	560	0	4010	4.40	176.44
1070	440	300	1810	3.20	57.92
					596.90

It is seen that □FMT accepts the printing of variables of different lengths, by completing the shortest columns with blanks.

A AND X SPECIFICATIONS

As well as the numbers above, we have a matrix of surnames (*SURNS*), and a matrix of Forenames (*FRNAMES*).

SURNAMES	FORENAMES
JOBERT	JEAN
PEGOUT	CLAUDE
RUIZ	MARC
BOUILLE	YVES
MARNIER	LOUIS

The characters are printed by means of the *A* specification. It should be recalled that in APL each character is an independant element of a matrix, and thus printing of each column will be controlled separately.

$$nAp$$

p = number of printing positions reserved for each letter

n = repetition factor (number of similar columns)

For example :

        '3A1 , A2 , A1 , 2A3' □FMT SURNS

        JOR ER   T
        PEG OU   T
        RUI Z
        BOU IL   L E
        MAR NI   E R

It can be seen that the first three columns occupy a single character, the following occupies two, the following one, the last two occupy three.

        '6A2' □FMT   FRNAMES

        J E A N
        C L A U D E
        M A R C
        Y V E S
        L O U I S

Apart from the case where it is desired to distincly separate the letters of a matrix as above, only the nA1 specification will be used.

The *X*p specification enables p blank columns to be inserted between certain columns of the result. This specification is rendered necessary in order to print matrices of characters side by side :

'7A1,6A1' $\Box$FMT (SURNS;FRNAMES)

```
JOBERT JEAN
PEGOUT CLAUDE
RUIZ   MARC
BOUILLEYVES  }        the surnames are stuck to the forenames
MARNIERLOUIS }
```

'7A1,X2,6A1' $\Box$FMT (SURNS ; FRNAMES)

```
JOBERT    JEAN
PEGOUT    CLAUDE
RUIZ      MARC
BOUILLE   YVES        Two blank columns have been inserted
MARNIER   LOUIS
```

$\Box$ SPECIFICATION

A text can be inserted between the columns of the result. This text must be
flanked by the $\Box$ symbols.
For example, in order to plot a vertical line between the columns, $\Box|\Box$ will
be written in the format.

FOR ← '$\Box|\Box$,7A1,X2,6A1,$\Box$ | $\Box$,3I5,I9,$\Box$ A $\Box$,F5.2,$\Box$ = $\Box$,F6.2'

FOR $\Box$FMT (SURNS ; FRNAMES ; BREAD ; SUM ; RATE ; ¯1↓CON)

```
| JOBERT    JEAN    | 1200  530    0     1730 A  2.50 =  43.25
| PEGOUT    CLAUDE  | 2300  210  540     3050 A 10.20 = 311.10
| RUIZ      MARC    | 1820    0    0     1820 A  0.45 =   8.19
| BOUILLE   YVES    | 3450  560    0     4010 A  4.40 = 176.44
| MARNIER   LOUIS   | 1070  440  300     1810 A  3.20 =  5792
```

THE E SPECIFICATION

The E specification is used like the F specification : nEp.s
It gives a print-out in an exponential form.

> p = total width of zone
>
> s = number of significant figures printed
>
> n = repetition factor.

'E10.4' $\Box$FMT 12553 0.0487 ¯62.133
```
1.255E04
4.870E¯02
¯6.213E01
```

As with the FORMAT function, the three positions on the right of the zone are
reserved for the exponent and its sign. It is thus essential to have :
$p \geq 5+s$.

9-10   PROPERTIES OF THE PRINTING CONTROL FUNCTION

1) The result of the ⎕*FMT* function is a matrix of characters; it can be
   assigned or used as an APL expression.

```
      ⍝ 'I3' ⎕FMT 9 10 562
   5
  16
 902
```

```
      'TOTALS' ,[1] 'I6' ⎕FMT  1290  1203  3027  989
 TOTALS
   1290
   1203
   3027
    989
```

2) If all the columns to be printed have to be presented following the same
   model, only a single descriptor need be used for all the printing.

```
      'A1' ⎕FMT SURNS is equivalent to 'A1' ⎕FMT SURNS
```

```
      'I8' ⎕FMT (SUM ; BREAD)
   1730    1200     530       0
   3050    2300     210     540
   1820    1820       0       0
   4010    3450     560       0
   1810    1070     440     300
```

3) The right hand argument of ⎕*FMT* can contain APL expressions; it is not
   necessary to separate them by brackets, the semi-colons serve as separators.
   Thus, we can write :

   FOR1 ⎕*FMT* (*A* ; *B*+*C* ; *U*)

   FOR2 ⎕*FMT* (*S*,[1] *B*,*C* ; 0,¯1↓*U*)

4) If a format zone is too narrow to contain the data required by the format,
   the zone is completely replaced by asterisks.

```
      H ← 240  70  420  2333  560
```

```
      'I3,X4,F4.2' ⎕FMT (H;RATE)
 240    2.50
  70    ****
 420    0.45
 ***    4.40
 560    3.20
```

In effect, 2333 does not fit into three positions, and 10.2 does not fit
into 4 positions if two decimal places are required.

In such a case, the FORMAT function would have diagnosed a domain error, and would not have printed anything at all, making it much more difficult to find the error or errors.

5) If a value does not occupy all the zone assigned to it, it will be position-ed to the right of its zone, and completed on the left with blanks.

```
      'A6' □FMT 'ABC'
   A
   B
  .C
```

5 blanks have been passed

6) There are two ways of printing a vector horizontally :

   - either reshape it as a matrix of one line :
     $$format \quad □FMT \ (1,\rho V)\rho V$$

   - or ravel the result of a printing with $□FMT$:
     $$, \ format \ □ \ FMT \ V$$

```
      'I6' □FMT 1 5 ρ SUM
   1730   3050   1820   4010   1810

      , 'I6' □FMT SUM
   1730   3050   1820   4010   1810
```

7) Repetition factors applying to several descriptors simultaneously can be included in a format. The descriptors to be repeated must then be placed between brackets.

'5A1,2(I4,F6.2)' is equivalent to '5A1,I4,F6.2 , I4,F6.2'

'6A1,3(I5,2(F6.2,A2))' gives the same effect as the following format :

'6A1, I5, F6.2,A2, F6.2,A2, I5, F6.2,A2, F6.2,A2, I5, F6.2,A2, F6.2,A2'

This possibility is not available on all APL's.

9-11   THE PICTURE SPECIFICATION

The use of the I, F, E, X and A specifications is very close to the FORMAT instruction of the FORTRAN language. APL also contains a specification to attract COBOL users who would have ventured into reading these pages : this is the G specification, or PICTURE, by analogy with the PICTURE instruction of the COBOL language to which it is similar.

                              n*G*⍞picture⍞

   G is followed by a "picture" of the line to be printed, placed between
quote-quads. A repetition factor, n, can also be specified.

The picture is composed of characters 9 and *Z*, each of which represents the
position which each of the figures of the result will have to occupy. All
the other characters which the picture contains will be reproduced in full,
in the exact position where they appear in the picture.

               '3*G*⍞ (9999) +⍞' ⎕*FMT BREAD*
        (1200) + (0530) + (0000) +
        (2300) + (0210) + (0540) +
        (1820) + (0000) + (0000) +
        (3450) + (0560) + (0000) +
        (1070) + (0440) + (0300) +.

It can be seen in this example that the blanks, the brackets and the + sign
have been reproduced, whereas the descriptors 9 have been replaced by the
figures of the result.
It can also be seen that if the descriptor 9 is used, all the positions are
occupied, the zeros being added as required to fill the empty numeric zones.

The *Z* descriptor, on the contrary, possesses the characteristic of replacing
the zeros whether <u>infront or behind</u> by blanks, even if they are significant.

               '3*G*⍞ ZZZ9⍞' ⎕*FMT BREAD*
        1200   530   0
        2300   210   540
        1820   0   0   the 9 which is at the end of the
        3450   560   0   picture prints a zero in every case.
        1070   440   300

If only *Z*'s are used, the zero values disappear completely, as seen below,
and the numbers are altered.

               '3*G*⍞ ZZZZ⍞' ⎕*FMT BREAD*
        12   53
        23   21   54
        182   therefore it will be advisable to
        345   56   always keep at least one 9 descriptor.
        107   44   3

SPECIAL FEATURES OF THE PICTURE SPECIFICATION

1) The *G* specification prints only whole numbers, and performs a preliminary
   rounding off of the decimal values.
   This can be seen on the variable *RATE*.

'G⎵ZZ9⎵' ⎕FMT RATE

```
      3
     10
      0
      4
      3
```
                                    The value 0.45 is rounded off to
                                    zero.

2) The figures of the same number can be separated by any characters .
   Thus, to print a telephone number :

'G⎵ TEL : (99) 999 999⎵ ⎕FMT 8694859 34001760

TEL : (08) 694 859
TEL : (34) 001 760
         ↑   ↑

            the advantage of the 9 descriptor can be seen here ; the Z
            descriptor would have printed (34) 1 760, which is unreadable.

This property is used by placing the decimal point in the picture itself,
and by making the number to be printed whole (for example by multiplying
it by 100).

'G⎵Z9.ZZ⎵' ⎕FMT RATE×100

```
    2.5
   10.2
    0.45
    4.4
    3.2
```

A more presentable result would be obtained by printing zeros.

'G⎵Z9.99⎵' ⎕FMT RATE×100

```
    2.50
   10.20
    0.45
    4.40
    3.20
```

9-12   QUALIFIERS AND DECORATORS

Qualifier codes which modify the presentation of the results and decorators
which print filling texts can be associated with the I, F, and G specifications
if certain conditions are met.

QUALIFIERS

B   Replaces the zero values with blanks (*B=B*lanks).

C   Inserts a comma every three figures in the whole number part of numbers, following the English use (*C=C*omma).

L   Positions the value on the left of the reserved zone (*L=L*eft).

Z   Fills up the left part of the zone with zeros, perhaps separated by commas if the *C* qualifier is used.

DECORATORS

M◫text◫   The text placed between ◫ will be printed to the LEFT of the negative numbers, in place of the minus sign (*M=M*inus).

M◫text◫   The text will be printed to the RIGHT of the negative values, and the minus sign will be printed normally.

P◫text◫   The text placed between ◫ will be printed to the LEFT of all the positive values (*P=P*lus).

Q◫text◫   The text will be printed to the RIGHT of the positive values.

R◫text◫   The reserved zone is filled with the text indicated (which is reused as many times as necessary), then the figures to be printed are positioned. All the places not occupied by figures will hance be filled by the text.

The effects of the qualifier codes and decorators are cumulative, and their order is of little importance.

For example, *BM*◫-◫*I*4   and   *M*◫-◫*BI*4   produce the same results.

Following are some typical examples of the qualifiers and decorators used. Further information on their use will be supplied in the supplement of this chapter.

Cancellations of non-significant zeros

         '*BI*5'   ⎕*FMT BREAD*
```
1200   530
2300   210   540
1820
3450   560
1070   440   300
```

Replacement of the ‾ sign by the - sign for people unfamiliar with APL.

        '*M*◫-◫*I*6'   ⎕*FMT*   45   ‾34   1220   ‾567   ‾569
```
  45
 -34
1220
-567
-569
```
In effect, the text placed between ◫ is printed to the left of the negative values in place of the APL minus sign.

We wish to produce the negative values of a series of bank balances by the reference DB (for DeBitor). We will use the *N* decorator to print this text to the right of the negative values.

> *REMAINDER* ← 1620 3466.30 ‾350.27 6980 ‾3708

>   '*M⎕ DB⎕F12.2*' *⎕FMT REMAINDER*
>   1620.00
>   3466.30
>   ‾350.37 *DB*
>   6980.00
>   ‾3708.00 *DB*

Printing of the reference DB has caused a shifting of three characters of the negative values towards the left. The presentation will be improved by printing three blanks to the right of the positive values by means of the decorator *Q⎕   ⎕* whose effect will be added to the precedent.

>   '*M⎕ DB⎕Q⎕   ⎕F12.2*' *⎕FMT REMAINDER*
>   1620.00
>   3466.30
>   ‾350.27 *DB*
>   6980.00
>   ‾3078.00 *DB*

The ‾signs can be cancelled by adding *M⎕⎕* to the descriptors.

A filling text can enable the dotted lines to be plotted.

>   '*6A1,R⎕.⎕I10*' *⎕FMT (FRNAMES; ‾1↓CON)*
>   *JEAN* 43
>   *CLAUDE*......311
>   *MARC* 8
>   *YVES* 176
>   *LOUIS* 58

A filling text can also be used in conjunction with the *B* qualifier, to replace zero values by a text.

>   '*R⎕   NIL⎕BI7*' *⎕FMT BREAD*
>   1200   530   *NIL*
>   2300   210   540
>   1820   *NIL*   *NIL*
>   3450   560   *NIL*
>   1070   440   300

Great care was taken to assure that the replacement text was the same length as the reserved zone.

Positive numbers can also be separated from the negative numbers by following the latter with a blank text. Thus two columns are obtained without having to run a test at the time of printing.

```
     REMAINDER
1620   3466.30   ⁻350.27   6980   ⁻3708


     'M⌷-⌷N⌷'                ⌷F20.2'  ⌷FMT REMAINDER
              1620.00
              3466.30
    -350.27
              6980.00
   -3708.00
```

NOTE

The M, N, P and Q decorators use a part of the zone reserved for a number
to write the decoration text there.   Therefore this zone must be large enough
to contain simultaneously, the numbers, the text and perhaps the inserted
commas, if the C qualifier is used.
This is why a width of 20 characters was requested in the last example.

SUPPLEMENTS

TO CHAPTER 9

THE EXECUTE FUNCTION

The EXECUTE function is a relatively late creation in the APL language, like SCAN and the FORMAT function, also there can be some working differences from one system to another.

For example, some systems accept the execution of a character string containing a semi-colon:

        ♣'4;6'
    46

Other systems accept the execution of system commands such as)*SAVE*,)*LOAD*,)*COPY*, etc.....
This possibility is attractive for carrying out very large data processing applications in modestly sized workspaces . In effect, it thus becomes possible to free the active workspace of most of the necessary functions, that will be stored in a library workspace.

All these possibilities do not exist on modern systems which have workspace control functions (□*SAVE*, □*LOAD*, □*COPY*) and functions enabling functions to be stored in the form of data (□*CR*, □*FX*, □*EX*), which will be studied in chapter 10.

Finally, we will point out that on early APL systems, the EXECUTE function is written ε. This notation has been abandonned on almost all the recent systems, in favour of the ♣ symbol, which recalls the complementary symbol.

HOW TO ECONOMISE

When an argument is conveyed to a function, it makes a copy of it on which it will work. Moreover, in order to carry out an operation on a variable, there must be the space to store the result.

Imagine a simple function :

        ∇ R ← DOUBLE X
    [1]   R ← 2×X ∇

        A ← 2 3 7 6

        DOUBLE A
    4 6 14 12

During the execution of the function, the workspace must contain :

  - The variable A

  - the copy X

  - the memory zone used in the computing of 2xX, which will be the
    result.

In all, there must be enough room in the workspace to house the equivalent
of three times the variable A. If A is large, it can lead to a saturation
of the memory space.

To demonstrate this phenomenon, we will use the control function $\Box WA$,
which will be studied in chapter 10, and which indicates the space still
available in the workspace .
A slight modification of the function $DOUBLE$ is carried out :

```
            ∇ R ← DOUBLE X
    [1]     'FREE PLACE ' , ⊤ □WA
    [2]     R ← 2×X ∇
```

We will attempt to execute with a large variable :

```
            □WA
    73376
```
                                    a little more than 7300 octets
                                    remain.

```
        A ← 65000 ρ 34 21 67 45 23 11 78
            □WA
    47360
```

The creation of the variable A has led to the occupation of 26016 memory
octets (4 octets per element + 16 octets of descriptors). We will carry
out the function $DOUBLE$.

```
        ρDOUBLE A
    FREE PLACE 21188
    WS FULL
    DOUBLE[2] R←2×X
```

At the time of the execution of line [1], the displaying of the remaining
space shows that the function, by creating the variable X, has caused the
occupation of about 26000 additional octets, and there are only 21188 of
them left.

Therefore, there is no longer enough space to house the result of the
operation 2xX, which is explained by the error diagnostic $WS/FULL$, which
indicates that the workspace is full.

It is here that the use of the EXECUTE function is attractive : in place
of conveying the <u>VALUE</u> of the argument to the function, we will convey its
<u>NAME</u> to it. The function $DOUBLON$ will carry out the same work as $DOUBLE$.

```
      ∇ R ← DOUBLON NAME
[1]   'FREE PLACE ' , ⍕ ⎕WA
P 2]  R ← ⍎ '2×' , NAME ∇
```

```
      →
```
pull out of the interrupted function.

```
      ⎕WA
47706
```
there remains perceptibly the same space as before the execution of *DOUBLE*.

```
      ρ DOUBLON A
FREE PLACE 47706
6500
```

the function is satisfactorily completed.

This time, at the time of the execution of the first insruction, there still remains a lot of space, it is possible to carry out the multiplication of line [2], and the function can proceed perfectly.

15   DANGERS OF THE EXECUTE FUNCTION

To convey the name of a variable in place of its value can have its advantages, but also its disadvantages. We will work on a function whose role is to exchange any two elements of a vector.


```
      ∇ I EXCHANGE NAME ; V
[1]   V ← ⌽ I
[2]   ⍎ NAME, '[I] ← ' ,NAME, '[V]'
      ∇
```

```
      WORD ← 'MORAL'
```

```
      3 5 EXCHANGE 'WORD'
```

```
      WORD
MOLAR
```

Advantage of this method : the variable *WORD* has been modified without which it would have been necessary to reassign the result of the function to it. We will attempt a second experiment on another vector :


```
      V ← 'RATS'
```

```
      1 2 EXCHANGE 'V'
```

```
      V
RATS
```

It could be expected that the variable V would become $'ARTS'$; why is this not so ?

The name of the variable to be processed, V, is conveyed to the function *EXCHANGE*. But, in the function there is a local variable of the same name; any reference to V will be taken as a reference to the local variable, and the global variable will not be altered. There is a conflict of names.

In line [1], V takes the value ϕI, that is to say 2 1.

In line [2], the string of characters $V[I] \leftarrow V[V]$ is obtained, which is hence supposed to be : $V[1\ 2] \leftarrow 2\ 1[2\ 1]$, and the local variable V takes the value 1 2, without which the global variable would be altered.

9-16   THE FORMAT FUNCTION

The monadic FORMAT function places a column of blanks to the extreme left of a matrix of numbers. This can be seen by catenating another character to it

```
      '|' , ⍕ 2 4 ⍴⍳8
 |  1  2  3  4
 |  5  6  7  8
```

This detail is significant because, if it were not the case, the expression ,⍕M would give the following string of characters :

```
    1  2  3  45  6  7  8
```

In such cases, $\underline{\cong},⍕M$ would not be equal to ,M. It can be seen that the blank automatically added on the left maintains this equality :

```
      ⍮ , ⍕ 3 2 ⍴ 1  9 2 8 3 7
   1 9 2 8 3 7
```

EXPONENTIAL FORM

The dyadic FORMAT can be used to print values in an exponential form. For this the second element of a pair of descriptors must be negative :

- the first term always indicates the width of the zone attributed to the printing of the value,

- the absolute value of the second term indicates the number of significant figures printed (and no longer the number of decimals as in the other cases).

These two forms of print-outs can be compared :

$$U \leftarrow 0.032 \quad {}^{-}6.87 \quad 9422.33$$

$$12 \ 3 \ \triangledown \ U$$
$$0.032 \qquad {}^{-}6.870 \qquad 9422.330$$

$$12 \ {}^{-}3 \ \triangledown \ U$$
$$3.20E{}^{-}02 \qquad {}^{-}6.87E00 \qquad 9.42E03$$

If this type of printing is used, it is advisable to define a zone width large enough to contain :

     - the significant figures,

     - the decimal point,

     - the E symbol

     - the two figures of the exponent

     - possibly the number sign

     - possibly the exponent sign

     - at least one space to separate each value from the following one.

To be sure, it is advisable to make the first term of a descriptor at least six more than the second.

PARTICULAR CASE

A scalar can be used as a left hand argument of FORMAT, for example $4\triangledown U$. In such cases, $4\triangledown U$ is equivalent to $0 \ 4 \ \triangledown U$, and the computer produces a print-out where the numbers are separated by a single space.

THE PRINTING CONTROL FUNCTION

RE-USING FORMATS

The left hand argument of $\Box FMT$ defines a certain number of printing zones. Each of these zones corresponds to a column of the result, and vice versa.

If the format defines fewer zones than there are columns to be printed, the computer re-uses the format, by starting from the beginning, as many times as necessary.

Hence, '*A2,2A5*' defines three zones of 2, 5 and 5 characters respectively.
The computer will have to re-use these descriptors twice in order to be able
to print the six columns of the matrix of forenames.

```
        'A2,2A5'  ⎕FMT FRNAMES
  J     E    A N
  C     L    A U    D    E
  M     A    R C
  Y     V    E S
  L     O    U I    S
  12       12345  12345          ⎱
     12345      12         12345  ⎰         zone references
```

In the same way, '*I9,I5*' ⎕*FMT BREAD* makes the computer re-use the *I9*
specification for printing the last column.

```
      'I9,I5'  ⎕FMT BREAD
        1200   530         0
        2300   210       540
        1820     0         0
        3450   560         0
        1070   440       300

    123456789      123456789   ⎱
          12345                 ⎰         zone references
```

But the computer places (or tries to place) each column to be printed in the
order in which the printing zones are presented :

```
        '8A1,3I6'  ⎕FMT (SURNS ; BREAD)
    JOBERT  *    530       0
    PEGOUT  *    210     540
    RUIZ    *      0       0
    BOUILLE*    560       0
    MARNIER*    440     300
```

The first seven *A1* zones have been used to print the seven columns of the
matrix *SURNS*; the computer has then tried to write the first column of *BREAD*
in the 8th *A1* zone, which was not possible, and has given rise to the printing
of an asterisk. Finally, the last two columns of *BREAD* have been printed in
the first two *I6* zones.

PRINTING HIGH VALUES

If a value to be printed exceeds the 16 significant figures which it is
possible to obtain with APL, the figures on the right are replaced by dashes:

      `'I30' ☐FMT !20`
             `2432902008176640___`

DIRECT PRINTING

If the result of $☐FMT$ is not assigned to a variable, the arranging and
printing is carried out line by line, without which there would in fact be
the creation of an array of characters containing all the print-out in the
memory as would be the case if the FORMAT function ⌻ were used. The $WS/FULL$
diagnostic can thus be avoided, even in the case of very large print-outs.

VARIATIONS

We have pointed out that the first ☐ FMT version had been created by the initiative of the American company S.T.S.C. The versions which have since been
developped on other systems sometimes present slight differences.

1) $☐FMT$ was called ΔFMT on the first systems,

2) it is called $☐FRMT$ on CONTROL DATA Corp.,

3) it is written ⌼ on HONEYWELL systems. This symbol is called the HOURGLASS
   and is formed by superimposing Δ on ∇.

4) On the version developped by NATIONAL CSS, the zones reserved for different
   variables to be printed must not be separated by commas, but by semi-colons.
   Moreover, the ⍠ symbol, which is tedious to type, is replaced here by the
   diaresis ¨.

   The commas are used as separators for the X specifications and diaresis.

   Here is one of the formats we have written, and the form which it would
   have to have on a CSS system :

      `'⍠| ⍠,7A1,X2,6A1,⍠ | ⍠,3I5,I9,⍠ A ⍠,F5.2,⍠ = ⍠,F6.2'`

      `'¨| ¨,7A1;X2,6A1,¨ | ¨;3I5;I9,¨ A ¨;F5.2,¨ = ¨;F6.2'`

REPLACEMENT SYMBOLS
─────────────────

When using the PICTURE (*G*) specification, the symbols *Z* and 9 are reserved
for the representation of the figures of the result. If we want to print a
text containing a *Z* or a 9, replacement symbols must be used in place of the
Z and 9 descriptors.

On some systems, the *H* specification enables replacement symbols to be designated for as many symbols as is desired :

      '*H*⌷*Z*09+⌷*G*⌷ *THERE IS* ooo+ *PUPILS IN ZONE* 9⌷'

                                                 ─symbols *to be replaced*

                                                 ── *replacement symbols*

Henceforth, the *Z* descriptor will be replaced by 0, and the 9 descriptor will
be replaced by +; which enables the term "ZONE 9" to be included in the
picture, which contains a *Z* and a 9.

On the NATIONAL CSS system, it is the *S* specification which plays this role.
Moreover it can be used to "qallicize" the print-outs, and put a comma in place
of the decimal point, and the full stops to separate the groups of three
figures :

           '*S*¯,..,¯*CF*15.2' ⌷*FMT* 4560.20 39067780.04 33711.80
             4.560,20
        39.067.780,04
           33.711,80

In effect, the format indicates that the comma is replaced by the full stop,
and vice versa, the *C* decorator indicating that the commas must separate
the groups of three figures.

      '*S*¨,..,¨*CF*15.2'

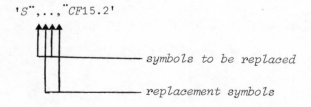

                     ── symbols *to be replaced*

                     ── *replacement symbols*

-18   SOME COMPARISONS

FORMAT users begrudge the $\Box FMT$ printing control function its clumsiness, and
its syntax which is very similar to other data processing languages.
On the contrary, one begrudges the FORMAT function the small choice of printing possibilities which it offers.

The following comparisons show that each function has its advantages and that
they complement each other usefully.

1)   ⊤ enables three dimension (and more) arrays to be printed, $\Box FMT$ does not
      allow this.

2)   The dyadic FORMAT function does not place zeros to the left of the decimal
      point for numbers lass than 1. $\Box FMT$ does this, thus producing documents
      which are more pleasant to read,

      For example :

                6 2 ⊤ 35.29 0.78 0.12 8.33
            35.29 .78 .12 8.33

              , 'F6.2' $\Box FMT$ 35.29 0.78 0.12 8.33
          35.29 0.78 0.12 8.33

3)   The FORMAT function eliminates the non-significant zeros on the left.
      It is possible to print these with the printing control function.

                4 0 ⊤ 073 03 96
            73 3 96

                'G⍈999 99 99⍈' $\Box FMT$ 730396
          073 03 96

4)   It is very difficult to cancel zero values with ⊤ , whereas $\Box FMT$ does
      this with ease by means of the B qualifier.

5)   It is quicker to use the monadic ⊤ than $\Box FMT$ for simple and rapid print-
      outs, or for joining a figure to a letter. For example, in order to
      dynamically create the character strings $S1$, $S2$, $S3$, ... $S10$, $S11$, $S12$,
      in terms of a variable N being able to take the values of 1 to 12, it
      suffices to write : $'S', ⊤N$

With $\square FMT$, the blank which would intercalate between the letter S and the values less than 10 would have to be eliminated :

$$'S','LI2' \quad \square FMT \ N$$

6)   In reality, these two functions complement each other. We will imagine that we want to print a variable number of columns of *BREAD* and the surnames side by side, by means of $\square FMT$.
According to whether one wants to print one, two or three columns of *BREAD*, one of the following three formats will have to be used :

$$' \ I6,X2,7A1'$$
$$'2I6,X2,7A1'$$
$$'3I6,X2,7A1'$$

If N is the number of columns to be printed, one will proceed as follows :

$$((\triangledown N),'I6,X2,7A1') \ \square FMT \ (BREAD[;\iota N] \ ; \ SURNS)$$

CHAPTER 10

INTERFACES WITH THE COMPUTER

SHARED VARIABLES

INTERFACES WITH THE COMPUTER

Up to now we have intentionally ignored the computer supporting the APL system on which we are working. However, it is sometimes necessary to modify the environment in which the processings are carried out, or to obtain information such as the date, or space still available in the work-space.

The aim of this chapter is to demonstrate the different tools available to the APL user for controlling the way in which the computer manages the objects (variables, functions, work-spaces), and carries out processings.

Before approaching these means of control, we will need to know some general concepts on the representation of data and the organisation of work-spaces.

REPRESENTATION OF DATA

In the computer, all the data are represented by series of binary numbers. Each binary number is called a BIT, the abbreviation of BInary digiT. The computer does not have access individually to each bit, but to blocks of fixed dimensions, called WORDS. The size of these words differs from one manufacturer to another : 16 bits on many mini-computers, 32 bits on IBM computers, 60 bits on CONTROL DATA computers. The larger the size of the words, the greater the precision of the computing. Another unit of measurement is the OCTET, which is a group of 8 bits. Beware of the term BYTE which, according to the manufacturer, designates either a word, or an octet(IBM).

The variety of the modes of representation of the data in the memory means that the units used to measure the size of a work-space are different from one manufacturer to another. As an example, here are the units in use on IBM computers :

- an alphanumeric character occupies an octet,

- a whole number between ¯2147483648 and 2147483648 occupies a word of 4 octets, or 32 bits,

- a whole number outside of these limits, and all decimal numbers, occupy a double word of 8 octets.

- finally, boolean variables are represented by means of one bit per binary number. Therefore, 32 binary numbers can be stored in one word. Of course, if we wish to represent a vector of 50 boolean values, the computer will occupy two words, i.e. 64 bits.

We will come back to the representation of data in greater detail in the supplement of this chapter.

10-3   ORGANISATION OF WORK-SPACES

When somebody is connected to a multi-user system, he must introduce himself to the computer by indicating his identity. This identity is most often comprised of the user's number (or name), usually followed by a confidential password. This is the usual procedure   but whose form can be different from one computer to another.
If the computer offers the possibility of working in several languages, a special procedure will then enable the language in which one wants to work to be specified.

On the other hand, if the computer is strictly to be used with APL, this procedure of connection is reduced simply to indicating an account number followed by a password :

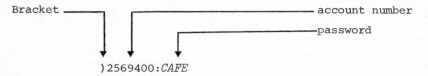

```
Bracket                                                    account number
                                                           password


            )2569400:CAFE
```

Each user has at his disposal a storage zone for working called an ACTIVE WORK-SPACE, whose size is usually unalterable. Some systems offer the possibility of varying the size of this zone within imposed limits, either before passing to APL, or during working. The active work-space is erased when the user disconnects, but it is possible to preserve the fruits of his labour by safeguarding a copy of his complete active work-space. The different copies thus safeguarded constitute the user's PRIVATE LIBRARY.

The libraries of the various users are referenced by means of a library number, which is the account number of their creator. Inside a library, each
work-space is referenced by an arbitary name attributed to it by its owner
when safeguarding it.
In order to designate a library space, the library number and the name must
therefore be specified at the same time; for example: 2569400 *HOME*.
The owner of the space can dispense with specifying the library number.

It is also possible to form libraries of work-spaces containing functions of
general interest, which are accessible to everyone, called PUBLIC LIBRARIES.
Usually, they carry a number less than 1000. The forming of public libraries is regulated, or reserved for certain privileged users.

Each APL user can create library spaces, or bring data contained in a library
space into his active work-space. Some of these operations are always
possible, others are under certain conditions, some, however, are prohibited.
For example, it is forbidden to gain access to another user's active work-space.

The following diagram shows the operations which are possible.

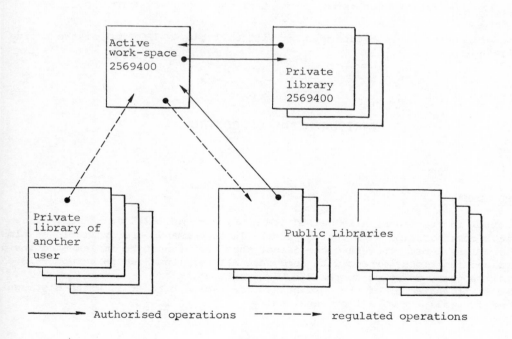

10-4   CHARACTERISTIC QUANTITIES OF A WORK-SPACE

After connecting to the system, or following a)*CLEAR* command, the APL user
has an active work-space which has no name, and which is called an EMPTY SPA
This empty space already possesses certain well defined characteristics, whi
can be modified as required. These characteristics have an influence on the
calculations, or the presentation of the results.

These are :

- origin of the indices,

- page width, or print-out width,

- precision of print-out of the numeric values,

- random root of random numbers,

- comparison tolerance,

- table of symbols,

- indicator of state of functions,

- latent expression, on most of the recent systems.

These quantities constitute what we will call the ENVIRONMENT of the active
work-space.

10-5   VARIOUS MEANS OF CONTROL

THE COMMANDS

Control instructions, also called COMMANDS, such as)*SAVE* or)*ERASE*, allow
for a communication with the computer. These commands are available on almo
all APL systems. They have the defect that they cannot be implemented insid
defined functions, except with some rare APL versions (see paragraph 9-13 on
this subject, relating to the EXECUTE function).
The first character of the commands is the closed bracket), which distingui
them from all normal APL expressions.

The commands generally induce an answer from the computer, which serves as confirmation that the command has been carried out.

)SAVE EXAMPLE   command
    SAVED 17.09.34 05/06/78   answer

On no APL system do commands provide control of all the parameters of the environment. Therefore, other measures are necessary. On early systems, the useful functions were stored in a public library; they carried a name like any other defined function (such as *SETFUZZ*), but could not be printed. This procedure has disappeared on modern systems, which have other means of control.

THE SYSTEM-FUNCTION I-*BEAM*

In order to complete the commands, the early APL systems had a "universal function" written I, by superimposing ⊥ and ⊤ . Because of the shape of the symbol, this function was baptised I-*BEAM*. This function reinstates different data according to the value of its argument.
The multiple uses of this function were rather difficult to retain, and the I-*BEAM* function has been abandonned on most modern systems, in favour of control functions and variables.
They remain, however, on some APL versions, for uses which are very specific to each equipment, for example to control the peripherals. There are even dyadic versions of the I-*BEAM* function, because the designers of APL systems are very creative people.

At the end of the chapter there is a table which recaps the most common uses of the I-*BEAM* function.

CONTROL VARIABLES AND FUNCTIONS

With the advent of the APL/SV product in 1973, IBM gives a new look to the interface between APL and the computer, and adds new possibilities to the language, such as scanning, the EXECUTE function and FORMAT functions, the canonicial form of function etc.....
Henceforth, the control of the environment will be undertaken by control variables, whose value will be fixed either by the user or by the computer, and by control functions.

In order to symbolise this communication between APL and its host computer, and to distinguish the control functions and variables from the other variables and functions, their name will start with the quad character (window of communication), followed by two letters which constitute a mnemonic recall of their use: $\square IO$, $\square CR$, $\square PW$, $\square DL$ ....

These control functions and variables are available in any work-space, in the same way as any primitive function. They cannot be erased. Consequently, this concept has been broadly used by most manufacturers, who have gone well beyond the initial possibilities presented by IBM.

IMPORTANT NOTES

There is no "standardized" version of APL, and there is a wide diversity in the means of control available to the user. We cannot state here the feature particular to this or that system, but simply give a picture of the common characteristics of most of the existing versions. Likewise, if the syntax of the commands, control functions and variables, is essentially the same on all systems, the form of the answers can present certain differences.

Thus it will be up to the reader to find out from the brochures issued by his supplier what the appropriate characteristics are of the version of APL which he is working on.

CONVENTIONS

Commands can be a mixture of optional signs. On the following pages, these signs have been placed between brackets { }.

The following conventions have been adopted :

      wsid   Work Space IDentifiers. {wsid} represents the name of a work-space belonging to the user (for example *CAVE*), or to another user. In the latter case, the name must be preceded by the owner's account number (5002341 *PERT*) or by the public library number (101 *UTILITIES*)

      key   this is an alphanumeric password used to protect access to an account number or a work-space.

Names   list of the names of variables, functions and groups of variables
        and functions of the work-space.

Other parameters will be stated explicitly, in normal lower case characters,
whereas the commands will be in APL characters (upper case italics).
For example :

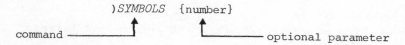

```
            )SYMBOLS  {number}
```

command ────────────↑   ↑──────────── optional parameter

PRESENTATION OF THE CHAPTER

The same effect can be obtained by different means, we will study the commands,
the I-*BEAM* function, and the control functions and variables simultaneously.
Four major themes will be dealt with :

  - control of the environment,

  - management of the work-spaces,

  - management of the objects in the work-space,

  - data and control of the processing.

At the end of the chapter tables which provide a synthetic view of various
means of control.

)-6   CONTROL OF THE ENVIRONMENT

ORIGIN OF THE INDICES

Normally, an index cannot be less than 1, but in some cases, this origin of
indices can be fixed at zero. This modifies the behaviour of the functions
and operators working on the indices (ι ? $\maltese$), or which have an index written
in them ($/ \setminus \delta$ .....).

)*ORIGIN* {0 or 1} is the command which enables the origin of the indices to be
modified.

$\square IO$ (for Index Origin) is the control variable which has the same effect.

The $\square IO$ variable presents the advantage that it can be local to a function, in
which it will be used. The)*ORIGIN* command cannot.

```
        )ORIGIN  0
WAS  1
        )ORIGIN  1
WAS  0
      □IO ← 0
      □IO

0
      V ← 67  30  21  88  29
```

Origin modification by the command.
The computer recalls what the preceding
origin was. Then reverse modification.
Modification, then consultation of the origin
of indices by means of the control variable

In origin 1, $V[4 \ 1 \ 5]$ equals : 88 67 29 , but $V[0]$ is prohibitted.

In origin 0, $V[4 \ 1 \ 0]$ equals : 29 30 64 , but $V[5]$ is prohibitted.

In origin 1, ι6   equals : 1 2 3 4 5 6

In origin 0, ι6   equals : 0 1 2 3 4 5

The INDEX-OF function is also affected, and $V \ ι \ 21 \ 67 \ 55$ would equal 3 1 6
in origin 0.

The GRADE UP and GRADE DOWN functions, which produce a set of indices, are
also affected by a change in origin of indices.

$ψV$ equals 3 5 2 1 4 in origin 1, ⎫
                                       ⎬   In every case, $V[ψV]$ provides
   and   2 4 1 0 3 in origin 0. ⎭   classification of the vector.

The ROLL and DEAL functions takes random integers in the vector ιN. This
vector being different in origin 0, the result of the ROLL and DEAL functions
will also be, and zeros may appear in the result.

?20 and 6?20 give values between 1 and 20 in origin 1,
         and give values between 0 and 19 in origin 0.

The origin of the indices also influences the functions and operators which
can be written with the line operator, i.e :

          - compression and reduction $A/[I]B$ and $+/[I]A$

          - expansion and scanning $A\backslash[I]B$ and $×\backslash[I]A$

          - reversal $φ[I]A$ or $⊖[I]A$

          - rotation $Aφ[I]B$ or $A⊖[I]B$

          - catenation and lamination $A,[I]B$

Finally, the left-hand argument of the dyadic transposition ($I⍉A$) must take
the origin of the indices into account.

As an example, we will take the following matrix M : ⎧ 20 17 43
                                                        ⎩ 60 23 30

If we are in origin zero, the following results are obtained :

```
        □IO ← 0

        +/[0]M
80   40   78

        1 0 0 1 1 0 \[1]M
20   0   0   17   43   0
60   0   0   23   30   0

        φ[1]M
43   17   20
30   23   60

        M,[0] 99
20   17   43
60   23   30
99   99   99
```

The lamination case is noteworthy, because it is the only case where an index
can become negative, as was demonstrated in paragraph 6-14.

```
        V,[⁻0.5] 33
67   30   21   88   29
33   33   33   33   33
```

Finally, it was stated in paragraph 6-17, that the left-hand argument of the
expression $A \Diamond B$ must comprise elements of the vector $\iota \rho \rho B$. Since the ι function
gives a different result in origin zero, the left-hand argument of a dyadic
transposition is different from what it would be in origin 1.

```
        □IO←3
        ι6
□IO IMPLICIT ERROR
        ι6
        ∧
```

This last example shows that □*IO* can be given a value other than 0 or 1,
but that it would provoke an error as soon as a function involving indexing
is used. A few rare systems, such as APLIXI, do accept it however.

PAGE WIDTH

By default, the computer assumes that a width of 120 characters is available
for the print-out of results. If a vector is too long to be printed on a
single line, the following lines will be printed with a shift of 6 characters.
According to whether one has narrower or wider paper, or if one wants to
transmit the results on a television circuit, etc...., this page width can
be varied from 30 to 390 characters (500 on some versions).

A command and a control variable are used to define this width.

)WIDTH 132
    WAS 120   ◄──────────── the command recalls the preceding   width.

This command has the major drawback on most systems that it can be used only in an empty work-space.

□PW, which is the abbreviation of Page Width, plays the same role, but has the advantage that it can be used anytime.

      □PW ← 70
      □←VEC←14ρ1452 6725 8910 3427 7681 2430 6003
1452 6725 8910 3427 7681 2430 6003 1452 6725 8910 3427 7681 2430 6003

      □PW←36
      VEC
1452 6725 8910 3427 7681 2430 6003   this time, the vector has had to be
    1452 6725 8910 3427 7681 2430   printed on several lines.
    6003

PRINT-OUT PRECISION

Numbers are normally printed with 10 significant figures (except on some mini computers). This precision can be reduced or increased up to a maximum of 15 to 16 figures according to the system. Of course, the precision of the calculations remains the same irrespective of the print-out precision.

          1÷3
    0.3333333333

)DIGITS 5
    WAS 10
          1÷3
    0.33333

The control variable □PP (for Printing Precision), which plays the same role has the advantage that it can be declared local to a function, thus enabling the display precision to be varied according to the functions used.

Outside the limits imposed by the manufaturer, the diagnostic □PP IMPLICIT ERROR is obtained.

RANDOM ROOT

A number called the random root, is used to produce each random number,
after which this root is modified, in such a way that the conditions for
generating the next value are different.

In an empty work-space, the initial value of the random root is fixed at 7*5
(or 16807). Consequently, identical generations of random numbers carried
out at several days interval in empty work-spaces give identical results.

The control variable $\Box RL$ (for Random Link) is the random root. It can be
consulted and modified to avoid, or artificially recreate the repetition
of identical generatings. This aspect can be reffered to in paragraph 8-27.

Any positive value strictly less than 2*31 with IBM, or 2*47 with CONTROL DATA
is suitable as random roots. Outside these values, the diagnostic $\Box RL$ *IMPLICIT*
ERROR will be obtained.

$\Box RL$ 16807	The initial value of $\Box RL$ equals 7*5
?10 2	A generating is carried out.
$\Box RL$ 282475249	
? 10 10 10 10 8 5 6 3	The root has been modified by generation. The initial value of the root is reestablished, then the same series of
$\Box RL$ ← 16807	generatings is carried out. It can be seen that the results obtained are
? 5ρ10 2 8 5 6 3	identical to the preceding ones.

COMPARISON TOLERANCE

Mathematically, 1 and $3 \times (1 \div 3)$ are equal quantities. But if there are only
6 figures to represent the numbers, $1 \div 3$ will be represented by 0.333333 and
$3 \times (1 \div 3)$ will equal 0.999999. This last value is not exactly equal to 1, and
the expression $1 = 3 \times (1 \div 3)$ would have to give the answer 0.

The same goes for the computer, where certain finite decimal numbers cannot
be represented by a finite series of binary numbers. Such is the case
with the decimal value 0.1, which gives rise to the unlimited binary series
.00011000110001100011.......

In order to avoid the comparison of two numbers giving abnormal results, the computer will consider as equal two numbers whose difference remains within a fork called "FUZZ". It is possible to fix the extent of this fuzz by assigning a value to the control variable $\Box CT$ (Comparison Tolerance). The definition of this COMPARISON TOLERANCE is slightly different from one APL system to another.

With CONTROL DATA, A and B will be said to be equal if $(|A-B|)\div|B|$ is less than or equal to $\Box CT$. In other words, the relative difference between the two numbers must be less than the comparison tolerance.

For example :

If $\Box CT$ equals 0.01   the numbers 5049 and 5000 will be declared equal, because (5049-5000)÷5000 equals 0.0098, which is less than $\Box CT$. On the other hand, 5051 and 5000 will be declared different.

If $\Box CT$ equals $1E^-6$ the numbers 5000004 and 5000000 will be equal, but not 5000006 and 5000000.

For this manufacturer, $\Box CT$ equls $5E^-11$ in an empty work-space, and can vary between 0 and 0.01. When the comparison tolerance is zero, the two values compared must be exactly equal for the computer to declare them as equal.

With IBM, the computer specifies that the two internal representations of two numbers have mantissas whose difference is less than $\Box CT$. For the human, this is translated by the fact that the two numbers A and B are declared equal if $(|\ A-B)$ is less than $\Box CT$ multiplied by the power 16 immediatly higher than $(|A|)\lceil|B|$. Some explanations would probably be welcome!

The powers of 16 are : 1 16 256 4096 65536 1048576 16777216 .....

- Between A and B between   16 and   256, a difference of $\Box CT \times 256$ is tolerated,
- between A and B between 256 and 4096, a difference of $\Box CT \times 4096$ is tolerated,
- between A and B between 4096 and 65536, a difference of $\Box CT \times 65536$ is tolerated,
- etc. ....

As an illustration we will give a comparison tolerance:

  20.00000 is equal to 20.00256, but not to 20.00257   the difference
200.00000 is equal to 200.00256, but not to 200.00257 } tolerated being equal to 0.00256

   65536 is equal to   65546, but not to   65547   the difference
1048000 is equal to 1048010, but not to 1048011 } tolerated being equal to 10.48576.

This method of computing leads to accepting relative differences starting from about $15E^-5$ for 65536, to only $1E^-5$ for 104800 for the same comparison tolerance. Much easier for the computer to carry out, this idea is very much more complex for the human to interpret, and is difficult to use. Many APL users have given up trying to understand it!

With IBM, $\Box CT$ can vary from 0 inclusive to 1 exclusive, and equals $1E^-13$ in an empty work-space.

SYMBOL TABLE

Part of the work-space is reserved for a list of all the names of variables, functions, groups and labels of the work-space. This list is called the SYMBOL TABLE.

On many systems, this table is a fixed size. Each new name is added to the table, even if it is incorrectly written and gives rise to the *VALUE ERROR* diagnostic. On the other hand, if an object is erased by the)*ERASE* command, its name remains in the symbol table.
As soon as the table is full it becomes imposible to create any new object, or the diagnostic *SYMBOL TABLE FULL* will be obtained. This situation is the more inconvenient the more tedious is the procedure for remedying it.

Recent APL systems have a symbol table which is dynamically managed by the computer, which increases as the need arises, and which is reorganised periodically. Is this the case with your system ?

)*SYMBOLS* {number}

This command enables the size of the symbol table to be fixed. In general, this is an operation which can only be done in an empty work-space. This restriction is very tedious when the *SYMBOL TABLE FULL* diagnostic appears. On some systems the state of the table can be consulted:

)*SYMBOLS*
  IS 256; 133 *IN USE*   133 symbols are already used, with an
                                   authorised maximum of 256.

STATE INDICATOR

In each work-space, a state indicator shows the functions whose execution has been interrupted, classified from the most recent interruption to the oldest. In an empty work-space, this indicator is also blank itself.

It is the)*SI* command (for <u>S</u>tate <u>I</u>ndicator) which causes the print-out of the
state indicator.
Its working can be shown by these two functions:

```
        ∇ CALL H;X                          ∇ R←INSIDE U
[1]     X←2+H                       [1]     R←3↑V
[2]     H←INSIDE X                  [2]     R←R[1
[3]     3×H ∇                               ∇
```

CALL 9 *VALUE ERROR* *INSIDE*[1] *R←3↑V* ∧	The *CALL* function is introduced. An error is detected and execution is inter- rupted.
)*SI* *INSIDE*[1] * *CALL*[2]	By consulting the state indicator, it is seen that *INSIDE* is interrupted on line [1], and that *CALL* is interrupted on line [2].

The asterisk signifies that after correcting, the execution of *INSIDE* can be
resumed by typing →1. On the other hand the continuation of *CALL* cannot be
resumed so long as *INSIDE* is interrupted. The *CALL* function is said to be
PENDING.

We will correct the error which has been diagnosed.

        ∇ *INSIDE*[1] *R←3↑U* ∇

CALL 2 *SYNTAX ERROR* *INSIDE*[2] *R←R[1* ∧	A complete execution is reintroduced, without finishing the execution which was interrrupted. A new error is detected.
)*SI* *INSIDE*[2] * ⟵ *CALL*[2] *INSIDE*[1] * ⟵ *CALL*[2]	In the first place the state indicator signals the interruption which has just arisen, but it conserves the trace of the previous interruption.
∇ *INSIDE*[2] *R←R+1* ∇	New correction of the function.
→2 15 3 3	The execution is reintroduced at the place of the interruption, and the required result is obtained.
)*SI* *INSIDE*[1] * *CALL*[2]	The state indicator no longer signals the last interruption, since the function has been successfully reintroduced, but it still signals the first one.
→)*SI*	By giving the out-put order of the interrupted function, and of all those which call it, the state indicator is cleared and becomes blank.

DAMAGE INDICATOR

It is possible to reintroduce an interrupted function at the place where it
is interrupted, or at any other place, by a branching arrow : →5. However,
this is possible only if the computer is able to recognise the function and its
line numbers. Consequently if the header or labels of an interrupted function
are modified, it will not be possible to resume its course.
During the modification, the computer indicates that the state indicator is
altered by the message *SI DAMAGE*. If the state indicator is then consulted,
a special notation indicates the function whose course cannot be resumed.
We will imagine, for example, the following state indicator :

```
      )SI
FUNC [3]      *
SURFACE [1] *
IN [8]        *
```

``` ∇ SURFACE [0] [0] SURFACES X ∇ SI DAMAGE ```	The header of *SURFACE* is slightly modified. When the definition mode is closed, the message *SI DAMAGE* is printed.

``
)SI
FUNC [3]   *
              *
IN [8]   *
``
	If the indicator is then consulted, a single asterisk, without a function name, marks the position of the function which can no longer be reintroduced (on IBM systems).

On other systems, the convention adopted can be slightly different, for example:
SURFACE [⁻1].

We will return to the use of the state indicator during the study of the setting
up aids. We will specify from now on that, except for exceptional cases, the
state indicator must always be cleared by typing as many niladic branching arrows
as there are asterisks in the indicator. This is a long procedure, and some
systems also have easier means of clearing the indicator.

LINE COUNTERS

The control variable $\Box LC$ (for <u>L</u>ine <u>C</u>ounter) reinstates the vector of instructio
numbers during the execution. The first term of the vector is the number
of the most internal function.

	▽ *OUTSIDE*		▽ *MIDDLE*		*INSIDE*
[1]	$\Box LC$	[1]	$\Box LC$	[1]	$\Box LC$
[2]	*MIDDLE*	[2]	$\Box LC$	[2]	$\Box LC$
[3]	*INSIDE* ▽	[3]	*INSIDE* ▽	[3]	▽

These three functions print $\Box LC$ at various stages of their execution. Here are
the values which would be obtained if *OUTSIDE* was executed. The layout of
the results has been deliberately modified to facilitate reading.

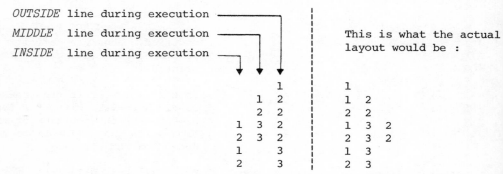

The easiest way of resuming the course of an interrupted function at the precis
place of interruption is to type $\rightarrow\Box LC$ or $\rightarrow I26$ or $I27$

The value of $\Box LC$ can be modified, but the computer immediatly re-establishes th
exact value :

```
      □LC
2 3
      □LC ← 1
      □LC
2 3
```

It is said that $\Box LC$ is a variable shared between
the APL user and the computer.

LATENT EXPRESSION

$\Box LX$ is the mn monic applied to <u>L</u>atent e<u>X</u>pression; this is a character string,
empty in an empty work-space, to which the user can give a value.

Each time that a work-space is loaded by the command)*LOAD* or the function
the computer executes the latent expression BEFORE handing over to the user,
by writting ± □*LX* .
If the latent expression is the name of a function, this function will be
executed from the time of loading.

            ∇ *NURSE*
   [1]   ⍞ ← '*DO YOU WANT THE USER MANUAL ?*'
   [2]   →('*N*' ∈ ⍞)/0
   [3]   *DESCRIBE* ∇

         □*LX* ← '*NURSE*'
)*SAVE MONITOR*
   SAVED 11.45.12   03/11/78

Having assigned a value to □*LX*, and safeguarding the work-space, we will imagine
that another user wants to work using this work-space; this is how loading will
be carried out :

)*LOAD* 3450012 *MONITOR*
      SAVED 11.45.12   03/11/78
      DO YOU WANT THE USER MANUAL?
      .....
            the *DESCRIPTION* function would be carried out here .....

The latent expression can be used to initial certain parameters, or to print
a message :

            □*LX* ← '*SCALE* ← 1 + *OPTIONS* ← 0 1 1'

      or   □*LX* ← '''*NEW VERSION, CONSULT THE USER MANUAL*'''

The latent expression is not activated by a)*COPY* command.

10-7   WORK-SPACE MANAGEMENT

<u>WORK-SPACE SAFEGUARDS</u>   :)*SAVE* idet {:key}

This command safeguards the contents of a work-space in a library. If,
following a)*LOAD* or a former)*WSID* command, the work-space already has a name,
it is of no avail to recall it in the)*SAVE* command.

)*LOAD GADGET*

SAVED 8.35.07 01/16/78   The user loads the work-space and carries
                                             out various tasks.

....work......

)*SAVE*   At the time of the safeguard, the computer
9.20.22 04/19/78 *GADGET*   confirms the time and the date of the
                                             safeguard (19th April 1978), and recalls
                                             the name of the space: *GADGET*.

On the other hand, if an active work-space does not have a name, it must be
given one. If this is not done the diagnostic *NOT SAVED, THIS WS IS CLEAR WS*.
will be recieved. This does not indicate that the work-space is actually empty,
but that it does not have a name.
A similar message is emitted if one tries to safeguard a work-space under a name
other than its own, and which already exists:

)*LOAD GADGET*

SAVED 9.20.22 04/19/78

)*SAVE TENTATIVE*
NOT SAVED, THIS WS IS GADGET

LOCKING

A library space can be locked by an alphanumeric key, separated from the name by
a colon, in such a way that antother user cannot gain access to it.

)*SAVE*   HOT : RABBIT

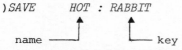

name ──────┘   └────── key

Henceforth, the key will have to be quoted in the commands)*LOAD*;)*DROP*; and
)*PCOPY*.
By using the single command)*SAVE* the key will be kept in action, whereas
)*SAVE HOT* or)*SAVE HOT* : frees the work-space from its key.

Finally, note that a work-space cannot be safeguarded in the private library
of another user.

SPACE LOADING :   )*LOAD* idet {:key}

This command is used to load the library space called idet in the active work-
space, by erasing anything which was contained in the latter.

The loaded work-space can belong :

- to the user's private library :)*LOAD GADGET*

- to a public library   :)*LOAD* 105 *STATS*

- to another user's private library :)*LOAD* 5002351 *PERT*

In the last two cases the library number must be quoted. Moreover, if a key protects the work-space, it must be quoted in the command:

$\qquad\qquad$)*LOAD   HOT:RABBIT*

At the time of loading, the work-space is loaded with all its characteristic qualities (see paragraph 10-4), and its latent expression is activated.

RESPONSES

The normal computer's response to the command)*LOAD* is *SAVED* followed by the time and date at which the safeguarding took place :

$\qquad$)*LOAD GADGET*
$\quad$ *SAVED* 9.20.22 04/19/78

The response *WS LOCKED* indicates that the work-space is locked, and that the appropriate key has not been given, or, on the other hand, that it is not locked and the wrong key has been specified.

The response *WS NOT FOUND* signifies that this work-space does not exist.

Some systems have a control function □*LOAD* , whose argument is a character string : □*LOAD* '*APL*50 *PLOT*'

PARTIAL COPY OF A WORK-SPACE :)*COPY* idet {:key} {names}

Whereas the)*LOAD* command erases the contents of an active work-space, the)*COPY* command preserves it, and enables objects recopied from a library space to be added to it, to which names are given. The syntax of this command is similar to that of)*LOAD*.

If no list of names is specified, the whole of the designated library space is recopied in the active work-space.

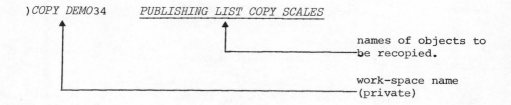

)*COPY DEMO*34   *PUBLISHING LIST COPY SCALES*

names of objects to be recopied.

work-space name (private)

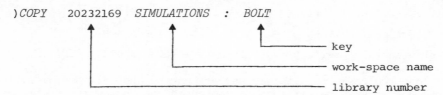

In this second example, the whole of the work-space *SIMULATIONS*, belonging to user 2032169, is added to the active work-space.

NOTES

If an object of the active work-space and one of the objects copied have the same name, the COPIED object erases the object of the active work-space, and takes its place.

During execution of a)*COPY* command, the characteristic quantities of the active work-space are not modified. Only the names of the copied objects are added to the symbol table. If a whole work-space is copied, its latent expression is not activated.

ANOMALIES

The normal response is the same as for a)*LOAD* command, and the same anomalies cause the same diagnostic to appear. Moreover, other anomalies may be detected:

>)*COPY GADGET PRINTING A MAMMOTH END*
> *OBJECT NOT FOUND : MAMMOTH*

This message indicates that the object *MAMMOTH* does not exist in the designated space.

>)*COPY* 8694859 *UTILITY*
> *SYMBOL TABLE FULL*

The names of the copied objects are added to the symbol table, which already contains those of the active work-space. The table is too small to contain them all, and the copy cannot be made. We will see later how to continue.

In the same way as there is a)*COPY* command, some systems have a control function □*COPY* . It has the following syntax:

> {'names'} □*COPY* 'wsid {:key}'

Example: '*EDITION   A   MAMMOTH   END*' □*COPY* '*GADGET*'

PROTECTED COPY :)*PCOPY* idet {:key} {names}

This command plays the same role as the preceding one, but it avoids an object of the active work-space being involuntarily erased by a copied object bearing the same name. In the event of similar names being produced, the object is not copied, and a diagnostic is emitted:

$X \leftarrow$ 12   34   25   16
)*PCOPY GADGET AGE TIME X SCALES*

SAVED 9.20.22   04/19/78
NOT COPIED : *X*

    X

12   34   25   16

The computer refuses to copy X, because there is already a variable with the same name in the active work-space. It is seen that it is not altered.

ERASING A WORK-SPACE :)*DROP* idet {:key}

This command abolishes a work-space of the user's private library. If this work-space is locked, mention of the key is essential (except on some systems, alas!). The computer responds with the time and the date of the operation. Some systems have the control funciton □*DROP*; the following will thus be' written :

- either :   )*DROP HOT:RABBIT*
- or   :   □*DROP 'HOT:RABBIT'*

SPACE NAME :)*WSID* {idet}

The)*WSID* command is used to consult, or modify the name of the active work-space.

)*WSID*
SYLVAIN

we consult the present name of the active work-space.

)*WSID CLAIRE*
WAS SYLVAIN

we modify this name.
The computer recalls the previous name.

The response *CLEAR WS* signifies that the work-space has not yet recieved a name.

The response 4772347 *OVNI* signifies that the active work-space arises from the loading of the work-space *OVNI* belonging to user 4772347, by a)*LOAD* command.

This command can be used to give a name to the active work-space before safeguarding it.
Some systems have the control function □*WSID* {'idet'}

STATE OF THE LIBRARY   :)*LIB* {number}

The list of all the work-spaces of one's own private library, or of a public
library whose number is given can be ascertained.

)*LIB*
     UTILITY
     CESAR
     BOOK
     EXAMPLES

The keys which may lock some work-spaces do not appear in this list; hence
this is not a way of recovering a forgotten key.

Likewise, for obvious security reasons, the contracts of another user's library
cannot be printed. Any attempts of this kind will result in the diagnostic
IMPROPER LIBRARY REFERENCE.   The same diagnostic is emitted when an incorrect
library number is specified.

10-8   MANAGEMENT OF THE OBJECTS OF A WORK-SPACE

LIST OF NAMES   :)*FNS*   )*VARS*   □*NL*

The)*FNS* {letter} command gives the list of all the functions of the active work
space, classified alphabetically. If a letter is specified, only the list
starting from this letter of the alphabet is obtained.

The)*VARS* {letter} command has the same effect for the variables.

□*NL* signifies Name List. This is a control function which gives a matrix of
characters as a result, of which each line is the name of an object. The
nature of the objects selected depends on the right-hand argument of the function, which has the following syntax :

        {'letter'} □*NL* scalar or vector

     - a 1 in the right hand argument extracts the labels of the interrupted
       functions,

     - a 2 in the right hand argument extracts the variable names,

     - a 3 in the right hand argument extracts the functions of the work-
       space.

The objects are not classified alphabetically, but it is possible to indicate a letter in the left hand argument, in order to obtain only the names which start with this letter.
Here are some examples of these possibilities.

> `)VARS`
> *A AGE EDGE END FULL LONG MONTH MORNING X*

> `)FNS`
> *EDIT MEF MOUNT RESET RESTORE*

> `'M' `$\square$`NL 2 3`
> *MONTH*
> *MEF*
> *MOUNT*
> *MORNING*

All the variables and functions whose names begin with *M* are requested.
The result is a matrix of characters.

> `ρ `$\square$`NL 3`
> 4 7

There are 5 functions.

CREATION OF GROUPS   :   `)GROUP` `)GRP` `)GRPS`

A set of variables and functions can be grouped under a single name, in a way which enables them to be manipulated collectively by the commands `)COPY`, `)PCOPY` and `)ERASE`. For this, the command `)GROUP` is used.

> `)GROUP` <u>*PACKET*</u>   <u>*GOLD A AVERAGE AGES WIGHTS ZERO MULE*</u>
>   ↑   ↑

name given to the group   names of the objects to be grouped

One group can be included in another one. This is also a means of extending a group. For example, to add the object *HOT* to the group *PACKET*, the following is done :

> `)GROUP PACKET PACKET HOT`

In the event of an attempt to group objects under a name which is already used for another object, the message *NOT GROUPED* would be received.

To DISSOCIATE the elements of a group without erasing them, the following is written :

> `)GROUP PACKET`

To ERASE all the elements of a group simultaneously, the following is written :

> `)ERASE PACKET`   These two possibilities must not be confused.

The objects contained in a group can be ascertained by the command)*GRP*.

)*GRP PACKET*
GOLD A AVERAGE AGES WEIGHTS ZERO MULE HOT

The list of groups of the active work-space can be requested by the command)*GRPS*.

ERASING OBJECTS   :   )*ERASE*   □*EX*

The command)*ERASE*, which has already been studied enables objects of the active work-space to be erased (variables, functions, groups). Normally, the computer gives no response. If certain objects, to be erased do not exist, the message *NOT ERASED* will be seen to appear followed by the names of these objects

The control function □*EX* can also be used (mnemonic of EXpunge), which accepts a matrix of characters as argument, each line of which contains the name of an object to be erased.
This function restores a binary vector, the 1's of which indicate the erased objects, and the 0's indicate the objects which have not been erased.

□*EX* 3 5 ρ'*WINE VAT MONTH*'
1 1 1

□*EX* □*WL* 2 3 would erase all the variables and functions of the work space.

This control function has the advantage of being able to be used during the course of a function to erase cumbersome objects which are no longer of use, so as to avoid saturation of the memory space.

VERY IMPORTANT DISTINCTION

The)*ERASE* command erases only GLOBAL objects, the □*EX* function erases only LOCAL objects.

Consequently,)*ERASE* enables groups and interrupted or pending functions to be erased, whereas □*EX* does not.
On the other hand, □*EX* can erase variables which are local to an interrupted function, whereas)*ERASE* cannot.

TOTAL ERASURE   :   )*CLEAR*

The)*CLEAR* command erases everything contained in the active work-space. The computer confirms its execution by the response *CLEAR WS*.
But this command is not satisfactory with erasing the contents of the work-space it has the failing of re-establishing all the characteristic quantities of the work-space to their values, as they were defined in the preceding pages.

☐*NC* (Name Classification) accepts a vector or a matrix of characters representing the names of objects as an argument. For each name, this function gives
a numeric result which means the following

> 0 : this is not used in the work-space,
>
> 1 : this name is used as a label,
>
> 2 : this name belongs to a variable,
>
> 3 : this name belongs to a function,
>
> 4 : this name cannot be used to designate an object, either because it
> is the name of a group, or because it does not answer to the cond-
> itions stated in paragraph 2-21.

```
      ☐ ← M ← 2 5ρ'FUNC 6TEEN'
FUNC
6TEEN

      ☐NC M                        (FUNC is a function, 6TEEN is invalid)
  3 4
```

CANONICAL REPRESENTATION   :   ☐*CR*

☐*CR* is composed of the initials of Canonical Representation. A matrix of
characters of which each line contains an instruction of the function is called
the CANONICAL REPRESENTATION of a function. The (DEL) carrots at the beginning
and end disappear, as well as the line numbers.

```
      ∇ R ← CONTRACT M;B
[1]   B←0≠R←,M
[2]   R←(ρM),B/R,[0.5]ιρR ∇
```
Here is any function.

```
      ☐ ← CANON ← ☐CR 'CONTRACT'
R←CONTRACT M;B
B←0≠R←,M
R←(ρM),B/R,[0.5]ιρR
```
The canonical representation of it is
taken.

Only the contents of the lines remain, relieved of their numbers and
carrots (∇) DEL.

```
      ρ CANON
  3 19
```

```
      ☐NC 2 8ρ'CANON    CONTRACT'
  2 3
```
It is confirmed that *CANON* is a
variable, and *CONTRACT* a function.

If a function is locked, its canonical representation is a matrix whose two
dimensions are zero.
Taking the canonical representation of a function does not erase the latter.
Whether in conjunction with $\Box FX$ or not, the canonical representation enables
functions to be modified like data, to abolish the lines of them, to retain
them in files and to re-establish them later, etc.....

FUNCTION ESTABLISHING   : $\Box FX$

$\Box FX$ is the mnemonic of Fi**X**. Whereas $\Box CR$ transforms a function into a matrix
of characters   transforms a matrix of characters into a function, when it
is possible:

)CLEAR   We have a totally empty work-space.
CLEAR WS

        $VAR \leftarrow 2\ 11\rho'R\leftarrow AVG\ V$ $R\leftarrow(+/V)\div\rho,V'$
        VAR
$R\leftarrow AVG\ V$
$R\leftarrow(+/V)\div\rho,V$ We create a matrix of characters, which
                                     is a canonical representation of the
        $\Box FX\ VAR$ function.
  AVG
                                 We establish the corresponding function.
                               The computer confirms this by giving
)FNS   the name of the function established.
  AVG
)VARS   We can check, by the)*FNS* and)*VARS*
  VAR   commands, that the creation of the func-
                               tion has not erased the matrix of charact-
        $\nabla AVG[\Box]\nabla$ ers which we started with.
        $\nabla\ R\leftarrow AVG\ V$
[1] $R\leftarrow(+/V)\div\rho,V$
        ∇
                             Here, we check that the funciton exists
        $AVG\ 11\ 12\ 13$ in its usual form, and that it is funct-
  12   ioning satisfactorily.

Normally, $\Box FX$ gives a vector of characters as a result which is the name of
the function established. But if an anomaly makes this operation impossible,
$\Box FX$ restores the zero value (or the number of the irregular line on some
systems).
The principle causes of anomalies are: the first line of the matrix does not
constitute a correct function header, or the name which the function to be
established would have taken is already that of a variable or an interrupted
function.

```
        A ← 1 2 3
        □ ← TRY ← 2 5 ρ'R←A XR←X*2'
R←A X
R←X*2
```

□FX TRY	As there is already a variable called A,
0	a function cannot be created which would have the same name. □ FX gives a zero result.

On the contrary, any errors which the text could contain do not prevent the
establishing of the function.
Finally, if the established function has the same name as a non-suspended function, the latter is erased.

By □FX a function can establish another function, whose name is declared local;
hence a LOCAL FUNCTION will have been created, which will cease to exist on
the conclusion of the calling function. This form of programming enables a
function and one or several of the funcitons which it calls during its course
to be grouped under a single name. The text of the local function is often
an extract of the calling function. Here is an example of this :

```
      ∇ R← A CORRELATION B ;USELESS;NORMALIZE
[1]   USELESS←□FX 4 0 ↓ □CR 'CORRELATION'
[2]   R ← AVERAGE (NORMALIZE A)×(NORMALIZE B)
[3]   →0
[4]   R ← NORMALIZE X
[5]   X ← X-AVERAGE X
[6]   R ← X÷(AVERAGE X*2)*0.5  ∇
```

The function *NORM* is established
appropriate computing

End of function

⎱ these three lines constitute
⎰ the canonical form of *NORM*.

TIME STAMP   :   □*TS*

Recent systems have the control variable □*TS* , abbreviation of T̲ime S̲tamp,
which gives a measurement of time in the form of a vector of 7 elements, which
are:

the year; the month; the day; the hour; the minute; the second; the
millisecond.

                              ☐*TS*
              1982   8   15   15   42   37   183

This information is used in any application where the date is of importance:
invoicing, accountancy, communicating messages, etc....

ACCOUNTING INFORMATION :   ☐*AI*

☐*AI* signifies <u>A</u>ccounting <u>I</u>nformation : this is a variable which groups the
information relating to the user's consumption of computer time. With IBM,
☐*AI* contains the user's account number, the time of central units consumed
(in milliseconds), the connecting time, the time of terminal inactivity
(in milliseconds). This time of inactivity corresponds to the time during
which the user was able to introduce data.
With other makes, the information can be different.

 ☐*AI*[1] is used to check that a programme is not used by an unauthorised person
 ☐*AI*[2] is used to compare the time two versions of the same function take to
perform.

WORKING AREA   :   ☐*WA*

☐*WA* , or <u>W</u>orking <u>A</u>rea, represents the work-space still available in the memory,
expressed in the units used by the maker.

With IBM, ☐*WA* is expressed in octets, and is not alterable. With CONTROL
DATA, ☐*WA* is expressed in words this is a vector of 4 terms, of which the
last two can be modified by the user. With this maker, each call for ☐*WA*
causes a reorganisation of the work-space.

ATOMIC VECTOR : $\Box AV$

$\Box AV$ (Atomic Vector), is the vector of the 256 characters representable by
8 binary numbers, thus the 256 characters available in APL.
Some of these combinations are, in fact, not used; others represent printable
characters such as $A\ \underline{G}$ ⱶ ⋆ ⎕ or ◊ . Finally, some combinations represent
characters which have a use, but are not printable. Some of these special
characters are useful to know, such as the carriage return (passing to the
next line and returning to the margin), the line feed (without returning to
the margin), the back space, which returns to the previous character, the
bell (if the terminal is equipped with one), etc....

These special characters cannot be placed between quotes; hence they can only
be obtained by extracting from the atomic vector. This is always indicated
explicitly in the maker's brochure; it differs from one to another, and
sometimes from one version of APL to another with the same maker.

However, it is preferable to use the global variables called $\underline{CR}$, $\underline{LF}$ and $\underline{BS}$,
previously initialized by means of $\Box AV$, in such a way that its value can
be changed without modifying all the functions if the maker decided to modify
its atomic vector (which happens), or if the user decided to change makers
(which also happens!).

Here are some amusing examples (with IBM equipment)

$\quad\quad\quad \underline{LF} \leftarrow \Box AV[\,202\,]$ This character is the line feed
$\quad\quad\quad \underline{BS} \leftarrow \Box AV[\,201\,]$ This character is the back space

$\quad\quad\quad\quad 'S',\underline{BS},'\,|\,'$

$\$$
$\quad\quad\quad\quad ,'DOWNSTAIRS',[1.5]\underline{LF}$ This is how to create the dollar sign
$\quad D$
$\quad\quad O$
$\quad\quad\quad W$
$\quad\quad\quad\quad N$ Here, the line feed is used to create
$\quad\quad\quad\quad\quad S$ an amusing visual effect. Generally,
$\quad\quad\quad\quad\quad\quad T$ it is used to jump several lines in
$\quad\quad\quad\quad\quad\quad\quad A$ printing. $\Box\leftarrow 5\rho\underline{LF}$ will jump 6 lines.
$\quad\quad\quad\quad\quad\quad\quad\quad I$
$\quad\quad\quad\quad\quad\quad\quad R$
$\quad\quad\quad\quad\quad\quad\quad\quad S$

The position of the special symbols not always being the same in $\Box AV$, IBM has
now grouped them in a particular control variable called $\Box TC$ (Terminal Control)
in the order Back space, carriage return, line feed.

The use of the atomic vector is equally useful for deciphering recordings of
files, when the read instructions are not carried out directly. Thus, it must
be ascertained that the binary representation of a character *CHAR* is given
exactly by : $(8\rho 2)\top^-1+\square AV\iota CHAR$
Conversely, we can find which character represents a binary vector of eight
elements, called *OCTET*, by writing : $\square AV[1+2\bot\ OCTET]$

DELAY   : $\square DL$

$\square DL$ causes a pause in the processing being carried out. The length of this
pause is given, in seconds, by the argument of the function.
As the user is not master of the total work carried out by the computer, $\square DL$
gives the time which has ACTUALLY passed as a result.

$\qquad\qquad\square DL\ 10$ A pause of 10 seconds is requested.
$\qquad$ 10.207133   After the pause, the computer gives its
                                 actual duration.

The DELAY function uses practically no central unit time, no matter what the
duration requested is. It is used to simulate physical processes in multi-
console programmes, or more simply to allow the user time to reorganise the
paper during a long printing.

Normally, the pause can be interrupted by the terminal's interruption key.
Some systems do not permit this (APL 2.0 of CONTROL DATA), which is extremely
hazardous, because nothing protects it from an error.

THREE PRACTICAL PROBLEMS

SAFEGUARDING A FUNCTION

Having created a function (or a variable) in a work-space which does not have
a name, we would like to store it in the library space *USEFUL*.
For this we must :

− Safeguard the accomplished work in a provisional work-space	*)SAVE WORK*
− load the desired work-space	*)LOAD USEFUL*
− add the function to it	*)PCOPY WORK FUNCTION*
− safeguard the modified work-space	*)SAVE*
− erase the temporary work-space	*)DROP WORK*

CHANGING THE SYMBOL TABLE

On some systems, the symbol table can be increased or the page width changed
only in an empty work-space. When the message *SYMBOL TABLE FULL* appears, the
following precedures must be carried out :

− consult the size of the symbol table	*)SYMBOLS*
− safeguard the present work	*IS* 300 ; 300 *IN USE* *)SAVE*
− create an empty work-space	*)CLEAR*
− modify the size of its table	*)SYMBOLS* 500
− recopy the contents of the safeguarded work-space (called *CHARLOTTE* here)	*)COPY CHARLOTTE*

− re-establish the characteristic quantities of *CHARLOTTE*, which the
)COPY command does not re-establish. Think in particular of
□*IO*, □*PW*, □*LX*

− change the name of the work-space	*)WSID CHARLOTTE*
− safeguard the result	*)SAVE*
− have a strong cup of coffee to recover.	□*DL* 600

CANCELLING LINES IN A FUNCTION

Even though it is easy to cancel a line of a function, few current APL systems
have a simple means of cancelling several lines. A simple function using
□*CR* and □*FX* solves this problem.

```
      ∇ R←L MODFUNC F  ;U;□IO        L is the vector of the lines to be cancelled
[1]    □IO←0                          F is the name of the function to be modified
[2]    U←□CR F                        Its canonical form is taken.
[3]    R←□FX (~(ι1↑ρU)∈L)/U           The cut down version is established.
[4]    R←0≠1↑0ρR                      We check that the operation has been correctly
      ∇                               carried out, by checking that □FX gives a non-
                                      numerical result.
```

It was preferred to work in origin zero, because the instruction [1] of a function becomes line [2] in its canonical form. So as not to disturb the work-space, □IO is declared local.

```
    1  3  4  MODFUNC 'RESEARCH'       Three lines of a function are cancell
                                      The reply 1 signifies that everything
1                                     has gone well.
```

10-10   SHARED VARIABLES

In 1973, IBM announced the product APL/SV, or APL/Shared Variables. This APL version enables two independent and simultaneously active processors to communicate by sharing one or several variables, of which either one can consult or modify the value.

These processors can be any tasks (programmes) handeled by the computer. Hence, an active work-space can share variables:

- with another work-space, for interaction purposes,

- with a process control system used to drive an automatic syste (pump, lift, underground train system....). The active work-space will receive measurements (temperatures, pressures, speeds, etc), and will send orders (signals to be tripped, electro magnetic valves to be operated,....).

- with the control programme which runs the host computer. The variables thus shared will hence be as many means of control, enabling the APL user to gain access to means of processing to which he had no right up to now: rapid printing, magnetic tape units, files created in other languages, etc....

As an example, when the user consults the variable □TS, it is the computer which gives its instant value. Likewise, if the user modifies the value of □LC, the APL system immediately re-establishes the actual value.

```
      □LC ← 3
      □LC
1 5
```

$\square TS, \square LC,$ and all the other control variables, are variables which are shared between the active work-space and the host computer.

A variable can be shared only between two given processors at a given time, but nothing prevents an active work-space from simultaneously sharing different variables with different processors.
There is nothing to distinguish a shared variable from another variable, it can be made local, be modified, erased, but its behaviour is special since its value can be fixed independently by its two owners.

0-11   SHARE FUNCTIONS

Four functions are used to share variables and to control their use. Their name starts with a QUAD (because these are control functions), followed by SV (for Shared Variables).

$\square SVO$ (Offer)   To offer a name for sharing, or to consult its present shared state,

$\square SVR$ (Retract)   To retract an offer,

$\square SVC$ (Control)   To control the communication procedure between the two owners of the variable.

$\square SVQ$ (Query)   To ascertain the state of the offers pending.

OFFER PROCEDURE $\square SVO$

The function $\square SVO$ enables one or several names to be offered for sharing to one or several processors. It returns as a result the COUPLING DEGREE of each variable proposed. This is a number which equals :

   0 - if the computer refuses the offer. This is the case if the name offered is invalid, is already the name of a function or a group or is already shared with another processor.

   1 - If the offer is valid, but the partner has not yet accepted it.

   2 - If the partner has accepted the offer by making a similar offer.

The left-hand argument is the vector of the processors' numbers, or the
account numbers of the user, to whom the offers are addressed. The right-hand
argument is a vector, or a matrix of offered names.
There must be as many names as there are partners, unless several names are
being shared with a single parner.

> I   6430 |□SVO 'FLAN'

> 2 2 1   7654 □SVO 3 7 ρ 'BREAD WINE BOURSIN'

We have successfully offered the name *FLAN* for sharing to user 6430, then the
three names *BREAD*, *WINE*, and *BOURSIN* to user 7654. Two of the offers are
already accepted, which means that user 7654 had already made an offer to us
for the variables *BREAD* and *WINE*.

A name can also be offered for sharing to any other user who might like to
accept it, by giving a zero left-hand argument. The partner will have to
explicitly specify the number of the first offering processor.

An offer can be repeated as many times as desired even after being accepted,
without any concequences. The monadic use of □*SVO* gives the coupling degree
of one or several names :

>   □SVO 3 5 ρ 'BED FLAN BREAD'
> 2 0 1

RETRACRION □SVR

□*SVR* 'HEAD' is used to retract a previously made offer, thus breaking any sharing
but does not erase the variable *HEAD*. On the other hand, if the name offered
is local to a function, and one is pulling out of the latter, or if one erases
the name by □*EX* 'HEAD', the offer is also retracted, but the variable is
erased.)*CLEAR* and)*LOAD* also break a sharing.

□*SVR* gives the coupling degree BEFORE as a result.

EXAMPLE OF SHARING

Here is the course of a work session, where we follow simultaneously what
happens to two different users whose account numbers are 7420 and 7100.
We assume that the two work-spaces are empty at the start .   The operations
are carried out chronologically in the order of the printed lines.

USER 7420	NOTES	USER 7100
1 7100 □*SVO 'SALAD'*	1	
	2	2 7420 □*SVO 'SALAD'*
SALAD ← 'OIL'	3	
	4	*SALAD*
	5	*OIL* *SALAD ← 'VINEGAR'*
		SALAD ← 'CATERPILLAR'
SALAD	6	
CATERPILLAR		
SALAD		
CATERPILLAR		
□*SVR 'SALAD'*	7	
2	8	□*SVO 'SALAD'*
		1
SALAD ← 'DDT'	9	
	10	*SALAD*
		CATERPILLAR

1. 7420 offers the name *'SALAD'* to 7100 for sharing. The computer answers 1, which signifies that the offer has been made. For the moment there is not yet a variable called *SALAD*.

2. 7100 offers the name for sharing to 7420 in reply; he therefore accepts the sharing, and the computer replies 2.

3. 7420 assigns a value to *SALAD*; the variable is created.

4. When 7100 requests the value of *SALAD*, he obtains the one placed by 7420 instead of obtaining the *VALUE ERROR* diagnostic.

5. 7100 successively assigns two values to *SALAD*.

6. When 7420 consults the variable, he no longer finds the value which he had assigned to it, but the last value placed by 7100. He has "lost" the value *'VINEGAR'*, even reading *SALAD* twice in succession.

7. 7420 decides to end the dialogue, and retracts his offer. The computer replies 2: a sharing has just been broken.

8. 7100, by a monodic ☐ *SVO* , states that the coupling degree has fallen to 1, hence that the sharing is broken.

9. 7420 assigns a value to *SALAD*.

10. 7100 consults *SALAD*, and finds the value which it had previously, and not that which 7420 has just assigned to it.

It can be seen that 7100 has not retracted his offer, it is consequently still valid, and if 7420 typed 7100 ☐*SVO 'SALAD'* on his terminal, the sharing would be renewed.

If we look only at what appeared on the 7420 terminal, we establish that *SALAD* does not have the value which its owner assigned to it at the begininin This phenomenon is characteristic of shared variables.
In a similar way, if a function contains the two following instructions:

        [1]   ☐ ← *'HOW OLD ARE YOU ?'*
        [2]   *AGE* ← ☐

the variable *AGE* will contain something other than what has been assigned to the QUAD. We can consider that ☐ is a variable which is shared between the user and the active work-space.

THE STATE OF OFFERS ☐*SVQ*

In the previous example, 7420 and 7100 knew in advance that they wanted to share a specific variable at a specific time. If such is not the case, the function ☐*SVQ* shows the list of pending offers.

        ☐ *SVQ* ι0   A blank argument gives the list of the processors who
    8301 7222   have made us an offer (two here).

        ☐ *SVQ* 8301   If the argument is the offering processor's number
    TOALL   the names of the variables which he is offering are
    HEART   obtained.

From the moment a varibale is effectively shared, it no longer appears in the result given by ☐*SVQ* (in APL/SV; it is different with VS APL).

ACCESS CONTROL

In the earlier example, 7100 gave two successive values to *SALAD* (*VINEGAR*,
then *CATERPILLAR*), without 7420 having had the time to consult the first,
thus perhaps losing important information. A little later, 7420 consulted
the value of *SALAD* twice in succession, and obtained the reply *CATERPILLAR*
twice, without being able to determine if 7100 has actually transmitted the
same character string twice, or if he did not have the time to modify it.
In order to ensure a greater security of transmission, a communications
protocol can be fixed between the two partners.

To each shared variable, the computer automatically assigns a binary matrix
of dimensions 2 2 : the ACCESS CONTROL MATRIX, which each partner can modify.
Moreover, he keeps track of the operations carried out by each one of the
partners on this variable.

Each 1 of the access control matrix represents a restraint imposed on one
of the partners on the use which he makes of the shared variable.
The following table gives the meaning of the 1's of the access matrix of a
variable *V* shared between two partners *A* and *B*.

Prohibiting double assignement	*A* cannot assign two successive values to *V* without *B* having used or modified the first	*B* cannot assign two successive values to *V* without *A* having used or modified the first.
Prohibiting double usage	*A* cannot consult *V* twice in succession without *B* having assigned a value to it meantime.	*B* cannot consult *V* twice in succession without *A* having assigned a value to it meantime.
	RESTRICTIONS IMPOSED ON *A*	RESTRICTIONS IMPOSED ON *B*

The performance of any instruction contrary to the restrictions imposed
by the access control matrix is deferred until favorable conditions have
returned. During the wait nothing functions in the work-space any longer,
but this wait leads to virtually no use of computer time.

For example, if the matrix equals $\begin{smallmatrix} 1 & 0 \\ 0 & 1 \end{smallmatrix}$ and user *A* types :

        V ← 12
        V ← 15

the first instruction will be carried out, but the second will be carried
out only if *B* has consulted the value of *V* meantime. Otherwise, the
instruction *V* ← 15 will be deferred until *B* consults *V*.

16 different access control matrices can be defined, but, all do not have
the same significance, here are four characteristic figures.

0 0   This is the state of the matrix after sharing. No control is exercised
0 0   with the advantages and hazards that this presents.

1 0   During transmission of values from A to B , the latter can neither read
0 1   the same value twice in succession, nor forget to consult one of them.

0 1   same effects, but in the direction B towards A.
1 0

1 1   The double assignment and double usage prohibition act in both direction:
1 1   This is the maximum degree of restriction, which provides certain
      transmission in both directions.

It should be noted that in all cases a partner can deliberately ignore the
values that the other transmits, by assigning a value to the shared variable
without consulting the transmitted value.

The sharing of a variable does not favour   either of the partners, and each
one sees the access control matrix symmetrically in relation to how the other
sees it, in such a way that the first column represents the restrictions
which are imposed on him.

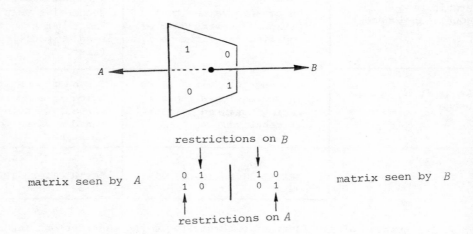

ESTABLISHING THE ACCESS CONTROL $\Box SVC$

By means of the function $\Box SVC$, each user can impose new restrictions, or lift
those which he himself has placed, but in no case can he lift those placed by
his partner.
The right hand argument of $\Box SVC$ is the name of the shared variable; the left
hand argument is the vector of the four elements of the access control matrix
as seen by the user. $\Box SVC$ gives the state of this vector as a result, as
defined by the combined action of both partners.

Hence, if two partners A and B place the restriction vectors CA and CB
respectively, the access control matrix will equal $MCA \leftarrow 2\ 2\rho CA \vee \phi 2 \phi CB$

$\qquad$ $1\ 0\ 0\ 0\ \Box SVC\ 'WOMAN'$
$\quad$ 1 0 0 0

$\qquad\qquad\qquad\qquad\qquad\qquad\qquad$ $0\ 0\ 1\ 0\ 0\ \Box SVC\ 'WOMAN'$
$\qquad$ $\Box\ SVC\ 'WOMAN'$ $\qquad\qquad\qquad\qquad\qquad\qquad$ 0 1 1 0
$\quad$ 1 0 0 1

Used in a monadic form, $\Box SVC$ indicates the state of the four elements of the
access control matrix, shown by the above example.

EXAMPLES

Two partners A and B share the variables X, Y and Z with the following restrictions :

	Matrix seen by A	Matrix seen by B
Variable X	0 0 0 1	0 0 1 0
Variable Y	1 0 0 0	0 1 0 0
Variable Z	1 1 1 1	1 1 1 1

Here are three typical examples of dialogues which could take place between
these two partners.

USER A	USER B
$X \leftarrow 1$	X 1
	X
$X \leftarrow 2$	2
	$X \leftarrow 3$ X
$X \leftarrow 4$	4
$Y \leftarrow 1$ Y	
1	
$Y \leftarrow 2$	
	Y 1
	Y 2
$Y \leftarrow 3$ $Y \leftarrow 5$	$Y \leftarrow 4$ Y
	5

DIALOGUE N° 1

B consults X for the first time.
While B attempts a second consultation,
his instruction is not carried out, and
his active work-space is placed in a waitin
position, shown here by the shaded part..

When A assigns a value to X, B's order is
activated, and the reply 2 is obtained.

B assigns a value to X, then tries to
consult this variable. As A has not assign
a value to X since B's previous consultatio
B's order is again placed in wait.

A deliberately ignores the value assigned
by B and assigns a value to X. B's order
is then carried out.

DIALOGUE N° 2

A assigns a value to Y, then consults it.
When A tries to assign a second value to
Y, B has not yet consulted the first, and
the assigning is placed in wait, shown by
the shading.

When B consults the first value of Y, the
second assigning of A is immediately carrie
out, and B can again consult Y.

A assigns a value to Y. B does not consult
it but replaces it by another value; this
is sufficient to allow A to again assign a
value to Y. Note that B has "lost" a valu
placed by A.

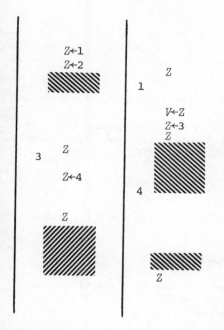

DIALOGUE N° 3

As in the previous example, A cannot assign two values to Z in succesion.

After B has consulted Z, the order Z←2 is validated, and B uses this value.
B decides to attribute a new value of his choice to Z. When B wants to re-read this value, his instruction is defered , because A has not given a value to Z since B's last consultation.

B's active work-space hence remains blocked until A assigns a value to Z.

A requests the value of Z for the second time, whereas B has not given a value to it: his order is defered.
B also consults Z for the second time, and his order is also blocked

It is seen therefore that it is possible to reach situations of total blockage if both partners try a prohibitted operation simultaneously. The interruption key enables one or the other work-spaces to be unblocked.

VARIABLES SHARED BETWEEN USERS

Sharing variables between users is a very good way of simulating physical, or automatic operations on several terminals with interactions between them.
For example, a mechanism can be simulated on a terminal by a function which loops indefinitely, whereas a second terminal enables outside orders which intervene at completely random moments to be sent to the first, which would be difficult to simulate with a single terminal.
A very significant example will be seen in the next paragraph with the simulation of a lift.
These applications are however rather rare, and the biggest use of shared variables is for access to auxiliary processors.

USING AUXILIARY PROCESSORS

With the APL/SV version of IBM, and then with the later APL CMS and VS APL
versions, variables can be shared with auxiliary processors which belong to
the computer's control programmes, or which the user could have written
himself in assembler language, or any other language.
Each processor has a specific role, and enables operations to be undertaken
which APL would not permit on its own.
Apart from functioning anomalies, the processors supplied by the maker are
always active (provided that they were initialized at the same time as APL),
and are known to the system under a number less than 1000, indicated in
the maker's brochures. For example:

In the APL version:

360 or 370 is a processor, called TSIO (Time Sharing Input Output), which
    permits access to the computer's general files.

In the VS APL version subsequently issued under CMS,

100 is the commands processor. It enables the computer's control language
    instructions to be carried out, while still in APL, transmitted in the
    form of character strings by a shared variable.

101 is the "stack" or "alternate input" processor. It enables commands,
    instructions and data to be stored   Each time the APL system is placed
    in waiting position, instead of handing over to the user, it uses the
    information in the stack. We can thus, for example, obtain an automatic
    safeguarding of a work-space.

110 is the disk I/O processor, which gives access to the files on the systems
    disk.

111 gives access to all types of sequential files.

With the IBM 5100 table computer, the processor 1 acts as an interface with
the peripheral memories, and with the printer.

The offers made to an auxiliary processor are automatically accepted,
provided that they are correct. Thus the computer usually imposes a complete
control on the communication. While the nature of the information transmitted after sharing depends on the processor used, some major principles can
however be redeemed.

1 - A variable, called control variable, is shared with auxiliary processor.
    It is used to control exchanges of information between the processor
    and the active work-space, and can also, in some cases, act as a vehicle
    for this information.

2 - Before sharing, the first value attributed to this variable is a
    character string comprising key words which are recognisable to the
    processor.

These key words indicate the nature of the processings to be undertaken.
For example, sequential reading of a file in APL/SV :

        370 ⎕SVO 'CTLA'
    2
        CTLA ← 'SR DSN=STOCK'

With a 5100 computer, sharing a variable with the printer :

        PAPER ← 'PRT MSG=OFF'
        1⎕ SVO 'PAPER'
    2

3 - Thus the computer assigns a value called code - return to the control
    variable, whose first element must be zero if the order has been under-
    stood and carried out. A non-zero value indicates either an error, or
    a technical impossibility forbidding the carrying out of the order.
    It is thus essential to consult the value of this code-return. ·

4 - Exchanges of information are established between the work-space and
    the auxiliary processor. As will be seen in the next chapter, this
    information is transmitted either by the control variable, or by a second
    shared variable, called the data variable.

5 - At the end of the exchange, we retract or erase the control variable.

We can imagine all sorts of auxiliary processors establishing communications
between the work-space and the outside. But the essential idea which led
to the development of auxiliary processors was to enable access to all the
types of files which a computer can accept. This is still their main
use at the present time; and it is this aspect which we will study in the
next chapter.

10-14   SIMULATING A LIFT

We wish to simulate the working of a lift. If we have only one terminal, the
calls will have to be introduced by means of a quad, thus always at the same
moment in the working cycle. In order to achieve a true simulation, we will
use two terminals communicating by shared variables :

    - On one terminal, a function which loops indefinitely scans the calls,
      causes the lift to continue and visualises its position on the paper.

 — the other terminal simulates the call and cabin buttons, which
allow the lift to move.

DATA

The function *START* is used to define the essential variables.
We will imagine that the lift serves two basement levels and 6 floors; the
variable *LEVELS* will be the vector : ¯2 ¯1 0 1 2 3 4 5 6

The calls will be memorized in the boolean matrix *CALLS*, of 3 lines and 9
columns (one per level):

0	0	0	0	0	1	0	0	0	calls to ascend
0	1	1	0	0	1	0	0	0	orders in the cabin
0	0	0	0	1	0	0	1	0	calls to descend

    ¯2   ¯1   0   1   2   3   4   5   6

In the first line, the 1's represent the levels from where the calls by
people wishing to ascend originate. Here, one person on the third level
wishes to ascend.

The second line represents the destinations requested by people who are in
the cabin. Here the people who are in the cabin want to go to levels ¯1
0 and 3 respectively.

In the third line are the levels where the calls by people wishing to descend
originate.

The position of the cabin is given by the variable *POSCABIN*; the direction in
which it is going, or was going before stopping, is given by the variable
DIRECTION: 1 for ascending, ¯1 for descending.

LEVELS, *CALLS*, *POSCABIN* are shared between the two terminals, as is the variable
DELAY, which enables the speed at which the process is carried out to be
modified, according to the computer's load.

OPERATION

The function *START* is introduced to the "lift" terminal. This function defines
the levels, initializes the variables and shares them with the other terminal
by means of the funciton *SHARE*. At the same time, the same *SHARE* function is
introduced to the "calls" terminal, so as to accept the offers.

Once the variables are shared, the calls can be sent by means of the three
functions *A*, *C* and *D*, whose syntax is as follows :

    *A*3   signifies that somebody on the 3rd level wants to ascend.

    *C*0   signifies that somebody in the cabin wants to go to the ground floor.

    *D*5   signifies that somebody on the 5th level wants to descend.

The position of the cabin is visualized on paper by the numbers of the levels reached and the characters   and X, which represent the opening and closing of the doors respectively.
An example of this operation will be seen on pages 296-297.

FUNCTIONS OF THE "CALLS" TERMINAL

```
      ∇ SHARE ;P;V;R;U
[1]   V ← 3 6ρ'CALLS DELAY LEVELS'
[2]   'PARTNER ?'
[3]   P←□
[4]   L0: R←P □SVO V
[5]   U←□DL 5
[6]   →(2∨.≠R)/0
      ∇
```

This function asks the partners account number, and offers him the three variables for sharing, until the offers are accepted, which is translated by a coupling degree equal to 2.

```
      ∇ U LVL
[1]   CALLS[1;LEVELS ι LVL]←1
      ∇
```

The three functions *A*, *C* and *D* are confined to placing a 1 in the appropriate place of the calls array. Note that it is possible to use a vectorial argument to send several calls simultaneously.

```
      ∇ C LVL
[1]   CALLS[2;LEVELS ι LVL]←1
      ∇
```

```
      ∇ D LVL
[1]   CALLS[3;LEVELS ι LVL]←1
      ∇
```

FUNCTIONS OF THE "LIFT TERMINAL"

The main function is the *LIFT* function, of which here is a complete description:

```
      ∇ LIFT
[1]   WAIT
[2]   ACTION:←→DECISION
[3]   GO
[4]   OPENCLOSE
[5]   UPDATE
[6]   →ACTION
      ∇
```

[1] Provided that no call is registered, the *WAIT* function, which loops
    indefinitely, maintains the lift in a waiting position.

[2] As soon as a call is detected, *WAIT* is left, and the *DECISION* function
    fixes the direction of the cabin and indicates which instruction should
    be followed. This will most often be instruction [3].

[3] *GO* simulates the movement of the lift by advancing *POSCABIN* in the direct-
    ion defined by *DECISION*. The cabin will stop at a level:

    - if somebody in the cabin has asked to go to this level,
    - if somebody on this level has issued a call to go in the same direction
      as the cabin,
    - if there are no more calls from levels situated in the direction in
      which the cabin is travelling. This is what happens when the cabin
      ascends to pick somebody up who wants to descend.

[4] At each stop, *OPENCLOSE* opens the doors, waits a few seconds and closes
    the doors again.

[5] The list of calls must thus be up-dated by puting zeros in the appropriate
    places.

[6] The cycle recommences with a new decision in line [2]:

    - if there are still some calls, we continue with *GO*,
    - if there are no more calls, we return to *WAIT*,
    - if the cabin is called from the level it is on, we jump straight to
      OPENCLOSE.

The following are other functions of this work-space; some, such as
CLOSING, could be improved by door or overload protection. It is also
possible to improve the graphic visualization of the cabins movements.

```
      ∇ START
[1]   'NUMBER OF BASEMENT LEVELS AND FLOORS'
[2]   LEVELS ← |2↑⎕
[3]   LEVELS ← (0,ι+/LEVELS)-LEVELS[1]
[4]   POSCABIN ← LEVELS ι0
[5]   CALLS ← (3,ρLEVELS)ρ0
[6]   DIRECTION ← 1
[7]   DELAY ← 5
[8]   SHARE
[9]   LIFT
      ∇

      SHARE
```

The function asks the levels to be
served, then places the cabin on the
ground floor.

Then various variables are initialized

These variables are shared
Then the principle function is
introduced.

This function has already been described
in the functions of the "calls" terminal.

```
     ∇ WAIT ;U
[1]    →(1∈CALLS)/0
[2]    U←□DL DELAY
[3]    →1
     ∇
```

This function loops indefinitely provided that no call is detected. The function *DC* prevents excessive use of computing time.

```
     ∇ R←AGAIN ;U
[1]    U←(DIRECTION<0)×1+ρLEVELS
[2]    R←1∈0,POSCABIN-U)↓CALLS
     ∇
```

The result (1 or 0) of this function indicates whether there are still any calls from levels which the cabin will reach.

```
     ∇ JUMP←DECISION
[1]    →(~1∈CALLS)/0,JUMP←1
[2]    → AGAIN/0,JUMP←3
[3]    DIRECTION ← -DIRECTION
[4]    → AGAIN/0,JUMP←3
[5]    JUMP←4
     ∇
```

If there are no more calls, the function is left, and *JUMP* ←1 will cause the *LIFT* function to be followed by *WAIT*. If there are still some calls we will follow on with *GO*, after having changed direction if need be. Finally, in the case where the call comes from the level where the cabin is, *JUMP*←4 will cause *OPENCLOSE* to follow on.

```
     ∇ GO ;U
[1]    U←□DL DELAY
[2]    DISPLAY POSCABIN←POSCABIN+DIRECTION
[3]    →(1∈CALLS[DIRECTION ↓ 3 2 1;POSCABIN])/0
[4]    → AGAIN/1
     ∇
```

The cabin travels until it meets one of the three conditions stated above. □ *DL* enables the travelling time from one floor to another to be stimulated and economises on computing time.

```
     ∇ DISPLAY N
[1]    ((3×N)ρ' '),2 0▼LEVELS[N]
     ∇
```

Visulizing the cabin's position on the paper.

```
     ∇ OPENCLOSE ;U
[1]    OPEN
[2]    U←□DL DELAY
[3]    CLOSE
     ∇
```

This function simulates stopping of the cabin at a level, the opening and closing of the doors, separated by a short wait.

```
     ∇ OPEN
[1]    ((3×POSCABIN)ρ' '),' □'
     ∇
```

Opening and closing of the doors are represented by the symbols □ and ×.

```
     ∇ CLOSE
[1]    ((3×POSCABIN)ρ' '),' ×'
     ∇
```

USER 4419	NOTES	USER 4420

USER 4419

```
        START
NUMBER OF BASEMENT LEVELS AND FLOORS
□:
        2 6
PARTNER ?
□:
        4420


            1
              2
                3
                  4
                  □
                  ×
                3
              2
              □
              ×

              □
              ×
                3
                  4
                  □
                  ×
                3
              2
            1
          0
          □
          ×
        ‾1
      ‾2
      □
      ×
        ‾1
          0
          □
          ×
            1
              2
                3
                  4
                    5
                    □
                    ×


              etc.....
```

NOTES

```
1




2
3




4
5




6
7
8

9




10




11




12
```

USER 4420

```
              SHARE
        PARTNER ?
        □:
              4419

              D 4




              C 2




              U 2
              C 4

              D 0




              C ⁻2




              U 5



              D 3




        etc.....
```

NOTES

1 - The partners share the variables. To begin with, the "lift" terminal must define the levels to be served.

2 - The variables are shared, and the *LIFT* function is introduced. No call has yet been registered, and the cabin waits on the ground floor (*WAIT* function).

3 - Call for decending from the 4th floor. The lift leaves waiting position and ascends. The cabin will stop when, on finding no calls for ascending it reaches the last call for descending.

4 - Opening the doors. The person enters the cabin and asks to go to the second floor.

5 - Closing the doors, the descent to the second floor, opening and closing of the doors.

6 - There are no more calls for the moment. We return to waiting position.

7 - Somebody calls from the second floor. We fully examine the *DECISION* function to realise that the call came neither from above nor below. Therefore we follow on with *OPENCLOSE*.

8 - Thus the doors are open, without the cabin moving. The person wants to go to the 4th floor.

9 - During the journey, other calls are registered.

10 - On the ground floor the cabin picks up a person who wants to descend, but the function *UPDATE* retains the call of somebody else who also called from the ground floor, but to ascend.

11 - The cabin picks up this last person.

12 - The cabin ascends directly to the 5th floor, without stopping at the 3rd where it will pass later to pick up somebody who wants to descend.

```
     ∇ UPDATE ;S
[1]   S←DIRECTION×1∈CALLS[DIRECTION↓3 2 1 ;POSCABIN]
[2]   CALLS[S↓3 2 1 ;POSCABIN]←0
     ∇
```

This function places zeros in two or three lines of the same column of *CALLS*, according to whether the cabin follows its course, or changes direction.

EXERCISES ON THE SUBJECT WITHOUT ANSWERS

1) Write a function *STOP* which instantly stops the cabin without cancelling the awaiting calls. A carriage-return will restart the lift.

2) Write the function *FIRE* which simulates a priority call: all calls are cancelled, the cabin descends to the ground floor and stays there. A carriage-return renders the lift ready to receive calls and operate again.

3) Write a function *WELCOME* which accepts offers for sharing from any other terminal, without either the partner or the names of the variables to be offered being known in advance.

DRAWING BY RUMWEISS

The function ⎕DL creates
a pause in the processing.

CONTROL VARIABLES

$\Box IO$	Index origin
$\Box PW$	Page width, in number of characters
$\Box PP$	Printing precision of numerical values
$\Box RL$	Random seed of random values (Random link)
$\Box CT$	Comparison tolerance
$\Box LC$	Vector of line numbers of interrupted functions (Line counter)
$\Box TS$	Time stamp: year; month; day; hour; minute; second; millisecond
$\Box AI$	Accounting information, variable according to the system
$\Box WA$	Memory space available (Working area)
$\Box AV$	Vector of usable characters in APL (atomic vector)
$\Box TC$	Terminal control charatcers (BS, RC, LF)
$\Box LX$	Expression executed at work-space loading (Latent expression)

PRINCIPLE ARGUMENT OF THE I-*BEAM* FUNCTION

I 19	Terminal inactivity time
I 20	Present time, in sixtieths of a second
I 21	Central processing unit time used, in sixtieths of a second
I 22	Number of octets available in the work-space
I 23	Number of terminals connected
I 24	Connection time at the beginning of the work session.
I 25	Date
I 26	Number of the instruction to be carried out
I 27	Line numbers of the functions awaiting execution
I 28	Type of terminal used
I 29	User's account number

PRINCIPAL CONTROL FUNCTIONS

□*SAVE* 'wsid'	Safeguarding active work-space under the name wsid
□*LOAD* 'wsid'	Loading the work-space wsid
{names}□*COPY* 'wsid'	Copy of the designated objects belonging to the work-space wsid
□*DROP* 'wsid'	Erasing the work-space wsid
□*WSID* {'wsid'}	Examining or modifying the active work-space's name
□*LIB*	Matrix of the work-spaces' name
□*CR* 'name'	Matrix of the characters constituting the header and instructions of the named function (canonical representation)
□*FX* C	Establishing the function of which C is the canonical form (Fix)
□*EX* 'names'	Erasing LOCAL objects whose names are given by the matrix of characters "names"
□*NL* types	Matrix of the names of the objects belonging to one of the types given by the vector "types" (name list) 1 = labels of interrupted functions 2 = variables 3 = functions
□*NC* 'names'	Class of local objects whose names are given by the matrix of characters "names" 0 = name unused up to now 1 = name of suspended functions 2 = name of a variable 3 = name of a function 4 = incorrect name, or group name
□*DL* N	Interruption of the processing for N seconds (delay)

The above list comprises the most common control functions. It could not cover every possibility offered by any particular system.

It would be appropriate to add all the variables sharing functions, the printing control function □*FMT* and functions for access to the files in some cases.

10-15   CONTROL FUNCTIONS AND VARIABLES

Control functions and variables are primitives of the language. They can neither be erased nor copied from one work-space to another. Furthermore, the control variables are SHARED between the computer and the user; also no matter what value can be attributed to variables $\square AI$, $\square AV$, $\square TS$, $\square LC$, $\square UL$ and $\square WA$, the computer immediately re-establishes the suitable value. Here are more notes which should interest the advanced reader:

REPRESENTATION OF NUMBERS, and $\square CT$

It was stated in paragraph 7-14 how whole numbers are represented on IBM computers. Decimal values are represented on a double word, or 64 bits, in three distinct parts which are:

- bit 1   : the number sign (0 for positive, 1 for negative),

- bits 9 to 64 : the mantissa, which is a number between 0 and 1
                 (exclusive) whose decimal value is : $(2\bot MANTISSA)\div 2*56$

- bits 2 to 8 : an exponent which indicates by which power of 16
                 the mantissa must be multiplied to obtain the number
                 represented. Its decimal value is obtained by:
                 $(2\bot EXPONENT)-64$

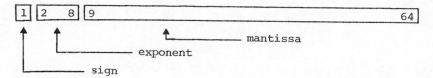

If we call the vector of 64 bits which represents a decimal number *WORD*, the value of the latter is obtained by:

$(1-2\times WORD[1]) \times ((2\bot WORD[8+\iota 56]) \div 2*56) \times (16*{}^{-}64+2\bot WORD[1+\iota 7])$

With such a representation, the smallest representable number is ${}^{-}7.2370E75$. and the largest is $7.2370E75$ with CONTROL DATA, where the representation is slightly different, these limits are reduced to $\pm 1.26501408E322$.

We understand that if we accept a difference equal to $\square CT$ on the mantissa, the difference tolerated on the number will be multiplied by the exponent, which gives:

$\square CT \times 16 * \lceil 16\circledast NUMBER$

Note that the definition of $\square CT$ is not symetrical with CONTROL DATA, which occasionally causes some surprises.

PAGE WIDTH

The upper limit of $\Box PW$ ranges from 390 to 500, according to the system, and even to $^-1+2*17$, or 131071, with CONTROL DATA. These high values are surprising when one considers that a terminal rarely has a width greater than 132 characters.

Actually, if we place a carriage-return character every 1000 characters an a vector of 1000 characters, a result printed on 10 lines of 99 characters will be obtained. If the page width is 132, the computer will pass on to the next line every 132 characters, thus preventing a wrong result.

According to the system, $\Box PW$ counts the total characters sent to the terminal (including the carriage-returns and back-spaces), or counts only the actual physical position of the printing system on the paper.

Which is it on your system? Test $\Box\leftarrow600\rho(100\rho\,'A')\underline{RC}$, where $\underline{RC}$ is the carriage-return and $\Box\leftarrow600\rho(50\rho\,'A')\,,\underline{LF}(49\rho\underline{BS})$, where $\underline{BS}$ is the back-space. If a daisy wheel printing terminal is used (ANDERSON-JACOBSON AJ 832 for example) curves composed of very close points can be plotted (1/60 of an inch). Hence a page contains more than 500 characters, and it is important to be able to give a high value to $\Box PW$.

RANDOM LINK

As an example, here is the algorithm used by IBM to generate random numbers by the monadic ROLL function:

```
        ∇ R←ROLL N
[1]     □RL←(⁻1+2*31)|□RL×7*5
[2]     R←□IO+⌊N×□RL÷2*31   ∇
```

The first line modifies the random seed, which will be used for the next generating. The use of the RESIDUE function ensures that $\Box RL$ is always less than $(2*31)-1$. This means that the quotient $\Box RL\div2*31$ is ALWAYS between 0 and 1. On multiplying it by the argument of the function, a number strictly less than N is obtained. On adding $\Box IO$, the required result is obtained. Moreover, two executions present a comparison:

$\Box RL \leftarrow 7*5$	$\Box RL \leftarrow 7*5$
? 10	ROLL 10
2	2
$\Box RL$	$\Box RL$
282475249	282475249
? 10	ROLL 10
8	8

OTHER CONTROL FUNCTIONS

Some systems have control possibilities other than those shown previously; without claiming to study them all, here are some interesting functions:

☐*LOCK*   enables one or several objects to be locked, given in the form of a matrix of names. Hence variables as well as functions can be locked, which is very useful (CDC)

☐*EX*   has already been encountered. This function sometimes accepts a vector of names separated by blanks, sometimes easier to write than a matrix.

☐*FMT*   Printing control function, described at length in chapter 9.

☐*STOP*   these two functions enable stop controls to be placed on the
☐*TRACE*   lines of a function, or tracing of its execution, as will be seen in the pages dealing with "programming aids". On other systems, these are ☐*SS* (set stop), ☐*ST* (set trace), ☐*RS* (reset stop) and ☐*RT* (reset trace).

☐*LTIME*   with CONTROL DATA is used to ascertain the time taken for execution of certain lines of certain functions. This type of procedure is also available with BURROUGHS by the functions ☐*SM* and ☐*RM*.

☐*SVQ*, ☐*SVO*, ☐*SVC*, ☐*SVR* are used with IBM to share and control variables between two users, or between a user and the computer.

On other systems, all the control possibilities are in the form of control functions, including handling work-spaces or disconnection of the terminal. This is certainly the path that future systems will take.

ERROR TRAPPING

What could be more disconcerning for somebody using programmes written in APL who does not know this language, than to see a *LENGTH ERROR* or *DOMAIN ERROR* message appear? The error could be attributed to the user, to the programme designer (who cannot foresee everything), or to outside elements, connected with the computer; whatever the reason, the user can continue only if he knows APL.

Also the designers of APL systems now offer the possibility of treating errors before they appear to the user. The methods proposed are rather diverse;

there will be demonstrated below the operation of the system of exceptions management set up by Scientific Time Sharing Corp. on its APL∗PLUS system since the end of 1978. It is definitely the most advanced system at this time, and it has the advantage of being harmoniously integrated into the general concept of APL.

This system uses five control functions: □*DM*, □*ELX*, □*ALX*, □*ERROR* , and □*SA*.

□*DM* (Diagnostic Message) is a niladic funciton which gives the last diagnostic sent out, in the form of a vector of characters containing ·carriage-returns.

          12+5)X7
SYNTAX ERROR
          12+5)X7
               ∧

          □*DM*   □*DM* contains the last diagnostic sent out
SYNTAX ERROR
          12+5)X7
               ∧

          ρ□*DM*   it is clearly seen that □*DM* is a vector.
    36

Of course, in an empty work-space, □*DM* is an empty vector.

□*ELX* and □*ALX* (Error or Attention Latent eXpression) are two latent expression very similar to □*LX* , which we know.

     □*ELX* is executed as soon as error is detected, BEFORE any other action
     □*ALX* is executed as soon as an interruption is brought about by means
            of the interruption key (Attention).

Even before an error message is sent out, it is possible to carry out a special processing, or to pull out of the function, or to introduce a correction module, etc.....

We will assume that we are using the QUAD function in a work-space as follows:

          ∇←R QUAD MSG;L   This function is very close to the *CALL*
    [1]   L←ρ □←MSG,' : '   function of paragraph 9-3.
    [2]   R←⍋L↓□
          ∇

          1979 — QUAD 'VECTOR OF AGES'
VECTOR OF AGES : 17 41 33 52 24   Normally, all goes well !
1962 1938 1946 1927 1955

But if the characters introduced do not represent a numeric vector, an error
will interrupt the QUAD.function.

Henceforth this type of error can be treated in the following way, by modifying
the QUAD function.

```
        ∇ R←QUAD MSG;L;□ELX
[1]     □ELX← '→LAB,ρ□←''ANOMALY, TRY AGAIN'''
[2]     LAB: L←ρ□←MSG,' ; '
[3]     R←⍎L↓□
        ∇
```

400 + QUAD 'ENTER NUMBERS'   An error is committed 45.78.99 is
ENTER NUMBERS : 45.78.99 11   incorrect. □ELX is activated, which
ANOMALY, TRY AGAIN   causes the processing to be taken up
ENTER NUMBERS] 45.78 .99 11   again at LAB.
445.78 400.99 411

No error message has been transmitted, but we can check that the APL system
had detected the error committed by consulting □DM :

```
        □DM
     SYNTAX ERROR
     QUAD[3]⍋45.78 . 99 11
                 ∧
```

□ELX and □ALX can be redefined at any moment, or be made local to a function
(as above), in such a way that the procedure employed to treat the anomaly
can differ according to the case.

In an empty work-space, □ELX and □ALX equal '□DM' , so that detection of
an error causes the usual message to be displayed. The user who does not
use these possibilities is thus not diverted at all.

It could be that an error committed in the environment of a function causes
an error inside the latter. In such a case it can be better to signal the
error at the level of the call sequence, rather than inside the function.
This is the aim of the monadic function, □ERROR.

If in a function, □ERROR is carried out with a non-blank argument, an error
will be signalled in the sequence which called this function, at its
completion.
Consider the two following functions

```
        ∇ R←A PLUS B                              ∇ R←BIZARRE A
[1]     R←A+B                          [1]        R←1↓A PLUS⁻1↓A
        ∇                                         ∇
```

BIZARRE 3 5 7 9
LENGTH ERROR   An error is signalled in PLUS,
PLUS[1] R←A+B   whereas the cause is in BIZARRE.
        ∧

We will modify the function *PLUS*. In case of error, the execution of □*ELX*
will cause □*ERROR* to be executed.


```
            ∇ R←A PLUS B;□ELX
     [1]    □ELX←'□ERROR ''ABNORMAL OPERANDS'''
     [2]    R←A+B
            ∇
```

```
        BIZARRE 3 5 7 9
  ABNORMAL OPERANDS
  BIZARRE[1] R←1↓A PLUS ¯1↓A
            ∧
```


This time, the error has been signalled at the level of the calling function,
and the error message displayed is that given as an argument to □*ERROR*.
In a way, *PLUS* behaves like a primitive function.

Thanks to □*ERROR* , we can make sure that the messages resulting from certain
errors are more explicit than the normal message.

Finally, it could be that no relevant action could cope with certain errors.
In such cases, the function □*SA* (Stop Action) assigns control to the computer
BEFORE handing over to the user. Three arguments are possible:

       □*SA* ← ''   nothing happens, the user finds himself in the normal
                                situation after an error,

       □*SA* ← '*CLEAR*'   the active work-space is cleaned; the user finds
                                himself in an empty work-space, which is useful
                                for assuring the security of certain applications,

       □*SA* ← '*EXIT*'   the computer leaves the interrupted function. It also
                                leaves the calling function, until it meets a function
                                in which □*SA* is either an empty vector, or the
                                value '*CLEAR*'. This allows a "return" to a function
                                whose state is well known and from which we can
                                continue.

Thus conceived, the control of exceptions is a big step towards the automation
of processings.
The other big step, equally due to Scientific Time Sharing Corp., is the
automatic control of execution (ACE), which enables tasks to be carried out
without a terminal needing to be connected during their processing.
In such circumstances it is important that the application introduced can
itself manage the exceptions encountered by means of the possibilities mentioned
above.

These two innovations open up the field of production data processing to
APL.

SCREEN MANAGEMENT

It must be said that the form of dialogue between the computer and the APL
user is rather poor, if one compares it with the methods available on computers
using the so-called "screen management" systems.
The principle consists of printing a series of questions on a screen in one go
the user then filling, or otherwise, the zones of the screen for which he
thinks he has information to be introduced. Checking of the form of these data
is carried out, and the screen is then filled again.
Such a method is more difficult to apply to APL, where a question can lead the
user to introducing a single number, or a long vector. However, some systems
are being studied by various makers, and IBM have put forward its APL FULL
SCREEN option already for some time.
It is no longer a question of simply speaking the APL language, but of means
of supplementary processings, to which one has access by an auxiliary
processor, and we will not take this any further in this work, despite all the
advantages which these devices present in management data processing.

10-16   COMMANDS

There are other commands on some systems. Hence, the command)*OFF*, which
ends the work session and cuts communication with the computer, is replaced
by other commands on some systems.
There are sometimes commands for ending the work session while maintaining
communication for the next user, for sending messages to the computer's
console operator, or to another APL user.

COMMANDS AND THE QUAD

According to system, it is either possible or not to release a command at the
moment when a quad causes a request for information.
For example:

□	A value request is relaxed.
□:	Warning symbol.
)*SI*	The state indicator is requested; the computer
□	indicates that the interruption is on a quad
□:	then re-asks the question.
)*SAVE*	A new command is introduced, which this time
INTERRUPT	causes defintive interruption of the quad,
□	signalled by the computer.
∧	

10.03.14 07/05/77 *EXPO*

Test this possiblity on your system, for commands)*SI*:)*SAVE*;)*LOAD*;)*CLEAR*.

10-17   SHARED VARIABLES

VALUE OF A SHARED VARIABLE

At the moment when two processors A and B share the name *VAR*:

- if the variable *VAR* exists neither with A nor B, it will take the fi
  which will be assigned to it by one of the two partners.
- If one of the users has already given a value to it , it keeps it at
  the time of sharing,
- if both partners have already assigned a value to it, at the time of
  sharing it keeps the value of the first user to have made the offer.

If one wants to share a variable between two work-spaces which already exist
it could be that the names used in the two work-spaces are not the same, or
that the name one user wants to share designates a function or a group belong
ing to the other. In such cases, surrogate names can be used, which does
not exist for either of the partners, and serves simply to establish
communication. In the offer, the name of the variable and the surrogate
name appear in this order, separated by a blank:

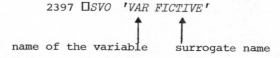

                2397 □*SVO 'VAR FICTIVE'*

           name of the variable   surrogate name

In order for there to be a sharing, both partners must use the same surrogate
name, or the surrogate name chosen by one of them must be the variable name
proposed by the other. For example, if user 5683 wants to offer the variable
ONE, whereas user 2487 wants to offer *TWO*, the sharing could be undertaken
in one of the three following ways:

USER 5683	USER 2487
2487 □*SVO* '*ONE I*'	5683 □*SVO* '*TWO I*'
2487 □*SVO* '*ONE TWO*'	5683 □*SVO* '*TWO*'
2487 □*SVO* '*ONE*'	5683 □*SVO* '*TWO ONE*'

STATE OF OFFERS

When a variable is shared, it no longer appears in the result of $\square SVQ$ (in APL/SV), but one can ascertain the names of shared variables by:

$$(2=\square SVO\ \square NL\ 2)\neq\square NL\ 2$$

On the other hand, there is no way of knowing with which processor a variable is shared. With VS APL, the function $\square SVQ$ has been modified to give also the names of variables already shared. A left-hand argument equal to 1 or 2 enables variables to be selected whose coupling degree is 1 or 2.

CONTROLLING SHARING

$\square SVC$ accepts the scalars 0 and 1 instead of 0 0 0 0 and 1 1 1 1 as left-hand argument. This function also accepts matricial arguments for fixing either the same degree of control on different variables, or different degrees of control on different variables.

If a variable is shared with a certain state of control, fixed by $\square SVC$, this state of control remains after the variable has been withdrawn, so that if this variable is shared again, it will be in the state of control which it was in before.

11-18   USING IBM AUXILIARY PROCESSORS

USE OF THE PROCESSOR 100

The processor 100 enables commands to be carried out, from among an authorized list of commands. Two uses of this will be seen in paragraph 11-9: to print-out the list of a user's files, and to erase one of these files.

USE OF THE ALTERNATE INPUT PROCESSOR

With the processor 101, a stack of commands, instructions or data can be formed by a programme. Each time that the work-space returns to waiting, instead of taking the next input from the keyboard, the system extracts the FIRST element of the stack, and uses it as if it had been typed on the keyboard by the user. The stack will thus be used at each quad, stop control (see this term in paragraph 12-5), at the end of execution of the function, and at each interruption of execution, whether voluntary or due to an error.

Knowing that the data placed in the stack are always used starting with the
first, the data can be stacked from the top of the stack (option *BEG* or
LIFO), or from the bottom (option *END* or *FIFO*) to obtain the required effect.

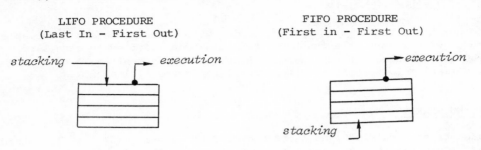

It can be stated also that the processor 101 will have to carry out conversa-
tions in the internal representation codes of the data in the stack (see IBM
brochures on this subject). The initial value of the variable to be shared
with the processor includes the following elements:

'CMS(conversation procedure)*'*

For example, a function named *PRINT* requires no introduction of data, but
requires a significant time in order to be executed. One would like to be
able to start execution and then leave. Therefore at the end of execution an
automatic safeguard is required which conserves the results elaborated, and
then the terminal disconnects itself automatically, for economic reasons.

The function *DISCAFTER* will perform this automatic operation.

```
          ∇ DISCAFTER FUNC ;STACK;U
    [1]   STACK ← 'CMS (FIFO APL'          Initializing
    [2]   →(2≠101 □SVO 'STACK')/ERR        Sharing the variable
    [3]   →(0≠STACK)/ERR                   Control of return-code
    [4]   STACK ← ')WSID RESULT'
    [5]   STACK ← ')SAVE'                  Stacking the desired commands
    [6]   STACK ← ')OFF'
    [7]   ⍕ FUNC                           Executing the function
    [8]   →                                Exit, and using the stack
    [9]   ERR: 'SOMETHING''S WRONG'
          ∇
          DISCAFTER 'PRINT'               Will execute the function with
                                          automatic safeguard and
                                          disconnection.
```

Use of the stack is also very good for proceeding with catenations of work-
spaces which are activated by □LX. A task can thus be divided into
several work-spaces.

CHAPTER 11

PROCESSING OF FILES

11-1   ## NECESSITY OF FILES

In standard data processing, data are generally recorded permanently on physical
media such as punched cards, magnetic tapes and disks.   These sets of data
called FILES, can be very large, because they are used only in successive
blocks.
In APL, stocking of data inside work-spaces means that all the data to be
treated are in the same work-space.   This design permits multiple interactions
between functions and variables, but unfortunately presents numerous disadvantages:

1 - The work-space is limited by the size of the computer's central storage,
    which prohibits working on very voluminous data.   This restriction is less
    critical with VIRTUAL STORAGE systems, where the computer "overflows" its
    central storage on to magnetic disks.
    From 70, 100 or 120 000 octets, the sizes of work-spaces pass to 2,5, or
    even 8 million octets, but, no matter how high it is, this limit always
    remains awkward.
    Moreover, it is unsatisfactory to store very large work-spaces which may
    be used only partly in each work session.

2 - The active work-space is not safeguarded automatically at the end of the
    work; the user must type)$SAVE$.   Some systems allow automatic safeguarding
    by ⋡)$SAVE$' or □$SAVE$, or by means of the STACK processor with VS APL.
    However, no system solves the problem of data security in the event of
    an accidental break in the liaison between terminal end computer, or in the
    event of clumsiness by the user.

3 - It should be noted that some data can be accessible to several users. If
    the)$COPY$ command allows data situated in other libraries to be used, it
    is imposible to return the modified values back to these libraries.
    Variables shared between users can solve this difficulty in very special
    cases, but it requires two simultaneously active processors.   It remains
    impossible to up date data which belongs to a user who is not working.

4 - One can work in only one work-space at a time, and one can gain access
    only to the variables in this work-space, except on systems which accept
    ⋡')$COPY$' or □$COPY$.

5 - Finally, no tie allows the APL user to use files formed in other data
    processing languages (not everyone uses APL), and vice-versa.

All this means that designers of APL systems have perfected possibilities fo
gaining access to files, while working in APL. The five problems raised abo
have thus been solved.

1 - Housed on inexpensive magnetic media, and used block by block, the files
    can be of almost unlimited size. Functions assure the transfer of data
    blocks between file and work-space. Of course each block must fit into th
    work-space.

2 - Data recorded on magnetic media remain after the end of the work, even i
    it is accidental.

3 - A file can be simultaneously consulted by as many users as desired, even
    if its owner is not active. Simultaneous modifications of a file by seve
    al users require some precautions, but they are still possible.

4 - One can work on several files simultaneously, and thus gain access to
    several sets of data.

5 - Finally, programs written in different languages can use the same files,
    provided that the utility programs assure suitable arrangement of these
    data.

The various solutions which have arisen favour one or other aspect, according
to the objectives which the designers have fixed for them.
The following are two examples illustrating two large groups of thought:
files specific to APL, of the *APL*PLUS* type, and general files accessible
through auxiliary processors, of the IBM file.

11-2   APL*PLUS FILES

In the early 1970's, the companies I.P. SHARP and SCIENTIFIC TIME SHARING
CORPORATION jointly conceived on APL system equipped with files, which they
called *APL*PLUS*. Even though it is a registered trade-mark this name was the
used to designate a whole range of systems inspired by it.
The description that we give of it conforms with the operating manual publish
by STSC, but we will see that other makers have applied some differences to
this basic system.

An *APL*PLUS* file comprises a succession of APL data, sequentially recorded on
a permanent physical medium (disk). These data are not designed by their name,
but by their order number in the file. They are called the COMPONENTS of the
file.
The file itself is known by a name of no more than 11 characters.

The creating functions and working functions are, according to the system,
either control functions (□*FCREATE,* □*FREAD,* □*FREPLACE,....*), or defined
functions (*FCREATE, FREAD, FREPLACE,....*) stored in the public library, which
thus call up a single "universal" control function, called *FF,* or □*FF* or
□*FI* with CONTROL DATA, or Ⅹ with HONEYWELL.
In this case, the access functions must first of all be copied before using
them, which is why we will retain the first solution here.

EXAMPLE

Some small businesses have created a purchasing co-operative, and each month
want to follow the orders placed by each member.
Each member is designated by a code of 4 numbers, and can place orders which
will be invoiced in total to him at the end of the month, to the amount of a
different limit for each one. In the event of exceeding the monthly limit
the member must settle the surplus immediately.
The orders are numbered from 1 to 1.

We have the following data (other data are also available, but will not be
needed for this short example).

       - list of all the numbers of the members of the co-operative.

       - value of the limit attributed to each one,

       - chronological list of the members who have placed orders during
         the month,

       - number of the last order received ,

       - for each member having placed an order during the month: the list
         of the numbers and total cost of each of his orders.

The following table gives the data already collected for the present month.

List of all the members	1202	2582	6330	4280	3611	4420	2145	3302	3172	8639	etc.....
Authorized limits	7000	5000	8000	5,000	5000	20000	5000	10000	4000	6000	

DATA RELATING TO THE PRESENT MONTH

members who have placed an order during the month	6330	4280	2145	3172	
number of the last order received	150				
For 6330 — Numbers	141	145	149		
For 6330 — total cost	1300	800	3600		
For 4280 — Numbers	140	143	144	147	150
For 4280 — total cost	1200	400	500	2700	600
For 2145 — Numbers	142				
For 2145 — total cost	3300				
For 3172 — Numbers	146	148			
For 3172 — total cost	5200	1400			

11-3   USING FILES

To keep these data up to date, it was decided to record them in two files
which will be called, rather originally, *MEMBERS* and *ORDERS*.

CREATION

Before being used, a file must be created by the function □*FCREATE*.   Thus it
is assigned its NAME, and a FILE NUMBER, or TIE NUMBER, which is easier to
handle than a name, and which will be essential for designating it later on.
This is an arbitary number.
From the time a file is created, any size can be given to it, which can be
modified later.   If no size is specified, the computer in its absence, will
reserve a size, for example, 50 000 octets.

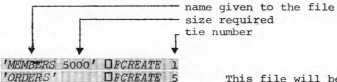

```
                                            ┌────────────────── name given to the file
                                            │ ┌──────────────── size required
                                            │ │ ┌── tie number
                                            ▼ ▼ ▼
        'MEMBERS 5000'  □FCREATE 1
        'ORDERS'        □FCREATE 5                  This file will be 50 000 octets.
```

At this stage, both files exist, but are empty.

SHAPE, RESHAPE

A file is formed by adding components to it one by one.   This is the role of
the function □*FAPPEND* , whose syntax is:

        value to be added □*FAPPEND* tie number to the file

We will fill file 1 with data already collected.

        1202 2582 6330 4280 3611 4420 2145 3302 3172 8639 □*FAPPEND* 1
        (1000×7 5 8 5 5 20 5 10 4 6) □*FAPPEND* 1

The file 5, i.e the orders file:

        6330 4280 2145 3172 □*FAPPEND* 5
        150 □*FAPPEND* 5
        (2 3ρ141 145 149 1300 800 3600) □*FAPPEND* 5
        (2 5ρ140 143 144 147 150 1200 400 500 2700 600) □*FAPPEND* 5
        (2 1ρ142 3300) □*FAPPEND* 5
        (2 2ρ146 148 5200 1400) □*FAPPEND* 5

At present, the files contain 2 and 6 components respectively, which each
represent data of entirely different dimensions (scalar, vectors, matrices).
The numeric components can be mixed up in a file, which is not the case in this
example.
The function $\Box FSIZE$ gives indications of the size of a file:

```
            ▯FSIZE 1
      1   3   3020   6040
            ▯FSIZE 5
      1   7   3020   51340
```

This information is:

- the number of the first component,

- the number of the next component to be created, being 1 more than
  the number of the last component,

- the space actually occupied, in octets. Minimal space is used
  throughout by the computer for managing the file.

- the total space reserved for the file, generally somewhat larger
  than was actually demanded.

On early systems, the function *FILM* gave the first two elements of $\Box FSIZE$.

Throughout the time spent working on a file, it is said that it is tied to the
work-space, or that it is OPEN. This is expressed by association of a number
to the files name. At the end of the work, the files are untied (it is also
said that they are CLOSED), by the function $\Box FUNTIE$, followed by the numbers
of the files to be untied.

            $\Box FUNTIE$ 1 5   in our case

As the data is recorded permanently no safeguarding procedure is required when
a file is untied.

To resume work on a file, during a new work session, it must be tied again,
i.e have a tie number assigned to it. This is performed by the function $\Box FTIE$

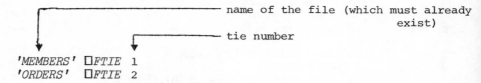

```
      'MEMBERS'  ▯FTIE 1
      'ORDERS'   ▯FTIE 2
```

Another file number has been used, which has no importance; the name is a fixed
feature of the file whereas the tie number can differ from one work session to
the next, since it is redefined each time.

READING, UP-DATING

The function □*FREAD* conveys the contents of any component in the work-space.
The file is not altered by this reading .

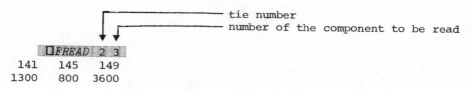

141	145	149
1300	800	3600

At the start of work, the function *HELLO* will gather all necessary data on the
files following the processings. These data will be placed in the global
variables of the work-space.

```
           ∇ HELLO
    [1]    'MEMBERS'  □FTIE 1
    [2]    'ORDERS'   □FTIE 2
    [3]    MEM ← □FREAD 1 1
    [4]    MAX ← □FREAD 1 2
    [5]    CODES←□FREAD 2 1
    [6]    ORD ← □FREAD 2 2
           ∇
```

Suppose that member 2582, who has not ordered yet this month, places an order
of 1500 F. It will have to have the number 151, and this value will have to
replace the value 150 in file 2, component 2.
The function □*FREPLACE* enables the value of a component to be replaced by any
other value, even of greater dimensions, or even of a different type.

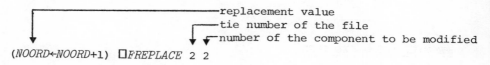

($NOORD$←$NOORD$+1) □*FREPLACE* 2 2

Likewise the cade 2582 will have to be added to the end of the component 1 of
the orders file; again □*FREPLACE* will achieve this:

($CODES$←$CODES$,2582) □*FREPLACE* 2 1

This last operation shows that a component can be replaced by a larger component.
Finally the order placed by the member will be added to the end of the file:

(2 1ρ$NOORD$,1500) □*FAPPEND* 2

In the event of a client having already placed an order during the month, for
example client 3172, we proceed as follows:

```
INDEX ← 2+CODESι3172
(ORD←ORD+1) ⎕FREPLACE 2 2
ORDER ← ⎕FREAD 2,INDEX
(ORDER,ORD,8510) ⎕FREPLACE 2,INDEX
```

——————————— total cost of the order

This is what the state of the orders file would be:

6330	4280	2145	3172	2582

152

141	145	149
1300	800	3600

140	143	144	147	150
1200	400	500	2700	600

142
3300

146	148	152
5200	1400	8510

151
1500

WE WILL FORMALIZE THIS

The limit imposed on each member must also be taken into account; the *MEMBERS*
file should be consulted for this. A function will secure all these processing

```
        ∇ MEM  ORDERED PRICE ;INDEX;ORDER;LIM;TOT
[1]     (COM←COM+1) ⎕FREPLACE 2 2
[2]     →((ρCODES)≥INDEX ← CODES ι MEM)/EXISTS
[3]     (CODES ← CODES,MEM) ⎕FREPLACE 2 1
[4]     (ORDER ← 2 1ρORD,PRICE) ⎕FAPPEND 2
[5]     →CONTROL
[6]  EXISTS: ORDER ← ⎕FREAD 2,INDEX←INDEX+2
[7]     (ORDER ← ORDER,ORD,PRICE) ⎕FREPLACE 2,INDEX
[8]  CONTROL: LIM ← MAX[MEM ι MEM ]
[9]     →(LIM≥TOT ← +/ORDER[2;])/0
[10]    'TOTAL COST TO PAY : ',▼PRICE ⌊ TOT-LIM
        ∇
```

At the end of the work, the function *BYE* will untie the files:

        ∇ *BYE*
   [1]   □*FUNTIE* 1 2 ∇

Here is an example of a work session, obtained starting from the last state
of the files :

                HELLO
                6330 *ORDERED* 1200

                2145 *ORDERED* 2400

        TOTAL COST TO PAY : 700
                1202 *ORDERED* 4000

                BYE

INFORMATION

User 88824 can obtain the list of files which he has created in his library
by the function □*FLIB* , followed by his account number:

                □*FLIB* 88824
        88824 *MEMBERS*
        88824 *ORDERS*

The result is a matrix of 22 columns. The first 10 contain the account number
of the owner of the files, the 11th is empty, the next 11 contain the names
of the files.

At a given moment, the names of the tied files and their tie numbers are
obtained by □*FNAMES* □*FNUMS* respectively, in the same order, which is the
order in which they were opened.

                □*FNAMES*
        77721 *TRUNK*
        77721 *ELEPHANT*

                □*FNUMS*
        3 7

The expression □*FUNTIE* □*FNUMS* therefore has the effect of untying all the
files.

ALTERING A FILE

The first or last n components of a file f can be withdrawn by:

    n □*FDROP* f $\begin{cases} n = \text{number of components to be dropped} \\ f = \text{tie number of the file} \end{cases}$

According to whether n is positive or negative, the first n or last n

components of the file are withdrawn. This is a useful operation for with-
drawing outdated components from an old file.

If the first 30 components of a file are withdrawn, the following components
keep their order number, so as not to require reorganizing of the working
functions.

$\qquad$ 2 ↑ □FSIZE 17

1   150

$\qquad$ ¯10 □FDROP 17
$\qquad$ 30 □FDROP 17

$\qquad$ 2 ↑ □FSIZE 17

31   140

A files name can be modified by the funciton □FRENAME, as follows:

$\qquad$ new name of the file □FRENAME present tie number

The new name can include an indication if size, in which case the size of the
file will also be modified: *'PLUS* 80000' □FRENAME 11
If however it is a question merely of modifying the size of a file, the funcito
□FRESIZE will sufice:

$\qquad$ 120000   □FRESIZE   14

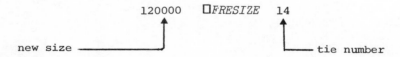

$\qquad$ new size $\qquad$ tie number

Finally, a file can be totally erased by the function □FERASE , provided that
it is tied exclusively (and not shared, as will be seen later).

$\qquad$ name of the file □FERASE tie number

Redundancy between the name and the tie number is a security factor.

11-4   SHARED FILES

When a file is created, only its owner has access to it. Afterwards, he can
decide to offer its use to other users.

SHARING PROCEDURE

In order to offer the use of a file to other users, an ACCESS MATRIX must be
assigned to it, which has three columns;

$\qquad$ - the first contains the account numbers to the people to whom access
$\qquad$ to the file is given.

- The second contains a representative number of the operations which he will be authorized to carry out, for each person.

- The third column, which is usually zero, can contain a pass number, whose use will be seen later.

The operations which can be performed on a file are assigned a weight. The total weight of the authorised operations must appear in column two of the access matrix.

FUNCTIONS	WEIGHTS	CORRESPONDING FUNCTIONS ON EARLY SYSTEMS
□*FREAD*	1	*FREAD, FILM, FSIZE*
□*FTIE*	2	*FTIE*
□*FERASE*	4	*FERASE*
□*FAPPEND*	8	*FAPPEND*
□*FREPLACE*	16	*FREPLACE*
□*FDROP*	32	*FDROP*
	64	*FHOLD*
□*FRENAME*	128	*FRENAME*
	256	*FRDAC, FSTAC*
□*FRDCI*	512	*FRDCI*
□*FRESIZE*	1024	*FRESIZE*
□*FHOLD*	2048	
□*FRDAC*	4096	
□*FSTAC*	8192	

The functions □*FCREATE*, □*FNAMES*, □*FNUMS*, □*FLIB*, □*FAVAIL* are authorized throughout; the function □*FSTIE* is authorized as soon as a user has the right to carry out any other operation on the file.

Hence, to authorize somebody to carry out the operations □*FAPPEND* and □*FREAD*, □*FREPLACE* on a file the following authorization will be given to him:

$$8 + 1 + 16 \text{ being } 25$$

It remains for us to discover the role of the new functions which have appeared in this table (□*FAVAIL* serving only to say, by a binary result, if the system of files is available on the computer).

EXAMPLE

Take the example of the co-operative from the previous paragraph.

The employees situated at the sales outlets have account numbers 77001 to
77003. They must be able to read, up-date and add to the *ORDERS* file. They
must be able to read the *MEMBERS* file to see if the limit is reached, but they
must not be able to modify this limit or accept a client an their own initiativ
They will therefore have authorization:

        – on the *MEMEBERS* file, to □*FREAD*   being 1

        – on the *ORDERS* file, to □*FREAD*, □*FAPPEND*, □*FREPLACE* being 25

The business director of the co-operative who has the account number 77721,
can accept new clients and fix their limit. He can also consult the month's
orders file, but cannot himself take orders, so as not to upset his salesmen,
who receive a commission on the orders they take.
Consequently, he will have authorization:

        – on the *MEMBERS* file, to □*FREAD*, □*FREPLACE*   being 17

        – on the *ORDERS* file, to □*FREAD*   being 1

The person responsible for data processing application, who has account 88824,
will construct two access matrices as follows:

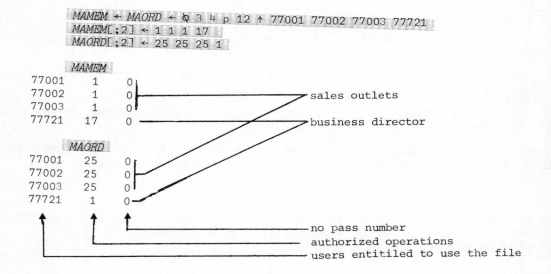

$MAMEM \leftarrow MAORD \leftarrow \lozenge\ 3\ 4\ \rho\ 12\ \uparrow\ 77001\ 77002\ 77003\ 77721$
$MAMEM[;2] \leftarrow 1\ 1\ 1\ 17$
$MAORD[;2] \leftarrow 25\ 25\ 25\ 1$

	MAMEM		
77001	1	0	sales outlets
77002	1	0	
77003	1	0	
77721	17	0	business director

	MAORD	
77001	25	0
77002	25	0
77003	25	0
77721	1	0

no pass number
authorized operations
users entitiled to use the file

The following operation consists of assigning each matrix to the corresponding file. This is performed by □*FSTAC* (ST̲ore A̲cess C̲ontrol) :

```
'MEMBERS' □FTIE 1
MAMEM □FSTAC 1

'ORDERS' □FTIE 2
MAORD □FSTAC 2

□FUNTIE 1 2
```

Henceforth, the access matrices are recorded permanently with the corresponding files. They can be consulted by the function □*FRDAC* (R̲eaD̲ A̲cess C̲ontrol)
or modified again by □*FSTAC*.

```
        )CLEAR
CLEAR WS
        'ORDERS' □FTIE 2
        □FRDAC 2
  77001   25    0
  77002   25    0
  77003   25    0
  77721    1    0
```

It is evident that nobody above has been authorized to read or up-date the
access matrix. Users recently authorized by 88824 to use these two files
can receive confirmation of this by typing:

```
     □FLIB 88824
     88824 MEMBERS
     88824 ORDERS
```

ACCESS PROCEDURE

People entitled to use the file can tie it by □*FSTIE* (for S̲hared TIE),
which authorizes several people to work SIMULTANEOUSLY on the same file,
contrary to □*FTIE* , which ties the file EXCLUSIVELY to one user at a time.
□*FSTIE* is used like □*FTIE* , except that the complete name of the file must
be mentioned, with its library number, in the left hand argument. Here,
the creator has the number 88824 so other people must write:

```
     '88824 MEMBERS' □FSTIE 6
```

As an example, here is the function which enables the business director to
admit a new member. The member's codes are generated at random, so as to
avoid fraud.

```
        ∇ ADMISSION ;MEM;C;P
[1]     '88824 MEMBERS' ⎕FSTIE 1
[2]     MEM ← ⎕FREAD 1 1
[3]     ⎕RL← +/⎕TS  [2 3 4 5]
[4]     ROLL: →((C←999+?9000)∊MEM)/ROLL
[5]     'THIS MEMBER WILL HAVE THE NUMBER ',⍕C
[6]     (MEM,C) ⎕FREPLACE 1 1
[7]     'WHAT IS THE AUTHORIZED LIMIT ?'
[8]     P ← 50000⌊⌊|1↑⎕
[9]     ((⎕FREAD 1 2),P) ⎕FREPLACE 1 2
[10]    ⎕FUNTIE 1
        ∇
```

If the business director tries to execute a function which he is not authorised
to use on these files, he will obtain the error message:
FILE ACCESS ERROR.

A person authorized to tie the file for exclusive use by ⎕*FTIE* can do so
only if nobody else has already tied it by ⎕*FSTIE* , so that no conflict can
arise. It is for this reason that a file can be erased only if it is tied
exclusively.

TRANSFERRING OWNERSHIP

The owner of a file is entitled to carry out all operations on this file (and
to pay for the invoices that this creates), unless he is careless enough to
make himself appear in the access matrix of his own file with reduced
authorizations.
If A has created a file FILE, and authorized B to execute the function
⎕*FRENAME* , B can rename the file. From this moment the file BELONGS TO HIM.
If A did not appear in the access matrix (which is likely), he will no
longer be able to carry out only the operations to which he was entitled.
This is just how a situation can be reached where nobody can any longer erase
a file   modify its access matrix. Hence the person responsible for data
processing service must be contacted.

SECURITY OF APPLICATIONS

Each time a user carries out ⎕*FAPPEND* or ⎕*FREPLACE* on a file, the computer
notes this operation without the user being able to avoid it. The owner
can then, by the function ⎕*FRDCI* (for ReaD Component Information), gain
access to the information recorded by the computer, for each component.

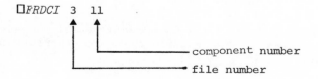

The result is a vector of three elements:

> - the first is the size of the component in octets. This information
>   can avoid having to read a component which is too large for an
>   already congested work-space.

> - the second is the account number of the last person to have modi-
>   fied this component by □*FREPLACE* or □*FAPPEND*.

> - the third is the exact date of this modification, counted in
>   sixtieths of a second since 1 March 1960 midnight. The function
>   *TIMEN* enables this date to be clearly expressed.

```
        ∇ R←TIMEN T;I;PSM
[1]     PSM ← 0 31 61 92 122 153 184 214 245 275 306 337
[2]     R ← 365.2501 | 1+1461|I+⌊T÷5184000
[3]     R ← (1+12|(~□IO)+(PSM≥R)ι1),⌈R-PSM[¯1+(PSM≥R)ι1]
[4]     R ← (1960+⌊(I+60)÷365.25),R, 24 60 60 60 ⊤ ''ρ⌊T
        ∇
```

```
        'HAM' □FSTIE 33
        CI←□←□FRDCI 33 5
    172 52331   34802808323
```

```
        TIMEN CI[3]
    1978  7  18  12  6   45   23
```

The last person to have written component 5 of this file is user 52331, and
this operation took place on 18 July 1978, at 12 h 16 mins, 45 secs and 23
sixtieths. Such information can be valuable in the event of an error.

However, security can go much further.
It has been said that a pass number can be given to each co-user of a file,
by placing it in the third column of the access matrix. Here is the advantage
of this.

Suppose we want to authorise user 55515 to calculate sales statistics from the
orders file, without his being able to find out who brought what, for reasons
of discretion. He must therefore not be able to read the first component of
this file.
We will add 55515 to the access matrix, be assigning an arbitary pass number
to him for example 6317 :

```
        'ORDERS' □FTIE 2
        AM ← (□FRDAC 2),[1] 55515 1 6317
        AM □FSTAC 2
        □FUNTIE 2
```

Henceforth, this person will have the restriction of catenating this pass
number to the argument of all the functions which he uses, except □ *FCREATE*
□*FUNTIE*, □*FLIB*, □*FNUMS*, □*FNAMES*, which do not apply to a particular file.

Hence instead of writting $\square FREAD$ 2 5, $\square FREAD$ 2 5 6317 will have to be written.

This pass number however, will not be communicated to the statistician, so that he cannot read the file without an aid. This aid will be the *READ* function below:

```
         ∇ R←READ V
[1]     →(1≠(V←2↑V)[2])/OK
[2]     →0,ρR←'PRYING VILAIN'
[3]  OK: R←□FREAD V,6317
         ▽
```

This function is locked (▽ see paragraph 4-42) and thus the user cannot find out the pass number which has been given to him. If he types *READ* 2 5, the function will catenate the pass number, and the reading will follow correctly. However, if he types *READ* 2 1 he will obtain a discouraging result (*PRYING VILAIN*).

Hence, it can be seen clearly that all sorts of controls can be accomplished. For this protection to work efficiently on systems which do not have control functions (*FREAD, FREPLACE, FAAPEND, ...*), it is IMPERATIVE to replace these by the equivalent control function.
If not, this is what an unrepresented prying person could do:

```
         )ERASE FREAD
         ∇ R← FREAD V
[1]      R ← ¯1↑V ∇

         LIRE 2 18    ◄
6317                  ◄
```

he may have the right to read this component

if *READ* does not call $\square FREAD$, but *FREAD* the modified function will display the pass number.

FILES IN SIMULTANEOUS USE

Simultaneous updating of the same file by several people can lead to serious miscalculations. Assume that two users A and B each decide to catenate a number to component 3 of the same file.

USER A	USER B
$\square$ ← *COMA* ← $\square FREAD$ 1 3	$\square$ ← *COMB* ← $\square FREAD$ 1 3
8 9 10	8 9 10
(*COMA*,17) $\square FREPLACE$ 1 3	
(at this moment, the component thus equals: 8 9 10 17)	

```
          ☐FREAD 1 3                              (COMB,81) ☐FREPLACE 1 3
   8   9   10   81                                ☐FREAD 1 3
                                          8   9   10   81
```

It is seen that the second person has erased the work of the first to avoid
such mishaps, the function ☐FHOLD permits someone to temporarily reserve
access to one or more files.

If a user wants to carry out delicate operations on the two files 1 and 8 by
means of a function *FUNC*, he must include the instruction ☐FHOLD 1 8.
Performance of *FUNC* will be suspended until all the other reserves sent out
previously by other users for these two files are satisfied.
When both files are simultaneously free, performance of *FUNC* will start again.
During, this time, other users who want to work on one or other of the files
1 and 8, and who have also used the instruction ☐FHOLD , are suspended.
The user who is working is thus the only one working on these files.
When he has finished using them, he will free the two files by ☐FHOLD 10, and
the next user will be authorized to work.

It is apparent that blocking a file for too long must be avoided; also the
action of ☐FHOLD ceases immediately in the three following cases:

- the user unties the file concerned, or disconnects himself, intentionally
  or otherwise;

- the user executes another ☐FHOLD instruction,

- the terminal returns to a waiting position.

This last use can arise due to several reasons:

- the functions being executed have been completed,

- an error has been detected,

- the user has intentionally interrupted the course of the function by
  typing the interruption key,

- a stop control had been placed in the function (see paragraph 12-5 for
  this term)

It is thus impossible to execute ☐FHOLD outside a function.

It is very important to note that the ONLY effect of ☐FHOLD is to suspend
execution of other ☐FHOLD 's concerning the same file. Consequently if a user
proceeds to an ☐FAPPEND, ☐FREAD without having preceded it by ☐FHOLD , his
instruction will be executed, with all the risks which this entails for everyone.
It is therefore up to the designer of all the functions to ensure that proper
use is made of shared files.

11-5   FILE PROCESSORS

*APL*PLUS* is a specialised system which operates on computers intended specif-
ically for use in the APL language. It requires specialised functions
($\square F$.... functions) and allows access to files created of that kind, except
for the obliging help of those responsible for the system.

At IBM, they have searched for a method which does not require any new functions, and enables access to any files: this represented the birth of
auxiliary processors.
The first files processor (360 TSIO) enabled access to all files, provided
that it was known how to describe them. Many people who started data processing with an APL bias have been discouraged by TSIO which, even when working
purely in APL, quickly causes to attend to the physical management of their
data (tracks, octets, conversions, blocking factor), from which APL had
been exempt up to then. Moreover, some characteristics of TSIO, such as the
impossibility of writing and empty vector in a file, constituted an abnormal
disadvantage. However, it must be recognised that TSIO was the first real
attempt to make the world of APL communicate with classical data processing.

With VS APL, used with CMS, VSPC, or TSO systems, the processors have appeared
each one specialized in the handling of a certain type of files:

> 110 is the CMS disk I/O processor,
> 111 is the Filedef I/O processor,
> 123 is the VSAM files processor.

It would be impossible to cover all these processors in detail. As an example
the following paragraphs develop the characteristics of the VSAPL 110 processo
used with CMS.
Readers wishing to obtain information on other processors will find no
difficulty in consulting the adaquate brochures issued by IBM.

11-6   ORGANISATION OF CMS FILES

With the CMS operating system, all the data are organised in files; even the
work-spaces are managed as special types of files. The files a re-housed
on "virtual disks", which are in fact zones of real disks, identified by
a letter and a number.

For example, the virtual disk A contains the user's private library, whereas the public libraries are housed on the Y disk.

The identity of a file thus contains three elements:

- its <u>NAME</u>, which is arbitrary, must not exceed 8 characters. For example, this can be CLIENTS or CHAP11.
- its <u>TYPE</u>, which is also arbitrary, enables the user to attribute a different type to files relating to different areas of activity:
    - ACCOUNT for all the accounting files,
    - PROD for files tied to production management etc....

  Some types of files are reserved for a special use:
    - VSAPLWS type designate work-spaces,
    - EXEC type designate procedures files,
    - ASSEMBLE type designate instruction files in assembler language etc.....
- its <u>MODE</u>, which is the name of the virtual disk where the file is housed.

Here are some typical file identifiers:

```
CLIENTS ACCOUNT       A1
PROFILE EXEC          A1
USEFUL VSAPLWS        A1
```

11-7   OPENING A FILE

In order to create or use files, two variables per file must be shared with the 110 processor:

- one is used for transferring data between the work-space and the file; this is the <u>DATA VARIABLE</u>,
- the other is used to control the number of the component which is being worked on, and to check that the exchange operations are proceeding satisfactorily; this is the <u>CONTROL VARIABLE</u>.

We will call them *DATA* and *CONTROL*, but any other name would be suitable.

In order to work on a file, the data variable and the control variable, in this order, must be initialized BEFORE sharing them with the 110 processor.

- The initial value of the control variable comprises the identity of the file, followed by the entry *(CTL* or *(CTL)*, which indicates that it is a control variable.

- The initial value of the data variable comprises the identity of the file, perhaps followed by three parameters: the format, the access mode, and the type of conversion to be applied to the file. These three parameters are detailed below.

$$CONTROL \leftarrow \text{'Identity } (CTL)\text{'}$$

$$DATA \quad \leftarrow \text{'Identity } (format\ access\ conversion)\text{'}$$

The final closed bracket is not obligatory; the open bracket of *DATA* is obligatory only if at least one parameter is given.
Certain parameters can in fact be omitted, in which case the computer assigns a conventional value to them, called "DEFAULT VALUE".

FORMAT

A CMS file is composed of RECORDS similar to the *APL *PLUS* components. They can all be the same length, in which case the file will be said to be of fixed length, and the *FIX* option will have to appear in the initial value of the data variable.
If this parameter is omitted, the file will be assumed to contain records of different lengths, and by default; it will be said to be of variable length.

ACCESS

A file can be opened in such a way that it can be used only for reading (option *R* for Read), only for writing (option *W* for Write), or for both at the same time (option *U* for Update). If this access parameter is not specified the value *U* will be taken by default.

CONVERSIONS

If the file must be used only in APL, the numeric or alphanumeric variables are transferred from the work-space to the file and vice-versa without any modification, keeping the rank dimensions and type descriptor attached to them in the work-space. The conversion option *VAR* is taken by default.

It may however happen that the file's data need to be exchanged between the APL
environment (work-space) and a non-APL environment (other languages, printer...)
where special APL characters do not exist, and where the descriptor attached
to any APL variable would have no meaning. In such cases, we can exchange with
the file only logical vectors (conversion option *BIT*) which will be suitable
for deciphering by a program, or character strings whose geographical aspect
will be more or less suitably converted (conversions option 370, 192 and APL).

IDENTITY

The mode of the file can be omitted, in which case it is assumed to be housed
on the Al disk. Its type can also be omitted, in which case it is assumed,
by default, to be of VMAPLcF type where c represents the conversion option
chosen. In the simplest case, the data variable thus receives only the name
followed by (*CTL*). The file will thus be of VMAPLVF type, will be housed on
disk Al, will be of variable length, without conversion option (VAR), and
will be accessible for reading and writing.

SHARING PROCEDURE

After initializing and sharing, it is ESSENTIAL to satisfy oneself that the
initial values of the variables offered for sharing have been recognised and
executed by the computer. If the operation has been successfully carried
out, the 110 processor assigns a value whose first element must be zero to the
two variables. If one or other of the values is not zero, it is because the
initial value could not be recognised or executed.

This is how creation is carried out of a file called CHAP11, of TRIAL type,
used to store APL variables, and having to be housed, in absence, on the Al
disk:

DATA ← '*CHAP11 TRIAL*'	Initializing the variables. All
CONTROL ← '*CHAP11 TRIAL (CTL*'	the parameters are taken by default .
110 □*SVO* 2 8ρ '*DATA CONTROL*'	Offer for sharing. Both offers
2 2	are accepted.
DATA	Verification of the return-
0 1 1 1	codes: creation of the files has
CONTROL	been successfully undertaken.
0	

Note that the 110 processor positions the access control matrix of the two
shared variables and the user does not have to concern himself with it:

          □*SVC* 2 8ρ '*EXCHANGE CONTROL*'
    0 0 1 0
    0 0 1 0

11-8   USING A FILE

With an open file,

> - each value assigned to a data variable will be registered in the
>   file, thus creating a new record, or modifying an existing record,
>
> - each consultation of the data variable causes a reading of a record
>   of the file,
>
> - after each read or write operation, one must satisfy oneself that
>   the first element of the control variable, called RETURN-CODE,
>   is zero. A non-zero value would indicate that the operation has
>   not been carried out normally.

The positions of the next record which will be read and of the following record
which will be written on the file, are given respectively by the 2nd and 3rd
elements of the control variable. These are called READING POINTER and WRITING
POINTER.

These two pointers are totally independent of each other and the user can freely
fix their value, in accordance with the procedure which will be seen later, so
as to read or write the record of his choice.
After each reading, or each writing, the 110 processor automatically increments
the corresponding pointer, in such a way that, if the user does not intervene,
the following reading or writing will concern the following record. Thus
we can work sequentially by leaving the task of managing the pointers to the
computer.

When opening a file, the reading pointer equals 1, so that the reading starts
with the first record, whereas the writing pointer is equal to the number of
records plus one, so that the next record to be written is placed on the end of
the file.

BLOCKING FACTOR

In the case of a file in fixed format, it is the length of the first record
written which obligatorily fixes the length which the following records must
be, otherwise an error will result. Moreover, the number of disk accesses
can be limited by reading or writing several records at once, in the form
of a matrix of characters of which each line is a record.
Hence, 10, 20, 100 ...... records can be exchanged in one go with the file,
provided that the virtual processor has buffers of sufficient size.

The number of records to which one has simultaneous access is called the
BLOCKING FACTOR; or blocksize this is the fourth element of the control variable.
It equals 1 at opening, and can only equal 1 for files in variable length, or
defined with the conversion options VAR and APL.

CONTROL OF THE POINTERS AND BLOCKING FACTOR (BLOCKSIZE)

When sharing is finished, the first value of the data variable comprises the four following elements:

- return-code, which must equal zero if everything has gone well,

- value of the reading pointer, always equal to 1,

- value of the writing pointer, equal to the number of records + 1,

- value of the blocksize, always equal to 1.

Consequently, it is the control variable which reinstates these values, and it is this which enables them to be modified.

When a value is assigned to the control variable:

- the first element fixes the value of the reading pointer,

- the second element, if there is one, fixes the value of the writing pointer,

- the third element, if there is one, fixes the blocksize.

If one or more elements are negative or zero, the corresponding parameter keeps its present value.

It is now time to see how these things actually appear

EXAMPLE

We will work on the file "CHAP11", created in the preceding paragraph, and which does not actually comprise any record. We can satisfy ourselves of this by consulting the control variable:

        CONTROL
    0 1 1 1

constituting the file

DATA ← 'FIRST STEP' *CONTROL* 0 1 2 1	Creation of the first record return-code test: the operation has been carried out (0) and the writing pointer has progressed from 1. We are ready to write the second record.

          DATA ← 'SECOND PROMPT'
          CONTROL
0 1 3 1

          DATA ← ι0
          CONTROL
0 1 4 1

          DATA ← 44 44 44 44   Now there are 4 records, and the reading
          CONTROL   pointer still equals 1.
0 1 5 1

sequential reading

          DATA   Reading of the first record.
FIRST STEP   Control of the return-code.
          CONTROL   The reading pointer has progressed.
0 2 5 1

          DATA
SECOND PROMPT
          CONTROL
0 3 5 1   The reading could be continued sequent-
                                                ally.

direct access to the records

          CONTROL ← 4   We fix the reading pointer
          DATA   Reading of the 4th record.
44 44 44 44
          CONTROL   Checking the return-code.
0 5 5 1

          CONTROL ← 1 1   We modify the two pointers, so as to
          DATA ← 'ONE'   modify the first record, then re-read
          CONTROL   it by way of a check.
0 1 2 1
          DATA   Re-reading.
ONE
          CONTROL
0 2 2 1

          ⎕SVR 2 8ρ'DATA   CONTROL'   We end the dialogue by retracting both
                                                variables, or erasing them by ⎕EX.

TWO CONSTRAINTS

The first constraint is not surprising: it is essential that a file be
constituted sequentially; there must be no "gaps".
The second constriant is more inconvenient: it is impossible to replace a
record by another of greater size.

This constraint, which is peculiar to files managed by CMS, considerably restricts their usefulness. The same constraint already existed with TSIO; it
disappeared with the VSAM file system (processor 123) therefore defer the
question of the validity of file processors.

11-9   MANAGING FILES

USING THE COMMAND PROCESSOR

The 110 processor serves only for gaining access to files, and does not enable
the list of them to be known, or enable them to be erased. These operations
are carried out by the commands of the CMS system. Hence the 100 processor
must be used, enabling such commands to be executed while remaining in the
APL environment.

To obtain the list of files, the following function suffices:

```
          ∇ LISTFILE TYPE ;COM
    [1]   →(2≠100 □SVO 'COM')/ERROR
    [2]   COM ← 'LISTFILE * ',TYPE
    [3]   →(0=COM)/0
    [4]   ERROR:'SOMETHING''S WRONG'   ∇
```

To obtain the list of "ACCOUNT" type files, we will type:
LISTFILE 'ACCOUNT', whereas we will obtain the list of all the files of
every type by *LISTFILE '*'*.

To erase a file, the procedure is as follows:

```
          ∇ ERASEFILE NAME;COM
    [1]   →(2≠100 □SVO 'COM')/ERROR
    [2]   COM ← 'ERASE ',NAME
    [3]   →(0=COM)/0
    [4]   ERROR:'BAD DAY FOR YOU'   ∇
```


A CRITICAL LOOK

While the principle of using the 110 processor is relatively simple in
appearance, its real use is less advantageous than appears, because each
access to a file is performed in three motions:

- positioning of pointer (usually),

- reading or writing,

- control of the return-code.

Separately programming each access would considerably increase the burden of
writing and maintaining the applications, hence one will construct defined
functions loaded to carry out these routine operations.
Functions such as *LISTFILE* and *ERASEFILE* will also be needed.
Finally, if various recordings of a file have been modified, the writing pointer has any value. If we suddenly wish to add a recording on the end of the
file, it is not possible to know the number of recordings already created.
This leads to managing, the number of the last recording written employing
a global variable.

With a minimum of humour, one could therefore define functions named *FCREATE*,
FREAD, *FLIM*, *FAPPEND*, ... but these functions will never have the efficiency
of control functions, and a significant waste of computing time would ensue.
Moreover, such solutions are very far from being satisfactory regarding
security of the applications in the event of an incident affecting the processings.

11-10   OTHER SOLUTIONS

Data can be safeguarded also in work-spaces. It is this which enables systems
which have control functions $\Box SAVE$, $\Box LOAD$, $\Box COPY$........, or which enable
the commands $)SAVE$, $)LOAD$, etc ..... to be dynamically executed, whether by
means of an auxiliary processor as in the VS APL version issued by IBM.

At present, the big manufacturers tend to favour *APL*PLUS* type solutions,
shared files excepted. CONTROL DATA, HONEYWELL, DEC, UNIVAC, have gone all
out for this formula, as have SEMS (France) on SOLAR and BURROUGHS equipment,
who have developed a special system, shown in the supplement.
It should be noted that most of these manufacturers, anxious to permit
communication between APL and other languages, offer access functions to
general files, whose syntax is very close to the handling functions for
purely APL files.

SMALL LEAP INTO THE FUTURE

In fact it is the file concept itself which is brought back into question.
It is completely abnormal to use different methods for gaining access to a
value when it is situated on a file (reading order) or when it is in the active
work-space (called by name). The present use of files creates confusion
between the ABSTRACT nature of the processings carried out (addition, classifying,
etc ....) and the PHYSICAL medium of recording the processed variables (disk,
central storage, tape ...).

We must expect that future APL systems will be totally free of the file concept
all the variables being addressed by name, and the duration of their retention
being fixed by other means (volatile data, permanent data, etc ..).
Since access to general files requires a suitable description of them, it is
probable that this will continue to be performed by means of variables
shared with a processor such as TSIO.

GENERAL ARRAYS

Most APL system designers have announced general array systems, and IBM has
just included them in the APL2 version just launched. This concept is very
significant.
The general arrays are arrays whose elements are themselves arrays, the elements of the latter also being arrays, etc... . All these arrays are, or
could be, of totally different types and dimensions. Hence we can solve what
could not be solved hitherto by APL, i.e the case of all data not lending
themselves to representation in the form of a rectangular array, hence another
reason for files to disappear.
Such a system, offered already some years ago by I.P.SHARP and S.T.S.C is
being developed without IBM initiative, it is undertaking, in relation to the
present APL, a step as big as APL in relation to classic languages.

A subset lacking these options is available on various mini or micro systems.

PROCESSING FUNCTIONS OF FILES
S.T.S.C. *APL*PLUS* SYSTEM.

FUNCTION	EFFECT	SHARING	
□ *FAVAIL*	Availability of the system		
□*FLIB C*	Files of user *C*		
N □*FCREATE F*	To create a file of name *N* and number *F*		
□*FNAMES*	List of names of tied files		
□*FNUMS*	List of numbers of tied files		
□*FSIZE*	Dimensions of file		X
□*FUNTIE V*	Closing files *V*		
N □*FSTIE F*	Shared opening of file *N/F*	*	
□*FREAD F,C*	To read the component *C* of file *F*	1	X
F □*FTIE F*	Exclusive opening of file *N/F*	2	X
N □*FERASE F*	Erasing file *N/F*	4	X
A □*FAPPEND F*	To add component *A* to the end of *F*	8	X
A □*FREPLACE F,C*	To replace component *C* by *A*	16	X
I □*FDROP F*	To cancel *I* components of *F*	36	X
M □*FRENAME F*	To change the name of *F* to *M*	128	X
□*FRDCI F,C*	Information on component *C*	512	X
T □*FRESIZE F*	To give the size *T* to the file *F*	1024	X
□*FHOLD V*	Reserving the files *V*	2048	X
□*FRDAC F*	To read the access matrix of *F*	4096	X
M □*FSTAC F*	To read *M* as an access matrix for file *F*	8192	X

F is an arbitrary file or tie number.
V is a file number, or a vector of numbers.
* □*FSTIE* is authorized as soon as the user is able to carry out all other operations on the file.
X The operations marked with a cross require indication of the pass number if there is one.

11-11   APL*PLUS FILES

Contrary to access by shared variables in use with IBM, the APL*PLUS system
does not require any shared variable in the work-space. Furthermore the files
remain tied even following the commands)*CLEAR* and)*LOAD*. Some systems even
keep the files tied for a few minutes in case of an accidental break in
connection between computer and terminal. The files are untied automatically
on disconnection by the user, even if he forgets to untie them. For this
reason, many users never use □*FUNTIE* , and leave their files tied. This
practice is not advised, because two different work-spaces can successively
want to assign the same tie number to different files.
It should be noted also that the number of files simultaneously tied is
generally limited.

VARIANTS

On early systems, a file could be constituted sequentially only by *FAPPEND*
or □*FAPPEND*. This was often a very embarrasing constraint. On some recent
systems, □*FAPPEND* and □*FREPLACE* have given place to a single function
FWRITE, and a file can be constituted starting with any component number,
for example the 20th, even if the 19 preceding components have not yet
been created.

Likewise, the APL 2.4 system of CONTROL DATA replaces □*FDROP* , which cancels
only the components at the begining or end, by *FRDEL* (Record DELete) which
enables any component of the file to be erased.
The function *FFREE* thus gives the number of the first free component in the
file.

BURROUGHS APL 700

The most elaborated version however is indubitably that offered by BURROUGHS
under the name APL700. Each file is considered here as a generalised vector,
whose components would be the elements.
Hence, most operations can be performed on the components of this file that
an APL vector supports special characters, all obtained from the quad character by superimposing.

As all systems which authorize the creation of files in any order, an APL
700 file contains "gaps" or blank components.

The files are not designated by a number but by their name and it is possible
to catenate several instructions on the same line without repeating this name
each function transmitting it, if necessary, to the next.

The files can be used as a FIFO or LIFO "stack" by means of four instructions
which enable a datum to be inserted at the head or tail of the file, and
a datum to be extracted from the head or tail by cancelling it from the file.

CHAPTER 12

FUNCTION DEVELOPMENT AIDS

MODIFYING FUNCTIONS

GENERAL RULES

One function will serve as an example throughout this paragraph; it contains two errors, and is of no special interest.

```
        ∇ R←DECOUPE V;N
[1]  'EN COMBIEN DE BOUTS ?'
[2]  U←(ρV) ÷ N←☐
[3]  R←(N,U)ρV
        ∇
```

1) We can modify or print out a function if we are in definition mode. This is the case when we are in the process of writing the function for the first time, if not, the definition mode must be opened again by typing a (del) carrot followed by the name of the function stripped of its arguments:

$$∇DECOUPE$$
(and not ∇DECOUPE V or ∇R←DECOUPE V)

Other conventional indications can follow, between square brackets:

∇DECOUPE [2]   opening and request for positioning in line 2,
or   ∇DECOUPE [☐]   opening and request for printing.

2) After all operations on a funciton line, the computer positions itself on the line following the numbering in question:

- after line [4] the computer positions itself on [5]

- after line [7.5] the computer positions itself on [7.6]

This automatic positioning, aimed at easing the user's work, is not a constraint. In fact, the user can impose any other line number for continuation of the work.

For example, we modify line 2.6 ————————➤ [2.6]   'ERREUR'
The computer positions itself on 2.7————➤ [2.7]   [4]→ENCORE

The user imposes another line number————————↑

3) We close the definition mode only when all necessary modifications have been made. It is only this moment that the computer re-numbers the instruction 1 by 1.

TO PRINT OUT A FUNCITON

The definition mode, being previously open:

[□]   causes all functions to be printed,

[5□] causes line 5 to be printed, and the computer repositions itse
      there,

[□8] causes the function to be printed starting from line 8, then
      the computer positions itself in waiting for a sequel.

If we follow the square bracket by a carrot (del) the computer re-closes the
definition mode without placing itself in the waiting state. For example:

         ∇ *DECOUPE* [2□] ∇
    [2] $U \leftarrow (\rho V) \div N \leftarrow$ □

TO INSERT A LINE

In order to insert an instruction between two òthers, it is sufficient to giv
it a decimal number between the numbers of the two instructions. For example
we will add a test between instructions 2 and 3.

∇*DECOUPE* [2.5]	Opening of the definition mode; we request
[2.5] →(U= ↓U)/OK	positioning on line 2.5 in order to insert
[2.6] →0,ρR←'*ANOMALIE*'	two instructions.
[2.7] [□].	Here we request printing of the function.

         ∇ *R←DECOUPE V;N*
    [1]   '*EN COMBIEN DE BOUTS* ?'
    [2] $U \leftarrow (\rho V) \div N \leftarrow$ □
    [2.5] →(U= ↓U)/OK   It is seen that the lines have not yet been
    [2.6] →0,ρR←'*ANOMALIE*'   renumbered.
    [3]   R←(N,U)ρV
          ∇   ←————————   The function actually ends here, and the
    [4]   ∇   computer places itself in waiting on line 4
                                       The user thus closes the definition mode.

On recent systems, it is sufficient to type the number of the line to be
cancelled preceding it with the Δ symbol.
For example:

    [8]   [Δ3]
    [3]

Only some APL systems such as APL*PLUS of S.T.S.C actually enables several
lines to be cancelled in one go by means of [∿ 2 3 5].

TO CORRECT A FUNCTION

To correct a line means cancelling characters and inserting others in it.
On equipment provided with screens, it is sufficient to display the line
and modify it by inserting and erasing functions of the terminal. When
the user types a carriage-return, the new line replaces the old.

With printing terminals or on screens which do not have correction possibilities,
the correction intentions must be signalled according to a conventional procedure, which has three stages.

As an example we will correct the error in line 2, and add the label *OK* which
is missing in line 5 (the lines have been renumbered).

       1 - We call the line to be corrected by asking the computer to posi-
           tion the printing head under an arbitary character, the 17th
           for example:

                ∇ *DECOUPE* [2☐17]
      [2] $U \leftarrow (\rho V) \div N$☐

                    ●
                    |
                    |position of the printing head

           Thus we correct this position by means of the spacing bar and
           the back-space key to bring the printing head under the characters
           to be modified.

2 - Thus we type the conventional characters in order to indicate the characters to be cancelled, and the places where we wish to insert their character

- each / typed under a charater signifies that this character must be
cancelled. This cancelling does not leave blank positions, since
the computer joins the two sections of the line.

- each figure 1, 2, 3, ... 9 typed under a character signifies that
it is desired to insert 1, 2, 3, ... 9 characters BEFORE that one.

In the present case, the closed square bracket must be cancelled and we
must request a space before the ÷ sign in order to insert a bracket there.

[2] $U \leftarrow (\rho V] \div N \leftarrow \square$
        /1

3 - The computer prints the line thus modified, and places itself in waiting,
on the same line, so that the user can type the characters to be inserted.
Here, the bracket has been indicated towards the bottom typographically to
show what the computer types and what the user types.

[2] $U \leftarrow (\rho V \div N \leftarrow \square$
)

In order to insert the missing label, it is sufficient to request the necessary
space. Here is the sequence of these two corrections, as they would appear
on the paper:

            ∇ *DECOUPE*[2□17]
[2] $U \leftarrow (\rho V] \div N \leftarrow \square$
                /1
[2] $U \leftarrow (\rho V) \div N \leftarrow \square$
[3]   [5□7]
[5] $R \leftarrow (N,U) \rho V$ After correcting line 2, we impose a corr-
                                            ection on line 5.
        6
                                            It is better to request too much space than
[5]   OK: $R \leftarrow (N,U) \rho V$ not enough.
[6]   ∇   Closing the definintion mode.

PARTICULAR CASES

When more than 9 characters are required to be inserted, a two figure number
can no longer be typed under a single character. Hence letters are used:
A is equivalent to 5 spaces, *B* is equivalent to 10, *C* is equivalent to 15,
D to 20 etc ....

The header is considered as line 0 of a function; it can be corrected as with
any other instruction.

In order to complete a line, it is sufficient to ask the computer the zero position of this line (for example ∇*FUNC*[18□0]. The computer will thus print the line and will place itself immediately in waiting at the end of the line. The user will be able to complete it directly.

For example, to add a local variable to *DECOUPE* the following will be done:

> ∇*DECOUPE*[0□0]
> ∇ R←DECOUPE V;N
>   ;UN   what the user types has been indicated.

If the message *SI DAMAGE* appears, consult page 263.

<u>TO DUPLICATE A LINE</u>

Frequently two lines of a function are very similiar. If they are long, rather than writing the second in its entirety, it is easier to duplicate the first while supplying the required modifications to it, and assigning a new line number to it.

For example:

```
        ∇  Y EXEMPLE X
[1]     X←(2,ρX)ρX,(ρX)↑'CECI EST UN EXEMPLE'
[2]     X←⌽X
[3]     [1□7]                                          request for correction
[1]     X←(2,ρX)ρX,(ρX)↑'CECI EST UN EXEMPLE'
        /9       /1                   / ///////
[1]     [3] Y    ←(2,ρX)ρ,Y,(ρX)↑'CECI EST UNE DUPLICATION'  insert characters
[4]     [□]∇                                           request for printing

        ∇ Y EXEMPLE X
[1]     X←(2,ρX)ρX,(ρX)↑'CECI EST UN EXEMPLE'
[2]     X←⌽X
[3]     Y←(2,ρX)ρY,(ρX)↑'CECI EST UNE DUPLICATION'     duplicate line
        ∇
```

INTERRUPTED FUNCTIONS

The execution of a funciton can be interrupted for several reasons:

- the user has typed the terminals interruption key,

- the computer has detected an error or encountered a situation which prevents continuation (full workspace for example),

- a stop control had been placed in the function (this term will be seen later in this chapter).

ACCESS TO LOCAL VARIABLES

When a function is interrupted, the user can consult and modify not only the global variables, but also the local variables already created by the interrupted function. He can thus reserch the cause of an error, and eventually correct either the function, or the incorrect variables so as to re-establish the values which they should have had, before continuing the particular processing.

RESUMING EXECUTION

The user can resume the execution at the point where it was interrupted by typing $\rightarrow \Box LC$ or $I26$ or $\rightarrow 5$ (if it is interrupted in line number 5), or at any other point p of his choice by typing $\rightarrow p$.
This is the best way of not losing the benefits of computing already carried out.

The function can also be terminated by typing $\rightarrow 0$. If it was called by anothe function, however, the course of the latter will resume, as if the interrupte function had been carried out normally; this can be dangerous.

Finally, one can decide to terminate any execution in progress by simply typing $\rightarrow$.

```
            ∇ R←FOREXAMPLE V;U;E
[1]      U←1+V
[2]      E←U⁻1↓V
[3]      R←AVERAGE E   ∇

        FOREXAMPLE  5 8 11 7 14
LENGTH ERROR
FOREXAMPLE[2]   E ←U-⁻1↓V
                  ∧
```

At this stage, the values of the local variables U and V can be consulted, but not those of E and R, which have not yet been calculated.

```
      U
6  9  12  8  15
```
here is the error, we have typed 1+V instead of 1↓V

```
      U ← 8 11 7 14
```
We correct the value of U

```
      →2
```
2.25

We resume execution at the point of interruption. This time all goes well.

Instead of modifying U, we could have, equally, corrected line [1] of the function, and resumed execution at this line by $\rightarrow 1$, as below:

```
      ∇FOREXAMPLE [1] U←1↓V∇
      →1
2.25
```

PENDING FUNCTIONS

Any functions which calls an interrupted function has to interrupt itself;
we say that it is PENDING.
On some systems, it is impossible to modify a pending function, or even to
print it. This is sometimes extremely inconvenient.
This is one of the resons why it is important always to take care to clear
the state indicator of a workspace (see chapter 10).

2-3   TRACE, STOP, MONITOR, PAUSE

Control functions enabling the course of a function to be followed so as to
facilitate its completion: trace and stop. These are very efficient aids
in seeking errors. On some systems, we can also measure the execution
time of a function line by line by placing it under a monitor.
We will now study these possibilities as well as an often extremely useful
PAUSE function

2-4   TRACE

We can ask the computer to display the course of certain lines of a function
by printing the last value calculated in the line, even if it is assigned to
a variable. This is called a TRACE of the execution. Here is an example
of this:

```
        ∇ R←SOMME X;I;N
  [1]    N←ρX←,X
  [2]    I←1+R←0                    This very simple function will suffice.
  [3]   ET: R←R+X[I]
  [4]    →(N≥I←I+1)/ET
        ∇
```

To request the trace of the four lines of the function, we write, according
to the system:


```
        T∆SOMME ← 1 2 3 4        IBM
        1 2 3 4 □TRACE 'SOMME'   CONTROL DATA
        1 2 3 4 □ST 'SOMME'      BURROUGHS (ST signifies Set Trace)
```

This is what happens each time we execute the function:

SOMME 8 15 9

SOMME [1]	3	3 is the value of *N*
SOMME [2]	1	1 is the value of *I*
SOMME [3]	8	8 is the value of *R*
SOMME [4]	→3	Some systems mark only 3.
SOMME [3]	23	New value of *R*
SOMME [4]	→3	
SOMME [3]	32	
SOMME [4]		No jump
	32	Result of the function

We can of course, trace the course of certain significant lines, or trace the lines of several interleaved functions.

NOTE: The state of trace of a function is safeguarded with it if a)*SAVE* command is executed.
To cancel the effect of a trace request, we write, according to the system:

   T⊼SOMME ← 0 or ι0

   '' □*TRACE* '*SOMME*' or (ι0) □*TRACE* '*SOMME*'

   □*RT* '*SOMME*'   (for Reset Trace)

Since the trace gives the result only of the extreme left of a line, it is not a very refined tool for analysing calculations, but rather a tool for analysing the order of execution of the instructions, thus the JUMPS carried out in the function. In order to obtain a refined analysis of the calculation we can use stop controls.

12-5   STOP CONTROLS

We can interrupt a function before execution of certain lines. This is the role of the stop. Thus, in order to place a stop control before execution of lines 2 and 3 of the function which we are using as an example, we will write:

   S△SOMME ← 2 3   IBM
   2 3 □*STOP* '*SOMME*'   CONTROL DATA
   2 3 □*SS* '*SOMME*'   BURROUGH (Set Stop)

Before executing each of the lines designated, the computer interrupts itself, indicating the point of interruption. Thus the user can proceed with all operations possible with an interrupted function, before resuming its course by a branching arrow.

                SOMME 4 2 7 5   The computer interrupts itself in line 2
SOMME[2]   The user consults a local variable,
            N   then resumes execution of the function.
4
            →2
SOMME[3]   New interruption
            R
0
            →3
SOMME[3]   The computer has executed lines 3 and 4 and
            R   stops again before the 3.
4
            I
2
            SΔSOMME←10   We remove the stop controls
            →3
18   Result of the function.

In order to remove the stop controls we will write, according to case:

        SΔSOMME ← 0 or 10   as above.
        ' ' □STOP 'SOMME'
        □RS 'SOMME'   (Reset Stop)

The stop controls, like the trace, are safeguarded with a workspace. They
permit refined analysis of the calculations carried out, but present the
disadvantage of interrupting the course of the function; we will avoid
including them in a loop requiring to be run through several times.

The trace and the stop controls are usually positioned outside the function,
but they can also be positioned by program. For example when certain conditions
are met.

2-5   MONITOR

The computing time consumed by a funciton line is obtained by the monitor.
It is operated by □SM and □RM (Set and Restet Monitor) with BURROUGHS, and
by □LTIME with CONTROL DATA. We will try a test with this version.

        3 4 □LTIME 'SOMME'
        SOMME ι1000
    500500

The function runs normally. We ascertain the time consumed by monadic □LTIME.

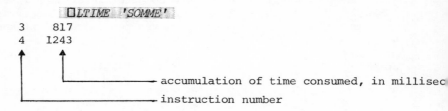

We cancel counting of time by '' $\Box LTIME$ '*SOMME*'

Since time is meaeured in milliseconds, instructions which consume little time at each execution can lead to a significant error which accumulated, as above, 1000 executions. The monitor is to be used only for seeking to optimise the calculating time of greedy lines.

12-6   PAUSE

In order to explore the variables local to a function, the user can interrupt it by means of the interruption key. On most systems however, if a request for data $\Box$ or $\Box\!\!\!\!U$ is included in a rapidly running loop, the interruption order will be understood as a correction of the value to be introduced, and will not produce the anticipated interruption.
It concerns an input $\Box\!\!\!\!U$, we can cause the interruption by typing three letters *O U T* superimposed (see paragraph 4-34). Unfortunately, on some systems, this prohibited character terminates the function without the possibility of resumin it, which is very regretable.

If it concerns an input $\Box$, we can produce part of the properties of the quad in order to explore the function during its execution. For this, it must always have the *PAUSE* function in its workspace as below:

```
         ∇ Δ ← PAUSE
[1]      U←6ρ' '
[2]      ± Δ ← 6↓U
[3]      →(0<ρΔ)/1
[4]      'RESUME PROCESSING'
[5]      Δ ← □
         ∇
```

Note that we have given a complicated name to the only local variable of this function (Δ), so that it does not mask a variable which we would like to test.

Here is a short function which will enable the use of *PAUSE* to be visualized.

```
         ∇ R←DEMONSTRATION X
[1]      R←ι0
[2]      R←R,1↑X
[3]      X←(1↓X)+□
[4]      →(0≠ρX)/2
         ∇
```

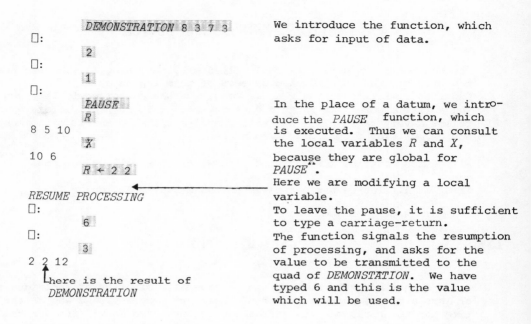

☐: *DEMONSTRATION* 8 3 7 3	We introduce the function, which asks for input of data.
☐: 2	
☐: 1	
☐: *PAUSE*	In the place of a datum, we intro-duce the *PAUSE* function, which
R	is executed. Thus we can consult
8 5 10	the local variables *R* and *X*,
X	because they are global for
10 6	*PAUSE*.
R ← 2 2	Here we are modifying a local variable.
RESUME PROCESSING	To leave the pause, it is sufficient to type a carriage-return.
☐:	The function signals the resumption of processing, and asks for the
6	value to be transmitted to the
☐:	quad of *DEMONSTATION*. We have
3	typed 6 and this is the value
2 2 12	which will be used.
here is the result of *DEMONSTRATION*	

It is very advisable to always have this function in the workspace during
testing.

12-7   FUNCTION PRINTERS

The methods for correcting functions shown above correspond to the options
normally offered to the users of terminals working in character mode (see
chapter 1).
Some systems offer more extended correction options, at the price, it is
time, of greater complexity of operation. For example, we can replace a
name or a character string by another in all or part of a function; we can
displace a group of lines; we can include in a function a group of
functions which have been extracted from another function, etc ....
Moreover, for terminals working in synchronous mode, IBM offers a "FULL
SCREEN" editor, which enables a whole function to be displayed on a screen
and enables its instructions to be modified directly.

For all these options it is advisable to consult the supplied by the
manufacturers' brochures.

CHAPTER 13

STYLES, METHODS AND ADVICE

You now possess a wonderful tool called APL, but how will you make use of it, how will you use the thousand aspects of this language?
Experience will teach you what is good, but the author would like you to spend yet a little more time in this exploration. This chapter therefore will not follow a very rigid plan, but will comprise rather a series of comments and advice, arising from application of APL.

All advice contains its share of errors; critics will be welcome!

First of all let us ask ourselves a fundamental question:

13-1   WHY USE APL?

For a long time, APL remained the reserve of a minority of individuals, more or less experts, who were users of their own programs, and who at the same time had to appreciate its attractive features and suffer its errors, gaps and shortcomings. APL increasingly serves to write sets of programs which will be used by third parties, often ignorant of APL. It is fitting to recall here that the applications which you will accomplish will have to answer certain criteria which in order of diminishing priority are as follows:

1 - SATISFYING THE NEEDS OF THE USER

The "client" is always right; it is not for the programmer to impose his options, even if he can and must advise his interlocutor.

2 - SECURITY OF PROCESSING AND DATA

It is out of the question to loose data or alter them by carelessness or error It is equally inconceivable that a user can find himself in a situation where he is not master. Even if he has committed a handling error, the user must never find himself in the presence of *LENGTH ERROR, INDEX ERROR, FILE FULL,* and other delights.
Only failure of the computer is unavoidable; again one must see to it that it never has irreparable consequences.

3 — <u>PLEASANT TO USE</u>

The priority which we give to this will certainly surprise data processors
However, it must be understood that most errors are due to fatigue, nervous
strain, or, frequently to lack of clarity and precision of the working
procedure.

4 — <u>EASE OF MAINTENANCE AND MODIFICATION</u>

There is always something to modify in a set of functions, because requirements
change. It is important therefore that the functions are easy to read back,
even by a third party, that the logic of the processings is clear, and that
documentation, complete and kept up to date, indicates the role of each function
and the structure of the data.

5 — <u>EFFICIENCY</u>

Efficiency must be one of the constant concerns of the programmer, but not
at any price. To gain a few seconds of processing on a function which is used
rarely at the price of several hours of work and thought is not always a good
move.
Care should also be taken that the performances obtained cannot be brought
into question by a change of equipment.

3-2   QUESTIONS OF STYLE

If your programs satisfy all these criteria, and moreover they are
"wonderful" and give you intellectual satisfaction, all is perfect, but
considerations of style must NEVER take precedence over all else.

However, we often find that the safest, the easiest to maintain and the
most efficient functions are also the most concise and the most satisfying
intellectually.
It is only in this spirit that one can tackle questions of style.

13-3   LOCAL VARIABLES, GLOBAL VARIABLES

All variables significant in relation to only one function must be made
local to it; this is the only way of preventing execution of this function
altering a global variable in error.

Preferably, one will avoid transmitting data to a function in the form of
global variables, unless it involves a sub-function called by a principal
function. If not, the use of arguments is certainly preferable, provided that
this does not lead to aggregating totally dissimilar data in the same argument
Sometimes, however, the use of a global variable can be advantageous in order:

- to group all the messages printed by function in a matrix of
  characters. This enables functions for bilingual usage to be
  easily created, or allows only abridged messages to be displayed
  to the experienced user.

- to alleviate reading of a function by representing the numeric
  constraints, or the formats of □*FMT* by global variables.

- to transmit the parameters of processing from one function to anothe
  when these two functions are not executed simultaneously.

- to modify the global environment of a whole set of functions. For
  example, a global variable can conserve for several successive
  processings a list of people on whom these processings have a
  bearing, or the numbers of data which one wants to see appear on
  successive print outs, etc .....

In all cases, global variables must immediately acknowledge themselves, both
in the reading of a function, and the list of variables supplied by)*VARS*.
If not it is to be feared that they have been erased by mistake.
For example, we can call them *GV*1, *GV*2, ..., *GV*23; this is simple and efficie
but not very revealing as to the nature of these variables. We can also
underline their first letter: *OPTION*, *DAY*, *LIST*, ...; this is disagreeable
to type, but clearer, and all the global variables occur at the end of the
list given by)*VARS*.

13-4   CHOICE OF NAMES

The names of the source functions (which do not call any other function) must
be perfectly clear: *PRINTING CONTROL*, *UPTODATE*, *SAFEGUARD*, and not *PROG*3
or *EDNM*.

Utility variables used in intermediate calculations can have short names, or
even be reduced to a single letter, but an important variable must also have
a clear name.
Evocative names can also be given to labels and this is sometimes a good
way of clarifying the meaning of a function.

Finally, in no case must the names of the formal requirements be indentical
with the names of variables actually used in the calculations, because,
in the event of an error, the local name would mask the global name, hiding
perhaps the real cause of the error.

13-5 RECURSIVITY

A function can call itself, directly or through the intermediary of another
function; we say that it is RECURSIVE. The most classic example is calculation
of $!N$ which is deduced from the calculation of $!(N-1)$ by the formula:

$$!N \equiv N \times !(N-1)$$

It is sufficient to know that $!1$ equals 1 to be able to calculate the
factorial of any other number. If the primitive $!$ did not exist we could
have written the following function:

```
        ∇ R←FACT N
[1]  →(N=R←1)/0
[2]  R ← N × FACT N-1   ∇
```

In line [2] there appears the recurring formula seen above, so that the
function calls itself $N-1$ times, until N becomes equal to 1.

```
      !5
120
      FACT 5
120
```

A stop control enables operating of this function to be scrutinized.

```
      SΔFACT ← 2            IBM convention

      FACT 4               Introduction of the function
FACT[2]                    First interruption, before line 2.
```

```
     )SI
FACT[2] *
     N
4
```
By testing the state indicator, we check that we are interrupted on line 2; N still equals 4.

```
    →2
FACT[2]
    )SI
FACT[2] *
FACT[2]
    N
3
```
We restart execution
New interruption

The function has called itself once, and N equals 3 in the internal function

```
    →2
FACT[2]
    )SI
FACT[2] *
FACT[2]
FACT[2]
    N
2
```
Now *FACT*4 has called *FACT*3, which has in turn called *FACT*2

```
    →2
24
```
↑
Final result

When we reintroduce the function, *FACT*2 calls *FACT*1, which equals 1. Each function can thus restore, to that which calls it, the value which it was lacking in order to end the calculation.

ANOTHER EXAMPLE

We wish to insert blanks in a character string. The number of blanks to be inserted is indicated by a second character string.

```
THE SUITCASE TRAVELS
     2 4    1 2
```

Here, we wish to insert 2 blanks before T, 4 before S, 1 before V, and 2 before L.

The following function will achieve this; note that it is recursive.

```
        ∇ R←NB EXPAND TEXT;I
[1]     R←TEXT
[2]     →((ρNB)<I←(NB≠' ')ι1)/0
[3]     R←((I-1)↑TEXT) , ((⍎NB[I])ρ' '), TEXT[I]
[4]     R ← R, (I↓NB) EXPAND (I↓TEXT)  ∇

        B ← 'THE SUITCASE TRAVELS'
        A ← '       2 4    1 2 '

        A EXPAND B
THE SUI   TCA    SE TRA VE LS
```

Recursivity is intellectually attractive, but beware at each stage of the
calculation, since the computer must store all the calling stages, with
their exact state, and their local variables. This can represent many
calculations and require a lot of space. It is often preferable to make
a single loop.
If recursivity tempts you, do not forget:

- that there must be a condition which enables one to pull out of
  the successive calls.

- that the names of the variables are the same in all the functions
  which call themselves; it is therefore essential to make them local,
  otherwise you will find that each stage alters the result of the
  calling stage.

13-6
USING THE QUAD

The use of the quad for data entry presents the disadvantage of consuming
a considerable amount of paper, so that it quickly becomes difficult to
find what was typed a quarter of an hour earlier. In this respect the *CALL*
function, written in paragraph 9-3, achieves much more concise entries.
However, the quad offers two considerable advantages:

- firstly, the computer takes charge of all controls of the data
  introduced, when it is difficult to control by program that a
  character string may serve as an argument of the EXECUTE function,

- next, we can profit from a quad for executing supplementary tasks
  by small functions restoring an explicit result. It is this property which the *PAUSE* function (§12-6) and exercise 22 of chapter 4
  makes use of. Hence we arrive at considerably improving the readability
  of a function by relieving it of processing a mass of special cases.

The quad still has sunny days ahead!

3-7
ALLEGRO, MA NON TROPPO!

Many APL users refuse to use some primitives which they consider too elaborate
(the inner product, scan, encode and decode), for fear of leading to obscure
programming. Such persons therefore use "periphrases" to achieve the same
thing.

This disregards the fact that repeated use of those "elaborate" primitives is the only means of making them so familiar that they end up by no longer engaging attention.

Moreover, a specialized function will always be much quicker than a whole series of equivalent instructions. We have seen, in exercise 17 of chapter 5 that the use of scan required a processing time one fifteenth of that taken by a loop. Precision pays.

To conclude: enjoy yourself, work happily, with the primitives which tempt you. But ....

But precision must not become an objective. Many apostles of APL have been tempted to completely solve each problem within a minimum of instructions, one only if possible. These *"one liners"* therefore elaborate expressions such as:

$(M \vee . \neq 0) \neq M \leftarrow \varnothing((+/S) - {}^{-}1\uparrow\rho M)\varphi(M-1\ 0\downarrow M,[1]0)\times(\rho M \leftarrow S \leftarrow BORNES\circ.<VALEURS[I])\rho I \leftarrow \psi VALEUR.$

Such instructions can be read back only by the person who wrote them; and often consume time in superfluous operations. Be warned against this type of deviation, which has done much wrong to APL, and which is commonly called "pornography".

In the same vein, it is advisable to use the instructions separator (DIAMOND) in moderation on systems where there is one.

13-8   METHODS

The first working procedure dictated by experience may be expressed in two sentences, mainly:

>   - *Ten minutes of thought is worth more than one hour of*
>   *fumbling on a terminal.*
>
>   - *Ten minutes of experimenting on a terminal can save hours*
>   *of thought.*

APL is a powerful, flexible, efficient tool and its high degree of inter-activity prompts working on the terminal; this is a danger to be avoided.

APL is only a tool and does not dispense with thought, particularly as regards the structure suitable for adoption for the data, and as regards which architecture of functions will be the best.

On the other hand, APL is a marvelous experimental tool, and it must be known. how to check hypothesis, or algorithms of processing on a terminal, before pursuing more advanced studies.

The second working performance consists of writing short and modular functions
in which each distinct task is delegated to a distinct sub-function.
A particularly characteristic example is simulation of a lift, demonstrated
in paragraph 10-14, where a pilot function shared the work between other
functions:

```
           ∇ LIFT
[1]        WAIT
[2]        ACTION: →DECISION
[3]        GO
[4]        OPENCLOSE
[5]        UPDATE
[6]        → ACTION   ∇
```

Such a function dispenses with commentaries and any programming flowchart.
This is of course, an extreme case, and it is not always possible to arrive
at such modularity. However, the approach will be attempted at all stages
of work. The required effort is always recompensated by incomparable
ease of use, testing and maintenance .

13-9   ORGANISING YOUR WORKSPACE

Should a large function be used to guide the user and ask him the necessary
questions, or again small independent functions which he will have to assign
himself, by assigning suitable arguments to them?
It all depends on the degree of experience of the end user, on the complexity
of the processings required, and on the security attached to the data.

Short functions with arguments will be used wherever possible. They offer
much more flexibility of assembly, they are quick to use and enable the
intermediate stages of the work to be controlled.
In the event of error in use, a language error will probably appear (*INDEX
ERROR, VALUE ERROR, ...*), which assumes that the user is capable of
clearing the state indicator and appropriately restarting its processing.

On the other hand, if the security of data or the nature of the processings
desired means that certain operations are carried out in a precise order,
without any omissions, it is no longer a question of placing confidence
in the user, and it will be preferable to write functions which take charge
of the operator from beginning to end, imposing and controlling inputs of
essential data.

This will be called INTERACTIVE or CONVERSATIONAL functions. Thus we can
have an interactive function for each separate activity. Sometimes we can
also achieve a monitor program instructed itself, to implement the preceding
functions according to the operator's answers to its questions.

We will study these two organisations of a workspace.

13-10   A PUZZLE OF FUNCTIONS

Here is an example which well illustrates the first type of organization.
It is a simple example which can be readily improved.

We have various information regarding the employees of a company. This
information is either represented in the form of global variables called
NAME, REG, BIRTH,...., or recorded in a file, and read by means of niladic
functions called NAME, REG,.... which amounts to the same thing.

> NAME   matrix of names of the employees
>
> REG   vector of their registration numbers in the company
>
> BIRTH year of birth of the employees
>
> SALR   vector of salaries, rounded off to the nearest dollar
>
> CHI   number of children of the employees
>
> CAT   socio-professional category (1, 2 or 3)

The employees are recorded in any order. The funciton PRINT enables information to be printed relating to the people whose order number in the file
is given. For example:

```
        PRINT 5 2 11
 |__|_____|_____|_____|_____|___|___|
 |NO|  N A M E  | REG |BIRTH | SALR |CH |CAT|
 |__|_____|_____|_____|_____|___|___|
 | 5|BUSNEL     | 935 | 1944 | 4006 | 2 | 2 |
 | 2|HUREL      | 949 | 1945 | 4194 | 1 | 2 |
 |11|HURTUBISE  | 285 | 1931 | 6243 | 5 | 1 |
 |__|_____|_____|_____|_____|___|___|
```

We have indeed caused the 5th, 2nd and 11th people to be printed.

In order to print all the contents of the file, we could write *PRINT*   ιρ*REG*.
It will be preferable to write a function:

           ∇ *R←ALL*
[1]   *R ← ιρ REG*
       ∇

     PRINT ALL

NO	N A M E	REG	BIRTH	SALR	CH	CAT
1	MARGERAIS	360	1929	5935	3	2
2	HUREL	949	1945	4194	1	2
3	VANNIEL	645	1933	4841	2	3
4	GENEGORD	823	1952	2844	0	1
5	BUSNEL	935	1944	4006	2	2
6	VARONIE	947	1937	4640	0	2
7	WANIEL	449	1945	3952	1	1
8	JOUSSET	639	1927	4945	2	2
9	SOMBOSSO	273	1934	4970	2	3
10	BAUMALE	289	1950	2813	2	3
11	HURTUBISE	285	1931	6243	5	1
12	VANIELLE	838	1933	4545	0	2
13	SENECHAL	904	1946	3070	1	3
14	BONENFANT	163	1918	5136	2	3
15	FURNAT	933	1944	4081	3	1

We will work here on a small company of 15 people who answer to certain
criteria. For example, those who earn more than \$4500, and are in category
2, which can be written:

$$(CAT=2) \land (SALR > 4500)$$

In order to pass the boolean result of this expression to a list of
numbers a function would be welcome. We will call it *PEOPLE* :

         ∇ *R ← PEOPLE CRIT*
[1]   *R ← CRIT / ALL*
       ∇

Moreover, since the symbols ∧ ∨ ∼ are unknown to the public, we will
incorporate them in three utility functions:

     ∇ *R←A AND B*   ∇ *R← A OR B*   ∇ *R←A EXCEPT B*
[1]   *R ← A∧B*   [1]   *R←A∨B*   [1]   *R←A∧∼B*
   ∇   ∇   ∇

We can now use them as follows:

PRINT PEOPLE (CAT=2) AND (SALR > 4500)

NO	N A M E	REG	BIRTH	SALR	CH	CAT
1	MARGERAIS	360	1929	5935	3	2
6	VARONIE	947	1937	4640	0	2
8	JOUSSET	639	1927	4945	2	2
12	VANIELLE	838	1933	4545	0	2

PRINT PEOPLE (CH <2) EXCEPT (CAT=2)

NO	N A M E	REG	BIRTH	SALR	CH	CAT
4	GENEGORD	823	1952	2844	0	1
7	WANIEL	449	1945	3952	1	1
13	SENECHAL	904	1946	3070	1	3

It would be much better however, to produce this information in terms of any
criterion. The function *ACCORDING* will achieve this:

```
       ∇ R←POP ACCORDING CRIT
[1]    R ← POP[⍋CRIT[POP]] ∇
```

PRINT (PEOPLE SALR>5000) ACCORDING REG

NO	N A M E	REG	BIRTH	SALR	CH	CAT
14	BONENFANT	163	1918	5136	2	3
11	HURTUBISE	285	1931	6243	5	1
1	MARGERAIS	360	1929	5935	3	2

it is seen that these
people are classed in
increasing order of
registration number

We can also class these people alphabetically, by using a function inspired
by that written in chapter 7 (for a small number of people).

```
       ∇ R← ALPHAORDER
[1]    R ← 27 ⊥ ' ABCDEFGHIJKLMNOPQRSTUVWXYZ' ⍳ ⍉ NAME
       ∇
```

It would be sufficient therefore to write, for example:

PRINT ALL ACCORDING ALPHAORDER

Many other functions could augment this embryo, but it can be seen already
that, with a few functions of a single instruction each, we can arrive at a
wide diversity of questions. We could not solve everything by such a device,
which we call pseudo-language, but we can thus open up the use of the computer
to widely diverse areas of population. This is also a means of carrying out
preparatory works whose result can be transmitted to a more significant
processing function, whether by means of an intermediate variable, or by means
of a quad.

We will not give the function *PRINT* here, so as to leave you the pleasure of writing it. It contains less than 12 instructions, and the global variable *ZONES* enables the number and order of the printed information to be modified:

```
ZONES ← 1 5 2
PRINT PEOPLE CH > 2
 |__|_____|___|_____|
 |NO|  N A M E |CH | REG |
 |__|_____|___|_____|
 | 1|MARGERAIS | 3 | 360 |
 |11|HURTUBISE | 5 | 285 |
 |15|FURNAT    | 3 | 933 |
 |__|_____|___|_____|
```

The zones are in the order:

1 → *NAME*
2 → *REG*
3 → *BIRTH*
4 → *SALR*
5 → *CHI*
6 → *CAT*

The number appearing on the left is automatically added by the function; a global variable contains the header.

13-11 CONVERSATIONAL FUNCTIONS

A conversational function expects from the operator either directives relating to the processings to be carried out or data. Due to the flexibility of APL, and in particular due to the possibilities of the EXECUTE function and the QUAD, these two types of information are often closely interwoven. Care must be taken however, that the system allows efficient working, without fatigue.

A few common sense rules for this should be observed.

CLARITY OF QUESTIONS

The operator must always be perfectly informed of the meaning of a question. This assumes preliminary training and a precise user's manual, complete and up to date. This assumes also that wording of the question is itself perfectly clear.
Nothing is more trying than a question, the length of a line, which is going to repeat itself 100 or 200 times in a run through like, for example:

WILL YOU INTRODUCE THE PRICE APPEARING IN COLUMN 3 OF THE CATALOGUE. THANK YOU.

It will be essential to be concise!

COMMENTARY

In case of doubt regarding a question with multiple answers a simple procedure
should enable the operator to obtain the list of possible answers, paired
with a brief commentary on their use. Normally, this list is obtained by
typing *?* or *SOS*. This does not exclude the user's manual previously quoted.

HOMOGENEITY

The same effect should always be obtained by means of the same directive. If
need be, a different procedure for an entry on ☐ and an entry on ☐ can
be accepted, but it is inadvisable that to pull out of a loop we must type
either *END*, or *STOP*, sometimes →, or even nothing at all, according to the
functions or the workspaces.

ENTRY BY DEFAULT

The more one limits the number of data to be entered the more one restricts
the causes of error and fatigue. In this respect, the maximum data will be
entered by default. For example, a company sells most of its products at
catalogue price, but is led sometimes to apply different prices (discounts,
sales, or supplements for special work). If we ask the operator to enter the
price of each product to be sold, she will type , 95 times out of 100, a
value already known to the computer.
It is thus safer and more economical to enter the price only if it is
necessary, by means of another question. For example:

> [17] '*QUANTITY ORDERED, PRICE*'
> [18] *QTY* ← 1↑*U*←☐
> [19] *PRICE* ← 1↑1↓*U, PRICECATALOG*

If the operator types only one quantity, the price will be the catalogue
price (designated here by *PRICECATA*); if she types two values, the first will
be taken as the quantity ordered, and the second as the special price.

VALIDATIONS

On the same theme, if we ask the operator to validate her system work, she
will finish by doing it automatically, without exercising real control, without
prescribing it, by means of another question.

For example, when the operator types the code of a product, we display its wording to verify that there has not been a code error.

Method not to be followed:

ARTICLE CODE ?
☐:
    3543

BALL AND SOCKET JACK HEAD	introduction of the code displaying
OK ? (YES/NO)	control
YES	request for systematic validation,
COLOUR CODE ?	which will soon become tedious.
☐:	

Here is a much better method:

ARTICLE CODE ?
☐:
    3534
50 BAR PUMP BARREL

COLOUR CODE [ERROR] ?	an incorrect code has been introduced
☐:	
ERROR	
ARTICLE CODE ?	By typing ERROR, we return to the previous
☐:	question.
3543	

Such methods of entry by default, we can save 10 to 20% of the entry work demanded of an operator.

DISPLAYING CONTROLS

On ending the control, the operator must be able always to display the stage in the operations being performed, or the data already entered. This possibility must be specially developed if the operator has a job where she may be distributed (landlady, sales person, receptionist ......).

OPTIONS

It is good form to recall in a question, processing options which are offered to the operator and which are not in systematic use:

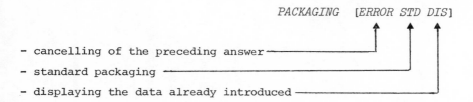

                                      PACKAGING   [ERROR STD DIS]

- cancelling of the preceding answer
- standard packaging
- displaying the data already introduced

CHECKING

Checking entered data is a tedious task. Essentially a check is made of the
number of values entered, their sign, their representation (whole or decimal)
their coherence to other data, and their probability (for example by means
of probability forks).

We must start from the principle that ANYTHING can happen. A file placed by
carelessness on a keyboard can bring about entry of a minus sign or a decimal
point; a typing error can lead to 12,30 (2 values), where one wished to type
12.30 (1 decimal value).

ERROR MESSAGES

Most errors are due to clumsiness or inattentiveness, and are generally very
apparent if one attracts the attention of the operator. Since printing of
an error message is always very much resented by the person who is at the
keyboard, one will be satisfied simply with asking the question. The
message will be printed if the nature of the error is not evident, or if
repetition of the question initiates normal running of the function.
On the other hand, there is sense at times in printing a message attesting
that an operation has been carried out correctly (safeguarding for example)

13-12   FINAL ADVICE

KNOW THE BULKINESS OF YOUR DATA

If we keep to IBM standards (see paragraph 7-14 and 10-2), a whole number
occupies 4 octets, a decimal occupies 8 and a binary value occupies 1 bit.
It is known however, that some operations always give a result in decimal
form, even if the value is whole ($\circledast$ o $\div$ ⊟ ...).
For example:

$$\Box \leftarrow V \leftarrow 2\ 4\ 8\ 16\ 32 \div 2$$

 1   2   4   8   16   These values occupy 8 octets, because they are
           $\Box WA$ the result of division.
 70240

          $V \leftarrow \lfloor V$ Without changing their value, we make the
          $\Box WA$ element of V whole, which frees some space.
 70260

In the case of bulky data, savings can be very significant. This is why
we often represent prices in cents, rather than in dollars and cents.

The gain is even bigger for binary values. The ONLY operations which give
a binary result are: $\in$ $<$ $\leq$ $=$ $\geq$ $>$ $\neq$ $\vee$ $\wedge$ $\sim$ $\curlyvee$ $\curlywedge$

$V \leftarrow {}^-1 + ?3200\rho2$ We have produced 3200 "binary" elements
$\quad \square WA$ In reality, they are represented in the
131160   form of whole numbers equal to 0 and 1.

$V \leftarrow 1=V$ By means of a boolean operation, we have
$\quad \square WA$ transformed representation of the values
143560   and achieved a saving of more than 12,000
                                             octets.

We will assume:

> - that all elements of a variable are represented in the same way.
>   Hence they occupy the smallest space between them.
>
> - that we can convert a decimal into a whole number by $X \leftarrow \lfloor X$
>
> - that we can convert a whole number into a boolean by $1 \wedge X$ or $1=X$.

AVOID LOOPS AND JUMPS

Each jump breaks the reading of a function, and renders its maintenance more
difficult. In exercises 17 and 35 of chapter 5 we encountered various ways
of avoiding jumps; moreover these methods must remain natural and simple to
read. Work on vectors, use of the means of avoiding numerous loops.
We must not however fall for the complete opposite, and arrive at unreadable
solutions, under the pretext of avoiding a loop!

EPILOGUE

It must be understood that APL is still a marginal language in the data
processing medium, and development is much more active in other sectors
of company business, among those concerned with statistical studies, management control, operational research, forecast management, and generally all
jobs of a high intellectual value.
Everything indicates that APL is the language which will undergo the greatest development in future years because it is the only one which offers
speedy profitability of the intellectual potential of a company service.

APL is still affected by the striking lack of adaptation of the data
processing equipment to vectorial processing. Nothing indicates whether
big manufacturers will invest in producing machines which are actually
vectorial and adapted for use with APL. If such is the case, there is no
doubt that data processing services will follow the change imposed by the
manufacturers, as they have always done in the past.

It is important therefore to know how to prepare for this development by
adequate training of personnel. In 1990, programs written in FORTRAN,
COBOL, and PL/1, will still be used, but new developments will occur
essentially with the aid of APL, or totally in APL.

Not everything has been said about APL, but you now have all the elements
for working efficiently, consulting other works to advantage and exploiting
possibilities available on your system, which the present work could not
enumerate.
Above all, you have the opportunity of discovering by yourself so many
things which could not be included in any book.
The author will be happy if he has been able to contribute, in no matter
how small a way, to enabling you to taste the joy and intellectual satisfaction
of using APL efficiently.

BIBLIOGRAPHY

GENERAL WORKS

APL, An interactive approach   Leonard GILMAN & Allen J. ROSE
John Wiley, 1974

Informatique par téléphone   Philip S. ABRAMS & Gérard LACOURLY
Hermann, 1972

APL, The language and its usage   Raymond P. POLIVKA & Sandra PAKIN
Prentice-Hall, 1975

Use and misuse of APL   Roy A. SYKES
Scientific Time Sharing Corp., 1973

WORKS ON PARTICULAR ASPECTS

A formal description of APL   R. H. LATHWEALL & J. E. MEZEI
Communication au colloque APL 1971
IRIA, 1971

General arrays,   Ziad GHANDOUR & Jorge MEZEI
operators and functions   IBM
Journal of research & development, 1973

Systems formulation & APL   R. H. LATHWELL
Shared variables   IBM
Journal of research & development, 1973

APL in exposition   Kenneth E. IVERSON
APL Press, 1976

PERIODICALS

Symposia of discussions at APL congresses

QUOTE-QUAD APL review   Published by STAPL.

SOLUTIONS TO THE EXERCISES

CHAPTER 2 EXERCISES

[1] *SHODDY* has 2 3 5 for dimensions, for rank 3, and its value is:

        5 0 1 6 6
        0 0 1 7 9
        2 5 12 72 0

        5 0 1 6 6
        0 0 1 7 9
        2 5 12 72 0

[2] The surplus elements are ignored by the computer.

[3] $V \leftarrow 1\rho S$ gives a vector of a single element.

[4] $S \leftarrow (\rho 1)\rho V$ gives a scalar. In effect, $\rho 1$ is indeed the dimension of a scalar, and it has been used as left-hand argument of ρ.

[5] *X* is the character string: '2 15 8 3'

[6] *D* equals 27, *C* equals 77, *B* equals 154, and *A* equals 155.

[7] $\rho\rho DOUGH$ equals 2 (this is the rank of this variable). Whereas $\rho DOUGH$ equals 2 6. $(\rho DOUGH)\rho(\rho\rho DOUGH)$ is thus equivalent to 2 6ρ 2.
     result of which would be:

        2 2 2 2 2 2
        2 2 2 2 2 2

[8] Answer: 6 6 ρ 1 0 0 0 0 0 0

[9] *THE CAT* of course!

[10] The matrix required will have the dimensions of the result, i.e. 3 6.
     In order to fill it, it suffices to note the space occupied by each
     character in the vector *STEAM*. Notice the blank, in the second position.
     TRAIN thus equals: 2 1 2 5 2 3
                            7 1 1 1 1 1
                            4 6 6 2 6 6

[11] *A* equals 0 5 0 9 0; and *B* equals 0, and not 0 0 0, as examination
     of the left-hand part only of the expression could leave one thinking.

[12] *TYRES*[; 2 ; 1 2 3 5] (every year; type 2; factories 1 2 3 and 5)

     TYRES[4 ; ; 1] (1977 is the 4th year ; NIORT is the first factory)

[13] *TYRES*[1;1 2;1 2 3] equals   3200   0 4100
                                           420   840   360

     TYRES[3 2 1;2 1;1] equals   440 3000
                                         400 3120
                                       420 3200

[14] Inside the square brackets, A is given the value 5 4 6 2 1 3
The expression given is thus equivalent to 5 4 6 2 1 3[5 4 6 2 1 3]
The result therefore is: 1 2 3 4 5 6

[15] M initially equals: *ABCD* and M[;3] equals: *CGKO*
                                EFGH
                                IJKL
                                MNOP

   The first transformation thus gives: *CGKO* and M[2;] equals: *EFGH*
                                               EFGH
                                             IJKL
                                             MNOP

   The second transformation thus gives: *CEKO*
                                               EFGH
                                             IGKL
                                             MHOP

[16] An attempt to proceed in two stages, will result merely in duplicating
one of the lines.
Conventionally one would proceed in three stages:

        BUFFER ← *PRESSURES*[;2]
        PRESSURES[;2] ← *PRESSURES*[;4]
        PRESSURES[;4] ← *BUFFER*

However, much easier to work: *PRESSURES*[;2 4] ← *PRESSURES*[;4 2]

[17] *ARRAY*[;1 5]←2 2ρ21 45 78 11 Remember to arrange the 4 values in a matrix
of two lines and two columns.

[18] *SOUP*[7 4] equals 2 1

   PRESSURES[2;2 1] equals 5 4

   DRALE[1;4] equals 3

The expression obtained is thus equivalent to *TYRES*[3;3;5 4], which
gives: 1560 0

[19] Aρ(ι14) is equivalent to 2 4ρ(ι14), and equals: 1 2 3 4
                                                               5 6 7 8

[20] The last term of 1+ι(ρV) is greater than the number of elements of V.
This expression cannot therefore act as an index to this vector.

[21] 1 2 11 11 1 7 8

[22] This exercise can be solved by stating that *ORIGIN*[3] equals 8, then
     that *ORIGIN*[1] equals 11, etc.....
     On the computer, it is easier to asign the values supplied by the
     statement to a vector of suitable dimensions:

             ORIGIN ← 6ρ0   the contents are of little importance
                                               only the size counts.
             ORIGIN[3 1 6 5 2 4]← 8 11 3 9 2 15

             ORIGIN
        11 2 8 15 9 3

[23] If we call *V* the given vector (9 2 7 4 5 1) then:

     V[*INDICES*[1]] is equal to *V*[4]. Thus *INDICES*[1] equals 4.

     V[*INDICES*[2]] is equal to *V*[2]. Thus *INDICES*[2] equals 2.

     V[*INDICES*[3]] is equal to *V*[1]. Thus *INDICES*[3] equals 1.

     The set of indices required is thus: 4 2 1 6 5 3

CHAPTER 3 EXERCISES

[1] $3 \times 2 + 6 \neq 3 \times 2$ It is advisable to proceed with the calcul-
                  $6 \neq 6$ ations from right to left, as shown along-
                $2 + 0$ side.
            3×2
                  6 The results obtained will thus be respec-
                                                   tively:

                                                        - a)   6

                                                        - b)   12 6 14

                                                        - c)   5 5 6

                                                        - d)   7 ‾3 6

                                                        - e)   42

[2] $2 + 2 \quad 2 + 2$ Remember that the left hand argument of a
          $2 + 4 \quad 4$ function extends up to the following symbol.
              $6 \quad 6$

[3] 1+ρ*A* is evaluated like 1+(ρ*A*) and thus equals 1+4 or 5.

ρ*A*+1 is evaluated like ρ(*A*+1) and thus equals ρ(9 3 8 6) or 4.

These two expressions are therefore not equivalent.
In the same way:

$$\bar{1}+\iota\rho A \quad \text{equals : 0 \quad 1 \quad 2 \quad 3}$$

$$\iota\bar{1}+\rho A \quad \text{equals : 1 \quad 2 \quad 3}$$

$$\iota\rho A-1 \quad \text{equals : 1 \quad 2 \quad 3 \quad 4}$$

[4] (2ρρ*A*) is equivalent to 2ρ4 or 4 4.

The expression given is thus equivalent to 4 4ρ*A* which equals:

        8 2 7 5
        8 2 7 5
        8 2 7 5
        8 2 7 5

[5] (ρ4⌊5) is equal to ρ4, hence this is the empty vector. Since the latter
is absorbant, the result of the given expression is also an empty
vector.

[6] 3 ⌈ ¯1 + ι4

7 ⌊ 3 ⌈ ι9

1 + 5 × ι 4 3 2 5 = ι5

[7] *A* ← 4 5 6 hence ρ*A* equals 3.

A + ρ*A* thus equals 4 5 6 + 3 or 7 8 9

Finally the last value of *A* is 12 7 20 - 7 8 9 or 5 ¯1 11

[8] *A* is a scalar if its rank is zero. The expression required is: 0=ρρ*A*

[9] *A*>*B* equals 1 or 0. The required expression is: *C* ← 3 + 4×*A*>*B*

[10] *C* ← (*A*≠0)ρ(*B*≠0)×3

[11] In both cases, *A* first takes the value 17. Then in the expression
(*A*←2)×*A* the computer evaluates the bracket, gives the value 2 to *A*;
and *A*×*A* equals 4.
In the expression (*A*←2)×⌊*A* the computer first evaluates ⌊*A* and stores
the result: 17. This result is then multiplied by 2, giving 34.

This is one of the rather rare cases where human logic is not respected
by APL.

[12]   1+2*2*ι5
            5 17 257 65537 4294967297

[13] $X \leftarrow (A+B) \div E+C \div D$ the brackets are essential

  $Y \leftarrow A*-B \div E+1$ the brackets are superfluous

  $Z \leftarrow ((-B) + ((B \times B)-4 \times A \times C)*0.5) \div 2 \times A$

[14]

  $x = a - \dfrac{b}{c+d}$

  $y = c^d - b$

  $z = ax^{2+b\,(x+c)}$ and not $ax^2 + bx + c$

  $t = a(a - 2c +d)$

[15] a) 1 1 1 0 1 1

   b) 0 1 0 1 1 1

   c) 0 0 0 0 1 0

   d) 0 0 0 0 1 0

   e) 1 0 1 0 0 1

   f) 0 0 0 1 0 0

   g) 0 0 1 0 1 0

   h) 1 0 0 1 1 0

[16] 1 0 0 1

   0 0 1

   1

   3

   7 0 7

[17] 0 1 1

   1 0 0 0 1

   1 1   in effect the scalar 11 is comprises the 2

   1 1   terms of the vector '11'

[18] The average of a series of values is equal to their sum $+/V$ divided by
   the number of values ρV.
   The required expression is thus $(+/V) \div \rho V$
   $+/V \div \rho V$ is equally valid, but if V has 1000 elements, one will carry out
   the sum of 1000 quotients, which will be less precise than the quotient
   of the sum of 1000 terms given by the first expression.

[19] ρCHI gives the number of couples questioned.
$+/CHI \leq 3$ indicates how many couples have at most three children.

The required percentage will be obtained by: $\lfloor 100 \times (+/CHI < 3) \div \rho CHI$

[20] $+/PH = 'T'$ or $+/PH \epsilon 'T'$ give the answer to 16.

[21] $A=B$ should give an answer composed uniquely of 1's. This can be ensured by proceeding with reduction by AND. The result will be 1 if the two vectors are identical, 0 if they are not: $\wedge/A=B$

After studying chapter 5, this expression can be replaced by an inner product: $A \wedge .= B$

[22] $Z=9$ indicates that the third element of Z equals 9, and indicates further that Z is a matrix of dimensions 4 1.
$2\rho Z$ indicates that the first two elements of Z equal 1 and 7.
$+/[1]Z$ enables us to calculate that the last element equals 3.
Z thus equals:

```
1
7
9
3
```

[23] $+/V=V$

[24] 8 0 ‾7 5
     0 7 ‾1 0

[25] $A-B$ is the vector of the two expressions $x_A - x_B$ and $y_A - y_B$.

$\div/A-B$ thus gives the inverse of the required relation.
The solution will be obtained by: $1 \div \div / A-B$

[26] $+/[3] \; TYRES$ or, more simply: $+/TYRES$

$+/[2] \; TYRES$

[27] $+/[2] \; EXPENDITURES$

[28] $(NOTES > 12)/[1]NAMES$ In effect, it is a question of cancelling the lines of the matrix of names by means of a mask.

[29] $(PH = 'T')/\iota \rho PH$

[30] $((\rho V) \; \rho \; 1 \; 0)/V$

[31] $\times/\rho \; TRYES$

[32] Since we wish to accumulate the productions of the factories, we must work on $+/TYRES$. The greatest productions over the years will be obtained by: $\lceil /[1]+/TYRES$

[33] 4 4   This is the sum of the vectors 2 2 and 2 2.

     2 4 4   2 , 2 gives 2 2; then 2 + 2 2 gives 4 4 we now catenate 2.

     6 6   2 2 + 2 in effect equals 4 4 ; and 2 + 4 4,equals 6 6.

     4 6   2 + 2 equals 4 ; 2 . 4 gives 2 4 ; and we add 2.

[34] The non-whole number values are not equal to their floor. Hence the
     solution: $(V=\lfloor V)/V$

[35] $((V>20)\wedge(V<30))/V$ or also: $(V=20\lceil 30\lfloor V)/V$

[36] 20 $\lceil$ 30 $\lfloor$ V this is the expression used in the previous exercise.

[37] The result is the pair of characters AB

     An apostrophe is inserted there between the characters A and B i.e: $A'B$

     We have inserted a comma here, as with any other character: A,B

[38] a) A closed bracket is missing

     b) $B2$ can represent a variable name, but $4AC$ can represent neither
         a product (which would thus be written $4\times AC$), nor a variable name
         (which cannot start with a figure).

     c) $(\iota 4)-3$ equals $^-2$ $^-1$ 0 1, we will thus divide by zero.

     d) The $^-$ sign is reserved for numbers; it cannot be coupled to a variable.
         ^-X is therefore incorrect.

     e) An operation sign is lacking between the two pairs of brackets

     f) 3 numbers (4 5 6) cannot be added to two numbers (1 2).

     g) We do indeed have the right to do this 4 0 $^-$4 ÷ 2 0 1 which gives
         2 1 $^-$4 but ι 2 1 $^-$4 has no meaning.

     h) Three variable names cannot be joined together. It is no longer
         a string of characters.

[39] 12 + 11 × ι17

[40] 25 × 1.2 $\star$ $^-$1 + ι20 or also: 25 × 1.2 $\star$ 0,ι19

[41] a) 8 5 8   b) 12 15   c) 3 10 7 1 5

[42] $+/FAMILY\in EARNERS$

      $(\sim TICKETS\in EARNERS)/TICKETS$

      $\wedge/EARNERS\in SOLD$

      $+/\sim EARNERS\in SOLD$

CHAPTER 4 EXERCISES

[1]
```
     ∇ R←REVERSE X
  [1]  R←X[(1+ρX)-ιρX] ∇
```

In effect, if X is the vector 8 3 2 5 11, then $1+\rho X$ equals 6, and $(1+\rho X)-\iota\rho X$ equals 5 4 3 2 1. $X[5\ 4\ 3\ 2\ 1]$ gives the result 11 5 2 3 8

[2]
```
       20   40   40   52   15   55  PAY 17
  340  680  680  884  255  935
```

Everything actually happens as if there were only one employee, who would have to have worked 17 hours. *NH* takes the value 17, *OH* takes the value 0, and the last line of the function calculates 20 40 40 52 15 55 × 17. The salaries will be correct for the employees who have not done overtime hours, false for those who will have. This is a nasty error because it is difficult to detect.

[3]
```
     ∇ R←N EXAM C
  [1]  N←N×(ρN)ρC
  [2]  R←(+/N) ÷ +/C ∇
```

The first line enables each mark to be multiplied by the coefficient which matches it. For this, as we cannot multiply a matrix (*MARKS*) by a vector (*COEFFICIENTS*), we must fill in a matrix of the same dimensions by the coefficients which the expression $(\rho N)\rho C$. achieves. The averages are obtained by dividing the horizontal totals by the sum of the coefficients applied.

[4]
```
     ∇ Z←N ROUND X
  [1]  Z←(⌈ ¯0.5+X×10⋆N)÷10⋆N
     ∇
```

If the left-hand argument is negative, it will cause rounding off of the number to the nearest tens, hundreds or thousands.

```
     ¯3 ROUND 8430  19680  47200
  8000  20000  47000
```

[5]
```
     ∇ R←LENGTH T
  [1]  R←(T=' ')/ιρT
  [2]  R←¯1+(R,1+ρT)-(0,R) ∇
```

The first line gives the position of the blanks. In one example, we would have obtained: 5 9 12 18. We now calculate the space between two blanks: (5 9 12 18 27)-(0 5 9 12 18) which gives: 5 4 3 6 9.

[6]
```
        ∇ P←C CALCULATE X
   [1]   P← +/ C×X*(ρC)-ιρC   ∇
```

In our example $(ρC)-ιρC$ will equal 4 3 2 1 0, then $X*4$ 3 2 1 0
gives the value of x^4, x^3, x^2, x, and 1. Each one of these values is
now multiplied by the coefficient which matches it, and we add up.

[7] Here are the four functions required:

```
         ∇ R←A UNION B
   [1]    R←A,(~B∈A)/B ∇
```

We catenate to A the elements of B which do not belong to A.

```
         ∇ R←A INTER B
   [1]    R←(A∈B)/A   ∇
```

We extract the elements of A which are also the elements of B:

```
         ∇ R← A INCLUDE B
   [1]    R←∧/ B∈A   ∇
```

A contains B if all the elements of B belong to A.

```
         ∇ R←A IDENTICAL B                ∇ R←A IDENTICAL B
   [1]    R←∧/(A∈B),(B∈A) ∇ or again:  [1]  R←(A INCLUDE B)∧(B INCLUDE A)∇
```

[8]
```
         ∇ RES ← COEF RESISTANCE TEMP
   [1]    RES←(1 TAKE COEF) ÷ * (1 DROP COEF) ÷ 273+TEMP
         ∇
```

[9]
```
         ∇ R←DERIVATIVE POL
   [1]    POL←((ρPOL)-1) TAKE POL
   [2]    R←POL×(1+ρPOL) - ιρPOL ∇
```

For example, for the polynomial 3 1 0 2, the first few lines give:
3 1 0. This value is then multiplied by 3 2 1, which gives 9 2 0.

[10]
```
         ∇ M←LONGEST T;L
   [1]    L←(T=' ')/ιρT
   [2]    M←¯1+(L,ρT)-(0,L)                The first three lines are close
   [3]    M←(M=⌈/M)/ιρM                    to exercise 5.
   [4]    M←L[M-1] DROP (¯1+L[M]) TAKE T
         ∇
```

[11]
```
         ∇ R←SIGN A
   [1]    R←(A>0) - (A<0) ∇
```

[12]   ∇ R←ABS X
   [1]   R←X×SIGN X ∇

Two other expressions are equally suitable :   R←X×1-2×(X<0)
                                          or :   R←X ⌈0-X

[13]   ∇ R←A ON B;DIM
   [1]   DIM←((ρA)+ρB)[1] , (ρA)[2]
   [2]   R←DIM ρ (RAVEL A),(RAVEL B) ∇

The first line gives the dimensions of the result required. The second
line calls the function *RAV* written in the course to constitute a
large vector comprising the vectors of *A* and *B*. It would not have
been possible to catenate *A* and *B*.directly.

[14]   ∇ NEW REPLACES OLD;POS
   [1]   POS ← (OLD=TEXT)/ιρTEXT   indices of the letters to be replaced
   [2]   TEXT[POS] ← NEW ∇   replacement by the given character.

[15]

          ∇ P INSERT VEC
   [1]   VALUES ← (P TAKE VALUES) , VEC, (P DROP VALUES) ∇

[16]   ∇ R←COMPLEMENT A
   [1]   R←(~ALPHA∈A)/ALPHA ∇

The complement is formed from the letters of the alphabet which do not
feature in the word given in the argument-

[17]
          ∇ LIMIT CONTROL VEC;M
   [1]   (⍕ρVECT) , ' VALUES'
   [2]   'AVERAGE = ', ⍕ AVERAGE VEC
   [3]   M ← +/VEC>LIMIT
   [4]   (⍕M),' VALUES GREATER THAN ', ⍕ LIMIT ∇

[18]
          ∇ MARRIAGE ;I
   [1]   'REGISTRATION ?'
   [2]   I← ⎕ IN REG
   [3]   'NEW NAME ?'
   [4]   NAMES[I;]← 12 TAKE ⎕,12ρ' ' ∇

We are seeking the position of the registration number by means of
the function *IN* written in §4-8. We then introduce the new name.
However, the latter could be less than the 12 letters required. By
adding 12 blanks, we are assured of being able to take at least 12
letters. This is the meaning of the last instruction.

[19] No, a value which has not yet been introduced cannot be modified.
      However the expression ⎕[2] would be accepted.

[20]
```
         ∇ POSIMAX M;L;C;Z
[1]     'THE GREATEST ELEMENT IS ',⍕Z←⌈/RAVEL M
[2]     L← 1 IN ∨/M←M=Z
[3]     C← 1 IN ∨/[1]M
[4]     'ROW ',(⍕L),' , COLUMN ',⍕C   ∇
```

The search for the maximum is accomplished either by ravelling the
matrix (as above), or by a double reduction: $⌈/⌈/M$.
A reduction by OR of the boolean matrix obtained by comparing this
maximum with all the terms of the matrix, gives the positions of
the maximum.

[21]
```
         ∇ CONNECTION ;OR;OD
[1]     'ORIGIN, DESTINATION ?'
[2]     OR ← ⌈/ OD←⎕
[3]     L←(⌊/OD) + 0.5 × (OR-1)×(OR-2)
[4]     'TAKE FLIGHT ', ⍕L   ∇
```

[22]
```
         ∇ HEADING N ; ALL
[1]     ALL ← (N=⌊ CODES÷100)/CODES
[2]     'THIS HEADING CONTAINS THE FOLLOWING CODES : ', ⍕ALL
[3]     'WHICH ONES DO YOU WANT ?'
[4]     N ← (CODES ∈ ⎕)/⍳⍴CODES
[5]     ''
[6]     'CODE    QTY      PRICE     SUPPL.'
[7]     CODES[N] , RENS[N;]   ∇
```

The search for the codes corresponding to the heading is accomplished
by dividing the codes by 100, and by looking for those whose whole
number part is equal to the value given as argument. To satisfy the
second part of the problem, the codes belonging to this item constitute
a vector which we called *ALL*.

We must now look for those codes which belong to the list introduced
by the user by means of the quad. We search for their indices,
which are in the variable *N*.
You will probably encounter difficulties in presenting the results.
The semi-colon does not enable a vector and a matrix to be printed side
by side. We have had to use catenation which, we will discover in
paragraph 6-3, applies in this case. It is also very difficult to
centre the heading above the columns of numbers. The FORMAT function
(§9-6) will help.

SECOND PART

Having by chance given the name *ALL* to the list of the codes of
the heading, it will be sufficient to type *ALL* in answer to the question
WHICH DO YOU CHOSE, so that the computer introduces the value of this
vector in the QUAD window. Hence no modification is necessary at
this stage.

Now two functions must be written, *TO* and *EXCEPT*.

```
        ∇ R←BEG TO END
[1]    R←((ALL≥BEG) ∧ (ALL ≤ END))/ALL   ∇
```

Since this function is intended for execution during running
of the *HEADING* function, it can make use of the variable *ALL*, which
will have been defined.. The function *TO* thus gives as result codes
between the two given limits. This value will be transmitted to the
HEADING function through the QUAD.

```
        ∇ R←LIST EXCEPT NO
[1]    R←(~LIST ∈ NO)/LIST   ∇
```

For example, if the *HEADING* function gives the variable *ALL* the
value: 1423 1427 1440 1451 1452 1466 1472 1480

   1440 *TO* 1466 will give the result: 1440 1451 1452 1466

   ALL EXCEPT 1427 1466 1472 will equal: 1423 1440 1451 1452 1480

[23]   If A is greater than B, jump to line 3, if not, pull out of the
        function.

[24]   If A is greater than B, 4×ι1 equals 1, and we jump to instruction 4.
        If not 4×ι0 gives an empty vector, and we pass to the following
        instruction (32).

[25]   If the value introduced is 10, we jump to instruction 5, if not,
        we pass to the following instruction (9).

[26]   This time, the expression 4⌊□⌈1 assures us that the value intro-
        duced will be brought back into the interval 1↔4.
        If we introduce a value greater than or equal to 4, we jump to line 19.
        If we introduce a value less than or equal to 1, we jump to line 8.
        If we introduce the value 2, 8 15 0 19[2] gives 15 and we jump to
        line 15.
        If we introduce the value 3, we pull out of the function.

[27] $(X>0)/S$ where S is the given scalar.

[28] $(∧/V=1)×3$

[29]   We will start by transforming the conversion formula:

$$C = \frac{5}{9} (F-32) = \frac{5}{9} F - \frac{160}{9} = \frac{9}{9} F - (\frac{4}{9} F + \frac{160}{9}) = F - (4F + 160)÷9$$

We then create two global variables C and F, equalling 0 and 1
respectively.
We now write the function:

```
        ∇ R ← N DEGREES U
[1]    R ← N - U×(160 + 4×N)÷9 ∇
```

When we type 17 *DEGREES C* the variable *UNIT* equals 0, and the result
is 17.
When we type 77 *DEGREES F* the variable *UNIT* equals 1, and the complete
formula gives the result 25. This style of programming is however,
not advised

[30]
```
      ∇ R←P INSERT VEC
[1]   →2×(P≥0) ∧ (P≤ρVALUES)
[2]   VALUES ← (P TAKE VALUES), VEC , (P DROP VALUES) ∇
```

[31]   Several solutions are possible. First of all here is the ABOMINABLE
       solution

```
      ∇ A AGAINST B
[1]   →(A≤B)/L1
[2]   'WON'
[3]   →0
[4]   L1:→(A<B)/L2
[5]   'DRAWN'
[6]   →0
[7]   L2: 'LOST' ∇
```

Here is a mediocre solution:

```
      ∇ A AGAINST B
[1]   ((A>B)/'WON'), ((A=B)/'DRAWN') , ((A<B)/'LOST') ∇
```

Here is the preferable solution:

```
      ∇ A AGAINST B  ;MSG
[1]   MSG ← 3 5 ρ'WON  DRAWNLOST '
[2]   MSG[2+SIGN B-A;] ∇
```

[32]
```
      ∇ R←SQUAROOT N
[1]   →(R≠ ⌊R←N*0.5)/0
[2]   R←(▼N), ' IS NOT A PERFECT SQUARE' ∇
```

It is sufficient to check that the root of the number is a whole
number, which is done by line 1. In line 2 we have used the FORMAT
function (§4-16) to catenate the given value and a message. Here is
another solution:
```
      ∇ SQUAROOT N
[1]   →(R≠⌊R←N*0.5)/ALAS
[2]   R
[3]   →0
[4]   ALAS: (▼N), 'IS NOT A PERFECT SQUARE' ∇
```

[33]
```
      ∇ R←FILL ;V;STOP
[1]   'WHAT ARE THE DIMENSIONS OF THE MATRIX ?'
[2]   R←⎕ρ0
[3]   STOP←*1
[4]   'GIVE THE ROW NUMBER, THE COLUMN NUMBER, THE VALUE'
[5]   ONEMORETIME: →NEXT × (~STOP∈V←⎕)
[6]   NEXT: R[V[1];V[2]] ← V[3]
[7]   → ONEMORETIME ∇
```

Observe the use of a global variable (*STOP*) for controlling the end
of the loop. Observe also in line 2, the direct use of the values
of the QUAD in an expression intended for initializing the matrix to
zero.

[34] and [35]

```
        ∇ CONSULT ACC ;STOP;S;C
[1]     STOP ← '*'
[2]     ENCORE: 'ACCOUNT NUMBER ?'
[3]      →(STOP=C←⎕)/0
[4]      →(~C∈ACC)/ZUT
[5]     S←BALANCES[S IN ACC]
[6]     POSITION[1+S≥0 ;] , ' DOLLARS'
[7]      ''
[8]      →ENCORE
[9]     ZUT: 'ABNORMAL ACCOUNT NUMBER'
[10]     →ENCORE ∇
```

This function answers the statements [34] and [35] in one go.
The search for the erroneous accounts is very easy: we detect the
numbers which do not belong to the argument *ACCTS*. The "*CREDIT*"
or "*DEBIT*" print-out could be undertaken by a new test and a jump
to a suitable instruction. This would be a very lengthy solution,
and we have preferred to use a global variable, created prior to
execution of the function, and which will print-out the first or the
second line according to case. This variable is called *POSITION*,
and equals:

> *DEBIT BALANCE*
> *CREDIT BALANCE*

A similar solution was used for exercise 31.

[36]
```
        ∇ R←ADDCOBOL N
[1]     I←1+S←0
[2]     LOOP: S←S+I
[3]      →(N≥I←I+1)/LOOP ∇
```

CHAPTER 5 EXERCISES

[1]   Calculation of a polynomial consists of multiplying the vector of the
       powers of X by the vector of the coefficients, then summating
       these products.
       The succesion of these two operations is a typed matricial product,
       extended to two vectors. Here is a different solution:

```
        ∇ R←C  CALCULATE X
[1]     R← C +.× X*(ρC)-ιρC ∇
```

[2] If we are looking for opened brackets, all we have to write is:

$$C = \text{'('}$$
```
0 0 1 0 0 1 0 0 0 0 0 0 0 0 0 0
```

Scanning by adding this vector will give, for each letter, the number of opened brackets which precede it:

$$+\backslash C = \text{'('}$$
```
0 0 1 1 1 2 2 2 2 2 2 2 2 2 2 2
```

A similar expression would give the number of closed brackets positioned before each letter:

$$+\backslash C = \text{')'}$$
```
0 0 0 0 0 0 0 0 0 1 1 1 2 2 2 2
```

We must state however that these two results must be shifted before subtracting them:

```
 0 0 1 1 1 2 2 2 2 2 2 2 2 2 2
 0 0 0 0 0 0 0 0 0 1 1 1 2 2 2
```
```
0 0 1 1 1 2 2 2 2 2 1 1 1 0 0 0
```

To operate this shift, the required expression will have to call the function *TAKE*, which has already been written.

$$(+\backslash C = \text{'('}) - 0, (\,^{-}1+\rho C)\ TAKE\ +\backslash\ C = \text{')'}$$

[3] $(\iota 4)\ \circ.\lceil\ 10\rho 0$ or also $(\iota 4)\ \circ.+\ 10\rho 0$

[4] $+\backslash\ 23\ ,\ 16\rho 11$

$\times\backslash\ 25\ ,\ 19\rho 1.2$

[5] 1 0 1 0 1 0   Beware of scanning with non-convertible operations.

5 1 4 2 3

720   This is actually equal to: $\times/1\ 2\ 3\ 4\ 5\ 6$

[6] 8   7   6   reduction takes place on the columns, the result is a vector.

16   this is the smallest term of the sum   20 16 19

0   this is actually the product of the following values: 3 2 1 0 0

15   this is the number of elements of the matrix.

[7] The easiest way of collecting the answers is to type the number of the answers supplied to each question. Hence, 2 1 1 3 1 2 will signify that the person interrogated gave the answer 2 to the first question, the answer 1 to the next two questions, the answer 3 to the 4th question, etc.....

This series of values can be introduced:

      - either by means of a quad, which will be presented thus:

        2 1 1 3 1 2

      - or in the form of a series of characters by means of a quote-quad, which will be presented thus:

      211312

It is evident that this second solution should be kept, because it saves the operator from typing a space between numbers, reducing the entry time by nearly a half!

Having introduced this string of characters; we will compare it with the R possible answers:

        '211312' ∘.= "1234'

```
0 1 0 0
1 0 0 0
1 0 0 0            This result is the true reflection of the answer
0 0 1 0            sheet filled in by the party interrogated.
1 0 0 0
0 1 0 0
```

Summation of these boolean matrices will directly yield the required totals. We will call the total thus obtained *RESULT*.

The first function will serve to initialize the processings:

```
      ∇ QUESTIONNAIRE ;R
[1]   'HOW MANY QUESTIONS ?'
[2]   Q ← □
[3]   'HOW MANY ANSWERS PER QUESTION ?'
[4]   REP ← '123456789' [ιR←□]
[5]   RESULT ← (Q,R) ρ0   ∇
```

This function creates three global variables which are the number of questions, the possible answers (for example 1234), and a zero matrix.

A second function will serve to collect the results. To pull out of this function, the operator will have merely to type "END", in which the letter E will be detected. Here, no control is carried out on the data introduced; there would be good reason for doing this in a real application.

```
     ∇ ANSWERS ;R
[1]    'GIVE THE ANSWERS TO THE ',(⍕Q),' QUESTIONS'
[2]    L0: →('E' ∈ R←⎕)/0
[3]    RESULT ← RESULT + R∘.= REP
[4]    →L0 ∇
```

When the operator wishes to interrupt, she types "END", and can then find out the result (partial or definitive). By typing simply the word *RESULT*.

This solution operates up to 9 answers per question, which is already a lot. Beyond this, a simple quad would have to be used.

[8] 1 2 3 4 ∘.< 1 2 3 4

(⍳4) ∘.= 5-⍳4

[9] 0

1 1 1 0 0 0

1

[10] We could write ∧/[2]$T=$ ' ' but it is easier to write:

T ∧.= ' '   to find the blank lines

' ' ∧.= T to find the blank columns

[11] Using the information of the previous exercise, we will write:

(0 ∨.≠ *MAT*) / *MAT* which is better than (∼0 ∧.= *MAT*) / *MAT*

[12] >/N>L is the succession of a reduction and a dyadic scalar operation; this expression can be replaced by an inner product: *N* >.> *L*

[13]
```
     ∇ S←AREA SIDES ;P
[1]    P ← 0.5 × +/ SIDES
[2]    R ← (×/P,P-SIDES)*0.5 ∇
```

The expression $P,P-SIDES$ equals: p , $(p-a)$, $(p-b)$, $(p-c)$
It is sufficient to find this product.

[14]
```
     ∇ Y ← YOTA N
[1]    Y ← +/ Nρ  ∇
```

[15] V ∘.= V enables each element of the vector V to be compared with all the others.
If all the elements are different, there will be only 1's on the diagonal, which will be verified by:

∧/ 1= +/ V∘.=V

[16] We will work on the series of numbers 10 12 14 10 16 18 12 16 16

In order to calculate the mobile averages of 3 elements, the following sums will have to be calculated:

(10+12+14) , (12+14+10) , (14+10+16) , (10+16+18) , etc .....

Rather than re-calculating each of these sums, it can be seen that it is easier, when one of them is known (for example 12+14+10), to subtract its first term (12) and add the following term (16) in order to obtain the following sum (14+10+16).

We will call S one of these sums, and I the index of the following value. The statement above teaches us that the next value of S will be obtained by:

$$S \leftarrow S + X[I] - X[I-N]$$

On calculating all these sums, and catenating them in a vector M, it will remain only to divide them by N to obtain the mobile averages.

```
        ▽ M ← N MOB X ;S;I
[1]       M ← S ← +/X[ιN]
[2]       I ← N+1
[3]     LAB: S ← S + X[I-N]
[4]       M ← M,S
[5]      →((ρX)≥I←I+1)/LAB
[6]       M ← M÷N    ▽
```

To initialize the process, we have calculated the sum of the first N terms, which is at the same time the first value of S, and the first element of M.

[17] There is an easier way however. Taking the first 4 sums, we can obtain them by a different method:

(10+12+14) is equal to (0+10+12+14)	minus (0)
(12+14+10) is equal to (0+10+12+14+10)	minus (0+10)
(14+10+16) is equal to (0+10+12+14+10+16)	minus (0+10+12)
(10+16+18) is equal to (0+10+12+14+10+16+18)	minus (0+10+12+14)

We can recognise, on both the left and the right, the succesive values of 0,+/X, shifted by N terms. The solution without a loop is thus rather simple:

```
        ▽ M ← N MOB X
[1]       M ← 0,+\X
[2]       M ← (N DROP M) - ((ρM)-N) TAKE M
[3]       M ← M÷N ▽
```

After the functions *TAKE* and *DROP*, in chapter 6, line [2] of this function will be written: [2] $M \leftarrow (N↓M) - ((-N)↓M)$
This function is apparently 15 times quicker than that of the preceding exercise.

[18] (ι6)∘.⌈(ι6)

CHAPTER 6 EXERCISES

[1]   2 ‾3↑P   ;   ‾2 4↑P   ;   3 ‾3 ↑ 3 4 ↑P   respectively.

[2]   ‾1 2↑P   1 ‾1↑P   and 0 1 ↑ 0 ‾1 ↓P   respectively

[3]   First method: 0,[1]Q,0   second method: ‾3 4↑Q

[4]   ∇ R←WORDING;NAME;WIDTH
       [1]   R←0 0ρ ''
       [2]   'INTRODUCE THE NAMES'
       [3]   LO: →(0=ρNAME←,⎕)/0
       [4]   WIDTH←(ρNAME) ⌈‾1↑ρR
       [5]   R←(((1↑ρR),WIDTH)↑R),[1]WIDTH↑NAME
       [6]   →LO ∇

[5]   In this solution we have assumed that the header contains fewer letters
       than the width of the matrix. If this is not the case, the function must
       be adapted.

                ∇ R←A HEADER B;BLANKS;WIDTH
       [1]   WIDTH←(ρB)[2]
       [2]   BLANKS←⌊0.5×WIDTH-ρA
       [3]   A←WIDTH↑(BLANKSρ' '),A
       [4]   R←A,[1]'-',[1]B ∇

[6]   ∇ UNTEL OBTAINS P;R;WIDTH   This function cuts down the new
       [1]   R← +/SCORE≤P≤   names to the width of the old.
       [2]   WIDTH ← (ρNAMES)[2]
       [3]   NAMES ←((R,WIDTH)↑NAMES),[1](WIDTH↑UNTEL),[1](R,0)↓NAMES
       [4]   SCORE ← (R↑SCORE),P,(R↓SCORE) ∇

[7]   TRAIN,(3 9↑WAGON) , (3 9↑WAGON)

[8]   U,[1.5]3600÷U←15+5×ι17

[9]   ∇ R←SHOW X
       [1]   R←X,[0.5] ' ↑'[1+Xϵ'0123456789']   ∇

[10]   ∇ R←CONTRACT C ;DIM
       [1]   DIM←ρM
       [2]   R←DIM,(M≠0)/M,[0.5]ιρM←,M   ∇

[11]   ∇ R←RE-ESTABLISH C ;DIM
       [1]   R←(×/DIM←C[;1])ρ0
       [2]   C←0 1↓C
       [3]   R[C[2;]] ←   C[1;]
       [4]   R ← DIMρR   ∇

[12]   (ρA) + (ρB) (ιρρA)=I

[13]

```
      ∇ R←C OUTOF T
[1]   R←C\(C←~T∊C)/T ∇
```

This solution is suitable even if *C* is a vector of several characters.

[14]

```
      ∇ Z←A MIX B
[1]   Z←((MODEL=1)\A)+((MODEL=2)\B) ∇
```

[15] It is of course the solution without a loop which we will keep; it consists of creating a boolean vector which serves to carry out expansion of the vector given.

1) we look for the lengths of the words: *L←POSITIONS - ¯1↓0,POSITIONS*

2) we constitute a boolean matrix whose 1's represent the positions of the letters in the required result: *M←L∘.≥⍳⌈/L*

3) this ravelled matrix gives the boolean vector required.

```
      ∇ R←POSITIONS SPLIT TEXT;M;LONG
[1]   LONG←POSITIONS - ¯1↓0,POSITIONS
[2]   R←(⍴M)⍴(,M←LONG∘.≥⍳⌈/LONG)\TEXT ∇
```

[16]

```
      ∇ R←SEP CUT TEXT ;POS
[1]   POS ← ((SEP=TEXT)/⍳⍴TEXT),1+⍴TEXTE
[2]   R ← POS SPLIT SEP,TEXT
[3]   R ← 0 1 ↓ R  ∇
```

We apply the same procedure, by referencing the position of the separators, then we drop a column.

[17]

```
      ∇ R←COL ADDING ARRAY ;TOT;EXP
[1]   EXP ← ~(⍳(⍴COL)+(⍴ARRAY)[2])∊COL←COL+⍳⍴COL
[2]   TOT ← +\R←EXP\ARRAY
[3]   R[;COL] ← TOT[;COL]  ∇
```

[18] If *A* equals 0, 3, 6, 9 , etc..... we pass to line 3
If *A* equals 1, 4, 7, 10, etc..... we pass to the following line
If *A* equals 2, 5, 8, 11, etc..... we pull out of the function.

[19] *YOU*
HAVE
WON ..... of course!

[20]

```
      ∇ R← A ADDLINES B
[1]   R←⍉ A ADDING ⍉ B ∇
```

you must know how to be lazy.

[21]

```
 1 3 2 ⍉ TYRES
```

[22] +/ 1 1⍉*T* would be the best solution, but calls on the use of the dyadic transposition which will not be studied until later. We will therefore undertake a series of reversals for the purpose of leading the appropriate elements on to the same vertical:

```
+/ ((¯1+⍳1↑⍴T)⌽T)[;1]
```

[23] ⍉ 10 4 ⍴ ⍳4

[24]   ∇ R ← C SUM V
      [1]   V ← (C≠1ϕC)/ +\V
      [2]   R ← V - 0,¯1↓V   ∇

[25]   ∇ Z←PALINDROME P   Do not miss this opportunity of
      [1]   Z←P∧.=⌽P←(P≠' ')/P   ∇   using an inner product.

[26]   ∇ R ← CUTDOWN V;B
      [1]   R←¯1↓(B∨1ϕB←' '≠V)/V←V,'□'   ∇

A supplementary terminal character has been added for the case where
the given vector possesses a blank at the begining and a blank at the end.
This character is then eliminated by the *DROP* function.

[27]   ∇ R ← M INTO P   This solution has a simple and readable
      [1]   R ← (¯1+ιρM)ϕM∘.=P   form, but it consumes space and
      [2]   R ← (∧≠R)/ιρP   ∇   computing time.

There are much better solutions, but writing them is a little more
demanding.

[28]   ∇ R ← N DIVIDE T;D
      [1]   D←ρT
      [2]   D←N, (⌈D[1]÷N) , D[2]
      [3]   T←D ρ ((D[1]×D[2]),D[3])↑T
      [4]   D← ρT ← 2 1 3 ⍉T
      [5]   D ← D[1],D[2]×D[3]
      [6]   R ← DρT   ∇

[29]   ∇ R←ENLARGE WORD;LETTERS;DIM
      [1]   LETTERS ← CARS['ABCDEFGHIJKLMNOPQRSTUVWXYZ ' ι WORD ;;]
      [2]   DIM ← 7 , 5×ρWORD
      [3]   R ← DIM ρ 2 1 3 ⍉ LETTERS
      [4]   R ← ((¯3+8×ρWORD)ρ1 1 1 1 1 0 0 0)\R   ∇

[30]   ∇ C←COMPARE P
      [1]   C←P=⍉6 10ρ⌊/P   This first version takes into account
      [2]   C←(ι10),(C+.×ι6),+/P×C   the actual dimensions of the proposed
      [3]   C←3 10ρC   ∇   array.

              ∇ C←COMPARE P   This version is usual.
      [1]   C←P=⍉(ϕρP)ρ⌊/P
      [2]   C←(ι(ρP)[1]),(C+.×ι(ρP)[2]),+/P×C
      [3]   C←(3,(ρP)[1])ρC   ∇

[31]   ∇ R← A MEMBEROF B
      [1]   R←(ρA),ρB
      [2]   R←∨/(RρB)=⍉(ϕR)ρA   ∇

[32]   ∇ R← A MEMBEROF B;D
      [1]   D ← ρA   Having noted the dimensions of *A* in D,
      [2]   R ← (ρA←,A),ρB←,B   we transform the two arguments into

[3] $R \leftarrow \vee/(R\rho B)=\lozenge(\Phi R)\rho A$ vectors and we apply the preceding method.
[4] $R \leftarrow D\rho R$ ∇   We then apply the dimensions of A to the
                                                                    result.

[33]   We wish to carry out the <u>SUM</u> (+) of the people who have chosen this
        activity <u>AND</u> the other. Hence the expression is evident:

$$(\lozenge M) +.\wedge M$$

We can prove this by calculating one of the elements of the array, for
example that of the 2nd line and 3rd column. It will be equal to:

$+/ \ (\lozenge M) [2;] \wedge \ M[;3]$ or again $+/ \ M[2;] \wedge \ M[;3]$

Note that the inner product +.× is equally appropriate.

CHAPTER 7 EXERCISES

[1]   We will use two variables representing the alphabet and the corresponding
       APL symbols: *ALPHA* and *APL*. Note that we have added to *ALPHA* a further
       symbol for the case where we would give, in the right-hand argument, a
       symbol not featuring in the APL alphabet.
       $ALPHA\leftarrow'ABCDEFGHIJKLMNOPQRSTUVWXYZ\star'$
       $APL \leftarrow ' \ \alpha\imath\cap L\epsilon\_\nabla\Delta\imath\circ' \square \mid \tau o\star?\rho\lceil\sim\div\cup\omega\supset\uparrow\subset'$

                ∇ $R \leftarrow TRANSLATE \ X$
       [1] $R \leftarrow ALPHA[APL \ \imath \ X]$ ∇

[2]   ∇ $R\leftarrow SORT \ TEXT \ ;U$ *ALPHA* being the vector of the letters
       [1] $U\leftarrow ALPHA \ \imath \ TEXT$ of the alphabet.
       [2] $R\leftarrow ALPHA[U[\Delta U]]$ ∇

[3]   If we work on the following vector V: 3 5 9 3 1 6 5 2 3
                            $V \ \imath \ V$ equals :   1 2 3 1 5 6 2 8 1
                            $\imath\rho V$ equals :   1 2 3 4 5 6 7 8 9
       Hence the duplicated elements appear :   ↑   ↑   ↑

            ∇ $R \leftarrow CLEAN \ X$
       [1] $R \leftarrow ((X\imath X)=\imath\rho X)/X$ ∇

       ___

[4] $NAMES[SCORE \ \imath \ 131 \ 144 \ 123 \ ;]$

[5]   ∇ $R\leftarrow A \ MIX \ B$
       [1] $R\leftarrow A,B$
       [2] $R[\Delta MODEL] \leftarrow R$ ∇

       Another solution is: $R \leftarrow (A,B)[\Delta\Delta MODEL]$

[6]
       a)
                ∇ $R\leftarrow F1 \ X$
          [1] $R\leftarrow^-1 +'0123456789'\imath X$ ∇

b)   ∇ R←F2 X
     [1]   R← +/ X×10*⁻1+ɸιρ,X   ∇

c)   ∇ R← VALUEOF X
   [1]   R ← F2 F1 X ∇

[7]   It is not necessary even to write a function: (A,B) [∇A,B]

[8]   ιρA of course.

[9]   The vector of weights will be: 0 0 0 0 1, which gives the result 19.

[10]   The vector of weights will be: 1 1 1 1 1, the result will thus be
       equal to +/V where V is the given vector.

[11]   If we encode in base ρM the vector ιρ,M we obtain: 0 0 1 1 1 0
                                                             1 2 0 1 2 0

       The solution is deduced thus: ∇ R←INDICES M
                                           [1]   R←1+(ρM) τ(ιρ,M)−1   ∇

[12]   We will use the global variable   HEXA ← '0123456789ABCDEF'

             ∇ R←HEXENCODE N
       [1]   R ← 16 16 16 16 τ N
       [2]   R ← , (HEXA[1+⍉R]),' '   ∇

             ∇ R←HEXDECODE H
       [1]   H←(H≠' ')/H
       [2]   H←⍉((0.25×ρH),4)ρH
       [3]   R←16⊥⁻1+HEXAιH   ∇

[13]
             ∇ R← CONVERT X
       [1]   X←(4ρ10) τ X   Separation of the figures of the
       [2]   R←'0123456789'[1+X]   number
       [3]   R←(~∧\'0'=R)/R ∇   The last instruction is intended to
                                       eliminate the zeros at the beginning with-
                                       out eliminating the significant zeros.

CHAPTER 8 EXERCISES

[1]   The matrix of the coefficients is: 1 ⁻1   0
                                            0   1 ⁻2
                                           ⁻1   0   1   we will call it M

       The solution is thus given by: 5 ⁻7 2 ⊟   M

[2]   M ← 3 3ρ 1 ⁻1 3 ⁻2 4 0 1 ⁻2 2 will be the matrix of coefficients.
       13 ⁻6 10 ⊟ M would give the vectors of a, b, and c.
       The expression required is thus calculated by: 3 5 ⁻1 +.× 13 ⁻6 10 ⊟ M

[3]   With fatigue beginning to show, we have written a function which carries
        out the calculation for a polynomial of any degree:

```
        ∇ R← FORESEE N;MAT;COE;U
  [1]    MAT ← MINUTES∘.*U←0,ιN
  [2]    COE ← DEGREES⊞MAT
  [3]    R ← (40*U) +.× COE ∇
```

For polynomials of degrees 1, 2, 3, 4 and 5, we have obtained (rounding
off)

487.45 ; 351.05 ; 80.48 ; 261.93 ; 1405.80 ; this is a result which

suffices to show that this mode of extrapolation is very dangerous.

[4]   We will let you carry out your own tests.

[5]
```
        ∇ R←MIX X
  [1]    R←X[(ρX) ? (ρX)] ∇
```

[6]   We obtain from 11 to 20 numbers between 11 and 20.

[7]   7+12?23   ;   36+?4 6ρ11   ;   ¯6+5 2ρ10?11

[8]   (99 + ? 15ρ801)÷1000

[9]   With repetition :   2+ ?(5+?11)ρ38

[10]   Without repetition :   2+ (5+?11)?38

[11]   Without repetition: L[5?8]   with repetition: L[?5ρ8]

[12]   2 12 ρ (12?21),(12?21)

[13]
```
        ∇ R←CHAR HIEROGLYPH DIM
  [1]    R←CHAR[? DIMρρCHAR] ∇
```

[14]
```
        ∇ R←CHAR TRIANGLE DIM;FORM
  [1]    FORM ← (ΦιDIM) ∘.≤ (ιDIM),ΦιDIM-1
  [2]    R← (' ',CHAR)[?1+(ρCHAR)×FORM] ∇
```

[15]
```
        ∇ R←GENERATE M;L;P
  [1]    R←L[P←?ρL←,M]       inspired by the function SPACEIN written
  [2]    R←R,,1+ρM)⊤P-1  ∇ in paragraph 7-9.
```

[16]
```
        ∇ GAME ;SCORE;CHOICE;ANSWER
  [1]    CHOICE ← ALPHABET[10?26]
  [2]    Ц ← 'ENTER 3 LETTERS : '
  [3]    ANSWER ← 18↓Ц
  [4]    SCORE ← 1+∧/ANSWERϵCHOICE
  [5]    (2 5ρ'LOST WON  ')[SCORE;],', I HAD CHOSEN ',CHOICE ∇
```

[17]   In order to simultaneously verify the two conditions, it is very simple
        to count the number of letters of the alphabet which appear in the answer.
        Hence we modify line 3 as follows.

        → (3≠+/ALPHABET∊REP←27↑⎕)/ 2

[18]   +/ ×N-L The sign of the function enables two comparisons to be made
        simultaneously.

        This solution extends to a vector of numbers to be placed in relation
        to a set of values, writing: +/×N∘.-L

[19]   + changes nothing in an expression, no matter what its value,

        ÷ modifies the value of an expression, but not its sign,

        × will give the value 1 or ⁻1 if the - sign has already made the value
        negative,

        - will make the result negative, no matter what its position.

[20]   -/(X⋆P)÷!P←0,2×ιN

[21]   (100÷ι4)⋆2
        3.041306665E⁻32   1   0.75   0.5   that is to say : 0 1 3/4 1/2
                  ⁻8|15 ⁻31 19
        7 1 3
                  2×0.5+⁻2○1○0.5
        3.141592654   that is to say Pi.

[22]   10⊛÷C

[23]   (0=(ιN)|N)/ιN

[24]   (((|V-M)>0.1×M←AVERAGE V)/V

[25]
              ∇ R←MINIDIFF V
        [1]   R←R=⌊/R←|V-1⌽V←V[⍋V]
        [2]   R←(R∨⁻1⌽R)/V   ∇

[26]   (SCORE ∨.≥ 21) ∧ (1< -/SCORE)

[27]   ∇ R←DINASA DIN
        [1]   R←⌊25×2⋆(DIN-15)÷3   ∇

              ∇ R←ASADIN ASA
        [1]   R←15+ ⌊0.5 +3×2⊛ASA÷25   ∇

        While if the second function gives the exact result, the first gives values
        which are slightly different from those in use. This is because the
        latter are merely values which have been rounded off for convenience.

INDEX OF SYMBOLS

ALPHABETICAL INDEX OF CONTENTS